Praise for Richard Kluger's

INDELIBLE INK

"[Kluger] brings . . . vivid storytelling built on exacting research, a knack for animating the context and an exquisite sense of balance that honors this country's essential press freedom without romanticizing its champions."
    —Bill Keller, *New York Times Book Review*

"*Indelible Ink* is a triumph . . . a new and very compelling take on the Zenger case. I found myself glued to Kluger's book and much in agreement with his findings, and he has written it all wonderfully well."
    —Stanley N. Katz, author of *Newcastle's New York: Anglo-American Politics, 1723–53* and director of Princeton University's Center for Art and Cultural Studies

"We've heard of the Salem witch trials. This is the trial from the 1700s you have not heard about. Mega-trial. Think Hamilton meets John Grisham. We have a First Amendment and we got into the American Revolution because of the explosive things that happened in this book."
    —Brad Thor, *The Today Show*

"Thoroughly engaging . . . packed with drama. . . . [I]t stands as a cautionary tale of what might happen if we let history repeat itself."
    —Amy Brady, *Los Angeles Review of Books*

"Lively, detailed . . . the most thoughtful, comprehensive and well-researched study of the 1735 criminal trial in New York City of newspaper publisher John Peter Zenger on charges of seditious libel."
—M. Kelly Tillery, *The Philadelphia Lawyer*

"Comprehensive."
—Richard Tofel, *ProPublica*

"Timely . . . well-written and thoroughly researched."
—James Srodes, *Washington Times*

"An outstanding book."
—*American Journalism*

RICHARD KLUGER

INDELIBLE INK

The Trials of
John Peter Zenger
and the Birth of
America's Free Press

W. W. NORTON & COMPANY
INDEPENDENT PUBLISHERS SINCE 1923
NEW YORK · LONDON

For information about permission to reproduce selections from this book,
write to Permissions, W. W. Norton & Company, Inc.,
500 Fifth Avenue, New York, NY 10110

For information about special discounts for bulk purchases, please contact
W. W. Norton Special Sales at specialsales@wwnorton.com
or 800-233-4830

Manufacturing by Quad Graphics, Fairfield
Book design by Brooke Koven
Production manager: Anna Oler

Library of Congress Cataloging-in-Publication Data

Names: Kluger, Richard, author.
Title: Indelible ink : the trials of John Peter Zenger and the birth of
America's free press / Richard Kluger.
Description: First Edition. | New York : W.W. Norton & Company, [2016] |
Includes bibliographical references and index.
Identifiers: LCCN 2016011040 | ISBN 9780393245462 (hardcover)
Subjects: LCSH: Zenger, John Peter, 1697–1746. | Printers—United
States—Biography. | Freedom of the press—United States—History—18th
century. | Zenger, John Peter, 1697–1746—Trials, litigation, etc. |
Trials (Seditious libel)—New York (State) | Printing—New York
(State)—History—18th century.
Classification: LCC Z232.Z5 K58 2016 | DDC 686.2092 [B]—dc23
LC record available at https://lccn.loc.gov/2016011040

ISBN 978-0-393-35485-0 pbk.

W. W. Norton & Company, Inc.
500 Fifth Avenue, New York, N.Y. 10110
www.wwnorton.com

W. W. Norton & Company Ltd.
15 Carlisle Street, London W1D 3BS

For Judy Crawford and John Doyle,
dear pals, wise and caring,
and bookpeople of singular devotion

CONTENTS

PREAMBLE

The Essential Liberty

A T THE BEGINNING of 1941, two months after he had become the first (and still only) U.S. president elected more than twice, Franklin D. Roosevelt delivered his ninth annual State of the Union address to Congress. Better known as the "Four Freedoms" speech and regarded by many historians as FDR's most memorable oration other than his First Inaugural Address, his remarks came sixteen months after the Second World War had detonated in Europe. Although Roosevelt had pledged to keep the country out of that global cataclysm as long as possible, his January 1941 address was phrased to justify eventual U.S. participation in the unfolding struggle against totalitarian powers that spurned the rights and liberties at the core of America's political creed.

"In the future days, which we seek to make secure," the president asserted, "we look forward to a world founded upon four essential human freedoms. The first is freedom of speech and expression—everywhere in the world." The other three he listed were freedom of worship, freedom from want, and freedom from fear. Only the first of these required no elaboration. Like Lincoln's Gettysburg declaration of universal equality and the imperishability of democracy, the liberty to express ourselves by whatever spoken and written words we choose without risk or reprisal was a self-evident—and the most imperative—blessing among the constellation of values said to be every American's birthright. It is the one form of freedom that, once lost, imperils all the others. Suppressing public grievances and dissent, history tells us, has been every dictatorship's fixed policy—and often its chief preoccupation.

In the wake of World War II, with the decline of Western imperialism and the confinement of communism, democracy spread around the world, and the accompanying human rights movement notably broadened the latitude of free expression. Still, stringent state censorship remains a malignant practice in many places—China and smaller Asian countries, Russia, much of Africa, most of Islam, and lands where democracy's foothold is fresh and tentative, like parts of Latin America and Eastern Europe. Even where paid lip service, liberty of expression is highly prone to manipulation by rogue rulers, while unapologetic police states train their shackled media to promote conformity of thought and compliance with regime commands. The world, then, while evidencing hopeful signs of enhanced personal freedom, remains in large part an unruly place that the United States has endeavored for a century now to liberate from tyranny. This mission—altruistic and providential to the minds of its advocates, arbitrary and delusional in the eyes of skeptics— has cost the nation an immensity of blood and treasure, to the point that cooler heads cry out for restraint; better to serve humanity as liberty's role model, not its armed redeemer. And how better to inspire other societies, especially those struggling to cast off the yoke of despotism, than to display with pride our devotion to free expression? The United States was indeed the first nation in history to monumentalize liberty of speech and the press as a fundamental right of its people.

It is tempting, then, at a time when political cynicism is rife and yearnings for social justice can sound more strident than stirring, to ask why Americans ought to bother themselves about, of all things, the sanctity of the first of Franklin Roosevelt's Four Freedoms. Hasn't the liberty of spoken and written expression been fixed long and securely enough in our firmament to withstand any challenge? Aren't we confronted with far more urgent and divisive issues? America faces an ever-widening gulf between unbounded wealth and dead-end poverty, between her compassionate and callous impulses. Our precious democracy itself may be coming apart at the seams, yet instead of trying to fix it, our public discourse grows more rancorous, driving government toward the outer banks of dysfunction and irrelevance. But it is folly to suppose in our present condition, with fanaticism abroad fanning heightened anxiety and violence at home, that any of our freedoms is immune from infection, with potentially fatal consequences if not diligently monitored.

There are signs, if we choose to notice them, that American press freedom—or media freedom, as we might term it now—has become tarnished of late, and that journalists, its professional practitioners, have been devalued as a group. Consider the 2014 World Press Freedom Index compiled annually by Reporters Without Borders (RWB), a nonprofit, unaffiliated organization headquartered in France and serving as a consultant to the United Nations. RWB's purpose is to track assaults on freedom of information worldwide, call them to the attention of global media, and work with governments to fight censorship and laws aimed at restricting liberty of expression. The organization's index is compiled from extensive questionnaires submitted by eighteen freedom-of-expression affiliate groups and 150 correspondents around the world and takes into account, among other factors, the legal framework for media and how they are regulated, penalties for press offenses, violence against journalists, and violations of the free flow of information on the Internet. Lamenting "a profound erosion of press freedom in the United States" over recent years, the RWB's latest survey of 180 nations rated America 46th in the world. This ranking placed the U.S. behind Finland (No. 1), Denmark (7), Germany (14), Canada (18), Uruguay (26), the United Kingdom (33), France (39), and South Africa (42). Lower-ranked than the United States were such nations with relatively recent or nonexistent democratic orientation as Argentina (55), Japan (59), Kenya (85), Indonesia (132), India (140), Russia (148), Mexico (152), Egypt (159), Cuba (170), Iran (173), and China (175). The main reasons cited for the low U.S. score as a citadel for press freedom among Western democracies were the Department of Justice's "aggressive prosecution of whistleblowers" and government security leakers and mounting pressure on investigative reporters to disclose sources of information greatly in the public interest but embarrassing to government officials. "Freedom of information is too often sacrificed to an overly broad and abusive interpretation of national security needs, marking a disturbing retreat from democratic practices," RWB commented.

Consider as well the latest Gallup Poll survey, taken continuously since the 1970s, asking the public to rate the honesty and ethical standards of people by their profession or occupation. In the 2012–14 results, nurses topped the list with 80 percent of the respondents rating them Very High or High in those qualities. Next came engineers at 70 percent; doctors, dentists, and pharmacists grouped in the 63–65 percent range; teachers at all levels, averaging 57 percent; in the mid-40s percent range came, in order, clergy, judges, funeral directors, and accountants. Below them were auto mechanics (29 percent) and building contractors (26 percent). And then came journalists, viewed as very highly or highly honest and ethical by only 24 percent of those polled—a decline from the 1976 percentage of 33. Journalists could salvage a sliver of consolation for ranking above such customary butts of group derision as bankers (23 percent rated as very highly or highly honest and ethical), lawyers (21 percent), business executives (17 percent), insurance salespeople (15 percent), car salespeople (8 percent), and lobbyists (5 percent).

Such data may be dismissed by free-expression champions as imprecise, transitory, or skewed by political bias—but at their peril, because the numbers would seem to suggest, at the least, a worrisome disaffection among Americans toward press freedom since Thomas Jefferson, in a 1787 letter to a Virginia friend, famously extolled its ascendancy over all others:

> The basis of our government being the opinion of the people, the very first object should be to keep that right; and were it left to me to decide whether we should have a government without newspapers or newspapers without a government, I should not hesitate a moment to prefer the latter. But I should mean that every man should receive those papers and be capable of reading them.

A student of history, Jefferson knew that oppressive governments habitually obscured their iniquities from those who most needed to know of them—and how else but from the press could the people determine whether to retain their government or replace it, rudely if necessary? Jefferson sensed that only an informed electorate, even if its information was at times willfully or unwittingly distorted by the deliverers, could make democracy thrive in America and not degenerate into mindless mob rule. His conviction would be shared by Congress four years later when it passed the First Amendment of the Bill of Rights.

It would be a miscalculation, though, to confuse this remarkably enlightened innovation in the annals of political history with a universally fond regard for the press among the American people. From the birth of the infant republic, newspapers and journals of opinion, however intrepid on best behavior, have never been without their critics, often among society's power elite, leery of the press's constant threat through revelation and protest to topple entrenched authority and warped values. In part, to be sure, the press has suffered rebuke for dishonoring itself by covert partisanship and crass defamation; Jefferson himself, viciously assailed in print throughout much of his career, would write another friend twenty years after his above-quoted paean to the press and six years into his presidency, "Nothing can be believed which is seen in a newspaper. Truth itself becomes suspicious by being put into that polluted vehicle."

On balance, the American press need hardly apologize. The disclosures of evildoing and injustice by earlier generations of U.S. journalists—about banks' malpractices, the inhumanity of slavery, graft and cronyism in government, religious charlatanism, imperialism, exploitation of labor, and chicanery by corporate trusts, to cite some obvious examples—goaded populist outcries for reform once industrial advances made print media more affordable by, and accessible to, the masses. But bearers of ill tidings, journalism's stock-in-trade, have always risked provoking kill-the-messenger sentiments, an occupational hazard of the profession (along with meager wages and alcohol addiction). And so, over generations, the public has taken an ambivalent view of the gentlemen (and, in time, the ladies) of the press. At their best, journalists have historically been cast as society's faithful watchdogs over public and private shenanigans—fearless, impartial, resourceful, bearing witness to our amazing feats and endless foibles while casting light into dark, sordid corners. At their worst, they have been vilified as scandalmongers, character assassins, hype artists, news-slanters, and self-appointed vigilantes on power trips.

Yet if the Gallup Poll is to be credited, this traditional ambivalence toward newspeople has escalated in the past few decades into a press-bashing tendency of puzzling origin. It may be attributable more to the speed and scale of advances in technology and their effect on society's collective psyche than to a decline in the skills, perseverance, or scruples among gatherers and deliverers of the news. We all live in cloudy cyberspace now, where computerized composition, data-processing, and transmission of raw information allow it to "go viral" almost instantaneously, before its content can be corroborated and its meaning assessed. We are afflicted with the evolutionary by-product of more than five centuries of ever-expanding press activity—cerebral overload from all the stuff floating around out there in medialand, which now encompasses virtually every PC, laptop, tablet, and smartphone screen on earth. Compounding this vast interconnective clamor has been the steadily growing encroachment upon authentic news content by artfully confected advertising, justified as essential to pay for it but inevitably demoting journalists from purveyors of intelligence to complicit pitchmen.

Lest we grow overly dispirited, though, over the assertion lodged in the latest survey by Reporters Without Borders that press freedom in the United States is seriously on the wane, a little perspective is in order. As suggested above, American journalism and freedom of expression have been radically recast over the past quarter-century by the tech revolution, greatly to the detriment of traditional hard-copy print media. Few communities are served by more than one newspaper. Those publications that survive have seen their circulation, advertising, and staff size hemorrhage, affecting the quality and range of coverage and leaving the public less informed. Arguably, though, this loss has been more than compensated for by the remarkable proliferation of the electronic news media. To speak of "the press" in alluding to today's collective outpouring from vehicles delivering news, information, and opinion to the public is to indulge in an antiquated misnomer. Purists may fault journalism on TV and the Internet for its triviality, herd mentality, and wildly uneven quality, but the same was true of the print media in their heyday.

Still, there is no denying the electronic media's shortcomings. Television coverage of local news remains abysmal by and large, starved by station owners and limited mostly to crime and weather news with emphasis on whatever graphics dictate; there is little or no investigative reporting on municipal government or anything else. TV network news, swamped by advertising, at least attempts to cover major events, but what gets on air is little better than a gloss, again with visual effects often governing story selection. The morning network shows are a hodgepodge of top-story nuggets, gentle interviews, happy talk, and entertainment gossip. The networks' evening "half-hour" shows (about eighteen minutes free of commercials) continue to do what pioneer news anchorman John Cameron Swayze called "hopscotching the headlines"—takeouts of a minute or two (three is an eternity) on a few important stories. The Sunday morning news-spotlight shows add some dimension but too often trot out the same camera-craving politicians and fail to press them for clear answers. The Public Broadcasting Service's *Nightly NewsHour* offers broader and deeper coverage than any other regular news show, though its budget forces it to stress a talking-heads format that can turn soporific. Friday night's long-standing *Washington Week* summary, however, suffers from its brevity; lucid analysis is rushed, and time is wasted on news clips. PBS's hour-long documentary show *Frontline*, while idiosyncratic in its selection of subjects, deals with them more informatively and with greater depth than any other TV news program.

Cable TV news outlets are a useful expansion of free expression but suffer as a journalistic enterprise from being either so wedded to nonpartisanship, like CNN, that all sides of a controversial story are treated equally regardless of merit, or so committed to political causes, like Fox News and MSNBC, that they wind up preaching to their choirs. CNN is, at least, dutiful, ubiquitous, and earnest, but its news acumen is challenged, substituting 24/7 presence for probing reportage. Two exceptional performers in the cable realm have been CNN's Fareed Zakaria, who offers more cutting news analysis and conducts more trenchant interviews than anyone else on the air, and Rachel Maddow, an avowed liberal, who at times sardonically documents her diatribes with enterprising investigative reports. Talk radio, too, can be credited for its contribution to our nationwide welter of free expression, but it can in no way be classified as journalism. Its principal aim seems to be to close its listeners' minds, not open them to fresh ideas. Public radio does just the opposite and merits praise for delving where others would rather drive by.

The most remarkable development in news coverage and the spread of free expression in the present generation has, of course, occurred on the Internet. A lot of what is generated on our screens is undisciplined, loosely written, and often carelessly sourced, but some of it—even what is churned out by lone-wolf bloggers—surely qualifies as journalism and compensates to a degree for staff and space cuts by old-line media that have put a serious crimp in investigative reporting. Imaginative talent has gone into the creation of website news magazines like Slate, Politico, Salon, BuzzFeed, and even the Drudge Report, earning them growing viewership even if their operators' political and social biases usually tell you where they're coming from.

All of which is to suggest that America's free press (to return to its traditional moniker) is alive and kicking, even if its liberty is under constant strain from powerful vested interests, starting with the lords of commerce and industry and the shadowy national security establishment. Well-intended critics like Reporters Without Borders seem misguided in faulting the United States for its "retreat" from press freedom by dwelling on its admitted lapses while blithely ignoring the torrent of free-flowing information, including much self-critical commentary, that the nation's news media produce, for the most part uninterrupted (if occasionally jeered) by those who fear or despise its content. America remains the world's splashiest fount of free expression.

Complacency, however, is never in order where liberty is concerned. Today, the free media's task of tracking government conduct and baring its meaner impulses has been turned on its head by regimes in many countries, the United States among them, as officials proclaim an urgent need—and their ordained right, above all others—to spy on, indiscriminately if they so choose, the behavior of the public in order to detect, monitor, and interrupt terrorist or insurrectionary activity anywhere it is suspected (or imagined) to exist. Thus, governments in garrison states and open societies alike are stealthily wielding sophisticated tools of surveillance in the name of national security, no matter the wholesale loss of personal privacy and dignity. One may therefore dare to suggest that on this ever-more-thronged and conflict-ridden planet, journalism, when practiced freely and conscientiously and not as an outlier in the realms of entertainment or partisan advocacy, is more important today than at any time since Gutenberg cranked up his printing press. Making government answerable for its behavior by the intrepid exercise of society's most essential liberty is, at the least, no less worthy a calling now than when it was first practiced in America. That time was the mid-1730s, forty years before the nation came into being. The place was New York City. The craftsman who carried out the task was named John Peter Zenger, but neither he nor the men whose words he printed—rattling the rulers of the British Empire—are celebrated these days. They deserve to be. *Indelible Ink* is their story.

—R.K.

AUTHOR'S NOTE ON STYLE

In excerpts from historical documents or statements quoted in the following text, the author has taken the liberty of modernizing the original spelling and punctuation for the purpose of facilitating reader comprehension. Bracketed words not found in the original texts have also been introduced liberally for the same reason, especially to clarify meaning and in excerpts when ellipses have been resorted to for the purpose of verbal economy. In doing so, every effort has been made to retain the intended meaning of the original texts.

INDELIBLE INK

I

A Perilous Trade

F OR MUCH OF his adult life, John Peter Zenger's name was widely
known and well regarded in colonial New York's vibrant little seaport at the apex of the largest harbor in British America. Along the
town's cobbled streets, pebbled lanes, and meandering alleyways, in its
hundred rollicking taverns and smoky coffeehouses, among the congregants at the old Dutch Reformed Church, where he sometimes played
the organ at the Sabbath service, and the dock workers and oyster fish-
ermen who labored not far from his shop, in the crowded open-air
marketplace and inside stately City Hall, where the colony's and city's
administrators shared quarters, almost everyone knew who Zenger
was—even if he ranked as runner-up to the leading, and only other,
printer in the province.

For the last thirteen years of his life, his name appeared constantly
in the four-page newspaper he issued every Monday. Much of its contents during the first two years of its existence took the form of letters
addressed to Zenger personally, though most were in fact written by
a handful of the smartest and most powerful men in the colony who
did not want their identities revealed and thus subject to prosecution
for demeaning the royal authorities. And yet, posterity knows very little

3

about Peter Zenger, as he preferred to be addressed—about his appearance, his character and personality, his education, his beliefs, his family (beyond its members' names and ages), or how he went about producing the journal that ushered in the dawn of press freedom in the New World. But copies of his paper survive, every issue, along with a probably reliable record of his trial, still celebrated as a monument in the annals of American jurisprudence. These documents and a few other archival materials permit us to recount his story. Zenger himself may be the least illuminating part of it, but without him the cause of free expression would have been denied an indispensable stalwart at a time when few cared—or dared—to stand up for it.

We can say at the outset that, based on anecdotal accounts and slender documentary evidence, Zenger was born in 1697 in or near the village of Rambach in the Palatinate, bordering the Rhine River in southwestern Germany. The Palatinate was part of the patchwork of loosely leagued principalities and duchies that were remnants of the Holy Roman Empire but, with the Protestant Reformation, had for the most part turned away from Catholicism. The region had been a garden spot, with a fertile, productive countryside and prosperous towns, until neighboring France's ambitious king blighted it.

Louis XIV, presiding over the most populous realm in Europe with the largest and best army, set out to re-create the Gallic dominion that Charlemagne had staked out nine centuries earlier and, while he was at it, to restore a thoroughly Catholic Holy Roman Empire under the Sun King's sway. For forty years starting in 1673, French forces were on the warpath to extend the nation's eastern boundary, establish an empire in the New World, and challenge Spain, Britain, and the Netherlands for global maritime supremacy. And no place in Europe was more severely victimized by the ceaseless marches, collisions, and cannonading of opposing armies than the Palatinate. Pillaging French troops devastated its towns and denuded its farmlands, forcibly requisitioning food, supplies, and living quarters and bringing famine, economic collapse, and religious persecution (one of the Catholic king's favorite pastimes) to the Protestant Rhineland. Louis's bellicose tendencies reached their zenith when the Spanish throne fell empty and he sought, with its line of succession sharply contested, to take control of his Iberian neighbor and its vast overseas holdings by installing one of his grandsons—Philip, Duke of Anjou—as the Spanish monarch. The step would have forged a French-dominated Catholic superpower encompassing as well the Spanish Netherlands (modern Belgium) and whatever German states Louis's army could annex. To check this threat of continental mastery, the alarmed and newly muscular British government carpentered a formidable alliance with the Netherlands, Hapsburg Austria, Prussia, and Savoy in northwestern Italy, another embattled French neighbor. What followed, beginning in 1702—when Peter Zenger was five—was the sprawling War of the Spanish Succession, involving immense armies in horrifically bloody combat that took a dozen years to resolve. In the end, thanks in large measure to the enduring heroics of Great Britain's generalissimo, John Churchill, better known as the Duke of Marlborough, Louis's dream died. French adventurism in Europe was contained for a century, while the British gained unchallenged title to easternmost Canada and bases at Gibraltar and Minorca, giving the Royal Navy control over Mediterranean traffic, and Louis's grudging acknowledgment of Parliament's Act of Succession, ensuring that no Catholic would again reign over Britannia.

The Palatinate did not fare so well. Beyond the ruination of war, the principality suffered a series of savage winters and crop failures, leaving a harvest of hunger and sickness. No surviving documents have enlightened us about Peter Zenger's boyhood, but a scholar writing under the auspices of the German Historical Institute of Washington, D.C. has reported that Peter was the oldest of four children of Nicolaus and Johanna Zenger and that his father was a schoolmaster in Rambach, close to the easternmost extension of France. Whatever his father's calling or wherever the family's residence was precisely, it can be safely ventured that the Zengers, like their neighbors, were near starvation and despair as long as the war dragged on. Then, in 1709, well before the fighting had run its course, a providential message reached the poor Palatines. It came, indirectly to be sure, from the Queen of England.

Had there been what we now call news media to inform the Zenger family of five—Peter had two younger siblings at the time—they might have learned a thing or two about the English monarch who was about to rescue them from doom. Queen Anne, then forty-four, was in the seventh year of her reign as the first female English sovereign since Elizabeth I's death a century earlier. Leaving no children when she died in 1714 (despite seventeen known pregnancies, courtesy of her consort, Prince George of Denmark), she would be the last—and best—ruler of the consummately egomaniacal Stuart dynasty. Anne reached the throne only because her sister and brother-in-law, Queen Mary II and King William III, had also died childless. Anne's prospects, despite the tranquil and increasingly vigorous realm she inherited, were not overly bright. She lacked Queen Elizabeth's shrewdness and the wiles to manipulate scheming courtiers, ministers, and politicians who were often less than respectful of a female ruler. Nor was she physically attractive or magisterial in bearing, and her health, already compromised by so many failed pregnancies, was poor. From her thirties on, she was stricken with gout, and possibly lupus and diabetes, which turned her more obese each passing year and limited her mobility—she moved about by wheelchair or was hauled, with effort, in a sedan chair. But she was far from a fool, attended to affairs of state with unusual diligence for a monarch, and understood the crown's need to bargain with Parliament's new potency. She was wise enough and fortunate to seek and gain the protection of the nation's most acclaimed soldier and statesman, the Duke of Marlborough, whose skills were so essential to victory in the central ordeal of her reign—the grinding war against the despotic and far more scintillating sovereign Louis XIV. In the midst of her tenure, she presided over the Act of Union, joining the kingdoms of England and Scotland in what has forever after been called Great Britain. Not for nothing was she widely known among her subjects as Good Queen Anne.

One of her most benevolent acts was the mercy she showed in 1709–10 toward the plight of the German Palatines. She invited 13,000 of those war victims to make their way, as best they could amid the surrounding hostilities, to the Netherlands and then across the channel to asylum and hopefully restored lives on British soil. The invitation, the Palatines were told, came with the queen's pledge of sustenance until gainful employment could be arranged for the immigrants, either in the home isles or by free passage across the sea—the going fare to America would otherwise have been at least £10 a head, a small fortune for an indigent family like the Zengers. In the British colonies, labor was in great demand, and workers who would surrender their freedom for up to eight years of indentured service were promised in return 50 acres (per family member in some cases), equipment and supplies for homesteading, and the return of their freedom.

Queen Anne's charitable gesture, to be sure, was not altogether altruistic. While she could not have supposed that these German refugees, like earlier French, Dutch, and Flemish dissenters from their state religions who had been welcomed to England, were skilled middle-class artisans, mechanics, or literate clerks—the Palatines were mostly rural farmworkers with rudimentary formal learning—nonetheless, Britain needed able-bodied newcomers. Her population was only one-third the size of France's, and military demands had absorbed a large portion of younger males. To increase the number and improve the health of Anne's subjects, an influx of German laborers could be useful, and the emerging industrial revolution could likewise benefit from additional brawny, hardworking manpower. If there turned out to be a surplus of Palatines, they could be shipped to America to clear primeval forests, turn the wilderness into a fruitful garden, build settlements, and otherwise increase the material value of the empire.

The vision would not quite mesh with reality, as the Palatines soon discovered. The Zenger refugee party must have had few amenities to comfort them as they made their way in the latter half of 1709 to Amsterdam, where they queued with masses of their uncomplaining countrymen, glad to have been delivered from the infernal war zone and anxiously awaiting salvation. When the transfer to England finally came, the immigrants learned that, even with good intentions, Her Royal Majesty's government could not cope with the scale of the influx. Feeding and housing the Palatines in tent camps on the outskirts of London cost more than anticipated, and dispersing them, mostly to Ireland and remote corners of Britain, where their labor was most needed, often caused problems due to language and other cultural differences, the depleted health of many of the arrivals, and almost surely an undisguised outbreak of xenophobia.

There is no record of where the Zengers dwelled or what labor, if any, they performed in England, but by the following spring, they were ready to gamble with fate and accept the government's offer to deliver them to America without charge but owing a considerable term of servitude to whoever would provide for their survival. We can only imagine the jumble of relief, hope, and dread that coursed through the Zenger children, thirteen-year-old Peter, his sister Anna, ten, and little brother Johannes, seven, as they boarded one of the ten vessels carrying roughly 2,200 Palatines to the colony of New York on what would turn out, sadly, to be a disastrous transatlantic voyage in the spring of 1710. The passengers might have taken some comfort from learning that the new governor of New York, Robert Hunter, a favored member of Queen Anne's court, was making the crossing at about the same time. Although not aboard any of their crowded vessels, Hunter had urged the Palatine project on the queen and pledged to protect the German travelers and provide for their orderly resettlement once they were safely ashore.

The new governor, not surprisingly, enjoyed far pleasanter shipboard accommodations than Peter Zenger's family and their displaced countrymen. Their vessels were small and tightly packed, the food was poor, sanitary conditions appalling, and the weather kept them below-decks in suffocating conditions much of the time—all factors spreading illness among the passengers. Governor Hunter would report back to London afterward that the crossing, intended as an act of benevolence, took the lives of 470 Palatines—one of every five who embarked. Almost certainly among the deceased, interpolating from the landing records, was Peter's father, since his mother, Johanna, listed herself as a widow on debarkation.

The grieving family, now to face life's certain hazards in a strange new land without their principal provider, must have scanned about with pounding hearts as their ill-fated ship slipped through the Narrows of New York Harbor on a mid-June day. The place they had come to was first reconnoitered by an English sea captain one hundred years before the German lad and his family arrived there.

II

The British province of New York was different from its twelve sister colonies in one decisive way. All the others were founded by Englishmen, and because it was not, New York—and especially the island seaport that served as the gateway to an immense hinterland—drew a far yeastier mixture of settlers than the rest. The other dozen colonies would each attract a preponderance of like-minded sectarians—royalist Anglicans favored Virginia; Puritans flocked to Massachusetts, Presbyterians to New Jersey, Quakers to Pennsylvania, Catholics to Maryland—but New York quickly evolved into a heterodoxy of nationalities, races, religions, and cultural affinities that foreshadowed the so-called American melting pot of diverse human ingredients unique among all nations to this day. Such an amalgam brought its share of stresses and misunderstandings, yet New York's diversity, traceable to its founding by the Dutch, would generate an intensity of commercial, social, and civic interaction more dynamic and more tolerant of otherness than elsewhere in the colonies. That ferment would one day make New York's capital city the receptive seedbed for America's first printed expression of overt political dissent.

Geography, first of all, distinguished the setting. No other colony could boast a harbor so ample or a connecting waterway so wide, deep, and far-reaching as those Henry Hudson, sailing under the Dutch flag, came upon in 1610 and claimed for his sponsors as the New Netherlands. The river that would bear his name was navigable for 150 miles north through a fertile, undulating valley and joined far upstream by a tributary of equal length, the Mohawk, which led west toward the Great Lakes and the interior of a seemingly boundless paradise. Another unmatched geographical asset was low-lying, highly arable Long Island, stretching 120 miles eastward from New York Harbor as the base of a vast arc of centrifugal settlement that radiated from the southern tip of Manhattan Island, the magnetic mid-harbor center of a colossal entrepôt in the making; the Dutch named it New Amsterdam.

Having appropriated this vector of lush territory as yet untouched by Europeans—a wedge-shaped expanse that had eluded English explorers' claims to the northeast and south—the Dutch officially designated New Netherlands a province in 1624. Their intention was less to plant a permanent, sprouting colony to reflect the greater glory of the Lowlands than to open a branch office of a national commercial enterprise to compete for trade with England, the other Protestant seafaring power, and the two preeminent Catholic leviathans of the age, France and Spain. By far the smallest of the four rivals, the Netherlands was nevertheless the richest of them, serving as Europe's banking and mercantile center for much of the seventeenth century while attaining its cultural zenith. It enjoyed as well a remarkable degree of acceptance of unorthodox spiritual, philosophical, and scientific thought in a period when the British Isles were wracked by religious and political schisms and did not welcome disruptive influences from abroad. Nervy Dutch cargo vessels defied Britain's proclaimed monopoly to trade with her American seaboard and Caribbean colonies, costing the royal treasury thousands of pounds a year in lost duties and making the Dutch republic a continuing irritant to the British ambition to dominate global commerce.

The bourgeois, acquisitive Dutch, extending their web of far-flung trading posts from Archangel in Russia to Recife in Brazil to Nagasaki in Japan, saw little prospect of profit from the soil of their North American colony, which did not yield durable crops, exotic spices, or precious metals like those their European rivals extracted from their colonies. The native peoples, moreover, were not amenable to serving as slave labor that might have transformed New Netherlands into a bountiful agricultural resource. Nor could the Dutch recruit many of their own people to abandon their cozy, prosperous homeland for a chancy transoceanic voyage and the likely far worse dangers, discomforts, and deprivations of frontier life. So the Netherlands government and the Dutch West India Company, the private compact of Amsterdam merchants it licensed as a monopoly to operate the colony, shied from investing the material and human resources that would have been required to establish the settlement and its environs as a fixture of Dutch hegemony.

Instead, the Hollanders settled on two expedients they hoped would

Parliament expressed the national will by inviting Protestant Prince William of Orange, the Netherlands' widely admired solider-statesman and husband of James's older daughter Mary, resistant to her father's Catholic faith, to take the British throne, provided the couple accepted a bill of rights that turned the kingdom into a true constitutional monarchy. The crown was prohibited from interfering with the administration of the law, imposing taxes without Parliament's concurrence, meddling with elections to the House of Commons, maintaining a standing army, and denying the people's right to retain arms for self-defense. The ascension of William III and Mary II prompted a massive sigh of relief throughout the realm and heralded a fourteen-year reign free of the religious, constitutional, and ideological tensions that had unnerved and bloodied the kingdom for most of the seventeenth century. Now a stabilizing evolution would produce government by consensus as a two-party parliamentary system emerged, allowing Commons—while still a far cry from a truly democratic institution—to determine the policies and control the national purse strings while the crown, through its Privy Council and ministry (soon to become the king's cabinet), operated the government under Parliament's oversight. Politics was no longer a deadly or even toxic game; ambitious men no longer sought office to impose divisive policies but to wield power for its own sake, with patronage and social standing as their prime spoils.

In that relatively serene setting, Britain underwent an unparalleled social transformation. Commerce and industry burgeoned with the expansion of the credit system and new debt instruments. Applied science—especially by the adaptation of Newtonian mechanics—spurred agricultural productivity, which in turn would sharply increase the nation's population over the course of the eighteenth century. The arts, too, flourished, especially literature, and the British military would beat back French, Spanish, and other foes to gain dominance of the seas and a widening empire in North America, the West Indies, and India. Still unaddressed by this expansive dynamism were the afflictions of the masses—poverty, poor health, ignorance, and the political subjugation of the unpropertied class, the nation's largest constituency.

people the colony sufficiently to ensure its prospective value. The government at the Hague made generous land grants, amounting in some cases to many thousands of acres of Hudson Valley farmland, to Dutchmen willing to gamble their future abroad with a license to rule their gratis estates like feudal landlords. The Netherlands concurrently sanctioned its American holding as an asylum for members of persecuted religious sects (Lutherans, Huguenots, Puritans, Quakers, and Jews most prominently), political fugitives (English, Scots-Irish, French, and German most commonly), and former petty criminals. All were welcome to earn a livelihood as artisans, laborers, and indentured or tenant farmworkers spread from New Amsterdam up the Hudson Valley as far as Fort Orange (later renamed Albany) and out across Long Island, which also drew English dissenters from rigidly Puritan New England.

Still, with little of value to export—by contrast, Frenchmen in the New World trafficked heavily in furs, the English raised tobacco, the Spaniards mined gold and silver—the Dutch colony's population grew slowly, outpaced by the surrounding British provinces. Only New Amsterdam, with its heterogeneous citizenry, was a thriving settlement, but by mid-century it was still little more than a struggling village. Though the Dutch West India Company's last director, Peter Stuyvesant, energized the colony, its defense consisted of too slender a militia manning rusty cannons—and, more to the point, its defenders lacked the willpower—to fend off growing pressure from the British. The Royal Navy, sailing with emboldened purpose now that the English Civil War and Cromwellian dictatorship had passed and the newly preening Stuart dynasty was restored in the person of the politic, high-living Charles II, moved in 1664 to displace the Dutch presence that had interrupted the British territorial expanse along the Mid-Atlantic coastline. The conquest was bloodless.

Unlike most British possessions, the new one was not designated a crown colony but a proprietorship given outright by the king to his brother James, Duke of York, for whom it was renamed. Because it was not granted a charter that would have placed clear limits on the royal prerogative within its boundaries, New York was autocratically and capriciously administered by governors and their retinues who counted on the gap of time and distance from London to tighten or slacken their reins on the colonists with little fear of reprimand. Indeed, the British were more controlling overseers than the Dutch, who had run the place like a company town, instilling little sense of communal or chauvinistic pride. Dutch landholders were allowed to retain their property, but British laws and taxes were quickly applied, all public offices were placed in British hands, and the colonists—mostly non-British—were denied a say in how they were ruled. There was no elective assembly or New England–style town meetings for airing grievances. Yet the British takeover never turned despotic. The few hundred troops garrisoned at the fort on the southwest tip of Manhattan were rarely called upon to whip the Dutch into civil obedience. For despite its new, officially Anglo trappings, New York remained during its first generation under crown rule largely Dutch in its culture. Freeholders in New York City and Hudson Valley land barons of Netherlandish descent still formed the local aristocracy; British immigration lagged as English newcomers to America preferred settling in Virginia, New England, and Pennsylvania, where their countrymen were already congregated.

But demographics soon gave way to acculturation. In religion, language, and acquisitive instincts, the English and Dutch proved highly compatible, though differing in temperament. Intermarriage grew, and the colony's—and especially New York City's—cultural porridge was thickened still further by the steady addition of immigrants from other lands, faiths, and races. They got along tolerably, by and large, and did not provoke their new rulers to apply the absolutist strictures of the Stuart kings. Which is not to say that New York was well or justly governed by its royal overlords.

Rather than playing martinets, the first two generations of colonial governors, most of them ex–military officers or minor aristocrats well down their families' hereditary ladder, took on their overseas posts as fortune-seekers out to maximize the spoils of their high office. Indifferent administrators at best, they were most adept at cadging fees and kickbacks for granting property titles, commercial monopolies, and appointments to public office—salable prizes typically bestowed on their friends, flatterers, and known clients of the crown. Some governors suc-

cessfully solicited the king and his councillors for assignment of t immense tracts of wilderness in their own or their relatives' nam future land speculation. Rule by elitist cronyism hardly invited dil administrative practices or policies aimed at meeting the colonists' needs or expanding their civil rights. This laxity and indifference, sy tomatic of rule by an absentee sovereign, were detectable in the freq turnover of governors—their tenures averaged three years and the between them was about eleven months. New York's economic and p ulation growth languished under early British rule even as it surged other colonies.

Charles II, for all his reputation as the philandering "Merry M arch," was a more wily and practical ruler than his Stuart forbears a reached a modus vivendi with Parliament as a brake on the rampa exercise of the royal prerogative. Accordingly, by the early 1680s, coloni governance of New York improved somewhat. The king granted its re idents a charter of liberties and privileges, and a legislative assembly wa authorized to raise taxes and codify the rule of law—albeit the governo retained an absolute veto over the colonial lawmakers' enactments. Bu when the Duke of York succeeded his brother as James II in 1685 and New York became a royal holding rather than the ex-prince's personal possession, the colony's fortunes soured. To consolidate his imperial domain in America, James assigned New York satellite status as part of the newly christened Dominion of New England, and its lately created assembly was no longer summoned. The colony's non-British majority in particular felt like subjugated residents of a conquered province as English newcomers with proper connections soon outstripped them in wealth and power. Domestic tranquility was yet more severely strained by news of the king's delusional behavior. A Catholic, he aspired to return the realm to the bosom of the Mother Church, a widely feared and reviled authority, and in the process subverted British laws and constitutional rights hard-won by Parliament. Impolitic and obstinate, James was hounded from the throne only three years after occupying it and fled to France, with whose regime he had clandestinely conspired.

With a renewal of full-scale civil war narrowly averted in the watershed year of 1688 by the so-called Glorious (and bloodless) Revolution,

III

News of the terrible shipboard toll of death and disease that had been inflicted on the arriving Palatine immigrants reached New York City's Common Council members even before the reduced cohort of Germans could set foot on Manhattan in the summer of 1710. While able-bodied labor was in demand throughout the colony, these reeling newcomers were likely far-from-healthy specimens, so the elected councilmen and their royally appointed mayor voted to quarantine the Palatines on Nutten Island (later renamed Governors Island), within swimming distance—if anyone dared to brave the harbor's swirling currents—of the Battery and British fort at the tip of the city until the arrivals could all be examined and efforts begun to rehabilitate them outside the city.

Young Peter Zenger's first home in America was probably one of the wooden huts that the City Council had ordered to be speedily thrown up on the island in the midst of the harbor, no doubt at the behest of safely arrived Governor Hunter, who wasted no time honoring his promise to Queen Anne and her ministers to provide for the Germans' sustenance. New York colonists, especially those in the city, were facing a serious shortage of bread just then, due to—according to City Council minutes—"the monopoly of the wheat by the inhabitants of the neighboring colonies." Under the circumstances, the council, also probably at Hunter's urging and in anticipation of what the Palatines might face as soon as they were freed from quarantine, decreed that local bakers and food purveyors would face penalties for raising prices exploitatively (besides costing the government more to feed the refugees who could not yet fend for themselves).

Hunter's next effort was directed toward placing the Palatines as indentured workers on manors and smaller farms up the Hudson Valley or as laborers to harvest timber and pine tar in the virgin stands on the colony's northern frontier. The latter materials were in heavy demand back in England, with its shrinking forests, to repair and expand the

Royal Navy and the growing fleet of cargo vessels carrying out the government's aggressive mercantile policy. Workers in the New York shipping trade, the colony's leading industry, and resident craftsmen and artisans were not eager for the German immigrants to vie with them for their livelihoods, so only 350 or so of the Palatines who had sailed with the Zengers remained in the city or settlements just across the harbor in New Jersey. That province, with a somewhat smaller population than New York's, was also under Hunter's jurisdiction in order to save the crown administrative costs, although it had its own elected assembly and slate of officials answerable to the governor.

Since her family had been villagers and her husband the local schoolmaster, not farming people like most of the Palatines, Johanna Zenger was likely resistant to being transplanted with her three children to a rural manor to perform hard agricultural labor under conditions akin to feudal serfdom or to be sent to a more distant region where the German men were wanted to fell forests and their families to serve as a human shield against the native tribes who sometimes menaced the uninvited white settlers. Governor Hunter, happily, had promised to arrange for apprenticeships for Palatine boys in their teens, but Peter was unlikely to enjoy a wide choice of masters; a harsh, hateful one might be imposed if a kindlier one could not be found. And the other two Zenger children might be taken from their mother by the authorities if she was unable to provide for them, or the family might suffer the indignity of assignment to the almshouse, so Johanna was on her mettle to rapidly discover what was going on in the colony's capital and how she and her brood might thrive—or at least subsist—there.

In 1710, Manhattan housed some 6,000 people, about 1,000 of them slaves, but small as it was compared with the Dutch metropolis of Amsterdam and Britain's immense seat of power, both of which the Zengers would likely have sampled en route to America, New York City was a busy place. Peter would have relished the noisy activity along the waterfront, where a newly arrived cargo ship tied up every few days; unloading them and refilling their holds with commodities for the outward voyage was at a peak during the fair-weather months when the Zengers were learning their way around. Sailors, haulers, draymen, people the colony sufficiently to ensure its prospective value. The government at the Hague made generous land grants, amounting in some cases to many thousands of acres of Hudson Valley farmland, to Dutchmen willing to gamble their future abroad with a license to rule their gratis estates like feudal landlords. The Netherlands concurrently sanctioned its American holding as an asylum for members of persecuted religious sects (Lutherans, Huguenots, Puritans, Quakers, and Jews most prominently), political fugitives (English, Scots-Irish, French, and German most commonly), and former petty criminals. All were welcome to earn a livelihood as artisans, laborers, and indentured or tenant farmworkers spread from New Amsterdam up the Hudson Valley as far as Fort Orange (later renamed Albany) and out across Long Island, which also drew English dissenters from rigidly Puritan New England.

Still, with little of value to export—by contrast, Frenchmen in the New World trafficked heavily in furs, the English raised tobacco, the Spaniards mined gold and silver—the Dutch colony's population grew slowly, outpaced by the surrounding British provinces. Only New Amsterdam, with its heterogeneous citizenry, was a thriving settlement, but by mid-century it was still little more than a struggling village. Though the Dutch West India Company's last director, Peter Stuyvesant, energized the colony, its defense consisted of too slender a militia manning rusty cannons—and, more to the point, its defenders lacked the willpower—to fend off growing pressure from the British. The Royal Navy, sailing with emboldened purpose now that the English Civil War and Cromwellian dictatorship had passed and the newly preening Stuart dynasty was restored in the person of the politic, high-living Charles II, moved in 1664 to displace the Dutch presence that had interrupted the British territorial expanse along the Mid-Atlantic coastline. The conquest was bloodless.

Unlike most British possessions, the new one was not designated a crown colony but a proprietorship given outright by the king to his brother James, Duke of York, for whom it was renamed. Because it was not granted a charter that would have placed clear limits on the royal prerogative within its boundaries, New York was autocratically and capriciously administered by governors and their retinues who counted on the gap of time and distance from London to tighten or slacken their reins on the colonists with little fear of reprimand. Indeed, the British were more controlling overseers than the Dutch, who had run the place like a company town, instilling little sense of communal or chauvinistic pride. Dutch landholders were allowed to retain their property, but British laws and taxes were quickly applied, all public offices were placed in British hands, and the colonists—mostly non-British—were denied a say in how they were ruled. There was no elective assembly or New England–style town meetings for airing grievances. Yet the British takeover never turned despotic. The few hundred troops garrisoned at the fort on the southwest tip of Manhattan were rarely called upon to whip the Dutch into civil obedience. For despite its new, officially Anglo trappings, New York remained during its first generation under crown rule largely Dutch in its culture. Freeholders in New York City and Hudson Valley land barons of Netherlandish descent still formed the local aristocracy; British immigration lagged as English newcomers to America preferred settling in Virginia, New England, and Pennsylvania, where their countrymen were already congregated.

But demographics soon gave way to acculturation. In religion, language, and acquisitive instincts, the English and Dutch proved highly compatible, though differing in temperament. Intermarriage grew, and the colony's—and especially New York City's—cultural porridge was thickened still further by the steady addition of immigrants from other lands, faiths, and races. They got along tolerably, by and large, and did not provoke their new rulers to apply the absolutist strictures of the Stuart kings. Which is not to say that New York was well or justly governed by its royal overlords.

Rather than playing martinets, the first two generations of colonial governors, most of them ex–military officers or minor aristocrats well down their families' hereditary ladder, took on their overseas posts as fortune-seekers out to maximize the spoils of their high office. Indifferent administrators at best, they were most adept at cadging fees and kickbacks for granting property titles, commercial monopolies, and appointments to public office—salable prizes typically bestowed on their friends, flatterers, and known clients of the crown. Some governors successfully solicited the king and his councillors for assignment of title to immense tracts of wilderness in their own or their relatives' names for future land speculation. Rule by elitist cronyism hardly invited diligent administrative practices or policies aimed at meeting the colonists' civic needs or expanding their civil rights. This laxity and indifference, symptomatic of rule by an absentee sovereign, were detectable in the frequent turnover of governors—their tenures averaged three years and the lag between them was about eleven months. New York's economic and population growth languished under early British rule even as it surged in other colonies.

Charles II, for all his reputation as the philandering "Merry Monarch," was a more wily and practical ruler than his Stuart forbears and reached a modus vivendi with Parliament as a brake on the rampant exercise of the royal prerogative. Accordingly, by the early 1680s, colonial governance of New York improved somewhat. The king granted its residents a charter of liberties and privileges, and a legislative assembly was authorized to raise taxes and codify the rule of law—albeit the governor retained an absolute veto over the colonial lawmakers' enactments. But when the Duke of York succeeded his brother as James II in 1685 and New York became a royal holding rather than the ex-prince's personal possession, the colony's fortunes soured. To consolidate his imperial domain in America, James assigned New York satellite status as part of the newly christened Dominion of New England, and its lately created assembly was no longer summoned. The colony's non-British majority in particular felt like subjugated residents of a conquered province as English newcomers with proper connections soon outstripped them in wealth and power. Domestic tranquility was yet more severely strained by news of the king's delusional behavior. A Catholic, he aspired to return the realm to the bosom of the Mother Church, a widely feared and reviled authority, and in the process subverted British laws and constitutional rights hard-won by Parliament. Impolitic and obstinate, James was hounded from the throne only three years after occupying it and fled to France, with whose regime he had clandestinely conspired.

With a renewal of full-scale civil war narrowly averted in the watershed year of 1688 by the so-called Glorious (and bloodless) Revolution,

Parliament expressed the national will by inviting Protestant Prince William of Orange, the Netherlands' widely admired solider-statesman and husband of James's older daughter Mary, resistant to her father's Catholic faith, to take the British throne, provided the couple accepted a bill of rights that turned the kingdom into a true constitutional monarchy. The crown was prohibited from interfering with the administration of the law, imposing taxes without Parliament's concurrence, meddling with elections to the House of Commons, maintaining a standing army, and denying the people's right to retain arms for self-defense. The ascension of William III and Mary II prompted a massive sigh of relief throughout the realm and heralded a fourteen-year reign free of the religious, constitutional, and ideological tensions that had unnerved and bloodied the kingdom for most of the seventeenth century. Now a stabilizing evolution would produce government by consensus as a two-party parliamentary system emerged, allowing Commons—while still a far cry from a truly democratic institution—to determine the policies and control the national purse strings while the crown, through its Privy Council and ministry (soon to become the king's cabinet), operated the government under Parliament's oversight. Politics was no longer a deadly or even toxic game; ambitious men no longer sought office to impose divisive policies but to wield power for its own sake, with patronage and social standing as their prime spoils.

In that relatively serene setting, Britain underwent an unparalleled social transformation. Commerce and industry burgeoned with the expansion of the credit system and new debt instruments. Applied science—especially by the adaptation of Newtonian mechanics—spurred agricultural productivity, which in turn would sharply increase the nation's population over the course of the eighteenth century. The arts, too, flourished, especially literature, and the British military would beat back French, Spanish, and other foes to gain dominance of the seas and a widening empire in North America, the West Indies, and India. Still unaddressed by this expansive dynamism were the afflictions of the masses—poverty, poor health, ignorance, and the political subjugation of the unpropertied class, the nation's largest constituency.

III

News of the terrible shipboard toll of death and disease that had been inflicted on the arriving Palatine immigrants reached New York City's Common Council members even before the reduced cohort of Germans could set foot on Manhattan in the summer of 1710. While able-bodied labor was in demand throughout the colony, these reeling newcomers were likely far-from-healthy specimens, so the elected councilmen and their royally appointed mayor voted to quarantine the Palatines on Nutten Island (later renamed Governors Island), within swimming distance—if anyone dared to brave the harbor's swirling currents—of the Battery and British fort at the tip of the city until the arrivals could all be examined and efforts begun to rehabilitate them outside the city.

Young Peter Zenger's first home in America was probably one of the wooden huts that the City Council had ordered to be speedily thrown up on the island in the midst of the harbor, no doubt at the behest of safely arrived Governor Hunter, who wasted no time honoring his promise to Queen Anne and her ministers to provide for the Germans' sustenance. New York colonists, especially those in the city, were facing a serious shortage of bread just then, due to—according to City Council minutes—"the monopoly of the wheat by the inhabitants of the neighboring colonies." Under the circumstances, the council, also probably at Hunter's urging and in anticipation of what the Palatines might face as soon as they were freed from quarantine, decreed that local bakers and food purveyors would face penalties for raising prices exploitatively (besides costing the government more to feed the refugees who could not yet fend for themselves).

Hunter's next effort was directed toward placing the Palatines as indentured workers on manors and smaller farms up the Hudson Valley or as laborers to harvest timber and pine tar in the virgin stands on the colony's northern frontier. The latter materials were in heavy demand back in England, with its shrinking forests, to repair and expand the

Royal Navy and the growing fleet of cargo vessels carrying out the government's aggressive mercantile policy. Workers in the New York shipping trade, the colony's leading industry, and resident craftsmen and artisans were not eager for the German immigrants to vie with them for their livelihoods, so only 350 or so of the Palatines who had sailed with the Zengers remained in the city or settlements just across the harbor in New Jersey. That province, with a somewhat smaller population than New York's, was also under Hunter's jurisdiction in order to save the crown administrative costs, although it had its own elected assembly and slate of officials answerable to the governor.

Since her family had been villagers and her husband the local schoolmaster, not farming people like most of the Palatines, Johanna Zenger was likely resistant to being transplanted with her three children to a rural manor to perform hard agricultural labor under conditions akin to feudal serfdom or to be sent to a more distant region where the German men were wanted to fell forests and their families to serve as a human shield against the native tribes who sometimes menaced the uninvited white settlers. Governor Hunter, happily, had promised to arrange for apprenticeships for Palatine boys in their teens, but Peter was unlikely to enjoy a wide choice of masters; a harsh, hateful one might be imposed if a kindlier one could not be found. And the other two Zenger children might be taken from their mother by the authorities if she was unable to provide for them, or the family might suffer the indignity of assignment to the almshouse, so Johanna was on her mettle to rapidly discover what was going on in the colony's capital and how she and her brood might thrive—or at least subsist—there.

In 1710, Manhattan housed some 6,000 people, about 1,000 of them slaves, but small as it was compared with the Dutch metropolis of Amsterdam and Britain's immense seat of power, both of which the Zengers would likely have sampled en route to America, New York City was a busy place. Peter would have relished the noisy activity along the waterfront, where a newly arrived cargo ship tied up every few days; unloading them and refilling their holds with commodities for the outward voyage was at a peak during the fair-weather months when the Zengers were learning their way around. Sailors, haulers, draymen, shipbuilders, sailmakers and ropemakers, ironmongers, coopers, and chandlers—all were in constant demand. Grog shops and dry-goods stores close by the docks enjoyed a steady clientele, and smiths, carpenters, and masons were raising brick and wooden houses along the lengthening, closely packed streets. Soldiers from the nearby walled fort mingled unabrasively with civilians, and many a civic construction project was underway that season. City Hall on Broad Street was having its graceful cupola repaired and painted, and permanent benches were being installed in the ornate Supreme Court chamber on the second floor for use by grand and petit juries. A short way below City Hall's triple-arched entryway, workmen were putting up a cage, pillory stocks, and a whipping post for the colonists' viewing pleasure at the expense of local miscreants. Other workers were applying the finishing touches to the new bridge linking the docks with the adjacent residential neighborhood. Over on Broadway, the vestrymen at twelve-year-old Trinity Church had ordered the addition of a spire atop the steeple that would soon make it the tallest structure in the colony.

At taverns and coffeehouses and tea shops and church suppers, in private parlors and public markets, and amid curbside auctions of every manner of merchandise, one curious topic was on everyone's lips—the reported sensation caused at the British royal court by a delegation of four sachems from the Iroquois tribe at the colony's northern frontier west of Albany, who were visiting London to beseech the great white queen to make an alliance with them to repulse French traders and their soldiers encroaching on the natives' hunting grounds. The queen and her courtiers were said to be fascinated by the appearance and customs of her primitive American subjects and inclined to grant their request. At City Hall, lawyers, clerks, and politicians were buzzing about the findings of a Common Council investigating committee that the treasurer's books showed a £645 shortfall in the municipal account—roughly $175,000 in twenty-first-century dollars—blamed on unpaid taxes and other debts to the city by "sundry persons." The city magistrates were promising a stringent crackdown on delinquent payers. The juiciest item of prattle that season was the ongoing speculation of the fate of Edward Hyde, better known as Lord Cornbury. First cousin of Queen Anne, Oxford scholar, hero of the Glorious Revolution, and seventeen-year veteran of the House of Commons, Cornbury had been governor of New York and New Jersey for seven years until he was ignominiously dismissed by the Privy Council in 1708 on charges of malfeasance and immorality and was still being held in prison in New York Harbor while the queen decided how to dispose of her errant relative. Among the claims against Cornbury, then forty-nine, were acceptance of bribes totaling at least £1,100 for political favors; diverting £1,500 in crown funds intended to outfit and arm the queen's garrison at the fort so that a mansion could be constructed on Nutten Island as the governor's summertime retreat (a charge Cornbury vigorously contested); attempting to prevent Quakers from holding public office in New Jersey; making land grants as large as 30,000 acres for excessive fees and gratuities so that the bankrupt aristocrat might hold off his creditors back in England, and that—the absolute choicest piece of tittle-tattle making the rounds throughout the colony— His Excellency would appear, on social occasions at the governor's residence, wearing a gown said to rival the queen's own most ornate finery. The queen was not amused, New Yorkers speculated, citing Cornbury's firing and detention, and mulled whether Robert Hunter would be an improvement or continue the crown's penchant for sending avaricious poseurs to govern them.

The colonists' tolerance of habitual misfeasance by the royal entourage is best understood if set against the political realities of the age. Great Britain may have been in the vanguard among nations with democratic leanings, but it was a glacial process. Déclassé and propertyless multitudes remained at the mercy of men of hereditary privilege and entrepreneurial zeal. In New York, colonial freeholders, men with substantial real estate, personal valuables, or cash income, qualified as voters; artisans, tenant and indentured farmers, and common laborers who made up well over half of the adult white male population were either denied the ballot or intimidated from voting by the aristocracy of baronial estate owners and mercantile moguls. In an age when exercising the franchise, for the minority who enjoyed it, consisted of openly declared voting, secret political allegiances were hard to hide or sustain. The lordly class held sway with the class-conscious governors, filled most of the twelve seats on the Provincial Council, which was tasked with consenting to gubernatorial decrees and patronage choices, and dominated the elected Assembly, whose two dozen or so lawmakers held the governor's purse strings by setting the colony's administrative budget and taxes. No governor could succeed without cosseting his best-off subjects, who reciprocated as accomplices to often abusive royal rule.

Still, times and communal needs were changing in a way that brought more than a sprig of hope for the prospects of the widow Zenger and her children and people like them to escape penury and social degradation. Marketplace laws of supply and demand were beginning to place enhanced value on the economic utility of every colonist. The large country estates granted to favorites of the crown were of little use or worth unless hands and heft were available to cultivate them. Similarly, the surge in oceangoing commerce and coastal trade among the Atlantic colonies that fanned out from New York Harbor required growing legions of workers at every skill level, and their aggregate industry was spreading wealth across society. The steady rise in immigration by manual laborers had its counterpart in a growing spillover of gently raised but disadvantaged victims of the Old World's law of primogeniture. These assorted arrivals, all hungry for a decent livelihood and secure future, added to an already fluid social structure that hastened the breakdown of unmanageably large landholdings and commercial monopolies. The result was a growing yeomanry of independent farmers and a rising entrepreneurial class of commodity traders, small-scale manufacturers, shopkeepers, and service-providers, of whom lawyers proved the most accomplished strivers. In New York more than anywhere else, the eighteenth century unfolded for a new world less and less beholden to orthodoxy and regimentation. Energy, talent, and ambition were given latitude unknown in European societies as New York men and families rose higher and faster in social, economic, and political standing than in most colonial settings. In such a place, where the dignity of the individual was becoming tacitly acknowledged, emerging discontent with government policies and conduct could not be blithely ignored forever.

IV

Within a few months of her fearful and fatherless family's arrival in the city, Johanna Zenger had made a suitable arrangement to improve her oldest child's prospects in the world.

For seventeen years, William Bradford had been the official royal printer for—and, in fact, the sole printer in—the colony of New York. Just recently his establishment on Hanover Square had issued the second version of the province's laws and the *American Almanack* edition for 1711. Inquiries about the forty-seven-year-old proprietor would have revealed to Peter Zenger's mother that Bradford, a leading vestryman at the Anglican Trinity Church, was regarded around town as a sober, hardworking, yet affable overseer, said to be a friend of the poor and needy, a category for which the Zengers fully qualified.

We can only guess what skills and aptitudes thirteen-year-old Peter might have had to offer the master printer. Even if the lad were quick-witted, he had probably heard English spoken only during the year or so that had passed since his family fled the Rhineland and would not likely have been fluent in it. But he must have seemed alert enough, and his mother was doubtlessly persistent in touting her boy's obedient and resourceful character, for Bradford to have agreed on October 26, 1710, to sign official papers assigning the German boy to his charge as a shop apprentice for eight years. The printer was to provide him with "good, sufficient and wholesome meat, drink and clothing"—and lodging, too, probably, the better to tend to his chores as printer's devil while allowing him to remain within brisk walking distance of his mother and younger siblings. In return, Peter pledged to serve his master "well and truly . . . not to absent or prolong himself" from Bradford's service at any time, and "to behave in all things as a good and faithful servant." In the event that their arrangement endured, the printer agreed to return Peter to the governor's custody at its conclusion.

The anxious teenager could hardly have found a better or more understanding mentor, for William Bradford himself had not had an easy time of it on the way to becoming a leading citizen of New York and its only purveyor of words in print.

The son of a printer, Bradford was born into a Quaker family in Leicestershire in the middle of the English Midlands. As was customary in most societies, he took up his father's trade and the family faith, apprenticed with the leading Quaker printer in London, and married his daughter. Given the competitive pressures of his strictly regulated trade, the twenty-two-year-old journeyman was pleased to accept the arrangement his father-in-law made for him to set up the first press to operate in the colony of Pennsylvania. William arrived in 1685, opening a shop in the outskirts of Philadelphia and enjoying the title (without salary) of official New World printer for the Society of Friends, the colony's dominant sect and not a persecuted dissident denomination as in England. Even so, it was not long before Bradford found himself in trouble of the sort that had plagued his trade ever since Johannes Gutenberg's 1439 invention of a printing press that used moving type.

A great irony had accompanied the arrival of one of civilization's most important tools. Even as mechanical reproduction of type-set texts superseded hand-copied work and began to liberate the human mind from thralldom to secular and ecclesiastical authorities, so did it alert those rulers and arbiters of society to the likelihood that an increasingly curious laity might soon awaken to subversive ideas that could incite demands for fundamental changes in the social order and spiritual realm. As literacy spread beyond the chambers of government, religious sanctuaries, universities, and counting houses, anxious authorities devised means to stunt the creation, production, and distribution of printed material and began imposing penalties on all who would flout the new controls. Governments would charge violators with disturbing the peace and sedition, and those convicted met with fines or prolonged incarceration or bodily disfigurement (or a combination thereof); the clergy would brand preachments against orthodoxy as heresy and demand confession of error from objectors whose only options often were excommunication or extermination. This relentless vigil over printed matter as the potential catalyst for revolutionary thought and behavior was more than misplaced zealotry; it was accurate recognition that the handwriting of change was no longer on the wall—printed messages had taken its place. Thus, the pace of the Renaissance quickened with the arrival of mass communication by print. The medieval mind was further flushed free of conformity by Luther's iconoclastic postings in 1517, leading to the Protestant Reformation and a yearning to contemplate one's place in life and eternity free from the dictates of temporal and clerical authority. Sacred texts and other forms of moral instruction could now be consulted directly as guides to personal salvation. Indeed, literacy was understood to hold the key not only to reaching a state of grace but to almost every phase of human advancement. Accordingly, soon there were books—primers—to help propagate literacy, and the Age of Enlightenment followed, spawning in turn the industrial, scientific, and political revolutions that would come to define modernity.

In sixteenth-century England, secular and religious officials were sufficiently fearful of printed material as a goad to social unrest that they collaborated to construct a two-part regimen to ration it. Tudor monarchs, in tandem with Parliament, the high clergy, and local magistrates, issued formal decrees that aimed at censoring whatever texts might be composed for circulation among the public and severely restricting the operation of printing presses. To ensure the peace of the realm, its ruling elements mandated that all dissenting opinion had to be suppressed, and the crown, through its proclaimed royal prerogative, unhesitantly appointed itself as the only instrument capable of carrying through such a program. Official press control began in 1529 with Henry VIII's issuing a list of 100 banned books. The next year the crown initiated a licensing system to certify who other than the royal printer had the right to operate a press and to import paper and ink from the Continent for that purpose. Censorship was similarly draconian: anything printed without the royal imprimatur was subject to prosecution. Because Henry was the head of both the state and the national church he established in his epochal quarrel with Rome, political and religious questions had become inseparably mingled, so all expressions of dissent or nonconformity were deemed to have the common effect of disturbing the king's peace and were thus punishable as subversive or even treasonable. Henry's daughters, Queen Mary I and, more so, Elizabeth I, expanded the licensing system as literacy grew and the menace of dissident thought and expression rose with it. The Stationers' Company, a crown-chartered guild of printers and publishers, was given two prime missions. Its first was to scrutinize all texts before publication to determine what was and wasn't fit for public consumption—the latter being mostly anything that smacked of Catholic theology, disparaged as cant and superstition. The Stationers' second duty was to restrict the issuing of licenses to printers and booksellers who, in return for their monopoly (limited early on to shops in London, York, and the university towns of Oxford and Cambridge), pledged full compliance with the crown's dictates. Under the eyes of an ecclesiastical Court of High Commission, the Stationers' wardens were directed to search out and seize propagators of objectionable material, who faced prosecution for their sins, particularly after the establishment of the Court of the Star Chamber. Under that demonic tribunal's 1586 decree, Star Chamber judges were granted royal exemption from defendants' common law right to a jury trial and freedom from giving self-incriminating testimony; the result was often predetermined and unappealable findings of what writings were iconoclastic, thus morally reprehensible—and harshly punishable.

The seventeenth-century expansion of British commerce and maritime power produced a newly vigorous mercantile class with accumulating wealth, expanding horizons, a yen for empire, and a hunger for practical information, fresh ideas, and news of happenings all over. Prominent among these was a nascent demand by commoners to share political power with the crown and end royal absolutism. One consequence of these developments was an outpouring of printed material, some of it illicit and placed in clandestine circulation, that was far different from the dry theological treaties, legal and commercial documents, and an occasional ancient classic that had been the standard output of print shops. Now pamphlets and books, often of a discursive or argumentative nature, appeared on a variety of subjects—philosophy, science, history; travel, literature (essays, poetry, and drama most often)—as well as broadsides and later the first so-called newsbook reports on foreign occurrences, although precious little about domestic events or the proceedings of Parliament. Journalism lay a century in the future.

This eruption of popular expression from below was decidedly unwelcome by the new Stuart dynasty and its first monarch, James I. He took the throne in 1603, openly disdainful of his subjects below the rank of nobility—"vulgar persons," he called them, who, in their massive ignorance, deserved no information about or say in their government's policies and ought to have contented themselves with mute allegiance to their rulers' mandates. Printers were placed under renewed surveillance, and two years into James's reign, the Star Chamber court reformulated the law of libel in a manner putting the realm on notice that any written or printed expression intended or serving to defame another's reputation—whether the target was a public or private person, alive or dead—would be punishable by fine, imprisonment, and/or "the amputation of the ears." By its very nature, libeling was defamatory and often contemptuous; it "robs a man of his good name, which ought to be the more precious to him than his life, and therefore when the offender is known, he ought to be severely punished." And there was a further reason, the Star Chamber said, for not tolerating scandalous accusations: they incited the victims' families, friends, and acquaintances to revenge and tended to produce quarrels, breaches of the peace, and even bloodshed. The court then extended its political outreach by holding that if the defamatory language was directed against a magistrate or other public person—from the king down to the humblest justice of the peace or municipal clerk—"it is a greater offense, for it concerneth not only the breach of the peace but also the scandal of government; for what greater scandal can . . . there be than to have corrupt or wicked magistrates to be appointed and constituted by the king to govern his subjects under him?" No worse sin could be attributed to the state than "to suffer such corrupt men to sit in the sacred seat of justice or to have any meddling in or concerning the administration of justice"—or, by implication, any other governmental function.

But what if the defamatory words were true? Were the targeted scoundrels nevertheless to remain in office, running the realm? Wasn't that a far worse sin? Why criminalize and prosecute whoever publicly unmasked royal employees who abused their power and denied the king's subjects knowledge of their malfeasance? No such irksome questions troubled the Star Chamber judges; near the beginning of their opinion in the case known as *De Libellis Famosis*, they wrote, "It is not material whether the libel be true or false." They did not say why— only that publishing any words, true or false, that tended to disturb the peace by maligning the government, justly or not, and thus presumably destabilizing the state was a crime and duly punishable. But in so declaring, the despotic Stuarts' pet court was ignoring a train of statutes, commonly referred to as *Scandalum Magnatum*, which ran back more than three centuries and were likewise intended to discourage aspersions on the crown, its retainers, and the nobility. All these laws took their cue from the first of them, passed in 1275 in the reign of Edward I, which stated, "From henceforth, none be so hardy to tell or publish any false news or tales whereby discord or occasion of discord or slander may grow between the king and his people or the great men of the realm." Indeed, one of the principal characteristics of these early antilibel statutes, according to Fredrick S. Siebert's *Freedom of the Press in England, 1476–1776*, was that "the matter objected to was *false* . . . which would lead to the conclusion that the falsity of the matter would have to be both alleged and proved by the prosecutor." That truth was a defense to a libel action "under the statutes," Siebert added, "is attested to by all the early seventeenth-century authorities." The tyranny inherent in the Star Chamber's condemnation of any and all criticism of the king's or his retainers' conduct of the realm—no matter how iniquitous that might be—had the desired chilling effect on writers and publishers. There was no outcry by the cowed masses; any protest against the regime would itself have been prosecutable before judges impaneled to quash it.

Under James's son and successor, Charles I, the muzzling persisted. In 1637, four years before its dissolution, the Star Chamber decreed still more stringent vetting of all printed matter produced within the kingdom or shipped in from abroad. As a further disincentive to the open exchange of ideas, the government also began to tax all texts approved for publication. By the 1640s, though, the rise of the entrepreneurial class and the lesser landed gentry had begun to breed resentment of the crown's obstinate hauteur as Charles embarked on a collision— and finally fatal—course with Parliament and its growing body of supporters. Subterranean opponents to the regime's oppressive ways now began to breathe fresh air, the fanatic Star Chamber was closed down, and unlicensed writers issued screeds proclaiming liberty of speech and the press an essential right of a free people as well as a benefit to enlightened statecraft. Continued suppression was seen through as dictatorship masquerading as defender of law and order. Among the pleas infiltrating the now lively, if not yet clamorous, national dialogue was one from the Netherlands, Britain's nearest Protestant neighbor, enjoying its heyday as the nexus of Western intellectual debate. To punish men's words so long as they were based on reason and not on "fraud, anger, or hatred," wrote philosopher Baruch Spinoza, served the interests of neither the wise ruler nor those he governed. Imprudent laws and unsound policies could be rectified by open discussion just as it would facilitate society's arrival at higher truths and fresh insights in the spiritual and philosophical realms—even if, Spinoza conceded, flawed or misguided thinking was aired in the process. Diverse ideas need not be divisive, he implied; liberty of expression would nurture harmonious communal spirit, not unsettle it as authoritarian officials insisted.

As government control over nonconformist thought was eased or averted, a passionate cry for uninhibited free speech and print was raised by Richard Overton, a leader of the English Levellers movement, dissidents who called on Parliament and the nation to embrace popular sovereignty through broadened suffrage, universal equality before the law, and religious tolerance in place of the schismatic turmoil wrenching society apart. To the privileged oligarchy in command of the realm, such demands were anathema, if no longer entirely unutterable. A more soaring anthem to free expression as the only pathway to ultimate wisdom and righteousness was John Milton's 1644 treatise, *Areopagitica*, justly celebrated by posterity though scarcely noted by his contemporaries. "Give me the liberty to know, to utter, and to argue freely according to my conscience, above all liberties," he beseeched. For all its fervor, Milton's luminous language was partially betrayed on closer examination by the conditional nature of his avowal of free expression—it did not extend, he allowed, to the beliefs of Catholics or atheists, whose convictions he loathed and whose utterances he would proscribe. Like many professed advocates of free expression, past and present, the immortal poet failed to grasp that its essence resides precisely in protecting the right to be read and heard of those whose words are repugnant to the listener as well as those whose words are in accord with one's own. Admiration for Milton's libertarian zeal must be tempered as well by his service, after the king's 1649 beheading, as an official censor during the Cromwell interregnum. His puritanical advocacy of free expression, furthermore, did not extend to what he regarded as licentious—in particular, obscenity and impiety.

During the English Civil War of the 1650s, both sides had more on their minds than curbing contentious speech and writing, but relaxation of control ended with the military dictatorship and the restoration of the Stuart dynasty. The realm, after enduring two decades of ceaseless religious and constitutional strife, had wearied of controversy. In the reactionary social climate of the second half of the seventeenth century, virtually all writing once again had to undergo prepublication screening lest it spread incendiary ideas that might, in the estimate of royal and church officials, lead to renewed domestic chaos. Crown officers snooped all over, violating without warrants the premises of writers, printers, publishers, and booksellers in an ongoing hunt for objectionable texts. Parliament, while striving to curb Charles II's genetically authoritarian impulses, connived with his regime to stymie social protest; in 1662, to cite an instance of such collaboration, Commons forced printers to affix their names to every item that went through their presses; violators risked the loss of their licenses. Champions of free expression, long out of season, had to find underground routes to the perilous marketplace of ideas, and some, like the defiant republican advocate Algernon Sidney, paid dearly for committing subversive words to paper even if retained within the confines of his own home. Sidney, while in his study, had the temerity to make notes suggesting that bad rulers deserved removal from office. When his private quarters were violated by crown agents and his musings discovered, he was tried for plotting the king's death, convicted of treason, and executed not for any act he had committed or words of incitement he had shared with others but for the indiscretion of writing down an idea. Could royal mind readers, ordered to club every suspect thought into submission, be far behind?

Five years after Sidney's martyrdom, the autocratic, cavalier line of Stuart kings was—as Sidney had prescribed—forcibly ended (though James II, unlike his father, managed to retain his head), and Parliament's long struggle for ascendancy was crowned by the realm's consensual embrace of Prince William of Orange and the establishment of constitutional monarchy. While the accompanying Bill of Rights that spelled out clear limitations on the crown's power was silent on the people's liberty to express displeasure with their government, it did allow members of Parliament to speak their minds with impunity as long as any derogatory words were delivered within the legislative chambers at Westminster. This "parliamentary privilege" was extended to the right of members to deny outsiders permission to report or comment on either house's proceedings and to prosecute those who dared to do so—and without a jury trial since the membership as a whole was supposedly to function as a jury. What the crown had surrendered in setting itself above the law and answerability to popular grievances Parliament seized up to make itself a sanctuary inviolable by criticism from any quarter.

Yet by a series of votes culminating in 1694, Parliament started to clear away the thicket of official suppression confronting all who wished to express their beliefs, wherever the chips might fall. The long-standing licensing acts that required a government or church permit prior to publication for any printed matter were allowed to lapse. Henceforth, all who could command a press or pay for its use were free to publish what they wished. The milestone seemed, momentarily, to mark an epochal advance in the liberty and dignity of every crown subject. But there was a barbed catch that accompanied the lifting of censorship. The action was not tantamount to a waiver of liability from prosecution for libel if freely published words of protest or vilification offended the sensibilities or reputations of those against whom they were directed, justly or not. And who was to determine if the defamation was merited, the courts or the public as represented by juries? The courts claimed that power, but the question was repeatedly contested over the next half-century. Either way, one still had to face the consequences of choosing to characterize villainy for what it was. Defamation of private persons could come at a high cost even if the writer was blackening the name of a blackguard. And the price could climb even higher if the writer chose to assail government officials, regardless of the validity of the accusation. In the view of most scholars and the barristers at London's Inns of Court, the doctrine of seditious libel as framed nearly a century earlier by the long-since-discredited Star Chamber had not in the least eroded, and Parliament exhibited no intention of granting statutory relief to libertarians who might then besiege the government with incessant protests over alleged abuses of power or acts of folly. Writers and printers remained subject to fine, jail time, and bodily insult for *any* defamatory words aimed at the keepers of the kingdom. Instead of a cause for celebration, the demise of official press censorship before publication was rather like winning the right to obtain a key to the lion's cage at the local zoo without first having to demonstrate the skill to tame the beast. Problematic or encumbered freedom of the press was no freedom at all, as William Bradford soon discovered upon transplanting his trade from England to Pennsylvania.

V

To understate the matter, the printing trade was not much encouraged in colonial America. Literacy was higher there, studies have suggested, than in Britain or on the Continent, but such demand as there was for reading material in a frontier setting, where survival was the prime concern and not intellectual development, could be largely satisfied by publications shipped in from the mother country. Books, moreover, were manufactured products, and Britain's mercantile system did not encourage manufacturing in the colonies, whose main function was to enrich the kingdom by sending home crops and raw commodities at a cheap price while serving as a captive market for items made in Britain.

Books and pamphlets fell into the category of luxury goods in America, and those most sought were of a practical nature—teaching primers, prayer books, instructive manuals, and almanacs containing vital information on seasonal weather and the tides, dates for court sessions, routes and schedules for postal riders—along with occasional snippets of wisdom from sages of the ages. Works of literature or of a reflective nature were less in demand; the colonists, after all, were busy making history, not contemplating it.

The overseers of the realm, moreover, were no more eager to promote the dissemination of provocative writing, casting doubt on the entrenched social order, in their overseas outposts than at home. American printers, too, had to be licensed and their numbers were restricted, and what they produced throughout most of the first century of British colonization required crown approval. Indeed, seditious thoughts planted among their offspring far away from hovering parents might take root more easily and resist weeding more fiercely. The government's prevailing attitude may be judged from a 1671 remark by William Berkeley, long-time governor of Virginia, the most populous of the thirteen colonies: "I thank God there are no schools and printing [here], and I hope we shall not have these [for a] hundred years, for learning has brought disobedience and heresy and sects to the world, and printing has divulged them. . . . God keep us from both." Fifteen years later, King James II's written instructions to Edmund Andros, on becoming governor of the newly designated Dominion of New England, were of like sentiment: "For [in]asmuch as great inconvenience may arise by the liberty of printing within our said territory under your government, you are to provide by all necessary orders that no person keep any printing press . . . nor that any book, pamphlet or other matters whatever be printed without your especial leave and license first obtained." Even after Parliament voided its licensing act following the Glorious Revolution, such repressive instructions remained standard in the American colonies. In New York prior to 1719, every governor was told that no press, book, pamphlet, or other printed matter was permitted without a license obtained from him or his office.

Given the risks of censure and punishment for attracting the displeasure of colonial officials—and the threat of prosecution for committing seditious libel, a crime as reprehensible in the eyes of the royal authorities in the colonies as in England—what few printers there were in America took pains to give as little offense as possible. And in fairness, the colonists by and large had little to complain about for the way the crown treated them. Their land cost them a relative pittance or nothing at all to obtain, food was plentiful, work was available for all willing to bestir themselves, taxes were low, nobody was pressed into military service, and the small garrisons of soldiers posted among them rarely if ever menaced the civilian population or had cause to. In truth, the colonial governments kept the crown's subjects under as light a rein, probably, as any imperial masters in recorded history. Nonetheless, colonial printers did not chance roiling still waters. Their staple printed items for most of the seventeenth century were government laws and proclamations, commercial and legal forms, orthodox theological tracts, moralizing sermons, hymnals, calling cards and stationery, and posters. Books were cheaper to import than produce in the colonies, so printers supplemented their incomes by selling imported titles.

Even while sticking to products devoid of politics or controversy, printers struggled to make ends meet, in part because production materials were hard to come by. The British government strictly limited the number of foundries that could make type, how much of it each could sell, and the variety of type fonts a print shop could own—hardly a subtle means to discourage the trade—and so the type available for export to colonial printers was often used long after it became old and broken. Paper, too, was in short supply and costly, and the locally produced kind was likely to be of inferior quality. One of William Bradford's better business decisions a few years after opening his own shop was to join in a venture creating the first paper mill in Pennsylvania. Ink was also a scarce commodity—lampblack and varnish, its chief ingredients, generally had to be imported—and printing presses themselves, complex devices to build, were as yet beyond the capability of colonial mechanics.

It is not surprising, then, in view of the obstacles to solvent operation, that by 1710, when Peter Zenger began his apprenticeship in William Bradford's shop, only fifteen printing establishments had opened throughout Britain's Atlantic seaboard colonies during their first century of settlement. That Bradford had survived as a printer for twenty-five years by then, considering the grief visited upon him for what, to modern observers, seem like entirely innocuous infractions, was a tribute to his sturdy backbone and unflagging industry.

One of his first undertakings in Philadelphia had been to offer the public an almanac for the year 1686—it was a product that would prove a popular seller for Bradford over his career—but soon after its appearance, the printer suffered a stinging official rebuke for no graver sin than naming in print the proprietary governor of the colony, William Penn. A pious enough Quaker himself (or he would surely not have been invited to open his shop under the sect's auspices), Bradford had not supposed that a passing reference to "Lord Penn" was contrary to the Society of Friends' tenet against any form of self-aggrandizement. He was told otherwise by the Provincial Council, Penn's pawns, and ordered to reprint the almanac with the proprietor's name omitted and not to print anything else without the consent of the council—especially nothing about the Quakers unless they agreed to it. The caveat seems to have slipped Bradford's mind—or he chose to risk defying it—for the Friends censured as well the 1688 edition of his almanac because it contained some playful passages offensive to the society's sense of rectitude, and they demanded that the publisher recall all copies thus far sold and destroy them. Bradford was paid £24 for his troubles and likely considered himself fortunate not to have been expelled from the sect.

A year later Bradford was at odds with the Provincial Council after one of its members had contracted with him to publish Penn's original charter of the colony along with the councilman's commentary, titled "The Frame of Government" and intended to let Pennsylvania citizens know their rights and privileges under a proprietary ruler—presumably a constructive purpose. Bradford was apparently unaware (or knew and disapproved) of an earlier vote by the council, perhaps in private, not to make the charter public knowledge in order to forestall any objections to their oligarchic rule over the colony. The councilman who engaged Bradford for the job was summoned before Penn's surrogate governor, John Blackwell, and the council to explain why the charter was published in violation of the rule against issuing printed material "of a dangerous nature" without benefit of an official license. The councilman remained mum except for invoking his common-law right not to testify against himself. Governor Blackwell, aware that Bradford's press was the only one operating in colonial America south of New England, hauled the printer before him but was unable to elicit self-incriminating testimony from him either. Angered, the governor bellowed that he had been empowered by Lord Penn himself to shut down the printing trade in the colony whenever he wished, so if the defiant Bradford cared to remain in business, he would have to post a heavy bond—reportedly as much as £500—to ensure his future printing of "nothing but what I allow." Bradford argued back that as a businessman he ought to be free to take on whatever jobs came through the door, adding boldly, "Printing is a manufacture of the nation, and therefore ought rather to be encouraged than suppressed."

Unchastened but wearying of harassment, Bradford accepted his father-in-law's offer to take over his press back in London, but the Friends Society, unwilling to lose their printer's skills, offered him a modest salary and, more important, a pledge to subscribe for 200 copies of any book they approved of his printing. The newly cordial relationship lasted two years until Bradford sided with a separatist faction of Quakers led by the master of the Friends' Philadelphia school. The teacher had dared to voice his dissenting views at meetings and with a collaborator expressed them in several pamphlets Bradford agreed to issue; in doing so, he omitted his name as printer, a thirty-year-old requirement by Parliament that applied in the colonies as well as in England. One of the pamphlets, moreover, accused the deputy governor of exceeding his magisterial powers. The co-authors and Bradford as their accomplice were charged with circulating "a malicious and seditious paper . . . tending to the disturbance of the peace and subversion of the present government." Summarily tried, without a hearing, by a provincial court packed with the deputy governor and other magistrates whom the offending tract had accused of abusing their power, the defendants were convicted—Bradford additionally for failing to list his name as the printer of the pamphlets—and fined the modern equivalent of $1,000 each. For good measure, the perpetrators were further humiliated in the public marketplace, where the town crier denounced them as subverters of the government and enemies of the king. Afterward, they were jailed until they agreed to recant their offenses.

But they would not. Bradford, for whose sins his printing equipment had been impounded by the government, demanded his Magna Carta right to a jury trial and, after being held four months in prison, was granted his wish. The prosecutor insisted at the outset that the jury could decide only whether Bradford had printed the pamphlets and, if so, it was then up to the judges to determine whether the publications amounted to seditious libel tending to cause a breach of the peace. Bradford, serving as his own lawyer, insisted the jurors were entitled to act as arbiters of the law as well as finders of the facts, so it was the jury's place, not the court's, to rule whether the pamphlets were an incitement to public unrest or merely an expression of the authors' personal opinions. The court ruled against the printer.

Bradford was left with only one defense—that, even though the sheriff's officers had entered his shop and seized the printing form containing the type for the pamphlets at issue, there was no hard evidence that the defendant himself had either set the type or printed the pamphlets. It may have seemed a lame argument, given the overwhelming circumstantial evidence against the shop owner, but it suddenly grew stronger. As the jurors were passing around the printing chase that held the schoolmaster's article, offered by the prosecutor as Exhibit A, the quoins securing the type within its frame loosened, scattering the letters all over the courtroom floor and ruining the only solid evidence against Bradford. After two days of deliberation, the jury was deadlocked nine-to-three in favor of conviction and was dismissed.

Bradford asked for release from custody and the return of his printing equipment while awaiting retrial, but his request was denied. Months passed until the anguished prisoner finally won a reversal of fortune. A year after his original arrest, Bradford was rescued by the intervention of the new governor of New York, Benjamin Fletcher, who had also been named temporary governor of Pennsylvania after Penn's charter had been suspended. Fletcher persuaded the Provincial Council that judging the libelous content of the pamphlets was really a theological matter, best settled among the Quakers themselves. Bradford was let out of prison and, his equipment restored to him, accepted Fletcher's invitation to quit Pennsylvania, with its press-baiting officials and forever-querulous Quaker elders, and become the royal printer for New York colony.

William Bradford may not have been a perfect craftsman—indeed, his publications often revealed poor design, broken type, uneven inking, muddled pagination, and lax proofreading—but he was hardworking, plucky in his dealings with the authorities, and notably innovative in certain aspects of his trade, such as type styles, bookbinding, and paper-making. In New York City, where he enjoyed the governor's sponsorship and greater social and religious tolerance than prevailed in any other crown colony, Bradford's business immediately flourished. His records for 1693 show that he issued thirty-eight publications, among them the laws and acts of the New York General Assembly and the ordinances of New York City's Common Council. It was likely more than happenstance that the first book he brought out was titled *New England's Spirit of Persecution Transmitted to Pennsylvania*. And when Governor Fletcher presided over the dedication ceremonies of the first Trinity Church on lower Broadway in 1698, among the newly welcomed Anglican congregants was the colony's lapsed Quaker printer.

Bradford's success was surely bolstered by being the colony's only printer for thirty-two years after moving there. His monopoly would be broken when a far smaller shop was opened by a struggling rival whom he had taken on as an apprentice fifteen years earlier.

2

Stormy Petrel

WHEN PETER ZENGER began his apprenticeship there in October of 1710, William Bradford's shop had lately finished printing a second edition of *The Book of Common Prayer* after selling out its initial run of 1,000 copies, a highly lucrative as well as spiritually satisfying outcome for the proprietor. Just what tasks he assigned to the new German boy or how much he taught him about the fine points of the craft, neither of them recorded, but Peter likely performed his chores well enough or he would not have been kept on for the full eight years of their contract.

Bradford's shop was a place often frequented by men of standing, and an attentive lad would have heard much talk about the commercial and political activities swirling within several blocks of the shop. Just a few weeks after he got there, Peter might well have absorbed his first lesson in local politics by listening in on reports of the sensational news on November 9. The New York Provincial Assembly, in session at City Hall, had voted that day to expel a recently elected member from Westchester for "falsely and scandalously [vilifying] the integrity and honor of the House" by calling his colleagues fools and knaves for denying the new governor, Robert Hunter, sufficient funds to administer the colony for the coming year. What the fledgling printer's devil could hardly have dreamed was that the ejected legislator, a fiery attorney and considerable property owner named Lewis Morris, was—despite the momentary rebuke by his offended confreres in the Assembly—on a trajectory to become the most powerful political and legal figure in the colony other than whoever was serving as governor. He would also prove to be one of the two people responsible for gaining Peter Zenger his niche in history.

Given the advantages of a keen native intellect, substantial inherited wealth, and exploitable family connections to go along with his burning ambition, Lewis Morris might have ranked high among major eighteenth-century American statesmen. A generation or two before the likes of Franklin, Washington, Jefferson, Adams, and Madison and more than any of his contemporary colonists, Morris registered the first unequivocal series of protests, aloud and in print, against the abuses of the royal governors who carried out Great Britain's proprietary—and at times contemptuous—rule over her American possessions. That Morris did not gain history's recognition as an icon for the ages had less to do with the sometimes overblown and unsubstantiated nature of his antigovernment tirades, which were far from groundless, than with the contradictory impulses that turned his many blessings and talents against his own best interest. His lone biographer, Eugene Sheridan, in a commendably balanced appraisal, painted Morris as "an assertive and combative landed aristocrat, whose long and stormy political career in New York and New Jersey [displayed] a thoughtful and articulate man whose intellectual and political gyrations reveal that colonial America had a richer and more complex ideological universe" than widely supposed. What most concerns us here was his insistence on being heard—and read—in both high and low places and challenging the officially sanctioned forces of repression aligned against malcontents who spoke their minds.

By all accounts, Lewis Morris had a quick, expansively curious brain that retained much of what it encountered. He put that deeply stocked mind to use as an obsessive communicator. His supple tongue, spewing opinions on every topic under the sun, was equally adept at delivering pleasantries and heaping scorn. No less expressive on fools-cap, he wrote voluminously—ten-page letters, caustic essays tending to meander, didactic dialogues, satiric poetry, lucid legal tracts—much of it brilliant but too often victimized by a surfeit of cryptic verbiage. Whether speaking or writing, he exhausted his subject, not to mention the endurance of his listeners and readers. Nobody, though, took him for a dilettante. Even at his most playful, Morris was a serious man who, as modern vernacular puts it, didn't just talk the talk—he walked the walk. As a player in the public arena, he was audacious, seemingly fear-less, habitually irreverent, and unyielding in combat—in which he was engaged most of the time, even in benignly hectoring talk around the dinner table with his adoring family. Both professionally and privately, his energy level was astonishing. Adroit at multitasking, he simultane-ously held active roles in the judicial, legislative, and executive branches of government; closely supervised his extensive properties and the labor force that made them flourish; continuously educated himself, acquir-ing in the process a library of 3,000 volumes, one of the largest private collections in the colonies; performed as devoted paterfamilias during a fifty-five-year marriage that produced fifteen children (of whom eleven survived to adulthood)—and played the fiddle when the spirit, or spir-its, moved him.

Yet a seemingly perverse streak in Lewis Morris's nature shadowed these abundant gifts. Equanimity, let alone serenity, eluded him for the most part. The most reliable near-contemporary chronicler of his era, William Smith, Jr., minimized Morris's flaws by describing him as "a little whimsical in temper." The totality of his behavior suggests, rather, that Morris suffered from an intemperate personality, often combusti-ble when challenged and vengeful toward those who had managed to thwart his ambitions. It was not enough for Morris to be in the right about whatever issue was up for debate; he was given to overstating his foes' aberrant conduct or skewing their views in order to drive home his point—an advocate's occupational tendency. His manner could become brusque, imperious, and dismissive toward his social and intellectual inferiors and less than deferential to those who outranked him. His self-assurance apparently derived from a decided sense of entitlement to rule society reserved for people like himself—endowed with high intelligence, wealth, and social standing.

Morris's self-centeredness, detectable in his notorious unpunctuality, fed a penchant for overindulging in both talk and drink, leaving him insensitive to his effect on others. Fond of the company of learned men who seemed to gravitate to his parlor or tavern of choice—the Black Horse, usually, when he was in Manhattan—he would avidly preside over freewheeling discussions on crown policies, Cicero's oratory, Montesquieu's *Persian Letters* and latest theories of government, or whatever his own recent readings may have been. He could outtalk, outdrink, and outlast his companions, then sleep it off overnight and well into the next day, at times (according to his detractors) keeping parties in lawsuits before his court waiting for hours after they had traveled great distances to arrive on schedule. One of the learned men drawn into Morris's orbit, Cadwallader Colden, who was New York's longtime royal surveyor and probably the colony's leading scientist, likely hit the mark when he wrote in a memoir that the boisterous and egotistical Morris was not by temper "fitted to gain popularity." He was respected rather than admired, inspired fear as much as fondness.

Two centuries after Morris's death, Princeton historian Gordon B. Turner offered a glowing retrospective on his career: "His insistence upon the letter of the law and his uncompromising integrity made him a formidable opponent of those who attempted to surpass the limits of their authority." A less charitable assessment of Morris's formidable character would, while acknowledging his virtues, concede that they suffered from their owner's chameleonlike habit of tailoring his jurisprudential convictions and political coloration to suit allegiances that he hoped would advance his ends and enhance his power. These purposes at times surely served the communal welfare of both New York and New Jersey, where he owned large estates and was a lordly presence, but primarily they were directed at advantaging and protecting his own elitist class. As a man of letters, Morris would likely have been pleased to learn that he is credited most of all on these pages for becoming the prime instigator of a heated controversy that culminated in the awakening of press freedom in his native land.

II

Even a bland recounting of Lewis Morris's ancestry and upbringing reads like a Dickens novel. Few children have been taxed with
more grief and less love than the lonely waif whose parents died scarcely
six months after he was born ten miles north of New York City. The
infant was handed over to the custody of colonial authorities until they
could determine whether his nearest relative, a soldier of fortune turned
Caribbean sugar planter living 1,500 miles away, could be bothered to
tend to the tyke's welfare. As it turned out, he could and would, seeing
that the child was his nephew and namesake, but it took a few years for
the childless uncle, a stern convert to Quakerism already in his seventies,
to get around to the task.

Little Lewis's father, Richard, had been raised at Tintern, the Morris
family's estate in southeastern Wales, and was said to have been gifted at
writing and interested in science. But the tumultuous times of his youth
steered him into a military career, abetted by his older brother Lewis's
decision to organize a troop of cavalry that fought on Parliament's side
against the legions of the Stuart dynasty during the English Civil War.
The doomed King Charles I stripped the elder Lewis of his inherited
estate, but Colonel Morris won it back for having fought on the winning side and, craving adventure, went to sea as a ranking officer in
Cromwell's navy. Assigned to advance the Commonwealth's commercial interests by subduing pirates and disrupting Spanish trade in the
West Indies, he helped lead the seizure of Jamaica from its diehard royalist garrison and, liking the sunny climate, invested in property on the
lush island of Barbados. With the Stuart restoration that would make
him persona non grata back in England, the colonel took up permanent
residence on Barbados, became a prosperous planter, married a much
younger woman named Mary, who was reputed in family chronicles to
have been of low birth, and summoned his younger brother Richard to
join him in the island paradise.

The pair were close, working together during the 1660s and overseeing the 200 slaves who harvested a fortune for the brothers that allowed

them to buy properties on other Leeward islands as well. After Richard married Sarah Pole, daughter of a suitably wealthy colonial family, Lewis promised his younger sibling he would look after any of the couple's offspring if Richard died before him. In 1670, likely chafing at his comfortable but subordinate role, Richard sensed a ripe opportunity to strike out on his own in New York, seized as a British colony just six years earlier and short on enterprising English gentlemen. With Lewis's blessing and cash investment in their joint venture, he and Sarah purchased a 520-acre estate from its original Dutch settler, Jonas Bronck, at the southern end of what was then Westchester County (but would later be annexed by New York City as part of the Bronx, as the borough was called—a corruption of "Bronck's" property). Though by no means the largest estate in Westchester, it boasted a highly advantageous location just across the Harlem River from Manhattan and within easy sail of New York City's waterfront, where the Morris manor's farm produce would find ready buyers.

Sarah Morris gave birth on October 15, 1671, and the child was named devotedly after his father's brother. In late spring of the following year, his parents succumbed within a short time of each other, possibly from a contagious disease, but no documented cause of their deaths has been found. The orphaned infant Lewis was assigned by the province to temporary guardians and the care of household servants while word of the family tragedy was sent to his uncle in Barbados. The aging Colonel Morris conveyed his intention to honor his fraternal pledge to look after little Lewis, but he had business matters to attend to first. Meanwhile, the Dutch had surprisingly recaptured New York, complicating the uncle's commercial prospects if he took up residence there under an alien government. Happily, the Dutch reoccupation lasted only a short time, and the colonel arrived in New York in 1674 to act as surrogate parent of three-year-old Lewis. It would not be a happy household for the child.

His uncle Lewis, still married but childless, may have been dutiful in assuming his family responsibility, but he was by nature frosty and withdrawn as well as too old and too preoccupied with commercial undertakings to nurture his small nephew. His wife was even less inclined to provide tender loving care for the child, whom she saw from the first as the inevitable rival to inherit her husband's rapidly growing wealth. Belying his age, the septuagenarian colonel enjoyed a surge of entrepreneurial energy almost as soon as he settled in at Morrisania, as the family estate would be formally christened. He made it his business to befriend the new British governor, Edmund Andros, whom he prevailed upon to grant the Morris estate 1,400 adjoining acres that allowed it to become—with the importation of slave labor the colonel was practiced at exploiting—a reliable provider of food to satisfy the colony's increasing appetite. Then the rejuvenated oldtimer partnered with a well-heeled New York merchant, trading with England and the West Indies, and turned into an industrialist and even larger-scale farmer in 1675 by buying 4,000 acres in Monmouth County at Shrewsbury on an inlet of the New Jersey shore thirty miles from New York Harbor. The estate encompassed the largest iron mine and smelting works operating in seventeenth-century America, along with orchards and a cider press, pastureland for raising cattle, sheep, and horses, and a flour mill and a sawmill to process the grain harvest and pine stands on Morris's and his neighbors' land. In time Morris's Monmouth County holding grew to 6,000 acres, among the most productive and valuable spreads in colonial New Jersey. Extending his canny investments in realty, Uncle Lewis picked up 1,500 acres on Long Island, where English tenant farmers had begun to arrive from Connecticut, and a house in New York City. His economic success won the senior Morris prestigious seats on the provincial councils of both New York and New Jersey. And when not traveling to and from Barbados to superintend his plantation, he spent what time he could spare corresponding with leaders of the Quaker faith he had adopted in later life. With great solemnity he proselytized its pious precepts and ascetic strictures, which he sought—but failed—to impose on his rambunctious namesake.

Young Lewis, all who knew him agreed, was an incorrigible scamp, attended in a strict Quaker household by servants, nursemaids, and tutors answerable mostly to his Aunt Mary in lieu of his distant old uncle, who was generally in transit—and distracted when present. That the high-spirited child turned into a hellion, rebelling against ceaseless pressure to learn obedience and reverence in keeping with the Friends' creed, is hardly surprising. His mischievous ways, moreover, suited Mary's design. As the boy's son, Robert Hunter Morris, would write nearly a century afterward, his great uncle's wife "used every means to set the old gentleman against his nephew, [so] that she and her poor relations might have his fortune, and . . . she so far succeeded to make his [young Lewis's] life uneasy." A misery, actually, as she missed no chance to paint the boy's wholesome exuberance—exhibited, for example, by his indulging in foot races or nine pins with non-Quaker pals on the Sabbath, or harmless hi-jinks, like teasing his austere tutors—as deep character flaws when reporting them to his uncle. The older he got, the more young Lewis resented the woman's tyranny and her husband's void where a compassionate heart might have resided. Around his eighteenth birthday, he flew the suffocating coop, making his way southward and finally finding refuge in Jamaica, where he worked as a scribe, perhaps the source of his precise penmanship as an adult.

Lewis's disappearance must have pained his old uncle, remorseful that he had failed to serve adequately *in loco parentis*, as he had promised his brother Richard, for he made wide inquiries after his nephew's whereabouts and, when he learned the answer, sent a ship to fetch him home. Its captain likely carried a message that Colonel Morris was in rapidly declining health and wished to patch things up with the runaway. In true Dickensian fashion, Lewis arrived shortly before his uncle's death in 1690 and, in a further novelistic twist, Aunt Mary died just eight days later, even as Lewis's parents had gone to their Maker in close succession. Now the young man was left with no immediate relative— and good riddance to the last of them. But, surely expecting to come into his uncle's riches, he discovered, when the will was produced, just how wicked a schemer Mary Morris had been. The document said the decedent had intended to make his nephew sole executor of his estate and principal inheritor, but because of Lewis's "many miscarriages and disobedience toward me and my wife, and his causeless absenting himself from my house, and adhering to and advising with those of bad life and conversation, contrary to my directions and example unto him," Mary was named sole executrix and bequeathed, with her heirs, most of his real estate, including his prime residence, the choice 2,000-acre barony of

Morrisania, and all his personal property. Lewis was to receive only the remote, but hardly insubstantial farm, mills, and ironworks in New Jersey. Mary's almost immediate death—Dickens or any certified novelist would surely have had Lewis suspected of foul play by the authorities—meant that the lion's share of his uncle's estate would go to Mary's unknown relatives back in Barbados or wherever they were.

Rather than turning despondent over the loss of his uncle and, more genuinely, of most of his fortune, the resourceful Lewis, who knew a thing or two about penmanship, engaged legal counsel to scrutinize Colonel Morris's will for tampering and ordered a painstaking search for Mary's will. No will of Mary's was found, and, better yet, as Lewis's lawyers and his own eagle eye focused on his uncle's will, they detected a number of interlineal insertions in inconsistent handwriting and other telltale signs of fraud. Pressed to explain, Mary's maidservant Becky confessed to conspiring with her mistress to alter the will and destroy all of the elder Morris's personal and business papers that might have bared their skullduggery. New York's governor and the Provincial Council voided the will and declared Lewis the sole heir of his uncle's estate. Even before reaching his majority, he was in possession of nearly 10,000 fertile acres conveniently close to New York Harbor (and sixty-six African slaves to work them), three homes, a lucrative partnership in the mercantile trade, and one sizable sloop to carry the farm produce from his estates to the Manhattan docks and their nearby markets. By any standard, and further taking into account his uncle's assiduously gathered social and political connections, Lewis Morris was a young man with a future.

III

The former unruly child, drifting through a loveless universe, may have felt that providence owed him his sudden reversal of fortune, but far from settling into a life of feckless luxury, Lewis Morris took a series of life-altering steps to enhance his prospective ascent to the highest rank among the American-born colonial elite. The first was to accept the very practical arrangement his ailing uncle had made with James

Graham, a Scottish lawyer and minor merchant, to marry his eighteen-year-old daughter Isabella. What her father lacked in riches he made up for in political power; at the time, he was the speaker of the New York Assembly as well as the official recorder of New York City, entitling him to a seat on its governing council. Of plain appearance, Isabella was to prove an otherwise ideal life's companion for her ambitious mate—smart, sensible, highly principled, demurely mannered, tolerant of Lewis's often uncontainable ebullience, and always the gravitational pull on the large Morris family and its demanding but affectionate male head. Benjamin Franklin, later an acquaintance of the Morrises' son Robert, noted that Lewis was fond of inciting his offspring "to dispute with one another for his diversion while sitting at the table before dinner." Theirs was a lively, closely knit family circle.

Secure in his marriage, Lewis redefined in his own way how a country gentleman in colonial America ought to occupy himself. For one thing, he should not be afraid of getting his hands dirty. To sustain a comfortable standard of living, Morris became a serious farmer, familiarizing himself over time with most aspects of agronomy and resolved to make his holdings a paying proposition. Even with dozens of laborers and foremen at his disposal, running his cumulative estates was a complex enterprise—a cornucopia of grain in several varieties (but wheat primarily), apple and pear orchards, livestock, poultry, dairy products, lumber, flour, and ironware—that could have easily degenerated unless vigilantly maintained. His letters to his children over the years revealed hands-on attention to and continuous concern for the farms' upkeep. Morris knew how the land should be drained, depending on the grade of each field; what tools and fertilizers worked best where; how to build a chimney and repair a mill; which of his foremen and their workers were diligent and which were malingerers in need of replacement. Toward the slaves who did the heavy lifting and bending for him, Morris was less conscience-stricken than Virginia's most renowned and obsessive gentleman farmer, Thomas Jefferson. Lewis regarded his black bondsmen as a lower order of humanity, childlike, unsuited for the Christian faith, "stupid and conceited and will follow their own way unless carefully looked to"—in short, best spared the responsibilities of freedom. His uncle's Quaker piety had not excluded racial bigotry and cruelty where money was to be made.

Pragmatism, then, dictated Lewis's immersion in the demanding regimen that yielded abundant harvests—his inheritance would plainly not be preserved or grow of its own accord. But a more profound impulse told him he would never amount to more than a cloddish yeoman or arrive at the high station in society he aspired to unless he deepened his intellectual capacity and broadened his cultural interests. His education during childhood and adolescence was marked by stubborn resistance to hidebound private instructors who almost certainly dwelled on theological concerns and Greek and Latin syntax rather than subjects that might awaken a bright boy's hunger to learn. So he steered himself in that pursuit, setting out on an autodidact's groping quest to become conversant with— or at least sample—every aspect of human knowledge he could wrap his mind around. He could afford to buy any imported books or journals he cared to, so he read greedily, and probably unsystematically, in law, history, philosophy, politics, and literature ranging from the classicists—Virgil's poetry was a favorite of his—to the masters from earlier in his own century, Shakespeare and Milton in particular. Family lore has him becoming something of a linguist as well, teaching himself to read, beyond the leading European languages, a smattering of more obscure tongues: Hebrew, Arabic, and a soupçon of Chinese. Spiritual concerns, too, absorbed him as his religious preference drifted from the Quaker precepts he had been force-fed in his formative years to establishment Anglicanism to the Deism favored by many of the leading American statesmen of the eighteenth century. The more he read as time went on and the wider his social and political orbit extended, the more Morris was inspired to write, becoming a prodigious correspondent and playful rhetorician who occasionally published, at his own expense, tracts about social issues on which he hoped to draw readers to his view.

With his metamorphosis from headstrong, lonely lad to widely informed, happily married country squire well underway, young Morris had one more life-altering choice before him. If Isabella provided him nearly ideal companionship, agriculture supplied his material sustenance, and books offered him steady mental stimulation, what was to be his life's consuming vocation and social mission? Commerce and finance struck him as grubby trades, beneath the dignity of principled men of genuine aristocratic standing; those in business, he was convinced, had scant use for anything that did not promote their own pecuniary advantage. That left him only the professions to choose from among. He lacked the ministering dedication that the medical calling required, the certitude and sanctimony that guided men of the cloth, the regimentation—perhaps the homicidal instinct as well—that a military career demanded, and the true scholar's patience and devotion to the arcane. There was just one occupation that appealed to his questing mind, his hunger for respectability, and his need to control whatever setting he occupied at the moment—and an exemplary practitioner was near at hand.

James Graham, Lewis's father-in-law, was one of the foremost lawyers of his day and an influential politician at a moment when the British monarchy was being regenerated under William and Mary and the New York colony was arising from the doldrums during the decline and fall of James II. What better time for an amply equipped novice to begin making his mark in that vibrant setting? And while we have no documentary testimony about Lewis's legal training, who could have better instructed him—and opened more doors for him around the city and beyond—than his devoted wife's father?

Morris was doubtless a quick learner, likely clerking for Graham by day and by his own fireside each night absorbing the minutiae of torts and contracts, crown decrees and Parliament's statutes, and the thick reports on the English common law by its august commentators at the Inns of Court. But his purpose was not to represent private clients in petty suits or to vet every last "whereas" in tiresome legal papers. From the start, Lewis Morris was devoted to the precept of noblesse oblige, which to him meant, to cite his biographer's definition, "those who had the greatest material stake in society should have the largest say in the direction of its political affairs." To Morris's way of thinking, his class's entitlement to that "largest say" would ideally result in enlightened and benevolent governance of the community as a whole even while it protected its own vested interests. Whether Morris ever recognized that he had gained his sizable "material stake" in society not by talent or any sustained exertion on his part but by accidents of birth and death, we have no evidence. What we do have, without imputing to him duplicitous motives or shallow character, is a cocksure but untested player striding onto the stage, eager to win the plaudits of a raucous provincial audience.

He made that debut in what may seem at first to have been an unpromising venue. Instead of New York, site of his family seat at Morrisania and where his father-in-law could have been most helpful, Morris expended the bulk of his energy in its satellite sister colony on the western side of the Hudson. Throughout his twenties and most of his thirties, he would become the leading political firebrand in New Jersey and chief instrument of its transformation from a loosely chartered fiefdom run by perpetually wrangling proprietors—an anarchic no-man's-land, as a practical matter—to a bona fide and secure royal colony.

IV

It was not a haphazard decision; Lewis Morris was a calculating young man. In turning to New Jersey to make his mark in public affairs, he was surely driven in part by a desire to become his own man as quickly as possible and not just James Graham's family dependent and personal protectorate. But there were more practical advantages to staking his claim beyond the Hudson. New Jersey was a less populous place, its settlements were a fraction of New York City's size and widely scattered, and its commerce decentralized and small-scale, leaving a power vacuum that a nervy, forceful newcomer might readily fill.

Besides, he was hardly a total stranger to the territory. His uncle had been among the colony's largest landowners and his holdings in Monmouth County on the Atlantic coast perhaps its most successful agrarian enterprise. At the time of his death, moreover, Colonel Morris had been a longtime appointee to New Jersey's Provincial Council, tasked with administering the colony in tandem with the governor and the elected Assembly. Soon after Lewis inherited the Monmouth estate in 1692, the governor and the consortium of proprietors who claimed legal control of the province awarded Morris, lately turned twenty-one, his uncle's place on the council, as if it, too, were a hereditary possession. And as if that was not enough inducement for Lewis to cast his lot in New Jersey, the callow lawyer-in-training was offered a place on the presiding panel of the province's highest judicial tribunal, the Court of Common Right. His legal experience may have left something—indeed, everything—to be desired, but his father-in-law's reputation as an eminent New York barrister and leading legislator added a glow of promise to Lewis's likely learning curve, soon reinforced by James Graham's appointment as the neighboring colony's royal attorney general. Besides, in a jurisdiction with fewer than 10,000 residents, there was a dearth of candidates more qualified to sit on its high court than the articulate and prepossessing young patrician.

To sense the appalling confusion of the New Jersey political map that greeted Morris, picture a football field with a 6-foot-high wall across the 50-yard line, the rest of the yard markers running both horizontally and vertically except in places where there were no lines at all, and no referees to enforce two conflicting sets of rules. Shortly after British naval forces captained by Richard Nicolls seized New Netherlands from the Dutch in 1664, the territory was presented by King Charles II to his brother James, Duke of York, as a private possession, not a crown colony even though still a part of the royal realm. Extending to the Delaware River, the western portion of this expanse was designated New Jersey, and Nicolls, serving for four years as the crown-appointed military governor of the colony, shortly began issuing letters patent conveying title to prime farmland in northeastern New Jersey to settlers from more crowded New England and Long Island. In doing so, Nicolls was unaware that James had already deeded New Jersey in its entirety to a pair of noblemen, Lord John Berkeley and Sir George Carteret, as a reward for their loyalty to the crown during the English Civil War of the 1650s. The two proprietors were free to subdivide the immense spread by gifts or sales to whomever they wished, free of crown oversight, with the colony's administration to be financed by quitrents, a small annual realty tax. By the time Nicolls learned of this transaction, the governor, as authorized by his original instructions from the king, had deeded away more than 750,000 acres of James's generous proprietary grant to Berkeley and Carteret. Trouble was at hand.

Although the duke later acted to rescind the governor's grants, made in good faith but oblivious of the Berkeley-Carteret arrangement, the already settled grantees—known as the Nicolls patentees—strenuously objected. Their titles were legitimate, they insisted, and could not be arbitrarily superseded by the duke's gift to his noble friends. They refused to recognize the Berkeley-Carteret ownership or apply for new deeds and pay fees for them to the two proprietors. Nor would the Nicolls patentees hand over quitrents to them, insisting that the so-called proprietors had no legal power to govern the colony—James was without constitutional authority to convey that right; only the king could. But he never did—kings were not in the habit of ceding their sovereignty. Confusion reigned. Withheld tax payments meant that government was virtually nonfunctional, boundary claims went unsurveyed, township limits were vague or in dispute, and health and safety concerns left unaddressed. Some hardy souls ventured into that jurisdictional quagmire, but immigration to New Jersey was understandably slowed.

By 1673, the two proprietors had given up the struggle to rule the unruly territory as a single entity—it was a costly and losing proposition financially—and divided it into two roughly equal provinces, each with an elective but impotent assembly. Berkeley sold off the undistributed land in the western portion, much of it to Quakers, under its own proprietary governing board. Carteret hung on to the eastern half of the colony for a time—it was from him that Colonel Morris obtained title to the ironworks and the surrounding 4,000-acre spread in Monmouth County in 1675. But in 1683, Carteret's widow sold East Jersey to a consortium of twenty-four mostly Scottish proprietors, many of them absentee owners, who claimed the right to govern it despite ongoing objections by the Nicolls patentees that they had a prior right to the land and were exempt from proprietary rule. The division of the colony settled nothing; disorder and rancor remained rampant, and civil authority was up for grabs where it existed at all.

By the time the youthful Lewis Morris arrived on this chaotic scene in 1692 as an appointee to the New Jersey Council, a joint body with nominal administrative and legislative oversight of both provinces, East Jersey's soil was held by eighty-five proprietors, who claimed title to all undeeded real property, revenue from new land sales, and payment of annual quitrents of 2 shillings per 100 acres owned, whether by Nicolls patentees or purchase from the board of proprietors. Enforcing tax payments where law and order were a chimera was a chancy business. Matters were hardly better in West Jersey, where disputes raged between local Quaker landowners and the West Jersey Society, a London-based consortium of Anglican merchants and land speculators who bought out what they claimed were all the proprietary holdings in the province, including the Quakers'. With the crown's consent, the proprietary boards of both provinces jointly chose a governor, who was charged with eliciting the cooperation of the intransigent disputants. Lewis Morris devoted much of the next decade of his life laboring to untangle the mess, at times placing himself in physical and legal peril.

He worked inconspicuously in his early years, making it no secret that he sided with the East Jersey proprietors, since it was from their ranks that his uncle had obtained Morris's Monmouth estate amid nearby holdings of the Nicolls patentees, now cumbersomely known as the antiproprietary party. Morris's avowed goal was not to let the colony's sorry political factionalism cripple efforts by the unusually competent governor, Andrew Hamilton, to foster civil order and commercial development. As a member of the joint Council, Morris repeatedly urged the assemblies of the two Jerseys to provide Hamilton with the funds he needed to improve public services and safety. Additionally, given his standing as a prominent Westchester estate owner in New York with a father-in-law in the highest echelons of its government, he played a leading role in the effort to have East Jersey's capital and largest settlement, Amboy (later renamed Perth Amboy), designated a free port able to operate independently of nearby New York City's landing facilities and thus challenge its ambition to monopolize the region's trade. As a judge on the Court of Common Right, meanwhile, Morris did not shrink from invalidating grants to Nicolls patentees when challenged by purchasers of tracts from the East Jersey proprietors, who hailed him as their champion. Morris's stature was further enhanced as Governor Hamilton welcomed his more selfless activities in the colony's overall interests.

The arrival of a new governor, Jeremiah Basse, in 1698 brought a renewal of fractious politics across the colony. Basse, an Anabaptist minister and the former London business manager of the West Jersey Society, inspired immediate opposition from the Quaker-dominated West Jersey Assembly for his history of animus toward that sect. Basse, moreover, had tried to hide the fact that he took the governor's chair without presenting the king's requisite confirmation of his appointment. Morris, whether out of righteous indignation or blatant opportunism, was among Basse's most vocal critics for alleged usurpation of power and hectored him continuously for a year and a half as a deceitful and illegitimate holder of royal office. The offended governor exercised his claimed authority to eject the outspoken Morris from both the New Jersey Council and his seat on the Court of Common Right, triggering a campaign of defiance by the rising political star. Appearing at the first session of the colony's high court after his ordered removal, Morris loudly—and in salty language, attendants reported—denied the governor's right to summon the court into session, to toss him off its bench, and by extension to perform any of his official duties. When words grew sufficiently heated on both sides, Basse's backers attempted to seize and arrest Morris, who reached for his sword, but his own partisans shielded him from a likely skewering. He was fined £50 and paid it; contrition, though, was not in his nature. Morris's whole agenda now was to have Basse stripped of the governorship.

Standing in his way was the proprietary party, whose interests had largely matched Morris's but now stayed loyal to the governor of their own choosing. Whether based on a cynical stratagem or genuine concern for the welfare of the colony as ungovernable in its current legal limbo, Morris suddenly shifted his political allegiance. The whole proprietary regime, he now proclaimed, echoing his former Nicolls patentee foes, had never been granted the right to govern New Jersey by the crown, and the only way to bring progress and civility to the colony was to dissolve the existing arrangement, starting with the replacement of Basse, and have New Jersey royalized—that is, designated a unified crown colony. Morris rushed all over the place, addressing town meetings and church gatherings, issuing pamphlets, and trying to persuade proprietary leaders and their adherents that everyone in the colony would be better off under a politically secure system. These relentless efforts prompted Basse to have Morris charged with sedition and imprisoned, but the heavy-handed suppression served only to win the fiery crusader more support; an armed mob broke into the jailhouse and freed him. Thereafter, the renegade redoubled his efforts and made deep inroads in the proprietary camp, where a majority was now amenable to the Morris-backed crown takeover of the colony, provided that all existing land titles would be honored and other rights granted, like religious toleration of dissenting Protestant sects, Quakers prominently among them. Morris's harangues reached London and the ears of the Board of Trade, the Privy Council's panel in charge of the crown's imperial holdings, and hit home. Basse was relieved of his office and replaced by former Governor Hamilton, still well disposed toward Morris, who was given back his seat on the Provincial Council and made its presiding officer, and had his judgeship restored as well. He had succeeded not only in hounding Basse out of office but also in uniting disparate elements throughout the colony in his crusade to end its chronic acrimony. In recognition of these bold initiatives, Hamilton decided—perhaps at Morris's suggestion—that the feisty pol was the only colonist with the credentials and popularity to press the case in London to royalize the colony on terms acceptable to the proprietors.

He arrived there in midsummer of 1701 with the formal backing of the East Jersey proprietors and the West Jersey Society as well as Hamilton's endorsement as his official negotiator. As a lawyer, jurist, and the well-spoken voice of New Jersey's landed gentry, Morris was cordially received at Whitehall and invited to submit a written blueprint for how to configure the royalizing process. But it was far from certain that New Jersey could survive as a separate colony. Pressure to dismember it was brought by commercial and political forces in both New York and Pennsylvania who sought to annex East and West Jersey respectively. Morris persevered, fighting to save New Jersey's jurisdictional and geographic integrity. To his wish list of settlement terms for surrendering proprietary control of the two provinces to the crown, he added one item that had not likely won approval by many of his fellow Jerseyans before he set sail for London: highly restrictive qualifications to vote in elections for the new unitary Assembly. Under his proposal, only freeholders of at least 100 acres would be allowed to cast ballots—and to serve in the legislature members had to own at least 1,000 acres. However earnest his desire to bring tranquility and prosperity to the colony that was his second home, Morris was conditioning his plea to the crown on its surrender of control over New Jersey's governmental machinery to the landed squirearchy, of which he was among the foremost members. As he confirmed in a letter to the Board of Trade, in charge of the royalization matter, Morris feared that unless men like himself—"of the best figure and estates"—ruled the colony, political stability would remain under constant threat by the "very dregs and rascality of the people."

After lobbying crown officials for nine months (and laying out £1,000 of his own money in the process), Morris prevailed, with his restrictive bias on voting rights and membership in the Assembly built into the deal. Composition of the legislature and the joint Provincial Council was to be equally apportioned between the former East and West Jerseys. The only question remaining was who would become the first governor of newly united and royal New Jersey. Ideally, the post ought to have been assigned to someone familiar with its political landscape and capable of conciliating the colony's contentious factions, but most of the obvious candidates had their detractors, and Morris, for all the ability he had evidenced in London, had just turned thirty.

Returning home, he was greeted as a hero for winning the crown's concession of existing property titles, a degree of religious tolerance, and other colonists' rights. The East Jersey proprietors, on the verge of having to yield their power to do so, rewarded Morris with a sizable new grant of land adjacent to his Monmouth estate out of gratitude as well as recompense for his outlay of personal funds in London. The West Jersey Society's directors in England designated him their American business agent, in charge of all new land sales of the unsold portion of its holdings and of collecting quitrents from the buyers (for a considerable aggregate fee). Morris, already well off, would nevertheless retain the lucrative position for thirty-three years. As he anxiously awaited word from London about who would be named New Jersey's royal governor, Morris learned that the Board of Trade had designated him, in his capacity as senior-ranking member of the Provincial Council, to act as the colony's interim chief executive—buoying his hopes to win the position outright, despite his relative youth.

After fourteen months as governor-in-waiting, during which he worked to widen his circle of supporters who he hoped would help him reform and solidify the colony's administration, Morris received crushing news from London. As a native-born colonist, he simply lacked enough backing in Britain's high political, social, and business circles to be awarded the garland. Powerful New Yorkers, moreover, were uneasy about the emergence of the freshly designated royal colony immediately to their west as a potential commercial rival. Better to keep New Jersey a satellite serving primarily as a customer and food supplier of its larger and far wealthier neighbor—and how better to ensure that subsidiary status than to give the governor of New York the added responsibility for administering New Jersey as well?

The Board of Trade and the Privy Council that supervised it agreed that the lately appointed governor of New York, Queen Anne's first cousin, Edward Hyde, better known as Lord Cornbury, would fill the role nicely. Free from embroilment in New Jersey's past civil strife, he could becalm long-troubled waters, so his territorial rule was extended over both colonies.

V

Chagrined, Lewis Morris nursed his wounded hubris but soon set about showing his new royal overseer who really ruled New Jersey. Their ensuing six-year hostility was all but guaranteed by Cornbury's instinctive biases against the two principal elements in the political coalition Morris had put together—the largely Scottish, antiroyalist proprietary leaders of East Jersey, who had only grudgingly ceded to the crown their claimed right to govern the colony, and the Quakers, with disproportionate membership in the West Jersey Assembly, whose pacifist creed Cornbury believed made them an obstacle to the defense of the colony against French or Indian attack.

Sure that his own popularity would prevail over the sway of the crown's new emissary, Morris, who remained the senior member of the Provincial Council, sent a package of proposed enactments to the Assembly that he professed would carry out the terms of the royalization agreement. In seeking to win financial and political advantage for his closest supporters, he was testing the limit of Cornbury's forbearance—and then exceeded it. Beyond directing the Assembly to certify the old land grants and sales to the proprietors and to minimize the size of the electorate, Morris pushed for undermining, if not outright quashing, the land titles of the old Nicolls patent holders and requiring all prospective buyers of Indian land to buy a license from the proprietors—and those who had made their purchases in the past would have to pay for the license retroactively. Such measures conflicted with the general understanding in the colony that the crown, in taking sovereignty over it, would validate all existing land titles—not cherry-pick among them—and strip the proprietors of any claimed dominion. Hopeful of gaining Cornbury's support for the hardly equitable program and mindful of his lordship's rumored heavy arrearage to debtors in England, Morris conspired with proprietary interests to collect a "gratuity" of £200, to be passed secretly to the governor despite the crown's standing instructions to all governors to reject any such compromising enticements from the colonists. The Assembly passed Morris's program, pending Cornbury's formal approval.

The unsavory scheme fell apart, though, when the Assembly, apparently determined to let Cornbury know he was beholden to the colonists to fund his administrative rule, voted him only a one-year £1,000 appropriation, briefer and stingier than the governor had in mind. He brushed aside the Assembly's claim that the colony could afford no more and, turning from his preoccupation with more congenial New Yorkers, met the challenge from Morris's New Jersey coalition by forming a bond with antiproprietary and Quaker-baiting allies. To counter Morris's influence as the Assembly's puppet master, Cornbury suspended the legislature—preventing it from enacting the Morris-crafted program—and threatened to dissolve it and call new elections likely to turn on the charge that Morris was advocating a policy of political and economic elitism at the expense of the common people. Infuriated, Morris minced no words at the next meeting of the Provincial Council. He accused Cornbury of violating his instructions to shepherd the royalization terms into law, goading the governor to reply he had no such instructions, then remark to aides that Morris "does give his tongue too great a liberty."

Their war of words only heightened thereafter. To stem the governor's threatened rebuff, Morris declared that the New Jersey Assembly had rights over the colony analogous to Parliament's constitutional mandate in governing the realm and, furthermore, colonists had the very same rights that Englishmen possessed at home. Both claims outraged Cornbury, who now took his verbal tormentor for more than a nuisance; Morris's incendiary words marked him as an undisguised seditionist and among the first American officials to challenge their subservient status as mandated by the royal prerogative, i.e., that colonists were second-class citizens whose rights and privileges existed at the pleasure of the crown.

Sensing that Morris's collision with the aroused governor presented an opening to check the landed gentry's domineering intentions, the antiproprietary forces reportedly collected a £1,000 gift as an inducement to Cornbury to follow through on his threat to dissolve the Assembly and order a new election. Cornbury would always deny having his palm crossed with anything so crass as an outright bribe—and there was, not surprisingly, an absence of "smoking gun" hard evidence that money changed hands; history has been left only the accusations of the governor's foes. Whatever caused it, Cornbury dissolved the old Assembly, a new election was held, the proprietary coalition was defeated, and Morris found himself again stripped of his political base on the Provincial Council until he agreed to apologize to the governor for his disparaging outbursts. The newly chosen Assembly, too, acted to clip Morris's wings. It extended the franchise and officeholding rights to all freeholders, regardless of how much acreage they owned; limited proprietors' rights to ownership of their soil—they were no longer privileged characters under the new royal regime—and voted to fund Cornbury's administration for two years at twice the previous Assembly's appropriation. The funding measure was particularly galling for Morris because it was based partly on a new tax on unimproved land, a burden that fell mostly on large landholders like him.

Defeat did not leave Morris subdued for long. Having sulkily begged Cornbury's forgiveness to regain his place on the colonial council, he renewed his defiance by boycotting council meetings and telling cronies he valued the governor "not a farthing." When his slur reached Cornbury's ears, as intended, he again suspended Morris from the council, this time for more than a year, and told his superiors in London that the troublemaker was a diehard advocate of proprietary interests without regard for or loyalty to royal authority.

If Cornbury supposed he had quelled the *agent provocateur* for good, he soon learned otherwise. Morris was not one to accept being bested, as Governor Basse had painfully learned. In exile, Morris again used his pen to skewer a gubernatorial target; he wrote to friendly acquaintances in the British ministry, who retained a good opinion of him for delivering up hapless New Jersey as a supplicant royal colony, and authored pamphlets for local distribution to explain why he refused to take his seat on the council. He accused Cornbury not only of failing to honor the settlement terms of royalization, thus denying the colonists their due rights and privileges, but also of neglecting New Jersey's urgent civic needs—indeed, rarely setting foot on its soil—and sacrificing the colony's interests to the wiles of London's commercial establishment.

In rebuttals sent to the Board of Trade and others in court circles where he was well connected, Cornbury tried to dismiss Morris's attacks on him as whining by a habitual malcontent. Soon, however, Morris's laments were backed by a gathering chorus of charges, in New York as well as New Jersey, not over policy issues but allegations of moral turpitude. The governor was said to be a bribe-taker, an embezzler of royal funds, neglectful of his duties, a persecutor of Quakers, and, after his wife's death in the summer of 1706, a social deviant for dressing in ball gowns and sashaying about on social occasions. Some of the testimony against him came from anonymous or otherwise questionable sources, but the desperate Cornbury was now reeling. Even the governor's aristocratic relatives could not shield him from the onslaught. Morris, meanwhile, exploited Cornbury's reduced stature to press for new Assembly elections, which resulted in his proprietary party gaining three-quarters of the seats, including the one Morris himself won in his first stand for public office. But Cornbury, hobbled yet still standing, continued to check Morris through his power to veto Assembly enactments and control appointments to public office. He rallied his cause by insisting that he had in no demonstrable way wronged the people of New Jersey and that, rather, as he implored his backers on the council to write to Queen Anne, the implacable Morris was largely to blame for the governor's troubles, thanks to "turbulent, factious . . . and disloyal principles" he had foisted on his backers, who were "men notoriously known to be uneasy under all governments." The Morris camp, Cornbury went so far as to charge, was bent on encouraging first New Jersey and then the other American colonies to overthrow British rule and set up their own government. Such a grave accusation of disloyalty, uttered scarcely forty years after New York and New Jersey became part of the British realm, had rarely if ever been directed at a prominent colonist. Morris, of course, relishing the contest, counterattacked in letters to the Board of Trade and members of Parliament, dwelling on Cornbury's alleged character flaws and administrative dysfunction and insisting that the complaints were motivated not by personal animus but by Morris's revulsion over the governor's abusive exercise of crown authority. Cornbury's worst error while governing New Jersey had been succeeding too well for a time in foiling Lewis Morris's self-interested aspirations.

By 1708, as Cornbury's Tory supporters lost control of Parliament and the ministry, the queen could no longer ignore the outcry to remove her cousin from his dual governorship. For the second time, Lewis Morris had played an instrumental role in bringing down a royal satrap. Cornbury's successor, Lord John Lovelace, another financially strapped aristocrat with military experience but none as a government administrator, signaled that the Whigs were sympathetic to Morris's political posture and pressed the ministry to have him restored as senior member on the New Jersey Council. Anticipating the renewal of his dominance over both the council and the Assembly, Morris greeted Lovelace with a fulsome tribute in verse on his arrival in the spring of 1709 and, with a vindictive impulse that would dog his whole political career, pressed the new governor to purge the council of its antiproprietary members.

Just when Morris saw clear sailing ahead, Lovelace died only six months after arriving. Morris's grief quickly yielded to his claim, by virtue of being senior councilman, to serve as acting governor of the colony until a replacement could be chosen in London. His reach for power was blocked, though, by New York's Lieutenant Governor Richard Ingoldesby, a holdover from Cornbury's tenure and a fellow Tory, who disdained Morris's wobbly claim and carried on business as usual with the New Jersey Assembly as if he was Lovelace's incontestably legitimate successor. When Morris persisted in his challenge, Ingoldesby ousted him from the council—the stormy petrel Morris's third such suspension in five years. Throughout most of the fifteen months that Ingoldesby hung on as acting governor, Morris kept on peevishly writing to London to remind colonial administrators of the great service he had rendered the crown eight years earlier in persuading New Jersey's proprietors to surrender the colony—reason enough, he artlessly implied, to reward him now with the governorship. But Morris's foes also lobbied the royal ministry, suggesting no more subtly that his proper reward for fomenting incessant political strife ought to be permanent disbarment from the council, not elevation to governor.

So with his fortieth year at hand, Lewis Morris was doubtless in a dour mood as he contemplated his violently gyrating political fortunes, which seemed to have delivered him to a dead end. Finally, word came in the spring of 1710 that a new governor was en route to New York Harbor—another soldier with personal ties to the queen and no record of achievement as an administrator. Reports from London said Robert Hunter had been en route to Virginia in 1707 to become its lieutenant governor in the midst of the War of the Spanish Succession when a French privateer seized his ship and brought him to France, where he was imprisoned for two years until exchanged for the Bishop of Quebec. Back home, he wrote Queen Anne in December 1709, soon after he was appointed governor of New York and New Jersey, proposing to relieve the Palatine refugee problem besetting England by bringing with him to the colonies 3,000 of the homeless Germans, many of whom could be put to work there as farm and forest laborers. The queen, always fond of Hunter, agreed, and, with his sizable contingent of Palatines in tow, he was due in New York shortly to serve as the queen's emissary and overseer. Morris could not have been sanguine at the prospect; the newcomer was likely to prove yet another in the line of grasping mediocrities the crown had seen fit to govern the colony since taking it from the Dutch.

3

Power Plays

ONE MARK THAT clearly distinguished Robert Hunter from his gubernatorial predecessors was that the year before his arrival in New York at age forty-four, he had been admitted as a fellow to the Royal Society, a crown-chartered, highly select fraternity of distinguished scientists, scholars, and litterateurs—in effect, Britain's intellectual *crème de la crème*. It was an unlikely achievement for a career soldier from a relatively obscure branch of the Scottish aristocracy who had made his way into the most influential circles of the realm by his wits, social adroitness, professional skill, and a knack for capitalizing on every chance that came his way.

Born in Edinburgh into an ancient clan, Hunter was a grandson of the twentieth Laird of Hunterston but inherited no title or land to speak of. His father was a lawyer of apparently modest eminence, for young Robert was placed as an apothecary's apprentice before he ran off to join the British military. An able and courageous soldier in King William III's army, he was by chance assigned to Princess Anne's honor guard, becoming a court favorite and acquainted with Anne's chief military and political counselor, the Duke of Marlborough, the most influential statesman in the nation once she took the throne. Marlborough caught wind of the bravery and administrative savvy young Hunter displayed when assigned to fight in Flanders against Louis XIV's forces and made him his aide-de-camp. As a dashing young officer off to a brilliant start in his military career, Hunter slipped seamlessly into aristocratic society by marrying the daughter of a baronet with an estate in Lincolnshire and a stylish house in London's Covent Garden.

Now certifiably acceptable in the social swim, Hunter's connection to Marlborough ensured his steady advance in rank—he would one day become a major general—and initiation into the political scene, where his eminent mentor served as the vital link between the queen and Parliament. Like Marlborough, a nominal Tory who claimed close friends among the rival Whigs as well, Hunter tried to keep a foot in both camps. Somewhere along the line he revealed a literary bent as a poet and essayist with a deft ironical touch that pleased *The Tatler*'s editors enough to run several of his unsigned pieces. A raconteur as well, he was soon a drinking crony and member-in-good-standing of the Whig literary establishment, including novelist and essayist Jonathan Swift, Joseph Addison, and parliamentary luminary Richard Steele, who coedited the famed if all too short-lived *Spectator*, and physician-satirist John Arbuthnot.

His varied talents had groomed Robert Hunter as a courtier of laudable service to the nation, but it may well have been his friendship with Dr. Arbuthnot, who happened to be Queen Anne's physician, that won him the royal governorship of New York. A quick and perceptive reader of the colonial social dynamics he had to contend with, Hunter sensed the mistrust and resentment engendered by the governors who preceded him. Few had seemed concerned with the welfare of the colonists; more than a few, like the lately defrocked Lord Cornbury, were venal and desperate in the gainful abuse of their delegated authority. To reverse the colonists' irritable sentiments toward the sorry crown officials sent to rule over them was Hunter's first task, and from the start it proved a thorny one; New York's socioeconomic structure was in thrall to four interlocking families presided over by merchant princes who were a law unto themselves. Hunter had to bend them to his will or vanquish them.

Curiously, none of the founding fathers of these clans of trade barons came from the English aristocracy—all their fortunes were self-made, with the timely assistance of wealthy spouses, even as Hunter's social and professional ascent had been similarly aided. The oldest of New York's dominant mercantile houses was founded by Olaff Van Cortlandt (1600–1684), who emigrated to New Netherlands as a soldier hired by the Dutch West India Company and soon promoted to commissioner (probably chief inspector) of cargoes, familiarizing himself with the import-export business. His entrepreneurial streak surfaced as he branched into the brewery business and began trading in and near the northern Hudson Valley with the fur-trappers from the Iroquois nation, exporting all the pelts he could get hold of to the eager European market. Marriage into a family of means added to his working capital, and the Van Cortlandt fortune grew steadily.

The Philipse family saga was similar. Its American patriarch, Frederick (1627–1702), was a carpenter who came to New Amsterdam in his early twenties, also in the employ of the Dutch West India Company, which designated him as its chief builder (probably inspector of construction). His wide-ranging work, like Van Cortlandt's, put him in contact with Indian fur traders, and what had begun as a sideline business bloomed into a fulltime enterprise. It became more lucrative through Frederick's marriage to a Van Cortlandt daughter, leading to a number of joint ventures between the two mercantile houses, as the British seizure of the colony opened vaster markets to the trade barons. By the time Adolph Philipse succeeded his father as head of the business in the 1680s, the family owned or shared in seven oceangoing cargo vessels, and Frederick's fortune of 80,000 gilders was reputedly the largest in the colony. On outgoing voyages, the holds of the trade barons' ships were crammed with timber, furs, hides, and hogsheads of nonperishable commodities like tobacco, flour, and tar, mostly for European markets. On the return legs, the New York–based ships would carry manufactured items and luxury goods for wealthier colonial buyers, but as time went on, the bulk of the westbound cargoes came from Madeira (the native nectar, an amber wine, won much favor in the American colonies), Guinea (where African tribal captives were wholesaled for colonial slave labor), and the West Indies (prolific suppliers of sugar, molasses, and rum).

The third of the major New York trade houses traced back to Philip Pieterse Schuyler (1628–83), an Amsterdam baker's son, who emigrated to Fort Orange (Albany after the British takeover of the colony), where he and his progeny would emerge as the kingpins of the fur market that was expanding far beyond the northern end of the Hudson region. Schuyler's commercial reach was extended by marriage into the Van Rensselaer family, whose original patroon was proprietor of a manorial grant so immense that it would be assigned a separate seat in the New York Assembly toward the close of the century. Much of the Schuylers' wealth derived from selling imported British-made merchandise to Quebec's French traders for barter with the Indian fur trappers who brought them most of the abundant catch north and west of Albany.

Last of the colony's four great mercantile tycoons to arrive in America was Stephen DeLancey (1663–1741), scion of a minor French aristocratic family, who in the early 1680s at the age of eighteen fled from his home in Caen, Normandy, and the persecution the Catholic French crown was inflicting on him and his fellow Huguenots. He took refuge in England for several years, but when James II, a Catholic, ascended the throne, Stephen sold the remnants of his family's jewels and other possessions and sailed for New York in 1686 with a reported £300 sewn into the linings of his clothes. Granted permanent legal residence a month after arriving, he took the oath of allegiance to the British crown a year later. DeLancey's cash stake was enough to launch his career as a merchant, operating a granary, a cargo warehouse, and a retail store before becoming a trader with, among others, Red Sea pirates and speculating heavily in cocoa. His marriage to a Van Cortlandt heiress opened more doors to him, and soon he partnered with Adolph Philipse in ventures that vaulted him into the ranks of the colony's foremost merchants.

The trade barons' web of commerce extended to every corner of New York, along the Atlantic Coast to the other British colonies, north to Canada, and across the ocean, giving them intimidating power throughout the entire colonial marketplace. They set the prices of the crops they bought from farmers and of the imported goods they sold consumers; the working and landed classes alike were beholden to them for determining the cost of living. The four trading dynasties added to their influence by assembling huge real estate holdings, the common measure of social prominence and civic stature in that period. They purchased parts of their manors, but much of their land was granted outright by the governors they consorted with and compensated by crown-sanctioned fees, under-the-table kickbacks, and complicity in their naked quest for the spoils of high office. All the trade barons asked from their cozy relationship with the government was that it not bollix up their commercial hegemony.

Their land accumulation contributed only marginally, if at all at first, to the trade barons' profits—much of the acreage was leased to tenant farmers or left idle for future improvement or sale. In that context, the merchant princes separated themselves from the colony's land barons, men like Lewis Morris, whose estates ran to thousands of acres and provided their owners a sizable livelihood from active farming. Morris, like other country squires, looked down his nose at the merchant princes as money-grubbers who lived most of the time in New York City townhouses and kept their vast upriver spreads as showplaces or retreats from muggy city summers. Smaller farmers and the artisan and working classes bore a similar animus toward the trade barons who, recognizing customer resentment as an occupational hazard of the entrepreneurial rich, acted to protect their joint self-interest by entering—and all but controlling—New York politics in the two decades before Governor Hunter's arrival. Stephen DeLancey and Adolph Philipse sat in the Assembly as outsize presences, and their allies presided over the colonial legislature by domineering both the rural electorate, who wanted to stay in the good graces of their baronial neighbors and landlords, and urban voters who depended on the maritime trade for their daily bread. The merchant coterie was also prominently represented on New York's Provincial Council, the governor's oversight attendants, where Philip Schuyler's son Peter, among other leading merchants, sat as a member for twenty-four years.

The biggest bone of political contention in 1710, as Hunter took office, was the Assembly's appropriation of funds to the governor for the salaries and day-to-day operations of the royal government. The crown did not subsidize the administration of its colonies; the genius of Britain's empire-building aptitude was its resolve to make the colonists bear the costs themselves, excepting only military costs to safeguard the outlying royal domain. A related concern among New Yorkers was how to ensure that the taxes their elected Assembly authorized were honestly and efficiently expended by their assigned—not elected—royal governors. Their tenures, for the most part, had been marked by administrative laxity, favoritism, and, in cases like Cornbury's regime, corruption, which, taken together, had saddled the colony with a sizable and growing debt. The issue had now gone beyond idle grousing by a servile population; the merchant princes were the most aroused because the bulk of the colony's revenue was derived from indirect taxes in the form of duties on trade—particularly imported spirits and other luxury goods—and a "tonnage duty" on foreign vessels offloading in New York. A related burden was the internal excise (or sales) charges levied against local manufactured goods and commodities and a use tax on chimneys and carriages. These trade-related imposts, accounting for roughly 60 percent of the colony's revenues, were anathema to the trade barons, especially the tonnage tax, which they argued discouraged imports and diverted maritime traffic to other markets.

The balance of the colony's revenues came from quitrents (direct taxes on realty, so called because they were the limit landowners could be charged as fealty to the crown, which technically still owned every acre in the realm) and a levy on personal valuables. Land barons like Lewis Morris were zealously vigilant against any increases in property taxes, especially on unimproved acreage; he had made his fierce opposition to them, along with any proposed restrictions on land speculation and engrossment (i.e., excessive accumulation), the centerpiece of his political endeavors for twenty years in New Jersey. But in New York, the country squirearchy lacked the economic cohesion and political clout to match the trade barons' collective might. As its new governor took office, the colony had to face up to the reality that more revenues were needed to run its long mismanaged government, meet a growing demand for civic services, and satisfy its obligations to creditors.

From his first months in office, Governor Hunter displayed political acuity leavened by a good nature that set him apart from his predecessors.

He grasped the need to avoid aligning himself with either set of the conflicting vested interests favored by the mercantile camp and the land barons and, instead, to play the conciliator between them while also addressing the disparate needs of the laboring class. His early patronage choices placed a priority on councilors and officers of ability and intelligence even if he found himself at odds with some of their attitudes and policy preferences. And he pledged to reform the civil service and make it efficient and honest. But there was no avoiding his first direct confrontation with New York's thirteenth colonial Assembly when it convened at the beginning of September 1710. Fifteen of its twenty-two members were allied with the trade barons' clique, and among their last names were DeLancey, Van Cortlandt, Schuyler, and Van Rensselaer.

Hunter tried disarming them at first. His inaugural address ran just 300 words, and he quipped afterward, "If honesty is the best policy, plainness must be the best oratory." But the Assembly, still aggrieved by the disgraced Cornbury's apparent abuses of the royal prerogative, was not to be charmed out of its pique. Hunter had to be taught a lesson at the outset—the colonists were no longer to be the playthings of inept royal courtiers nor were their tax payments to be squandered. The legislators adamantly declined to appropriate Hunter's requested funding until they could wring concessions from him that the crown traditionally denied to its colonial subjects. He was offered only half the usual governor's salary and a paltry sum to run even a shadow government unless he met the colonists' insistence on setting the salaries of crown officials and empowering the Assembly to police the government's disbursal of tax revenues—a calculated challenge to unbridled royal authority.

This rude rebuke disheartened Hunter, who was amenable to some sort of compromise with the legislature but not abject surrender to political blackmail. He rapidly concluded he had better enlist a wily, respected, and strategically placed colonist as his confidential adviser on how to overcome the Assembly's animosity. The most obvious choice would have been Stephen DeLancey, three years Hunter's senior and in his eighth year as a member of the Assembly. Though a member of the merchant princes' high command and among the wealthiest men in the colony, DeLancey was regarded as the soul of probity and open to reason. But he might also prove a hard nut to crack, with little motive to do the governor's bidding without first extracting a promise to reform the administrative system to the colonists' satisfaction. So Hunter made a far chancier selection—a choice that would have a decisive bearing on both men's careers.

II

The new governor was likely told during his presailing briefing by the Board of Trade, with its institutional memory of how Lewis Morris had skillfully masterminded the royalization of New Jersey at the beginning of the century, that the land baron was a formidable character—ambitious, self-assured, quick-witted, but combative at times to the point of unmanageability. Indeed, at the moment of Hunter's arrival, Morris was still under suspension as senior member—or president, as the position was designated by then—of the governor's New Jersey Provincial Council. That Morris had spearheaded efforts to have two former governors ousted was perhaps more to his credit than not, especially since Cornbury had proven such an embarrassment to the government, and it was his understudy, Acting Governor Ingoldesby, who, when challenged by Morris as claimant to rule New Jersey, had thrown him off the council.

A little investigation likely revealed to Hunter, a Scotsman from an ancient clan, that Morris's core supporters in New Jersey's long-running political wars were the colony's Scottish proprietors—a strong point in his favor. Morris, moreover, was a country squire with large estates in both the colonies Hunter was sent to govern and thus a promising counterpoise to the mercantile tycoons who dominated the New York Assembly and were threatening to make the governor's tenure a misery. Early on, the two men found in each other a kindred spirit; both had an energetic, outgoing disposition (though the governor's was more circumspect), a sprightly intellect, a passion for literature and composition, and a drive for power that was more pragmatic than ideological. Hunter lost little time in restoring Morris to his place as president of the New Jersey

Council, making him in effect the colony's political boss and administrative director. Gradually, with the governor's assent, Morris replaced unfriendly councilmen, judges, sheriffs, and minor officeholders with men of his own choosing, and for the first time, with his delegated grip on the perquisite of patronage, he was the de facto vizier of New Jersey, albeit serving at the governor's pleasure. The arrangement suited Hunter's priorities; New York was where his paramount challenge lay—and where Morris, happily incentivized, was also now invited to direct his purposeful efforts as the governor's ranking, if unofficial, confidant.

Morris would shortly discover that New York was a still more hazardous battleground than New Jersey, with more numerous, deeply entrenched combatants, bearing heavier weaponry for him to contend with. His first foray in Hunter's behalf, as well as establishing himself as a serious entrant onto the colony's political stage, had been to get himself elected to the Assembly. It was almost as easy for him as for the landed British aristocrats who were regularly returned as Members of Parliament by the docile electorate of their districts. Morris had a ready-made Assembly seat representing the borough of Westchester, an enclave composed largely—thanks to his uncle's political connivance a generation earlier—of his family manor, Morrisania, and its immediate environs, whose employees, suppliers, and neighbors massed behind his candidacy. It did not hurt that one of Morris's friendliest neighbors was a fellow country squire, with a good deal larger estate than his own, named William Willet, a Quaker of influence among his local and plentiful co-religionists, who was fully apprised of Morris's ongoing efforts to gain political equality for the Quaker community in New Jersey. Willet had held one of Westchester County's three other Assembly seats for nine years and became a staunch Morris ally from the first.

Willet, though, may have been as shocked as the majority of his legislative colleagues when Morris, almost immediately upon taking his seat in the Assembly, flayed them in vituperative language for rejecting Hunter's request to fund his administration. Miscalculating the latitude of parliamentary privilege to speak his mind within the Assembly chamber—and likely forgetting he was no longer addressing deferential New Jersey pols, newcomer Morris in effect was calling his fellow members dunces for their manifest unfairness to Hunter and ingratitude to the crown, which he pointed out paid dearly to defend the colony's safety on land and sea. Appreciative of such fiery, if a touch strident, support, Hunter sent a copy of Morris's remarks to London, where they were passed approvingly around the high councils of government and even brought to the queen's attention. But in New York, where the trade barons ruled the Assembly, Morris was expelled on November 10 and did not return until his loyal constituents sent him back the following autumn—and would allow him to remain for more than twenty years.

The solid backing Hunter received from Morris, Willet, and their small band of cohorts was no match for the trade lords' insistence on reining in the governor's purse strings. For the next two years, he was on partial pay and forced to administer New York's government on a hand-to-mouth basis. It was a testament to Hunter's generous and conscientious character that when the paltry appropriations ran out, he dipped into his personal resources to pay colony officials and keep the administration from shutting down. To make matters worse for him, a new Tory government took power in London and declined to honor more than a quarter of the vouchers that Hunter had sent back to the Board of Trade to cover the costs of relocating and subsidizing the upkeep of the Palatines he had brought to New York with Queen Anne's blessing and promise to pay for the program aimed at improving the realm's economic health. Before long, Hunter was the crown's creditor for more than £30,000 and nearly broke. For all his amiability and evident rectitude, however, his foes in the mercantile establishment remained adamant. The Assembly would neither provide the revenue essential to run the government unless accorded substantive oversight of its financial operations—an abject acknowledgment, to Hunter's way of thinking, of past royal governors' shortcomings—nor consider a rise in taxes to cover debt service. Something had to be done, or the kindly Hunter would face a fate as ignominious as Cornbury's.

To break the deadlock and solidify his position as the governor's indispensable ally and savant, Morris began knitting together a political coalition, as he had done in New Jersey, fashioned from seemingly divergent elements—the hallmark of his political aptitude. Its home base may have been Westchester, contiguous to New York County (Manhattan Island), but it was not uncontested turf; the Philipse and DeLancey families also owned great estates there, but unlike Morrisania, theirs were largely undeveloped. What Morris needed most to combat the trade barons was to enlist under his captaincy a land baron whose wealth and territory were of a magnitude comparable to theirs. He found just the right man well up the Hudson Valley in lower Albany County, where the Schuylers championed the traders' cause largely uncontested.

Robert Livingston, of Scottish Presbyterian stock, had fled Britain as a youngster after the Stuart Reformation made life uncomfortable for dissenters from the Anglican faith and found refuge in Rotterdam. A resourceful lad with a good business head, he learned Dutch and became a precocious merchant—by sixteen he was shipping cargoes on his own account. His success convinced Robert there was a fortune to be made in the American colonies, where he arrived in 1674 and set up shop in Albany. His dealings with the established Dutch traders were greatly facilitated by his fluency in their native tongue and made him useful to the British authorities attempting to control the Indian trade centered there. Like so many other fortune-seekers past and present, Livingston married well—exceedingly so, wedding the widow Alida Schuyler Van Rensselaer, connecting him to two families whose landholdings were among the colony's largest. When his wife's family contested the couple's claim to a sizable share of their domain, Livingston struck out on his own, subordinating his trade operations to land accumulation. His acquisitive appetite and practiced politesse netted him the proprietorship of a 160,000-acre riverfront spread, granted by Governor Thomas Dongan, who in the 1680s set the standard for lavishly dispensing royal land to those who could afford to show him appropriate gratitude. Livingston Manor established its owner as a lordly presence and a suitable collaborator with Morris's new political venture, as soon evidenced by Governor Hunter's assigning his manor its own seat in the New York Assembly, first occupied unabashedly by Livingston himself.

Morris now reached out to attract multitudes, not grandees, to his emergent party. He cast his net to ensnare anyone nursing a grudge against the trade barons and the Anglican establishment. Prominent among these were smaller farmers, especially the Dutch yeomanry in the Hudson Valley and their kinsmen among the lesser merchants, and town tradesmen and laborers who sensed their reduced standing since the British took charge of the colony and showed partiality to the elite international shippers catering to London's moneyed interests. The common political denominator among Morris's targeted partisans was that, like him, they favored indirect taxes from trade duties and the sale of luxury goods to cover the bulk of government costs. He then drew up a legislative agenda with populist appeal. On it were calls for better roads for farmers, fewer barriers to land acquisition, a larger money supply and cheaper credit for consumers, protection for the petite bourgeoisie and local manufacturers to spur domestic commerce and thwart cheap imports, and mandatory tolerance of religious dissenters.

But how to win support for his program in an age when word-of-mouth—from street corner orators, Sunday sermonizers, coffeehouse gossips, and the town crier—were the principal means of communication? As he had done to make political headway in New Jersey, and because he had both the literary skill and financial resources to do so, Morris honed his powers of persuasion by putting his pen to work. In 1713, with Hunter doubtlessly approving the text, he published a widely distributed pamphlet in the form of a manifesto that laid out his populist program and called for funding the colonial government by modestly boosting duties on imported goods and the tax on retail liquor sales. While candidly admitting that shopkeepers would no doubt pass along the increased tax burden to the public by raising prices, the step was socially justifiable because, Morris argued, "it is not the sober, industrious, prudent or needy part of mankind who will bear that charge, but the rich, vain, and extravagant; for those who can satisfy themselves with being clad in homespun, and instead of wine, brandy and rum, make use of cider, beer and such spirits as we can distill from our own produce, will be entirely freed of paying anything towards the support of government," whereas wealthy folk who spent up to £300 a year "in good living" could well afford the extra few pounds needed to provide essential public services. The appeal may have been grounded in class conflict, but it got the message out. Morris appended another argument that was likely still more persuasive because of its alarming nature. If the Assembly did not act promptly to fund Hunter's administration, Parliament would have to step in and forcibly impose the required tax payments, ending any semblance of self-government the colony enjoyed and relieving the governor of all answerability to its citizenry. To assuage the legislators' demand to oversee royal officials' revenues and expenditures, Morris proposed joint scrutiny by a crown inspector and a watchdog officer assigned by the Assembly.

Slowly, the tide began to turn, driven in part by fear the British authorities might indeed intercede—by force of arms, if necessary—and in part by growing commercial traffic in the port that undermined the trade lords' caveat the economy would suffer from higher taxes. There were signs, too, that the electorate was wearying of the political standoff and that Morris's populist pitch was paying off at the polls. The 1713 Assembly elections netted the "court party," as his and Hunter's supporters were now known, five new members and brought the two factions to almost equal numbers in the legislature. Accordingly, Morris, as his party's floor leader in the Assembly, devised a plan the year after to pay off the colony's growing debt that was both fiscally manageable and too irresistibly popular for the antitax merchant princes to scuttle.

Hundreds of New Yorkers were owed money by their government, some for over a generation. Among them were investors (like Robert Livingston) who had made interest-bearing loans to the colony, laborers who were owed for services performed, suppliers for goods delivered, and militiamen for participating in three fruitless attacks against French Canada since 1690. Most telling politically, the colony had a moral obligation to followers of martyred vigilante leader Jacob Leisler whose properties were destroyed or confiscated when royalist forces brutally retook command of the colony after it had been left without a crown-certified government for the two years following the Glorious Revolution. At Morris's relentless prodding as floor manager of the bill, the Assembly passed the Public Debt Act of 1714. It provided for paying off £28,000 of the colony's debt by issuing bills of credit—paper money—to be retired periodically by revenue from a twenty-year tax on liquor sales. The payments were particularly welcomed by the Dutch community, many of whose members had sympathized with the Leisler rebellion as a protest against the absolutist Stuart monarchy and had never been compensated for their property losses as the uprising was quelled. Hunter himself was the largest beneficiary of the debt repayment, receiving £5,000—belated recognition by the Assembly that he had nobly sustained the government with his personal resources—but he was still owed five times that amount.

Although the wealthy merchants grumbled for years that the debt act was primarily a scheme for Morris to gain party adherents and that it cheapened the value of money, hurting creditors both in London and locally, the infusion of circulating cash in fact spurred New York's economy. The popularity of the measure softened resistance to Hunter's plea for adequate funding for his administration, and the closely divided legislature passed the Support Act of 1715, a five-year revenue bill based on a modest increase in import duties and excise taxes, ending the financial crisis that had hog-tied Hunter since he took office. His only concession was to authorize the Assembly to appoint an officer to track the government's disbursements.

Emboldened by these gains, Morris now won Hunter's backing for a package of decrees by the Provincial Council and measures by the legislature for a social and economic welfare program aimed at safeguarding and growing local business. To help shopkeepers, for example, the Assembly required their principal competitors—unlicensed and often unscrupulous street peddlers, smugglers, and sidewalk auctioneers—to pay fees for the right to do business. New York manufacturers and artisans were aided in a variety of ways—tanners were protected by a small duty on imported hides, coopers by a like charge on barrels brought in from elsewhere, local distillers by exemption from the levy on imported rum. To encourage producers of vital commodities, established makers of lampblack and pressers of linseed oil were granted monopolies, and like protection was given to operators of porpoise fisheries and the harbor's fertile oyster beds. No less important were steps to strengthen the maritime trade, heart of the colony's commerce, most notably by subsidizing shipbuilders and creating jobs as well for satellite workers. For the same purpose and against the wishes of the big mercantile families, Morris put through a tonnage duty on cargoes entering New York aboard vessels built or owned elsewhere. While the trade lords also kept moaning about the devalued "New York pound" because of the issue of paper money and other debtor-friendly measures by the Assembly, like the 6 percent ceiling placed on loans to stamp out usury, doing business became easier in New York, where coin currency (specie) was in short supply. Commerce grew and trade duties and excise receipts jumped in tandem, giving Hunter the revenue he needed to keep his administration solvent. The government was even able to undertake a number of infrastructure projects like extending the highway from Manhattan's Battery through the farming village of Harlem at the northern end of the island to connect with the Kingsbridge ferry, improving coach service and transportation of farm produce from nearby Westchester and Connecticut.

All of this progress must have greatly gratified Morris since it was achieved almost wholly with trade-based revenues and not from higher taxes on big landowners like himself. Ever opportunistic, he further strengthened his political hand by winning Hunter's backing for the Assembly's naturalization bill, confirming full British citizenship for all New Yorkers of foreign birth and the Protestant faith. Their previously indeterminate status had long concerned a good many Dutch and Huguenot families, especially in rural Dutchess, Orange, and Ulster counties, where the measure stoked the popularity of the Morrisite coalition, as did Hunter's political gambit of allocating, with his Council's backing, an additional Assembly seat to each of the three Hudson Valley counties. This political connivance, which the outmaneuvered trade lords were powerless to head off, allowed the Morrisite coalition to score a resounding victory in the 1716 election—even Morris's archenemy, the flinty merchant prince Stephen DeLancey, lost his seat representing New York County—and capture two-thirds of the Assembly membership.

There was a further, and even sweeter, reward for Morris. No mere political manipulator, he was a lawmaker with a scholarly knowledge of, and often worshipful respect for, jurisprudence, having served for seven years on New Jersey's Court of Common Right, though with what distinction there is no reliable way to determine. When the chief justiceship of the New York Supreme Court, the colony's highest tribunal, fell vacant, the governor, who was perhaps Lewis Morris's keenest admirer, appointed him to the post. His enemies could—and did—object, but the man's cerebral capacity could not be denied. Speaking for the contemporary generation, historian (and lawyer) William Smith, Jr., remarked of Morris, "Not many in the colony equaled him in the knowledge of the law and the art of intrigue." The latter talent left him unloved by many, even his closest political allies like the Livingston family, who noted that Morris was inclined to take up arms only when his own interests were affected. In fairness, the embattled posture Morris so often assumed grew out of the conviction—or delusion, as his enemies contended—that his own interests and the public's largely coincided.

A telltale footnote to the friendship and political likemindedness of the governor and his new chief justice was their co-authorship in 1715 of a satirical play, *Androboros: A Biographical Farce in Three Acts*, mocking their foes, either by name or thinly disguised, as fatuous nitwits. The story was set in a secret room in the basement of the governor's mansion, where a venal cabal plots to seize control of the colony. The work, believed to be the first play both written and printed in the American colonies, was almost certainly never staged at the time (if ever), but copies of it were doubtlessly passed around for the private pleasure of the co-authors and their circle. The likelihood is that the text was circumspectly run off in William Bradford's print shop, where eighteen-year-old Peter Zenger had three years remaining of his apprenticeship.

By the last years of Robert Hunter's governorship, then, in an age when collecting simultaneous public offices was not forbidden, Lewis Morris was serving as president of New Jersey's Provincial Council and was the most powerful member of the New York Assembly, the chief justice of New York's highest court, and the confidential strategist for the governor in charge of both colonies. Probably no other American colonist surpassed him in political influence.

III

The thunderous political comeback Hunter enjoyed and Morris had engineered allowed them to put through a second major debt retirement act in 1717, which served to intensify the frustrated trade barons' grievances, but to no avail. New York's economy prospered further, Robert Livingston became Assembly speaker in 1718, and the British ministry at Whitehall, weathering criticism from London financiers that their American debtors were settling their accounts with cheap colonial money, supported Hunter's financial program. But then he made one of his rare policy blunders.

The Board of Trade ordered Hunter to bar all illicit French shipping in and out of New York Harbor, evidently intending to halt smuggling and piracy. But the governor took the command to include all vessels carrying cargoes, legitimate and contraband alike, to and from the French West Indies, one of the most lucrative markets for New York merchants, whose ships carried flour, bacon, and lumber to the Caribbean and returned home loaded with sugar. The embargo put a detectable crimp in New York's economy, which soon worsened when the Spanish West Indies market was also closed due to Britain's renewed hostilities with that empire. The New York trade barons heaped renewed scorn on Hunter and the whole Morrisite endeavor.

Hunter's health suffered a setback as well—it had been a stressful eight-year tenure—and he chose to return to England for a more sedate form of public service, overseeing the collection of customs duties at British ports, and to lobby Parliament for the repayment of the £22,000 the crown still owed him for out-of-pocket expenditures while governor. All he ever got back was an acknowledgment of the debt. But posterity has repaid him with honor. One chronicler of the period, Rex Maurice Naylor of Dartmouth College, expressed the historical consensus by calling Robert Hunter "probably the best of the [colonial] New York governors."

Soon after Hunter departed from New York, twenty-one-year-old Peter Zenger, who had arrived in the colony at virtually the same time as the governor with the influx of Palatine refugees he was safeguarding, also left the city. His eight-year apprenticeship in William Bradford's print shop had evidently ended amicably, for in late 1718 or early 1719, Zenger went to Philadelphia, where Bradford's son, Andrew, had become a successful printer despite his father's long-ago misadventures in the trade there. A reasonable guess is that the senior Bradford thought Zenger, now well schooled in their craft, could be an asset to his son as he was about to launch the *American Weekly Mercury*, the first recognizable newspaper in the colonies. If so, the plan faltered; the only known reward of Zenger's stay in Philadelphia was his marriage on July 28, 1719, to Mary White in that city.

The couple moved to Maryland, where Zenger aspired to become the colony's official—and only—printer. But instead of setting up his shop at its capital, Annapolis, where the legislature, government administrative offices, and a royal naval base might have provided convenient work for his press, he located his business in the wealthy little port of Chestertown, thirty miles to the northeast on Chesapeake Bay's Eastern Shore. How Zenger found the means to buy his printing equipment is a puzzle—perhaps with a loan from William Bradford, his former master, for his faithful services as apprentice or, more likely, from his wife's dowry or family. What is evident, however, is that he could not attract enough business to make a go of it. He tried, probably repeatedly, to win the colony's appointment as printer of its official documents, but the only surviving record of his success is a onetime payment to him of 500 pounds of Maryland tobacco in 1720 to print the laws of the colony's counties. Zenger lacked the political connections and geographic proximity that might have made his shop financially viable. To add to his anguish, Mary Zenger died soon after giving birth to their son, named after his father.

Defeated and downcast, the young widower took his son back to New York with him and in September of 1722 at the Dutch Reformed Church married Anna Catherine Maulin, a woman who had come to the colony about the same time he had. With a growing family to support—the couple would soon produce four sons—he resumed working in William Bradford's busy printing establishment, this time as a valued journeyman. By then New York and New Jersey had a new governor, a younger friend of Hunter, as it happened, who had recommended him for the post and urged him to retain Lewis Morris as his chief adviser and political operative. Morris, a veritable potentate among his fellow colonists at the moment, did not object.

IV

At first reckoning, William Burnet likely struck Lewis Morris as a reversion to the usual sort of governor Britain packed off to the colonies—a privileged character with high connections and an empty purse that he had come to America to replenish. Burnet's advantaged social position, though, stemmed not from noble breeding but immediate proximity to ecclesiastical and intellectual figures of distinction.

His father, Gilbert Burnet, had been the foremost theologian in the court of William, Prince of Orange, and accompanied him to England, where he delivered the sermon at the prince's coronation as King William III. In time, the elder Burnet would be rewarded with the appointment of Bishop of Salisbury; his son William would later marry the daughter of the dean of Canterbury. By then William was regarded as a highly promising scientist, elected to the Royal Society at age nineteen under the sponsorship of no less a luminary than Sir Isaac Newton, the most eminent scientist in the world, who tutored young Burnet after he had dropped out of Oxford. His membership in the Royal Society was not based solely on pull—he delivered serious papers on subjects like the Grindelwald Glacier in Switzerland, conjoined twins he observed in Holland, and eclipses of the moons of Jupiter. To earn a living, Burnet worked as a civil servant in good standing with influential Whig friends, holding the post of the crown's comptroller of customs. Like many other political insiders, he invested heavily in the South Sea Company, a government-chartered monopoly to generate trade with South America—its projected profits were intended to help reduce the national debt—but after the scheme collapsed in 1720, Burnet found himself in need of a better-paying job. When he learned that his fellow Royal Society member and friend Robert Hunter had retired as governor of New York and New Jersey and was seeking a respectable sinecure back in

London, the two men prevailed on the Board of Trade to allow them to swap positions.

Seeking a mentor steeped in the rough-and-tumble of colonial politics, Burnet took up Hunter's advice to rely on Lewis Morris, who had served him so well and no doubt struck the incoming governor as socially agreeable and highly erudite—for a provincial. For his part, Morris likely shared the widely held first impression that the thirty-three-year-old Burnet made as a man of good sense, goodwill, and a sprightly manner like his predecessor, and was no more inclined to put on airs while mingling freely with colonial society. But he erred, as Hunter had not, in allowing himself to be drawn off too easily into undisguised partisanship by Morris, who appears to have found the young governor highly suggestible. At any rate, Morris's manipulative hand was visible in two major policy decisions Burnet took within weeks of his arrival.

Customarily, a new governor dissolved the sitting Assembly and invited voters to exercise their democratic right to confirm or replace their legislators, as was always the case with Parliament when a new monarch took the throne—and as colonial New York had done upon every change of governor except one. But there was no statutory requirement for every new governor to call for an Assembly election, nor did Burnet come bearing such an instruction from the Board of Trade. The legislature, moreover, its composition intact for four years, retained its heavy Morrisite majority, which had taken six years to achieve—and Morris understandably did not wish to risk losing it. Aware that Burnet was in financial straits and could not, as Hunter had, endure a hostile legislature bent on denying him sufficient funds to run his government, Morris pledged, as de facto Assembly leader, that if the governor kept the house membership in place he would ensure passage of a long-term, adequate appropriation bill. To lend the color of legitimacy to their arrangement, Morris—in his capacity as chief justice (and in an era when the separation of powers between branches of government was not a recognized civic principle)—presented Burnet with a legal memorandum rationalizing why the governor could keep the sitting Assembly in place. Whereas the succession of a monarch of the British realm marked a break in sovereign authority that necessitated the election of a new

Parliament as well, Morris contended, a colony was not a sovereign entity but a territorial dependency, whose governor was similarly not a sovereign but a representative of the crown, worn in this case by King George I, who remained on the throne, so New York had no need to dismiss its Assembly and elect a new one.

The anti-Morrisites were of course infuriated by this attempted quasi-judicial interference. As the colony's commerce slowed, they had hoped to make political hay out of the departed Hunter's erroneous embargo on trade with the French West Indies and Morris's protectionist policies to stimulate local business. Members of Burnet's Provincial Council bellowed their objections and vowed to complain to London officials, but the governor held firm. In the Assembly itself, the mercantile bloc declared that Burnet was abusing the royal prerogative by denying colonists their fair turn at self-determination; in response, the governor blithely invited the outraged lawmakers to read the chief justice's learned opinion on the subject. Switching his political hat from judge to iron-fisted floor leader of the Assembly, Morris doubled down on his position by stifling all debate over the call for a new election. When one assemblyman from Suffolk County, Long Island, a chronic complainer against any display of crown muscularity as tyranny, kept protesting, Morris switched back to his role as chief justice and issued an *ex cathedra* threat to have the offending legislator prosecuted for undermining royal authority "if he so much as declared his opinions to his neighbors." It was not the first time that Morris, cocksure he could get away with it, used his judicial office to intimidate political foes.

As promised, the now firmly ensconced Assembly under Morris's whip hand passed a five-year funding bill to secure Burnet's administration and added a temporary 2 percent duty on all imported European goods, further angering the trade barons, who charged the measure would only discourage foreign carriers from putting in at New York. Then Morris and Burnet, claiming to act in imperial Britain's patriotic interest, dealt a still more painful blow to their provincial enemies.

France, in control of the Canadian heartland, had lately made deep incursions into the upper Ohio Valley as well. Bonding with the native tribes who were their major trading partners, the French were grow-

ing rich from the fur business while advancing their territorial aspirations by urging their Indian allies to block further British settlements
west of their Atlantic seaboard colonies and open the entire Ohio and
Mississippi basin to the uncontested dominion of New France. Burnet
and Morris contended that the big New York and Albany merchants
were collaborating with the enemy by selling British-made merchandise
particularly valued by the Indians—tools, guns, knives, blankets, coarse
fabric for clothing, and liquor—to French traders in Quebec and Montreal to barter for native-trapped pelts that drew high prices (beaver fur
especially) when sent back to Europe. The fur trade was a major source
of wealth for the New York mercantile families, who imported five
times as much from England (a lot of it for sale to the French Canadians)
as they exported. Burnet and Morris, hoping to disrupt French designs
to dominate Indian country and foil Britain's westward expansion, convinced the Assembly to ban New Yorkers' sale of imported merchandise to the Canadians; the purpose was to force the French to offer the
Indians inferior but costlier merchandise from other sources instead of
the British goods they favored, thereby encouraging tribes in the region
to deal directly with British merchants in Albany. Then, to challenge
the French pressing on New York's western frontier, Burnet authorized
construction of a fort and trading post at Oswego on Lake Ontario, 150
miles from Albany, at the edge of white habitation, in order to open up
trade with tribes on the Great Lakes and in the Ohio and Mississippi
valleys, where French *voyageurs* had had free rein.

The strategy may have made good sense so far as it promoted Britain's
expansionist interests vis-à-vis France, but loss of their French-Canadian
trade embittered the largest New York import merchants, who insisted
that bad government policy was being foisted on the colony by an illegally
sitting Assembly. Burnet and the Morrisites prevailed, though, and over
the next several years as the Indian Trade Act of 1720 was found to be easily circumvented by smugglers, both white and tribal, Morris put through
a supplementary act to stiffen enforcement by a crackdown reminiscent
of despotic Star Chamber practices in Britain a century earlier. Anyone
who was suspected of selling French traders items of British manufacture
sought by the Indian trappers was required to take an oath not only that

he himself refrained from the practice but that he knew of no one else engaged in such commerce. Whoever refused to swear to it was assumed guilty and susceptible to being jailed without a judicial hearing, let alone a jury trial, until paying a heavy £100 fine. An army of local officials was enlisted to administer the oath, and any recruits found less than fully diligent about their assignment were subject to a £200 fine and lifetime disbarment from government service. Such an exercise in witch-hunting suggests the extent of Morris's dictatorial control of the Assembly and sometime arbitrary abandonment of the rule of law—charges he was quick to level against his political foes whenever it suited him.

Still, their opponents could not deny that by 1725, the Burnet-Morris criminalization of trafficking with French fur traders had proven effective. The quantity of beaver pelts exchanged by native trappers for British merchandise at New York trading posts and shipped to London's booming luxury-goods market—no longer to Paris or other European destinations—rose markedly, bringing prosperity to English hatmakers in particular. Burnet was advised that the Board of Trade supported his aggressive policy toward the French. That policy, though, came at the price of fuming resentment that Morris was muzzling all dissent within the Assembly.

Unfazed, Morris was not done accumulating power under a permissive superior. His final prey was the governor's Provincial Council, created to advise on and consent to all Burnet's decrees, land grants, patronage choices, disbursement of funds, and when to summon or dismiss the Assembly. By Board of Trade directive, the membership of up to twelve councillors was to be composed of "men of estate and ability . . . not necessitous people [who needed the job] or much in debt"—in short, colonial aristocrats. Five of the councilmen when Burnet took office, certifiably upper-crust, were hostile or at best neutral toward Morris's policies, especially trade barons Adolph Philipse and Peter Schuyler, whom the governor soon purged as the chief justice/Assembly leader asked. Their replacements, less lordly but more enlightened men, included two remarkable Scots, younger acolytes of Morris, justly called by historian William Smith "men of learning and good morals."

James Alexander was always close-mouthed about his pre-American youth, but his meteoric ascent to the top of New York's legal profession so soon after emigrating suggests he had already been introduced to the law in Edinburgh or London. Later, while serving in the royal army as an engineering officer, he was suspected of sedition for sympathizing, and perhaps even plotting, with those opposed to handing the British throne to the German Elector of Hanover to prevent a Catholic from claiming it after Queen Anne's death in 1714. Alexander fled to the colonies the next year at age twenty-four and settled in Amboy, New Jersey's provincial capital, where Lewis Morris held forth as president of the council and must have soon encountered the young man's penetrating mind, varied and useful vocational training, and writing ability—traits very like his own. Morris, almost certainly instrumental in Alexander's appointments as Amboy's town surveyor and recorder and then surveyor general for New Jersey, no doubt called Governor Hunter's attention to his fellow Scotsman's abilities. On shifting his activities to New York, Alexander soon excelled as a private practitioner in commercial law, a field congenial to him not least because the woman he married had inherited one of the city's most prosperous dry-goods establishments from her first husband. As part of his intellectual development, Alexander became a close student of the leading European commentators on political philosophy, prompting him as his income grew to amass a splendid library, said to hold more legal tomes than any other in the colony. After a spell as apprentice to Provincial Secretary George Clarke, he was installed—again surely at Morris's urging—as attorney general of New York in 1721, just six years since his hasty departure from Britain; then he joined Burnet's council after Morris swept his foes from it, became the governor's personal lawyer, and, in further extension of his powers, was also designated attorney general of New Jersey and placed on the Provincial Council there as well, serving as a colleague to his guardian angel, Lewis Morris, its senior member.

Among Alexander's close friends—the two likely met while they were surveyors general of their respective colonies—was Cadwallader Colden, who had come to America at about the same time but was a more recent arrival in New York. Colden brought with him a remarkable array of knowledge and interests—medicine, physics, engineering, astronomy, botany, cartography, economics, and anthropology, and while he revealed streaks of stubbornness and vanity, he struck most who knew him as a man whose integrity matched his intelligence.

Son of a rigid Presbyterian minister, Colden was sent off at fourteen to the University of Edinburgh, considered at the time a seat of learning more liberal in its intellectual range than Oxford or Cambridge. Immersing himself in botany and Newtonian physics, he graduated in two years and went to London to study anatomy and chemistry in preparation for practicing medicine. After struggling for five years to make his living as a physician, he accepted a widowed aunt's invitation in 1715 to change his luck in Philadelphia, but his medical practice fared no better. At loose ends, he visited New York in 1718 and was introduced to Governor Hunter, a fellow Scot, who was struck by the polymath's astonishing breadth of knowledge and urged him to join New York's colonial government as surveyor general—and to sweeten the offer, Colden was granted 2,000 Hudson Valley acres. By the time his appointment was confirmed in London, Burnet had become governor; Colden served him with a zeal rarely found in a royal retainer.

The surveyor general's post, which Colden was to hold for forty-two years, carried real authority; no land grant could be certified unless fully surveyed by his office, posted, and its title officially registered. Few in the vast, still sparsely settled colony ever possessed greater familiarity with its terrain, flora and fauna, and the native tribes in the northern sector, where Colden played missionary to ally the Indians with the British traders in Albany and wean them from their French suitors to the north and west. To educate the colonists and spur amicable relations between the races, he wrote an anthropological study of the Iroquois tribes, the first such scholarly work written in British America, published by William Bradford's shop in 1727. As royal surveyor, Colden bristled with indignation when he discovered slovenly record-keeping in the colonial land office, along with rampant favoritism and corruption in the administration of crown grants. Besides laboring to correct the abuses, Colden put his analytical powers at the governor's disposal as a one-man think tank by composing papers—forwarded to the Board of Trade in support of Burnet's policies—that dealt with New York's climate and diseases, its commerce and potential to become the empire's foremost mercantile hub in the New World if not strangled in the crib by imperial restrictions and the Morrisite arguments for cutting off French fur traders from imported British goods. Named to the Provincial Council as part of Morris's political housecleaning, Colden would serve on it for forty years—a testament to his valued learning, honesty, and judgment.

Morris's other three nominees to Burnet's council bore more suspect credentials—his lawyer son, Lewis Morris, Jr.; a nephew of James Alexander's wife by her first marriage, and a scion of the Livingston land barony, all beneficiaries of Morrisite nepotism. The chief justice further extended his web of political mastery by allowing only his partisans to be named as mayor, sheriff, and lesser officials of New York City (the elected councilmen excepted)—he was the forerunner, by a century and a half, of William Magear Tweed, ruler of New York's Tammany Hall and the paradigm of political bossism. Morris left his adversaries few scraps of patronage, even in their home counties, where the governor controlled all appointments down to the clerical level. Besides the offices they held, leading members of the power-wielding Morrisite contingent—the chief justice, his son Lewis Junior, and Councilmen Alexander, Colden, and ambitious attorney Francis Harison among them—were rewarded by the governor with further political spoils in the form of generous land grants, many encompassing thousands of acres along the banks of the Mohawk River west of Albany.

But then Morris, already surfeited with power, made a supremely imprudent move that alienated the one politician in the colony whose sway rivaled his own.

George Clarke, a self-taught lawyer like Morris and a minor British government functionary, had become a colonial land magnate upon marrying the daughter of Lord Cornbury, cousin to Queen Anne, who authorized Clarke's crown appointment (i.e., not subject to dismissal by the governor) in 1702 as New York's provincial secretary and deputy auditor—posts he would retain for more than thirty years. He was also assigned the jobs of clerk of the Provincial Council, the Supreme Court, and all the colony's circuit courts. These multiple appointments meant that through his offices passed every document requiring the royal seal—civil commissions, land grants, marriage licenses, death certificates, pardons, conveyances—as well as all revenues collected and all payments made by the crown to colonial officials and creditors, along with all the minutes, pleadings, rulings, and dockets for the provincial and county courts.

An aloof and somewhat shadowy figure whose estate at Hempstead Plains, Long Island, twenty-five miles east of Manhattan, insulated him from the New York social scene, Clarke took pains to league himself with no political faction. His noninvolvement may explain why he was regarded, if we accept the word of contemporary historian William Smith, Jr., as "sensible, artful, active, cautious; had a perfect command of his temper, and was in his address spacious and civil." While hardly a scintillating personality, Clarke had a far cooler temperament and deeper supply of patience than Morris, which made him a canny political operator when required. Hunter named him as a neutral and conciliatory figure to the Provincial Council—on top of all his other posts and possibly over the objection of newly named Chief Justice Morris, who likely detected in Clarke a potential brake on his control of the colony's judicial system. Clarke may have used his power sparingly, but he had a firm grip on virtually all the levers of New York's governmental machinery. So, when Morris and his partisans were invited five years later by new Governor Burnet to purge his administration of obstructionists, real or potential, they began to question whether the multiple offices under Clarke's oversight were handling royal funds scrupulously and to hint that their service fees might be exceeding the limits set by the crown. It was time, Morris eventually counseled the pliable governor, to bring Clarke down a peg; he was endowed with more offices than any man was entitled to hold—except Morris himself, of course—and, at any rate, the independent-minded squire with powerful patrons was not a Burnet loyalist.

Accordingly, the governor removed Clarke as clerk of the circuit courts, where the bulk of the colony's cases above the level of petty crimes and disputes was adjudicated. The slight would not have riled Clarke unduly, in view of all his other retained offices, save for Morris's request that the vacancy be filled by his son, Lewis Junior—a glaring exercise in favoritism that strengthened the chief justice's dominion over the colony's courts but at the cost of turning a prominent and well-respected officer of the king into Morris's unforgiving enemy.

V

It is undeniable that Lewis Morris contributed significantly to the prudence and utility of public policy and the improvement in honesty and diligence of the men who performed public service under governors Hunter and Burnet. Yet at the zenith of his power, Morris displayed no generosity toward whoever disputed the programs he had advocated and the strong-arm methods he applied to achieve them. His intransigence left him dismissive of the gathering insurgency mounted by men of wealth with a compulsion to yank him from his high horse.

In 1722, almost immediately after Morris had trade baron Adolph Philipse, his fellow Westchester resident, fired from Burnet's council, Philipse won an Assembly seat in a by-election to represent their county and used it as the base to organize an anti-Morrisite uprising. Its war cry dwelled on two claims: Burnet, while an able administrator, was acting despotically in refusing to call a new election for the Assembly, entrenched since the Morrisite sweep of 1716. And Morris's protectionist policies were hurting New York's commerce and making merchants unfairly bear the cost of government while sparing large landholders like himself. The message began to resonate. By 1725, eight of the Assembly's twenty-seven seats changed hands in by-elections due to the death, retirement, or defection of Morris's allies, giving his foes a narrow majority, including the seat recaptured by Philipse's close ally, Stephen DeLancey.

When the legislators convened that autumn, seventy-one-year-old Assembly Speaker (and Morris ally) Robert Livingston had been delayed by illness and lost his leadership post to Philipse. Desperate to reverse the narrow defeat, Morris made a blunder even worse than his captious strike at George Clarke; he persuaded Burnet to declare DeLancey ineligible to sit in the Assembly on the ground that he had never become a fully naturalized citizen since emigrating forty years earlier. Yes, DeLancey had been legally admitted as a permanent resident and, yes, Hunter's 1715 decree granting naturalization rights to all non-British, Christian residents of the colony applied to DeLancey. But Morris claimed that neither act necessarily gave him full citizenship rights—and specifically the right to sit in the Assembly (where DeLancey had earlier served for twelve years) unless an act of the Assembly had so provided. The Philipse faction assailed the governor for gullibly submitting to Morris's transparent chicanery and interfering with the Assembly's right to determine its membership qualifications. Even some of Morris's allies in the legislature accused him of overreaching, and strong objections were raised by some of his usually staunch Dutch supporters, who feared their own citizenship and land tenure rights might be similarly questioned. Under siege, Burnet had no choice but to retreat, send a note of apology to the Assembly, and contritely call for new elections the following year. After a vitriolic campaign, the result was a clear-cut triumph for the mercantile establishment and a repudiation of Morris's career-long fight to protect his own landed class.

Over the next two years the trade barons' party pushed through a series of retributive measures. Tonnage duties on unloading foreign ships were eased. The prohibition against selling British goods to French Canadian fur traders was lifted. Paper currency was taken out of circulation as a deflationary measure that helped creditors but hurt small farmers and the working class. Sidewalk peddlers were freely allowed to hawk their wares, hurting shopkeepers. Real estate taxes were boosted to help cover higher government expenses; the Assembly voted to slash the salaries of officials, including the chief justice's, and the governor's administrative funding was limited to two years rather than the stabilizing five-year appropriation Hunter had finally extracted from the lawmakers a decade earlier. Desperate, Burnet tried to slow the deluge by appealing to Provincial Secretary and Councilman Clarke, the only potential mediator between the polarizing factions, but Burnet had lost all credit with that adroit tactician by trimming his sails at Morris's behest. The governor had to dissolve the Assembly and order a new election in the hope that the Morrisites could regain majority control by blatantly appealing to laborers (through, for example, a proposed end to duties on staples like salt, molasses, and rum) and to their debt-conscious base of city artisans, small traders, and the country yeomanry. But the Philipse-DeLancey crowd had made inroads among Morris's landed class, now swinging over to the pro-business side, and offered populist measures of their own. This time the trade barons and their backers emerged with a two-to-one majority in the Assembly. The whole Morris-conceived coalition and its policies now unraveled even faster, and in the 1728 election, Morris lost his own Assembly seat when even his country neighbors and formerly loyal supplicants rebelled against him. He had badly overplayed his hand.

Morris still retained his longtime offices of chief justice of the New York Supreme Court and president of the New Jersey Council, but these were dependent on the pleasure of the sitting governor. And at year's end, Burnet, against whom complaints of partisanship were being filed in London in steadily heavier volume, was transferred by newly crowned King George II to Boston as governor of Massachusetts and New Hampshire.

With the demise of Morris's protectionist program and the ascent of the free-trade advocates, New York's economy faltered. Currency was devalued by design. The price of wheat, pork, and other commodities fell, hurting farmers. Foreign vessels, more lightly taxed now, increasingly dominated the carrying trade; New York's shipbuilding industry slowed accordingly, affecting allied trades as well, so joblessness rose. But while unprotected local productivity languished, the merchant moguls feasted on the colony's worsening imbalance of trade due to the surge of imported goods.

None of these tribulations—or much of anything else—seemed to perturb Burnet's successor as governor, John Montgomerie, an affable but flaccid figure devoid of the civic awareness that had animated his two immediate predecessors' terms. A military officer of small distinction, Montgomerie could claim only one dubious credential for his appointment—he had been a favorite groom of the Prince of Wales's bedchamber, and upon his master's coronation was duly rewarded with the New York governorship. Said to be "little acquainted with any kind of literature," Montgomerie was more than familiar with the bottle and a hedonistic lifestyle—at his death he left an estate brimming with 2,000 gallons of Madeira. His ambition as governor, according to Councilman Cadwallader Colden, was "to live as much as possible at ease and at the same time retrieve his fortune[,] and for this purpose his administration was entirely directed to the humors of those men who . . . had the Assembly under their influence."

Treading the path of least resistance, the new governor avoided the temperamental and now degraded Lewis Morris and relied instead on Assembly Speaker Philipse and Provincial Secretary (and Councilman) Clarke as his prime advisers. Nonetheless, Montgomerie tried to act in a conciliatory manner by retaining Morris's loyal supporters on the council—his son, Lewis Junior, Colden, and James Alexander, and other Morrisite appointees to office under Hunter and Burnet. But he dealt Morris's judicial hegemony a crushing blow by filling two vacancies on the three-member Supreme Court with young relatives of the chief justice's archrivals—Stephen DeLancey's son James, and Philipse's nephew Frederick, who were able to outvote him on the colony's highest tribunal. Even Morris's long-standing political base as senior member of the New Jersey Council, which Montgomerie had the grace to let him keep, was undermined by growing hostility among the panel's other members toward his protracted tenure.

The New York Assembly under Philipse applied the *coup de grâce* to Morris's shrinking hubris by voting to slash his salary as chief justice from £300 to £250, claiming it was part of a general cost-cutting drive that left his pay no lower than it had been when he was appointed fourteen years earlier. In high dudgeon, Morris objected that the Assembly had no right to set the salary of royal officers without the crown's approval, but Montgomerie, mindful of the political groundshift, approved the indignity. Morris's appeal to London was unavailing, and when Lewis Junior, with more filial devotion than prudence, loosed repeated strident denunciations of the vengeful insult to his father, Montgomerie dropped him from the Provincial Council for his "many scandalous, unjust and false reflections."

Morris likely shed few tears when Montgomerie died suddenly at the beginning of July 1731 after three listless but soothing years on the job.

His passing provided a fourteen-month season of solace for Morris, who, still senior member of the New Jersey Council, was elevated to acting chief executive of New York's satellite colony until the king picked a new governor. Still hungry at age sixty for executive power, Morris urged the Board of Trade to allow New Jersey its own governor and in his most florid prose (e.g., "Tho' I [have] not vanity to hope such favor, nor ambition enough to put me upon asking for it . . .") shamelessly applied for the job himself as unsubtly as he had done thirty years earlier. Again, he would be bypassed.

VI

For Peter Zenger, 1725 ought to have been an auspicious year. Having returned to William Bradford's employ as a journeyman printer for three years, he was taken in as a junior partner of sorts and listed with the owner as copublisher of one of the books the shop issued that year. It was also the year that Bradford decided to launch the colony's first newspaper, a weekly he called the *New-York Gazette*—a project that presumably would have made good use of Zenger's skills and enhanced his earnings potential.

The *Gazette* was something of a risky venture for Bradford, who knew of the troubles encountered by the publishers of two papers begun recently in other colonies. In 1719, six years earlier, his son Andrew had earned the distinction of bringing out the first recognizable newspaper in the British colonies, Philadelphia's *American Weekly Mercury*, conceived primarily to drum up business for his print shop. In truth, it was not a very newsy sheet, filled largely with articles cribbed from months-old British journals. Even so, the *Mercury* managed to get into hot water with Pennsylvania's council the year after it premiered for carrying an article taken from an anonymous pamphlet his shop had printed that remarked on "the dying credit of the province." Offended by the implication that the council and government as a whole should be held accountable for the colony's economic woes, the councilmen summoned Bradford and threatened him with severe punishment. In an age when no one stood up to demand freedom of the press—especially nobody who owned one—Andrew was reduced to claiming he had been away from the shop when the supposedly scandalous pamphlet and issue of the paper were printed. After an abject apology, Bradford was let off with a reprimand never again to publish anything concerning the affairs of the government in Pennsylvania or any other colony.

James Franklin started his *New-England Courant* the following year in Boston—a far more literate undertaking, notable for pieces of social and political satire (including a witty series mocking busybodies by the publisher's teenage brother Ben under the pseudonym Silence Dogood) and columns of dueling letters to the editor on pressing issues such as the benefits and perils of smallpox inoculation. Franklin first ran into a storm for a brief report in 1722 on the Massachusetts government's intention to outfit a ship to pursue coastal pirates—"and 'tis thought," the article added, "he [the captain] will sail some time this month, wind and weather permitting." The colonial council took the straightforward wording to mean officials were being dilatory in their duty, charged Franklin with perpetrating "a high affront to this government," and ordered the publisher to be jailed for a month until he expressed remorse. But his troubles were far from over. The *Courant* carried "An Essay Against Hypocrites" the next year, and this time the Massachusetts legislature read the piece as a rebuke to Cotton Mather, the colony's celebrated Puritan clergyman, revealing a tendency on the paper's part "to mock religion and bring it into contempt . . . [so] that the Holy Scriptures are therefore profanely abused" and society's "peace and good order" disturbed. For this transgression the publisher was ordered never again to print editions of his paper, or any other papers or pamphlets, without first submitting the contents for approval by the colonial secretary and to post a sizable bond to ensure his compliance. This stricture was imposed nearly a generation after Parliament had repealed prior censorship in the mother country. Franklin proved incorrigible, soon resuming the paper's caustic commentary without first seeking government license, but knowing the authorities would likely again pounce on him, he went into hiding for a time while brother Ben ran the paper. Apprehended and brought before a grand jury, Franklin managed to escape indictment—public opinion mounted against such outdated government repression—but he was weary of battling Boston bluenoses, gave up his paper, and moved to Providence, where he put out a lackluster sheet for a time while kid brother Ben moved to Philadelphia and over time became an icon.

William Bradford was therefore careful, in founding his *Gazette*, to avoid publishing any material that might jeopardize his status as the longtime royal printer for New York and New Jersey. Its contents were even less daring than those in his son's paper; they consisted mostly of official notices and proclamations, lists of ships arriving at and departing from New York Harbor, an occasional speech by or message from the governor, clippings from elsewhere, and classified advertisements. The text was loosely edited, poorly proofread, and typographically unappealing; subscribers, not surprisingly, were hard to come by. Whether the drabness of the paper troubled Zenger or he and Bradford fell out over something else entirely—neither man ever expressed rancor over their breakup—the journeyman decided to strike out on his own in 1726, opening a small print shop on Smith Street, a strip of modern William Street, in competition with his former boss. Zenger's place of business was ideally located to win the city's attention: directly across the street from the Black Horse Tavern, the leading dining and drinking establishment in the colony, where Morrisite members of the Assembly gathered for informal skull sessions.

The move likely took all of Zenger's savings—and probably then some—but unlike his earlier, ill-fated effort in Maryland, this one was mounted in the commercial midst of a busy maritime colony, and he found customers, though fewer than he had hoped. His principal publications were sermons and religious tracts, with titles like "The Adorable Ways of God" and "Remarks upon a Discourse Presented to the Reverend Synod of Dissenting Ministers Sitting in Philadelphia," and works in German, his native tongue, and Dutch, his wife's first language, like the 1730 volume *Arithmetica*, credited as the first mathematics text published in New York. Citing the large share of foreign-language works among his output, some modern observers like Vincent Buranelli have concluded that Zenger's "grasp of the English language remained defective." But this seems unlikely—he had probably been setting and proofing type in English for more than fifteen years before he opened his own New York shop. A more probable explanation is that the Zengers' national origins caused them to gravitate not toward British social circles but to New York's still sizable Dutch community and particularly to the company of their fellow parishioners at the Dutch Reformed Church, where they had been married, Anna Zenger taught Sunday school, and Peter earned £12 a year as "organ blower."

Slowly, though, he made contact with influential colonial officials. Among them was Councilman and Surveyor General Cadwallader Colden, whose election campaign polemic "The Interest of the Country in Laying Duties" in support of Morris's protectionist trade policy was printed by Zenger in 1726. His acquaintance with crusty old Rip Van Dam, a pillar of the Dutch Reformed Church, wealthy shipyard owner, and longest-serving member of New York's Provincial Council, was probably the source of a July 31, 1730, grant of 1,000 acres in what is now Schoharie County in central New York to "John Peter Zenger and others." The acreage was remote—Zenger may never have seen it—yet the gift suggests he was well regarded in the colony.

The next year, however, an event occurred that revealed how close to the financial edge Zenger was skating. To make ends meet in those hard times, Peter had won a moonlighting job as a "collector of sundry public taxes in the City of New York," according to the September 8, 1731, entry in the *Journal of the Votes and Proceedings of the General Assembly of the Colony of New York*. But he was unable to account for "forty pounds and upwards" he had collected and owed the colony "by reason he fell under some trouble from his creditors . . . by the removal of some and insolvency of others . . . for which he is informed writs [of arrest] are issued against him. And that being unable to pay the same, has been forced to keep out of the way [probably meaning fired as a collector], but proposes to discharge in his way [by] printing at the most moderate and reasonable wages. And therefore prays the prosecution against him may be stayed, and he be employed in printing for the public." All of which apparently meant that Zenger did not make a practice of segregating his tax collections from the income he earned from his print shop but instead used the mingled funds to pay for his living and business expenses—and when some of his creditors failed to pay him, either because they had gone broke or fled the colony, he could not pay the government the modern equivalent of roughly $10,000 in taxes he had collected. To stay out of prison, he was asking the Assembly to let him work off the debt by printing for the public's needs without charge.

Zenger was almost certainly more careless than devious as a handler of public funds. While no record survives of the Assembly's response to his request, it was apparently affirmative, for the matter was addressed again in an August 19, 1732, entry of the Assembly's *Journal*. It reported a petition for relief from the printer, who said he still owed the public £47 "and that if he could be free from arrests [*sic*] . . . for two years, he should be in a capacity to satisfy the public." The Assembly must have voted compassionately again to allot him the requested time because the historical evidence shows that Zenger was not only left at liberty but that his print shop was at the center of a broiling political fracas during the second of the subsequent two years. When he was actually arrested and jailed, it was for a very different and far nobler cause.

4

Bending the Rule of Law

COLONEL WILLIAM COSBY, accompanied by four members of his family, set sail from England in early June of 1732 on the H.M.S. *Seaford*. He was the twenty-fourth of thirty-seven men who would serve as governor or acting governor of the province of New York and, in the estimate of some authorities on the colonial period, he was the vilest of the lot. His foul reputation is due in no small part to the enemies he made, among them some of the most talented and influential men in the colony, whose interests they believed Cosby imperiled, and so they set out to brand him a tyrant worthy of removal from office. Whether his detractors were largely justified in their charges or merely self-interested in their vehement finger-wagging, their efforts were the first to shatter the chains that bound free expression in America.

Cosby was the surrogate of George II, then in the fifth year of his thirty-three-year reign after his father had become the first of the German-born Hanoverian kings in 1714. Neither George, *père* nor *fils*, was brainy or charismatic, and both spoke English with a Teutonic accent that was less than endearing to their subjects. Yet they were hardly putty in the hands of the ascendant Whig Party leaders who took control of Parliament on George I's arrival in England and retained it for half a century. Having gained the British throne by chance rather than inheritance, war, or intrigue, the two sovereigns were sufficiently comfortable in their majestic robes to defer on most policy issues to parliamentary primacy. Whatever their limitations, the first two Georges presided over an age marked by Britain's arrival at the apex of world power, its prosperity restored and surging after the South Sea Bubble crisis had nearly bankrupted the realm.

Much of the credit for this advancement has been assigned to Robert Walpole, a country squire without an aristocratic title (but with a Cambridge education) who made himself a master political manipulator and the first leader of Commons to be labeled prime minister. No subsequent P.M. has held the position longer. Walpole, in high command of the government that sent William Cosby to rule over New York and New Jersey, was a gifted orator and something of a financial wizard—for much of his prime ministry, he doubled as Chancellor of the Exchequer—but his great prowess was as a conciliator who pressed hardest for economic and political stability by heading off inflammatory disputes. His oft-cited motto, "Let sleeping dogs be," was a wily caution, not a symptom of apathy. He kept taxes and government expenditures down and Britain out of wars by diverting both Hanoverian kings' ancestral yen to dabble in continental conflicts at the likely expense of Britain's solvency. Walpole's deft deployment of patronage to purchase influence, if not ardent loyalty, was especially effective in heading off divisive policy clashes and wars to gain or defend national honor—for him, acquiring and wielding power were not means to an end but themselves the overriding purpose of politics. In his elegiac history of the English-speaking people, Tory Winston Churchill, while himself a latter-day prime-minister-in-waiting, wrote demeaningly of Walpole's reign: "Public life was degraded by materialism and politics became a mere striving for office and crown patronage by rival groups of Whigs."

Among those striving for office most avidly in Walpole's shadow was Thomas Pelham-Holles, first Duke of Newcastle, who at age twenty-one, upon the demise of his father and uncle, became one of the largest landholders in the kingdom, with vast holdings in Sussex

County near the channel. A textbook case of noblesse oblige—with a need for self-validation that playing the great feudal lord evidently could not provide him—Newcastle devoted himself to public service through Whig politics as a prominent Walpole protégé. Overcoming a plodding, notoriously forgetful mind by obsessive attention to detail, the dutiful duke was appointed to Walpole's cabinet as Secretary of State for the Southern Department, whose responsibilities included oversight of Britain's New World possessions. Not in the least a policymaker, Newcastle was in his element as ex-officio chairman of the Board of Trade, a data-gathering panel with a staff that monitored foreign commerce and all aspects of colonial affairs except military operations. He pursued his task with what Stanley Katz, author of *Newcastle's New York*, called "indefatigable industry for the minutiae of public administration," which he mistook for serious policy issues to avoid formulating a coherent colonial program. Without need to enhance a fabulous fortune, he was personally honest, witness his departure from office £400,000 poorer than when he entered public service. His principal compensatory perk seems to have been dispensing jobs to financially needy cronies and relatives, regardless of their qualifications. This unfortunate habit was most conspicuous in his selection of royal governors.

In fairness to Newcastle, the pool of able and available candidates to administer the crown's overseas holdings was limited. Men of accomplishment and high standing in British social, commercial, and political circles had little motivation to undergo the privations and dangers of colonial life; the most willing prospects were also the most hard up for money. Those chosen invariably had a powerful friend within the royal court or the peerage or had rendered noteworthy service to the crown, often military—useful training to combat the perils of frontier existence alongside natives unhappy over their displacement. Newcastle's choice to succeed Montgomerie as governor in New York had performed no great service to the kingdom, but he was a military man, a relative of the duke—Cosby's wife was Newcastle's first cousin—and indeed financially needy. That his troubles were due directly to reprehensible conduct in his previous post as a colonial administrator did not disqualify him in Newcastle's befogged eyes.

II

Born in 1690 on a Laois County estate in south central Ireland, William Cosby was either the sixth or tenth son—accounts vary—of an aristocratic British father and an Irish mother in a family that had settled in Ireland in Queen Elizabeth's time. Little else is known of his formative years, but at nineteen he reportedly went to Italy to sow his wild oats and gamble at cards. When his money ran out after a year, he joined the British Army's 5th Dragoon Guards, fought in Flanders and Iberia during the War of the Spanish Succession, and married well at twenty-one to Grace Montague, sister of George Montague, Earl of Halifax, who would soon sit in the king's Privy Council, and cousin of Thomas Pelham-Holles, three years Cosby's junior and shortly to be made the Duke of Newcastle. The couple had five children, a London home on Soho Square, and a country place at Windsor. Cosby's connections likely sped his advance in rank; by twenty-seven he was a colonel with the16th Royal Irish Regiment and named both military commander and civil governor of Minorca in the Balearic Islands in the Mediterranean, one of Britain's trophies from the long war against Spain. He served in that cushy, if obscure, posting for nearly ten years (likely with frequent home leave) and might have escaped the Walpole administration's notice forever but for a single, rash transgression.

As in most colonies, rumors arose on Minorca about irregularities in tax collections and crown expenditures but nothing that materialized as a scandal. In 1718, though, Cosby's second year on the job and a few months before Britain resumed hostilities with Spain, his officers seized from an arriving English ship 234 sacks of snuff, valued at £9,000, consigned by Catalan merchant Bonaventura Capadevilla, operating out of Lisbon, to a British buyer, one Joseph Bow. Cosby ordered the snuff impounded as contraband because, he falsely claimed, it was being shipped from an enemy nation, and confiscated documents testifying to Capadevilla's title to the cargo and Bow's letter of intended purchase. Royal governors were allowed to retain such booty as a prize of office, provided it was truly contraband and fully accounted for to crown officials, but the seized snuff met neither requirement. Cosby sent fifty of the sacks to Italy for his personal gain; the rest, he alleged, was held on Minorca on orders received from London, but the snuff never surfaced. When lawyers for both the shipper and the buyer complained to local legal authorities and sued to recover the precious powder, Cosby never produced the papers for judicial scrutiny—or the snuff.

His larceny and stonewalling succeeded for several years until the deceased Bow's estate lawyer called the matter to the attention of the Privy Council, which determined that, contrary to Cosby's claim, no order from British trade officials at Whitehall had ever been sent authorizing confiscation of the snuff. Cosby was asked repeatedly for the documents in support of his predatory behavior, but the papers were never forthcoming—the miscreant likely claimed they were lost or stolen, like the snuff itself—and Cosby supposed the whole fuss would subside in time. On a home visit in 1722, however, he was summoned before the Privy Council to answer the charges against him, and when he could not, he was eventually ordered to pay Bow's heirs £10,000 for value and damages. Even if Cosby had managed to dispose of his illicit trove for a portion of its original value, the judgment caused his family finances to crumble. But his cousin Tom Newcastle would not fire him, and Cosby stayed on in Minorca until 1728 while the scandal was hushed up back in London.

Apparently contrite on his return home, he reportedly was placed as a royal equerry for a time, but to help pay his heavy debt and restore his blighted honor, he applied to Newcastle for another, preferably more lucrative, governorship. In April of 1731, almost certainly at the urging of his cousin Grace Cosby, the duke assigned her husband to serve as governor of the Leeward Islands (including Antigua and Monserrat) east of Puerto Rico. Rather than a reward, Newcastle and the Board of Trade may have regarded the new post as a form of banishment, or at least a demotion, since the sugar islands he was to be sent to in the Caribbean were a more remote and even smaller territory than Minorca. With the usual relaxed attitude toward colonial affairs countenanced by the ministry, Cosby did not ready himself to leave until the end of summer. While boarding ship, he learned of Montgomerie's death and immediately postponed his voyage to apply for the far more lucrative job as governor of New York and New Jersey. His wife's cousin did not disappoint him.

One of Cosby's contemporaries soon to become acquainted with the appointee expressed retrospective revulsion at Newcastle's blind family loyalty. Cadwallader Colden, in a later account of Cosby's tenure, remarked, "How such a man after such a flagrant instance of tyranny and robbery [in Minorca] came to be entrusted with the government of [another] English colony . . . is not easy for a common understanding to conceive without entertaining thoughts much to the disadvantage of the honor and integrity of the king's ministers." Colden allowed, however, for the possibility that cousin Tom had had a few brisk words of warning for Cosby and convinced himself "that what [Cosby] had suffered by the complaints made against him from Minorca would make him for the future carefully avoid giving any occasion of complaint from his new government. . . ." The king formally appointed him in mid-January 1732, and late the next month in New York, James Alexander wrote Colden, his Scottish kinsman—before word of Cosby's heinous conduct in Minorca had reached America—of an advisory from London that the new governor was of good character and lively spirit, "has the Earl of Halifax's sister as his wife," and would arrive with two nearly grown daughters and a son.

During the four months it took the laconic Board of Trade to prepare his papers, Cosby wrote to advise the acting governor, Rip Van Dam, senior member of New York's Provincial Council, that he was conscientiously mobilizing his political contacts to plump for defeat of the Molasses Act then pending in Parliament—a bill that would impose an onerous duty on colonists for buying molasses and sugar imported from non-British territories, especially Haiti and Martinique in the French West Indies, and thus providing British colonial planters a pricing advantage. As an afterthought, Cosby prayed that "care be taken of the garden [at the governor's house] and proper things sow'n in for the season; and care also be taken of Nutton Island and the game preserved" for fair-weather hunting. As they left for the New World, the Cosby family had to repress thoughts of the primitive surroundings, meager luxuries, and coarse manners they were likely to encounter in such a rough-hewn outpost—a prospect perhaps most dreaded by the governor's aristocratic wife, Grace, used to the elegance of London's highest society and country manors serviced by battalions of servants. No doubt allaying their anxiety was an awareness that, however far Cosby's family had fallen, he would, as the king's personal deputy, outrank everyone else in both colonies under his charge—and he intended to let them all know it.

III

Free of virtually all timely restraint on his conduct in office, a royal governor's influence on the political, economic, and social life of a British colony in America was formidable indeed. In an age long before civil service codes set standards to winnow the best-qualified applicants, the governor's patronage power allowed him the liberty of staffing almost the entire colonial administration from top to bottom, ranging from the Provincial Council, which advised on and consented to many of his actions (but dissenters ran the risk of being dropped from membership), to all judges and local justices of the peace, sheriffs, tax collectors, and down to the lowliest clerks. New York's governor also chose the mayor and chief officers of the colony's two most populous settlements, New York City and Albany (except for the aldermen composing their city councils). While the General Assembly, the legislative branch of government, was elected, the governor could summon and dismiss it at will—it could not gather on its own—and veto every bill it passed (though at the peril of having his administration starved for tax revenues that only the lawmakers could authorize, as Hunter had painfully experienced for more than half his term in office). The governor and his council sat as the colony's appellate court of last resort, while he himself served in the ex officio role of chancellor, presiding, either alone or with associates of his choice, over the Court of Chancery to determine equity disputes without a jury. A governor's power was further enhanced by his right to distribute land to whomever His Excellency wished, subject to approval of his council, composed mostly of men who already held substantial property themselves and were disinclined to cavil with the governor's wishes for sharing the wealth. He could also enforce the law in whatever manner he chose, with little fear of reprimand; he picked the colony's attorney general, sheriffs, and their deputies and could order the arrest and prosecution of lawbreakers as he divined them and press his judges to impose harsh sentences. Furthermore, he acted as military commander of the colony, authorized to pay for all its garrison's needs down to their uniforms and rations. New York's royal governors, as Stanley Katz has suggested, were "virtually unrestrained in the day-to-day . . . exercise of power"—a heady license that even the best of them, like Hunter and Burnet, at times succumbed to abusing.

Given the lure of nearly omnipotent sway that governors enjoyed, one might suppose the office held wide appeal for men of ambition who would have relished the challenge of taming the royal wilderness and transforming it into a prospering paradise. In reality, few worthy men pined to shoulder the thankless responsibility of reigning over bleak settlements of unruly colonists (not to mention hordes of threatening "savages," as the natives were routinely referred to). Thus, marginal men were usually sent, with a single driving ambition—to make the job pay. In this regard, Cosby's designs were no more inglorious than most of his predecessors'.

The material rewards of his new office derived from two main sources. The first was the New York governor's salary, which in Cosby's era was £1,650, with a supplement of £400 for fuel and candles, £150 for travel to Albany and the north country and gifts to the Indians there, and £1,000 for presiding over colonial New Jersey as well. The second and likely far more lucrative source of the governor's income were fees for use of his royal seal to certify nearly all official transactions in the colony and, still more remunerative, gratuities (the purchase price, in reality) in return for the award of public offices and land grants, which could run into hundreds of pounds sterling apiece. Another source of income Cosby was all too familiar with: the right to seize cargoes as contraband for violating Britain's Navigation Acts aimed at penalizing foreign shippers. A further resource available to less-than-scrupulous New York governors was the fund provided him for supplying the troops at Fort George in what is modern Battery Park; by keeping the enrollment list at less than full strength (of about 400), a governor could pocket the unspent allotment for the soldiers' salaries, mess, uniforms, and weaponry. Thus, during his seven-week voyage to New York, Cosby had cause to savor his financial prospects: an income of somewhere between £5,000 and £10,000 a year, exclusive of the speculative value of land grants presented to him by the crown for his personal use or disposal.

The political climate he was sailing into was auspiciously balmy as well. As in Walpole's Britain, provincial New York in mid-1732 was torn by no clamorous ideological disputes. The principal concerns of the moment were the sluggish pace of the colony's economic recovery and how enlightened or benighted the new governor would prove to be, given his hegemony over nearly every aspect of the colonists' lives. The last incumbent, mild-mannered John Montgomerie, though only three years in office, had had a salutary effect on public affairs and private enterprise by maintaining an unobtrusive profile and defusing factionalism. Meanwhile, New York's most volcanic politician, Lewis Morris, lay dormant, and the colonists' principal forum, the Assembly, was a conquered province under the rule of Morris's avowed antagonists.

On the eve of Cosby's arrival, New York's heterogeneous population stood at somewhere between 50,000 and 55,000 with an additional 40,000 or so living in the satellite jurisdiction of New Jersey. The combined number of residents in the two colonies Cosby was about to preside over would have placed it in an approximate tie with Connecticut and Pennsylvania for third place in size among the British provinces and far below Virginia and Massachusetts. New York City circa 1732, which then extended about a mile north of the Battery, was home to approximately 10,000 people, of whom 1,700 were slaves (only the city of Charleston had more); Boston and Philadelphia were larger, but New York was steadily closing the gap.

Although the little city was crowded compared to the other urbanized settlements in British America, it was considered a healthful place with a temperate climate, sea breezes to fan the summer's muggy heat, and a safe harbor that reached for enough inland to calm wintry blasts off the ocean. New Yorkers could enjoy a diverse and nutritious diet, thanks to an abundance of grains, fruits, vegetables, and animal protein—plump oysters were a specialty—from the surrounding countryside and waters, much of it arriving by boat from Long Island's fertile fields and Hudson Valley farms and orchards. This cornucopia kept prices in line and hunger at bay in a community where the demand for labor usually outstripped the supply. Religious tolerance prevailed; two dozen or more houses of worship had been founded by then, including a synagogue, and while nearly every Christian denomination was represented, Catholic parishioners were relatively scarce. The well-being of the soul was better provided for than the life of the mind. There were no schoolhouses and few organized schools; teaching was done in classes at home or at church, but good masters were hard to come by. Nor was reading much in favor nor the arts widely pursued, though a new theater had been opened lately on Broadway, offering occasional productions. Most entertainment was presented at the Exchange, a large open room raised on brick arches—one of the town's few public buildings, along with City Hall and the almshouse—and used mainly for meetings, concerts, and dances. It was a convivial town, by all accounts, where hoi polloi had their pick of taverns and grog shops, while gentlemen repaired to their stag evening clubs for weekly gatherings. Women of refinement held musicales for one another, and well-off couples regularly hosted dinner parties, polite society's staple recreation.

The informal character of colonial life Cosby was about to encounter differed radically, of course, from what he was used to in the empire's great thronged metropolis; the scale of everything in compact New York was miniature by comparison, tastes were modest, and social and commercial interaction unceremonious. Though women took their fashion cues from London, time and distance left them perennially out of style. Yet we have the word of reliable contemporary chronicler William Smith, Jr., that by and large, the women "are comely, dress well, and scarcely any of them have distorted shapes." Smith, a prominent lawyer who served on the Provincial Council in the decade prior to the American Revolution, left us an engaging portrait of the colony he grew up in—a two-volume history of British New York that began to appear in 1762. While he did not paint the lily, noting, for example, that education was abysmal and "our common speech is extremely corrupt," Smith nonetheless celebrated the virtues of his fellow New Yorkers, who for the most part he found to be "modest, temperate, naturally sprightly, sensible, and good-humored" folk. While he believed them to be taller and healthier than Europeans, they were curiously shorter-lived, an oddity he attributed to a severe scarcity of competent physicians while "quacks abound."

IV

Cosby arrived in New York on the first of August, 1732, and lost no time presenting himself to his subjects. He emerged the next day from the governor's house, received a volley of musket fire in salute from waiting rows of garrison soldiers and militia volunteers drawn up on the parade grounds at next-door Fort George, and proceeded on foot— likely a bonding gesture toward curious onlookers—to City Hall. There he was greeted by provincial and municipal officials, leading merchants, and other local notables and presented with the royal seal of the colony by Rip Van Dam, the acting governor, who may also have administered the oath of office. Possibly the Anglican rector of Trinity Church, the city's ranking clergyman, did the honors, but the swearing in was evidently not conducted by the colony's august senior jurist, Chief Justice Lewis Morris, who was apparently at his estate in New Jersey, where he had been happily reigning as acting governor of that colony for the long interval before Cosby's arrival.

The new governor was almost certainly on his best behavior for most of that day of pageantry, but there is reason to believe he may have suffered a momentary lapse when the acclaim subsided. We have the usually credible word of Cadwallader Colden for it that on his second day in town Cosby was "willing to show his disposition of governing . . . by going out in his coach and, meeting a loaded wagon in which one of the planters sat with his wife, ordered his coachman to whip him because the man did not drive so quickly out of the way as he expected." As with many of the defamatory charges to be directed against Cosby, in this first alleged display of foul temper we have only one of his antagonists'

account of the happening, with no attempt on his part to find or identify witnesses or elicit the governor's version of the occurrence, if factual.
True or not, the incident gained circulation as evidence, almost as soon
as he arrived, that Cosby was intolerant of all, no matter their rank, who
stood in his way.

He would soon meet his match in hauteur. In narrating his first
encounter with Lewis Morris, Cosby showed he was as liable as his
detractors to tell a one-sided story, uncorroborated by attendants, that
cast his enemy in the worst possible light. In a letter he sent to Newcastle
about a year afterward, Cosby reported having traveled to New Jersey's
capital building in Amboy on August 6 or 7 to meet with Council President (and Acting Governor) Morris, whom he had given "timely notice"
of his arrival so he might be presented the royal seal of the second colony
he had been sent to govern. But Morris was not on hand to greet him and
instead kept him waiting in an anteroom for "an hour or two." Morris
was said to be closeted with fellow councilman (and his close friend)
James Alexander while they put the finishing touches on a decree being
issued in their capacity as the colony's Chancery Court, which settled
disputes on matters of equity. The matter at hand, according to Cosby,
was their ruling in favor of one of Morris's daughters-in-law or perhaps
her sister—Cosby's vagueness here typified many of the charges he
would hurl at Morris (and vice versa); the issue to be resolved in the case
had to do with a disputed land title, which Morris and Alexander were
in the process of awarding to the former's relative. Cosby inserted parenthetically that the decision had been made without giving the other side
a chance to state its case—a shocking instance of partiality and judicial
malfeasance if true. Cosby claimed that Morris, compounding the disrespect shown him, sent out word from the council chamber that he would
promptly hand over the royal seal the governor had come for if he agreed
to affix the seal, immediately upon Morris's surrendering it, to the ruling
Morris and Alexander had just rendered; otherwise, Morris would apply
it himself while still the acting governor of New Jersey before handing
over the crown's imprimatur. In short, Cosby was accusing Morris of
trying to do his own family a rank favor at the last moment before he
left office.

Almost surely, Cosby spurned the devious proposition, or else he would not have cited it to Newcastle, overseer of all British colonial governance, as evidence of Morris's dishonorable methods. Whatever the facts of the episode, one thing seems clear—bad blood began to flow between the two men from the first; it would shortly become a torrent.

Cosby got off on a far friendlier footing with other, more useful political potentates. He retained New York's seasoned, sensible colonial secretary, George Clarke, also a member of the Provincial Council, as his chief adviser and tactician, the same role he had served for Montgomerie, and befriended the barons of trade, especially Adolph Philipse, the Assembly speaker, and young James DeLancey, who sat on both the Supreme Court and the council. Like Burnet, the governor exercised the privilege not to call for new Assembly elections, last held in 1728 when the mercantile junta and its allies had captured a strong majority. To solidify his support among the ruling faction, Cosby went before the Assembly on August 10 to deliver a cordial greeting and blamed his delayed arrival on his efforts in London "to give the best assistance I was able to defeat a bill then [pending] in Parliament in favor of the [British] sugar islands."

Despite skepticism over Cosby's effectiveness as a lobbyist against passage of the Molasses Act (which passed), his good intentions were accepted at face value and generously rewarded by the colonial legislators. Not only did they "cheerfully" (Colden's word) vote to amply fund his administration for the next five years—Smith said it was for six years, which would have made it the longest such appropriation ever voted to a governor by the New York legislature—but also awarded him a gift of £750 for his "vigilant and generous assistance" in allegedly opposing the Molasses Act. No substantiation was asked for Cosby's claim nor has any ever been found; the large gratuity was nevertheless presented despite the Assembly's almost certain awareness that the governor's written, publicly posted instructions from the Board of Trade, like those given to all royal governors, forbade their acceptance of gifts from colonial legislators (or anyone else), presumably to discourage attempts to purchase their favor. Possibly Cosby regarded the gift as acceptable because his rewarded activity had occurred prior to his formal assumption of office, but that would have amounted at best to splitting hairs. Even if so, Cosby displayed an avaricious nature, flouting the crown's rules as he complained that the Assembly's expression of gratitude (equivalent to roughly $280,000 in 2014 currency) was ungenerous. William Smith cited Lewis Morris, Jr., just entering the Assembly after winning a by-election for his father's old seat representing Westchester borough, as the source for the governor's alleged complaint, "Damn them—why did they not add shillings and pence? Do they think I came from England for money? I'll make them know better." Not anxious to ruffle their preening new commandant and likely hopeful of gaining a louder say in both his patronage choices and handling of public funds, the assemblymen added £250 to their gift.

"Our party differences seemed over," James Alexander, soon to become Cosby's adamant adversary, would later recall of that transitional period, "and everything seemed to promise an easier administration than any governor had ever met with in this place." Despite his disreputable history, Cosby had been given every chance to redeem himself with a lush colonial governorship. And all the auguries were positive for him. He had come wreathed with fresh self-confidence and the backing of major figures of the realm, found the colonies he had asked to preside over to be free of civil unrest, allied himself at once with some of their most powerful residents, and exhibited courtly manners and a smooth if transparent charm that won over the Assembly. Early signs emerged, nonetheless, that Cosby's reign would not remain tranquil for long.

Within a few months of his arrival, the governor's manner was being faulted as dismissive toward his colonial subjects, whom he seemed to regard as inferior denizens of the realm. One leading historian of the period has called him "a man of rather strong personality, self-willed and resourceful, accustomed to command, with the contempt of men in general which was characteristic of the soldier and of the ambitious courtier." As a military officer of high rank, he was unused to back-talk, and his ineffectuality as a civil administrator may be inferred from an early letter to Newcastle, lamenting that those under his command "think themselves entirely independent of the governors and . . . act accordingly, which is a very great hindrance to the king's affairs." He was apprehensive as well about an undercurrent of civil restlessness, he confided, because regrettably, "the example and spirit of the [obstreperous] Boston people begins to spread among these colonies [New York and New Jersey]."

The souring of Cosby's abbreviated grace period is readily traceable to his fixation on money. His greed seemed to exceed the usual gubernatorial syndrome. While still in London, even before spending a single day on the job, he was awarded some £6,400 in fees, commissions, and emoluments payable to New York's governor for the thirteen months since his predecessor had died in office. When he finally arrived in America, as we have seen, he wheedled a £1,000 gratuity from the Assembly for his doubtful efforts to block the Molasses Act. As if these were not rewards enough in advance of any labors, in his third month in office Cosby asked London to approve the appointment of his son William, Jr., scarcely out of his teens, as provincial secretary of New Jersey at an annual salary of £450, which was £200 more than the pay of New York's Chief Justice Morris. There was more than a whiff of insolence about the man, as if certain of his license to extract whatever he could from the royal purse. A few weeks later, before his egregious request in behalf of son Billy was halfway across the Atlantic, Cosby reached for another £1,000 boodle, this one from the pocket of someone who strenuously objected, even though the governor may have been well within his rights. The attempt would end his political honeymoon.

V

Ten days or so before he sailed for America, Cosby asked for and was given a supplementary instruction by the Board of Trade, allowing him on his arrival to collect half the salary and other income that had been paid to the acting governor. It was customary but not mandatory for the temporary occupant of the office to split the salary paid during an installed governor's absence from the colony. The rules were murky, however, when it came to who was paid what for services rendered by the acting governor in the interim between the appointment of a new governor and his actual takeover of a colony. Cosby was not one to leave such a question to chance and so came to New York armed with a crown directive to Rip Van Dam, the seventy-year-old acting governor then in his thirtieth year as a member of the unpaid Provincial Council, to hand over half his wages for temporarily presiding over the colony (even as Lewis Morris had simultaneously been acting governor of New Jersey). Cosby was either tactful or foolhardy enough to let several months pass before breaking the bad news to the venerable Dutchman, who was born in Albany two years before the British seized New Netherlands. On November 14, Cosby advised members of his council, including the dismayed Van Dam, that he was entitled by royal directive to half the money Van Dam had been paid as temporary governor, which came to precisely £1,975 7s. 10d.

Cosby's wisdom may be questioned for pressing the issue—why penalize a popular and influential figure and risk antagonizing his fellow colonists who had been so hospitable to the incoming governor? But a shade under £1,000 in 1732 New York currency, it should be borne in mind, was not pocket change—and Cosby was a needy man, probably more so than Van Dam. Besides, the government had authorized the pay split, so why not take his due? Rip Van Dam, though, as Cosby failed to intuit, had not won respect throughout the colony by being anyone's pushover. Proud of his heritage, he still spoke English with a pronounced Dutch accent, but it had hardly kept him from great commercial success. His shipyard behind Trinity Church on what would come to be called the Hudson River may have been the busiest in the colony. He held ownership stakes in a number of swift cargo vessels. He owned considerable real estate in the commercial district, including the building that housed the city's new theater. And he was likely the richest and most respected parishioner in the older and larger of New York's two Dutch Reformed churches. Among his close friends were Chief Justice Morris and James Alexander, Van Dam's lawyer, who counted on his support in the Morrisite political cause. He could also turn mulishly stubborn in his righteousness when challenged.

After pondering Cosby's demand and consulting with Alexander, he told the governor and council at its session two weeks later that he would not comply. He had earned his payments fair and square, had performed dutifully, and no one could claim the colony had suffered under his temporary oversight. In disregarding custom, he growled, the Board of Trade was practicing arrant favoritism at his expense toward an aristocrat who had done nothing to earn the funds he craved. But Cosby's allies on the council were in the majority and ruled for the governor. Undaunted, Van Dam offered a nervy counterproposal; he would consent to the governor's order provided he, in turn, reciprocated by giving Van Dam half of the funds Cosby had collected as the governor's perquisites while still in London—which, the Dutchman had discovered, came to precisely £6,407 18s. 10d. Just how Van Dam unearthed this figure is a mystery—perhaps the well-connected Alexander, who corresponded often with lawyers and merchants in London, employed a spy on the Board of Trade's staff to provide intelligence useful to his clientele—but suffice it to say, Cosby never challenged the accuracy of the claim. Van Dam's breathtaking defiance clearly got the governor's silk britches in a twist, for he petulantly decided to sue the prickly codger for the £1,000; crown authority had to be upheld.

But which court best promised to provide the governor a satisfactory outcome for his suit? It was not a cut-and-dried procedural matter. Ordinarily, given the amount of money involved, the case would have been brought in the colony's Supreme Court, which handled both civil suits and criminal matters, combining the functions of Britain's Court of Common Pleas and the King's Bench. But in either capacity, New York's high tribunal operated as a common-law court under the jury system, and Cosby was not so obtuse as to suppose a panel of Van Dam's peers would favor the governor's claim, even with its royal imprimatur, over the resolute objection of one of their foremost fellow colonists. To avoid a jury trial, the suit could have been filed in the Court of Chancery, the colony's equity tribunal, established by the Assembly in 1683, which issued its rulings without jury participation. As a court of equity, Chancery had the power to override, in the name of justice or fairness, decisions by lower courts that it believed had erred, perhaps based on too rigorous or oppressive an application of common or statutory law or perhaps on faulty interpretation of conflicting court rulings or statutes. But Chancery also acted as a court of original jurisdiction over disputed rights and duties, usually involving crown funds (e.g., tax payments or, say, governors' salaries), and property, such as contested land titles.

The Chancery Court would have suited Cosby's purpose had it not presented two problems. The first rub was that Chancery was presided over by the governor himself serving as chancellor and consisted of himself alone or, if he so chose, with some members of his council. Since Cosby, however, could hardly sit in judgment of a suit he himself had brought before the tribunal, he might have nominated a surrogate chancellor, serving alone or with councilmen. But this solution, too, was problematic. Equity courts like Chancery were exceedingly unpopular among New York colonists, who saw such panels as a potent weapon in the hands of oppressive governors—and, at any rate, most of them lacked legal knowledge and, acting without jury restraint, could arbitrarily usurp colonists' rights and rule on the basis of favoritism, not justice. Nevertheless, Governors Cornbury, Hunter, and Barnet had all chosen on occasion to call the Chancery Court into session and handed down controversial rulings, despite the Assembly's loud denunciation of the practice four times between 1700 and 1727. Cosby, too, would doubtlessly have disdained the Assembly's perennial objection if an appropriate dispute arose requiring him to resort to such an expedient. Ruling as chancellor on his own suit against Van Dam, though, might have got him tarred and feathered by the colonists—even Cosby grasped that autocracy had its limits. And since any surrogate chancellor or participating councilmen he might have named to hear his claim against Van Dam would be suspect as the governor's pawns, the juryless Chancery Court option was out.

Cosby's guileful legal advisers, led by the colony's veteran Attorney General Richard Bradley, an avid champion of the royal prerogative, promptly crafted a gimmick to have the case of *The King v. Van Dam* heard in a court controlled by judges friendly to the governor and empty of unfriendly jurymen. The tricky stratagem relied on some tortured history. In 1691, the Assembly had established a single "Supreme Court of Judicature" to be installed in New York City and empowered with "cognizance of all pleas, civil, criminal and mixed, as fully and amply, to all intents and purposes whatsoever, as [respectively] the Court of King's

Bench, Common Pleas and Exchequer within his majesty's kingdom of England have or ought to have." This passing reference to the Court of Exchequer provided a useful device for Cosby's legal team to latch on to. The English Court of Exchequer, an ancient tribunal whose activities had changed markedly over the centuries, sometimes heard equity disputes and always without a jury, and so Cosby's claim against Van Dam might have qualified as falling within the statutory language of the New York Assembly's 1691 Judiciary Act. This would arguably have meant that in its Exchequer function as a court of equity—operating without a jury—Lewis Morris's Supreme Court could have heard Cosby's suit, even though in its other two functions as a common-law court hearing civil and criminal matters, a jury decided cases. The 1691 act, however, had required the Assembly to renew it every two years, and after it failed to do so in 1698, it lapsed, leaving the Supreme Court without equity jurisdiction. But the previously established (1683) Court of Chancery, however much it was despised by colonists as a tool for tyranny, remained intact to hear equity cases whenever a governor so chose. Since Cosby could not bring his Van Dam suit before the Chancery Court over which he himself presided, he induced his council to pass an ordinance early in December that empowered the Supreme Court to hear cases as a juryless court of equity, in effect reactivating the language of the lapsed 1691 Judiciary Act but without bothering to obtain the Assembly's approval. As Cosby's head legal gunslinger, Attorney General Bradley argued the legislature's consent was not required; in his view, only the crown, or its royal representative, the governor, could create a court of equity in the colonies. And now the Supreme Court, two of whose three justices belonged to the anti-Morrisite mercantile families allied with Cosby, had been licensed by the governor and his council to hear his suit to recover half of Van Dam's wages—and with no jury to stop Justices DeLancey and Philipse if they outvoted Chief Justice Morris, to whom Van Dam had long pledged political allegiance.

As soon as he caught wind of Bradley's legal gymnastics, Morris tried to intervene. For him a much graver issue was at stake than the £1,000 Cosby so coveted. In Morris's view, the new governor was manipulating the colony's entire legal system for no reason other than spite over Van Dam's defiance. In doing so, as the chief justice's letters and memos reflect his thinking, Cosby was riding roughshod over two fundamental objections to such despotic abuse of his executive power. First, the governor had no right to dictate by a council-approved ordinance what the Supreme Court's jurisdiction was—only the Assembly or Parliament could assign it an equity function. Second, New York already had an equity tribunal, the Chancery Court; it did not require another one merely because Cosby, in his capacity as chancellor, could not sit in judgment of his own case and, more to the point, was determined to circumvent a jury trial of his suit, despite Van Dam's constitutional right to one. Yet Morris, too, had a self-serving motive in registering his fervent disapproval of Cosby's subterfuge. While Morris hardly acknowledged as much, he was not oblivious to the likelihood that if Cosby prevailed in his Van Dam suit, he would similarly demand from Morris half the salary he had been paid as acting governor of New Jersey for the period before Cosby's arrival—a little over £300. So the chief justice had a personal incentive to make sure that Cosby's suit never got heard by his court—or any other.

Accordingly, Morris sent a timely message to the governor, objecting that the pending council ordinance installing a court of equity within the Supreme Court was contrary to law, and he asked that the enactment be delayed until Cosby heard him out. In response, the governor sent an intermediary, Joseph Warrel, a lately bankrupt London merchant whom Cosby had just appointed attorney general of New Jersey, to say—as Morris recounted it in a letter to Cosby the following April—that "you [Cosby] would neither receive a visit or any message from me; that you could neither rely upon my integrity nor depend upon my judgment or opinion; that you thought me a person not at all fit to be trusted with any concerns relating to the king; that ever since your coming to the government I had treated you . . . with slight, rudeness, and impertinence, and that you did not desire to see or hear any further of or from me."

The extremity of this rebuke was likely prompted in part by Morris's far-from-deferential conduct when Cosby had come to Amboy to receive the royal seal of New Jersey and in part by the governor's embrace of the trade barons who had surely filled his ears with tales of Morris's twenty years of political militancy. Whatever the reasons behind Cosby's sharp slapdown, the equally aroused chief justice now mobilized his energies to shred the governor's contrived ordinance. He did so in close and wholly unethical collaboration with James Alexander, who was defending Van Dam against Cosby's suit. If there was one colonist who had inspired the governor's displeasure more than Morris, it was Alexander, with whom he must have suffered an almost immediately contentious relationship at the Provincial Council's meetings. The governor's animus reached such a height that, after October 1732, he pointedly failed to notify Alexander when council meetings were scheduled—a clear dereliction of the governor's duty—and it was probably no coincidence that his claim on Van Dam's purse was raised only after Alexander, the Dutchman's friend and attorney, was deemed *persona non grata* at the council sessions and not on hand to deter the governor's aggression. "He is the only man who has given me any uneasiness since my arrival," Cosby wrote Newcastle in December—seeming to have forgotten how gravely Morris had also offended him—and added, "[H]is known very bad character would be too long to trouble your grace with particulars, and stuffed with such tricks and oppressions too gross for your grace to hear." Such wholesale, undocumented character assassination spoke more to Cosby's dark tendencies than to Alexander's. The New York attorney's gravest sin had probably been his failure to genuflect adequately to suit His Grace, a talent evidently perfected by Joseph Warrel, the man with whom, Cosby told Newcastle, he wished to replace Alexander on the council.

Morris and Alexander colluded to quash Cosby's suit not on the merits of his salary claim but on the jurisdictional ground that the Supreme Court could not hear the case based on the governor's invalid directive that it function as a court of equity, especially since the colony already had one. Morris pored over every volume and legal treatise in his own and from Alexander's even more extensive library to survey the relevant statutory and common-law history of the English court system. Alexander, meanwhile, sketched out the motion he would deliver asking the Supreme Court not to hear Cosby's suit and sent it to Morris to critique. The chief justice, improperly complying with the improper request by counsel for one of the parties in the suit, replied on January 11, 1733, with an extensive memorandum aimed at refining the arguments Alexander would raise to have the case thrown out by the Supreme Court—or, rather, to insist the court disqualify itself from hearing the matter.

VI

By the time the crown's suit against Van Dam was docketed for a hearing before the Supreme Court in mid-March of 1733, the chief justice would not have been surprised to learn that early in the previous month the Board of Trade had granted Cosby a new instruction entitling him to half of Morris's salary while acting governor of New Jersey. Had word of it reached New York in time, Attorney General Bradley would likely have demanded that Morris vacate the bench when the Van Dam case was to be heard on the ground that the chief justice's impartiality would appear to be fatally compromised as a prospective defendant against Cosby's second salary claim. But Morris was spared that necessity and instead sprang a tactical surprise of his own on Bradley at the March 15 hearing.

Rather than listening to opening arguments on Cosby's claim against Van Dam, Morris as the presiding judge ruled the court would first hear the litigants' views on whether the Supreme Court was duly authorized to sit as an equity tribunal (i.e., without a jury) to decide the outcome. Alexander, of course, fully cognizant of Morris's thinking, reeled off an argument that closely parroted the chief justice's instructive pretrial memorandum to him preemptively refuting the legitimacy of the Provincial Council's ordinance granting the Supreme Court equity jurisdiction. Bradley, representing Cosby, had not been prepared to argue the jurisdictional question and had to improvise. The attorney general argued that because the New York Assembly's 1691 Judiciary Act had authorized the Supreme Court to function in the same way the Court of Exchequer did in Britain, Cosby and his council could justifiably invoke the expired 1691 act as precedent for their December ordinance renewing the Supreme Court's equity function. Omitted from this facile line of argument, of course, was acknowledgment that the colony had fifty years earlier assigned the equity function to the Chancery Court and never withdrawn it. And so, as Alexander contended, there was no rationale—absent the Assembly's blessing—for the governor to suddenly construct a second equity court by decree for his own transparent financial benefit.

Rather than taking the arguments under advisement and ruling after due deliberation, Chief Justice Morris immediately—and injudiciously—produced a lengthy written opinion rejecting Bradley's contentions. Plainly, Morris had made up his mind before hearing both oral arguments. Determined not to cave in to Cosby's disdain for the rule of law, he asserted that "giving a new jurisdiction in equity by letters patent to an old court that never had such jurisdiction before, or creating a new court of equity . . . by ordinances of the governor and council without assent of the legislature are equally unlawful and not a sufficient warrant to justify this court to proceed on a course of equity. And therefore, by the grace of God, I as chief justice of this province shall not pay any obedience to them in this point."

But there were two other justices to be heard from, and Cosby was relying on both to side with him. He had ample reason to suppose that Justice James DeLancey would support him; his trade-baron father, Stephen, was Morris's long-standing political foe and nursed a grudge against the chief justice for trying to get him expelled from the Assembly for allegedly lacking full citizenship rights. Young DeLancey had been educated at Corpus Christi College, Cambridge, and schooled in the law at Lincoln's Inn in London. With the help of his father's wide commercial and political connections—Stephen was still an Assemblyman—and a £3,000 stake from him, James opened his own practice in New York, where he won immediate prominence as a learned and skilled practitioner. He was further blessed with a wife who inherited Scarsdale Manor in Westchester and whose first cousin was a member of Parliament and a confidant of Prime Minister Walpole. At twenty-six, DeLancey was named to the Provincial Council and headed a commission to write a new charter for New York City, largely his handiwork and duly approved by the Assembly. At twenty-eight, James was made a justice of the Supreme Court—

and now, his thirtieth birthday still eight months off—he voted after a few days' reflection against the chief justice and for upholding Cosby's ordinance allowing the court to hear his suit against Van Dam.

That left the decision up to the third member of the court, Frederick Philipse, nephew of the Assembly speaker, who still headed one of New York's leading mercantile houses. But Frederick had minimal legal training and owed his judicial post to undiluted nepotism, then as always and in every field the surest avenue of swift career advancement. But even as a callow jurist, Philipse recognized the power contest unfolding over the Van Dam salary issue and wisely asked to ponder the matter until the court reconvened the following month.

Upon hearing the gist of Morris's extensive opinion recited to him, Cosby reportedly flew into a rage, assailed the chief justice as unfit for his high office—in words similar to his response to Morris's earlier request to be heard before the ordinance at issue had been promulgated—and demanded to see the written text of Morris's ruling. Whatever its explicit language, to Cosby it amounted to nothing other than a public demonstration of Morris's disrespect for the governor. By then, word of Cosby's intemperate responses to any show of resistance to his will had given rise to reports that he was ruled by his aristocratic wife and, as Patricia Bonomi wrote in *A Factious People: Politics and Society in Colonial New York*, might have "made up for his lack of authority at home by playing the petty tyrant in public affairs." Word of Cosby's outburst against Morris's ruling prompted James Alexander, writing to a London lawyer friend soon after the court hearing, to observe that "the governor's general behavior gives the chief justice reason sufficient to expect that [Cosby] will suspend him from his . . . office and will use his interest at home [in England] to have such suspension approved." When Justice Philipse delivered his opinion on April 17 siding with DeLancey and holding that Cosby's ordinance expanding the Supreme Court's jurisdiction did not require the Assembly's concurrence, it was Morris's turn to fly into a rage. Speaking from the bench and without a scintilla of legal authority to support him, the chief justice said he could not be overruled by his two very junior colleagues, who he claimed were essentially his assistants and surely not his coequals in knowledge or experience, witness their rulings in the matter at hand, which he characterized as "mean, weak, and futile." Then he stalked from the Supreme Court chamber on the second floor of City Hall, vowing he would never preside over that tribunal if it tried to exercise an equity function at the governor's dictate—even though Morris's two judicial brethren had now ruled that the governor had acted legally.

Three days later, Morris finally complied with Cosby's request to see a written copy of his (by then) dissenting opinion in the Cosby–Van Dam case. But the chief justice did so in a way that further infuriated the splenetic governor by publicizing his defiant stand; Morris had his opinion set in type and printed by Peter Zenger's shop as a pamphlet on sale to the public with an open letter to Cosby appended to it. He explained that he was resorting to this step because the governor had so abruptly dismissed Morris's request to discuss prior to its passage the council's intention to assign equity powers to the Supreme Court—and in so doing had harshly impugned Morris's integrity and professional conduct. "I am neither afraid nor ashamed to stand the test of the strictest inquiry you can make concerning my conduct," he wrote the governor in his public letter. "I have served the public faithfully and honestly . . . and dare to appeal to them for my justification." He expressed puzzlement over why Cosby had so vilified him, but conceded he might possibly have been impertinent, "for old men are too often so." But if the governor's ire had been stirred "by a bow awkwardly made or anything of that kind, or some defect in the ceremonial of addressing you . . . I beg it may be attributed to the want of a [royal] court and polite education . . . rather than the want of respect to his majesty's representative." Still, the real issue between them was the need for mutual respect, meaning that Cosby had to grasp that the chief justice had simply been fulfilling his duty in rendering the opinion attached to the letter, for "if judges are to be intimidated so as not to give any opinion but what is pleasing to the governor and agreeable to his private views, the people of this province who are very much concerned both with respect to their lives and their fortunes in the freedom and independency of those who are to judge them, may possibly not think themselves secure in either of them as the laws of his Majesty intended they should be."

Rather than chastening Cosby, Morris no doubt hoped these ringing words would revive his own faded public reputation by portraying himself as a dauntless defender of the people's sacrosanct right to jury trials and staunch foe of a governor who seemed set on destroying any obstacle to his selfish ends. This studied assertion of principle, which Cosby took for gross insubordination, was all the more an affront to the governor because it was openly designed for public consumption. English libel law was clearly intended to discourage printers from issuing such criticism of government authority, no matter how abusive it might seem. William Bradford, long and painfully aware of such repressive legal strictures, would not have risked his appointment as the colony's royal printer by daring to issue, as Zenger did, Morris's pamphlet, damning Cosby's action as lawless and his denigration of the chief justice's integrity as wholly unwarranted. Mindful, of course, of Bradford's vested interest in placating the governor, Morris had brought his provocative printing job to Zenger, who owned the only other press in the colony and whose financial struggles made him the chief justice's willing accomplice. Zenger likewise accommodated Morris's co-agitator, James Alexander, by printing copies of the brief he soon filed with the Supreme Court in a civil suit in Van Dam's behalf, formally demanding half the funds Cosby had received back in London following his appointment as New York governor. For Zenger, who had no known previous political affiliation, printing and selling Alexander's brief on top of publishing Morris's court decision and nose-thumbing letter to Cosby marked the beginning of an alliance that would soon embroil him in a conflict that made him famous throughout the colony—and well beyond.

Cosby's fury must have been stoked still further when Justice DeLancey recused himself from hearing the Van Dam suit because he had sided with the governor in supporting his instruction from London to force Van Dam to surrender half his pay as acting governor and afterward voted in favor of the council ordinance assigning equity jurisdiction to the Supreme Court. However irksome to Cosby, DeLancey had taken the high moral ground by avoiding the appearance, or at least the strong suspicion, of partiality to Cosby's cause. With both Morris and DeLancey off the case and Philipse dubiously qualified to sit in solitary judgment, Cosby's suit fell into limbo; Morris had foiled his scheme. And now he would be made to pay for it.

In a May 3 letter to Newcastle complaining of Morris's courtroom conduct and public rebuke to him by resorting to Zenger's press, Cosby labeled the chief justice "a man under a general dislike for his want of probity" and charged him with a catalogue of sins. Among them were excessive pride and fondness of liquor, a propensity for bullying, and abuse of his office by lack of impartiality and failure to conduct court in a punctual manner—claims all possessing a degree of validity but none substantiated in Cosby's petulant letter or relevant to the larger legal issue that Morris had ruled on. Regarding one specific instance of Morris's alleged injudicious conduct, the governor cited a dispute between two factions of congregants vying for control of a church in Queens County and said the chief justice ruled on it summarily without giving both sides a fair hearing—admitting, however, that he had no proof of the claimed impropriety. "I mean either to discipline Morris or suffer myself to be affronted," he wrote the duke, "or, what is still worse, see the king's authority trampled on and disrespect and irreverence to it taught from the bench to the people by him who, by his oath and his office, is obliged to support it." He added that he soon intended to replace the chief justice with young DeLancey.

Had Cosby been aware of all the evidence that history is now privy to, he could have cited persuasive reasons for the crown to remove Morris from the bench, or at least severely censure him, solely on the basis of his conduct in the Van Dam suit unrelated to the legal reasoning behind the chief justice's decision or to any alleged insults to Cosby or the crown. Morris had behaved with flagrant disregard for judicial rectitude remarkable even in that day and age, starting with his secret pretrial collusion with defense counsel Alexander, his intimate friend, aimed at having the suit dismissed before it could be heard. His reading of a prepared ruling right after the close of oral arguments on the legality of the Cosby-sponsored ordinance expanding the Supreme Court's jurisdiction bespoke a shuttered mind, not to be enlightened by any arguments the governor's counsel might have raised. Morris was still further culpable for his public outburst that the votes against his ruling by the two other members of his court could not outweigh his own because they were so greatly his inferior in experience and legal acumen—and so he feigned justification for marching out of the courtroom in an effort to nullify the whole proceeding. That Morris may have been in the right on the legal issues did not mitigate his otherwise execrable behavior.

Even Solomon would have been hard pressed to decide whether Cosby or Morris, for all their posturing and protests against each other, had acted more deplorably in the Van Dam fracas—and which of them, if either, could claim cause to don the robes of righteousness in the more heated conflict to follow.

5

Battle Lines

BESIDES TRYING TO manipulate New York's judicial system during his first year in office, Governor Cosby showed signs of abusing his authority for personal gain in another area under his office's control, the issuing or confirmation of land-grant titles. A ripe source of crown-approved income, this function had been exploited by a number of his predecessors in an arbitrary or despotic manner. The most intrigue-filled example of this low-lying fruit that tempted Cosby early on implicated him in a scheme fabricated by a treacherous henchman the governor had entrusted with a surfeit of delegated power.

At issue was a 50,000-acre tract (nearly 80 square miles) of some of the lushest unassigned land in the colony, ceded to New York by Connecticut in 1725 to settle a long-standing boundary dispute that had simmered ever since the British seized New Netherlands. The boundary line was more or less settled by a decree of William III in 1700, but cartography was far from an exact science at the time, and what seemed clear on paper grew clouded when field surveys were undertaken. The border between the two colonies was to have run from Long Island Sound on a roughly north-south course about twenty miles east of and parallel to the Hudson River. But surveyors eventually discovered that such a line in fact crossed the river near West Point and would have grossly expanded Connecticut's territory.

To relocate the boundary in a way agreeable to New York, Governor Burnet appointed a three-man commission in 1725 to confer with its Connecticut counterpart. The New York team was headed by the colony's highly regarded surveyor general, Cadwallader Colden, and included another insider among the Morrisite allies whom Governor Hunter had relied upon—Francis Harison, a smooth-tongued lawyer ever on the make, with a knack for collecting lesser public offices. Little is known about Harison's origins, but it is believed he came to New York in the first years of the eighteenth century and persevered sufficiently for Hunter to appoint him sheriff of New York County (the city and county were co-terminus, as they remain three centuries later) in 1710. Among other official posts Harison snared were surveyor and searcher (inspector) for the Port of New York, judge on the provincial admiralty court (with jurisdiction over disputes involving the laws and regulation of trade), recorder for New York City's Common Council, membership on the governor's Provincial Council, and, as mentioned, a member of the commission to finally settle the New York-Connecticut boundary. Taken together, his offices made Harison someone to be reckoned with and fueled reports that he used his power wantonly.

The boundary agreement stalled over the redrawn line that ran north for fifty miles from the inland eastern corner of the stub of territory that makes up the southwestern extension of the modern state of Connecticut. The projected new line would have shifted the Connecticut village of Ridgefield across the boundary into New York, alarming residents in the area that their land titles might be jeopardized or that they might be required to pay a stiff fee to New York to retain them. To keep the negotiations from collapsing, Colden pushed through a compromise— the boundary line would jog a few miles northwest before resuming its northerly course, thereby allowing Ridgefield to remain in Connecticut. To compensate New York for the lost land, Connecticut agreed to cede it a skinny 60,000-acre tract, only two miles across at its widest point, that came to be known as the Oblong. The agreement could not be sealed, however, because the New York Assembly, where the Morrisite coalition had lost control to the Philipse-DeLancey mercantile party, refused for five years to pay for the final surveying and staking of the line.

It was at this point that Colden stepped in to rescue the settlement and, while he was at it, arranged a land-speculation deal participated in by close friends including Lewis Morris and James Alexander—some of "the most considerable men in the province had shares," Colden would recount in a later memoir but fail to mention he was among them, lest he feed suspicion that he used his insider information to get in on prospectively lucrative real estate schemes. To lend the color of propriety to their syndicate, the legal aspects of which Alexander seems to have handled, they enlisted Ridgefield's leading citizen, the Reverend Thomas Hauley, the community's Harvard-educated pastor, town clerk, and schoolmaster, to lend his name to the enterprise and bring along other Connecticut residents among the twenty-two principals. In 1730, Hauley & Company petitioned New York's Governor Montgomerie to grant them title to all but 10,000 acres of the Oblong for a fee of £750 on the proviso that the syndicate would gain final title only after it completed, at its own expense, surveying and running the line that would then become the official intercolony boundary.

Among those not invited to participate in the Oblong venture was Francis Harison, who, as a member of the boundary commission that approved the settlement and of the governor's council that approved the conditional grant to the Hauley syndicate, felt entitled to be rewarded for his help. Harison's initial exclusion had not been accidental. When Burnet's political missteps, following Morris's overbearing guidance, cost the governor his allies' control of the Assembly, the always opportunistic Harison saw which way the wind was blowing and switched allegiance to the trade barons' camp when Montgomerie became governor. His desertion riled the Morrisite group enough to cut him out of the Oblong syndicate until Harison pleaded to be included, likely promising to use his influence in behalf of the enterprise with the new governor, into whose good graces he had insinuated himself. Colden and Alexander relented, and political turncoat Harison was allowed a full Oblong share and access to the details of the undertaking.

But Harison was a vindictive viper. Instead of forgiving the Morrisite group for its original snub, as they had behaved mercifully to him, he plotted to take over the whole venture rather than settling for the scraps Morris and his friends had dished him. During the months Colden's crew was completing the boundary measurements required before title could formally pass to Hauley & Company, Harison alerted a group of titled aristocrats back in England about the availability of the beautiful Oblong tract while neglecting to point out it had already been provisionally granted, if not officially transferred, to a syndicate of American investors who had paid a large fee to obtain the title. For an appropriate stipend Harison offered to serve as the British speculators' New York agent if they petitioned the crown directly to grant them the Oblong acreage. As a rule, land grants in the colonies were the governors' privilege, but the king had the final word when it came to gifting any portion of his dominion, and Harison's group of investors was headed by Sir James Eyles, aka Lord Chandos, with easy entrée to H.R.M. George II. The royal seal was affixed, granting the Oblong to the peer of the realm et al., on May 15, 1731, not quite a month before Governor Montgomerie—unaware of the king's kindness to the Chandos consortium—gave final approval of the Oblong transfer to the Morrisite group of grantees in New York. A few weeks later, Montgomerie was dead and could never testify to Harison's treachery once it became known. But the betrayer had to await the arrival of a new governor before putting forward his British clients' claim to have Hauley & Company's title to the Oblong revoked.

Once Cosby took office, Harison applied his perverse talents—flattery, gossip, tattling, and pretense—to gain the confidence of the vain and avaricious governor. According to Colden, who had a seat on the governor's council along with Harison and knew as much as any man about how the colony's government functioned, Harison parlayed his pull with Cosby to extract payoffs from officeholders who wanted to keep their jobs and to collect hefty fees to the governor and kickbacks to himself from those he managed to place on the royal payroll. Another potentially profitable racket Harison was suspected of pursuing in the governor's behalf—though no documented proof ever surfaced—was threatening to have imprecise or otherwise flawed land titles vacated unless the landowners paid what amounted to an extortionate fee for the governor to confirm their holdings. In a word, Harison was Cosby's bagman. His adeptness in the role soon permitted him to broach to the governor the conflicting Oblong grants and seek his aid.

The usurping Harison knew that ordinarily there would have been no justification for a New York governor to set aside a provisional grant duly issued by his predecessor and to be confirmed as soon as the condition (that is, staking out the boundary) had been fully satisfied—which turned out to be three weeks after the crown's irregular grant to the elite Chandos bunch had been sealed. Nor, as a practical matter, could Harison file suit in the Supreme Court to have the Hauley group's title vacated; no jury of New Yorkers would vote in favor of British aristocrats and against their fellow colonists, even if technically the king's seal might have trumped Montgomerie's final certification. But Harison had a third option and took it, urging Cosby to rule on the disputed title claim in his capacity as chancellor in the equity Court of Chancery—and solitary judge in the matter—and supplying him at least three reasons to do so. Cosby would ingratiate himself with Lord Chandos's circle back in England, where his future best interests lay. He would deal a blow to the Hauley group's key participants—Morris, Alexander, and their compatriots who had bedeviled him in the Van Dam fiasco. And the governor could collect a handsome fee from the British group when title to the Oblong was transferred to their hands. Harison was given the nod and filed a motion in Chancery to have the Hauley group's title to the Oblong land vacated, prompting Colden to remark afterward that "such a course of proceeding would not have been attempted before any chancellor but such a one as Colonel Cosby, who had no notion either of natural justice or of equity or the law of the land."

Alexander vehemently countered Harison's motion, arguing that the grant to the Hauley syndicate was a *fait accompli* by the time the Chandos group was improperly awarded the Oblong—Montgomerie's approval had been conditioned only on the completion of the survey and formal installation of the boundary markers, as Chandos's counsel (i.e., Harison) had been perfectly aware. For Cosby as chancellor to take jurisdiction over the title dispute would constitute "ruthless disregard" of the circumstances. The governor, no lawyer, likely sensed the knotty nature of the dispute and, wary of entangling himself in a fresh legal squabble with formidable adversaries like Morris, Alexander, and Colden, was in no hurry to adjudicate the Oblong matter. But donning his chancellor's wig, neither did he dismiss it out of hand—all the better, perhaps, to hold it as a club over the Morrisite troublemakers. There was a price to pay, though, for the governor's apparent willingness to hear Harison's guileful motion in the colony's equity court, where the chancellor's ruling could not be challenged. It raised the specter that Cosby might intervene in a similarly arbitrary fashion to cancel any or all land titles open to dispute on even the flimsiest technical ground—documentation was notoriously error-prone in that era. Reports began to circulate among those of all political persuasions that Cosby was intent on the wholesale disturbance of land titles in certain sectors of Long Island and northern New Jersey unless tribute money was paid to him through operatives like Harison—a fearsome prospect and deeply unsettling power "in the hands of such an ignorant, willful, avaricious man as Colonel Cosby," Colden would later reflect.

For the scholarly, thoughtful Colden to apply such words to him suggests how rapidly Cosby slipped from grace. Deservedly or not, the locals were soon tarring him as intellectually shallow, lacking political finesse, disdainful of their want of pedigree and manners, incapable of suffering criticism, prone to act on impulse instead of sound judgment, and highly susceptible to the advice of toadies. Character flaws aside, his worst strategic blunder, carried out at a meeting of his council on August 21, 1733, was to humiliate Lewis Morris for having dared to defy him.

II

According to the formal instructions given by the Privy Council and the Board of Trade for half a century starting in 1702, all royal governors were required to seek the advice and consent of their councils before appointing or dismissing judges in their colonies. In Cosby's case, seven of the twelve councilmen were aligned with him, and since the crown procedures required only five council members for a quorum and thus only three of them would constitute a majority, it would have been a simple—if deceitful—expedient for the governor to conduct business with an entirely friendly and compliant council by failing to notify its five opposing members when meetings were to be held. Or summoning some of them only when it suited his purpose, as Cosby did at the council's August 21 meeting to announce—without bothering to give an explanation—that he had suspended Lewis Morris as chief justice of the Supreme Court and replaced him with James DeLancey, who was half Morris's age.

At least one pro-Morris councilman was on hand for the announcement—Cadwallader Colden, who left an account of the event. Cosby had summoned him from his home in rural Ulster County, feigning that there were matters for him to attend to in his capacity as the colony's surveyor general, and "When I came into the governor's house, he received me into his arms with, 'My dear Colden, I am glad to see you.' I was caressed for two or three days by everyone of the family. Just before I went in to council, he took me upon the couch with [him] and seemed to entertain me in the most friendly manner but spoke not one word of removing the chief justice and appointing another till we were sat in council. . . ." Almost certainly Morris's other two close friends who were councilmen, Van Dam and Alexander, were not on hand, having teamed with Morris to defeat Cosby's suit against the Dutchman, but Colden had not yet fallen out of favor with the governor. He did so the moment after Cosby broke the news that Morris was off the Supreme Court and its two younger members, DeLancey and Frederick Philipse, had each moved up one rank; the third justiceship remained temporarily vacant.

Colden, stunned by the decision Cosby had brooded over for nearly four months but never consulted him about, recalled the exchange that followed: "Upon which [announcement] I said, 'Then your excellency only tells us what you have already done,' to which he answered yes, and I replied, 'It is what I could not have advise[d],' and he very briskly returned to it, 'I do not seek your advise.' This put his having the consent of the council out of the question." Colden's asserted disapproval "defeated the whole design he had . . . of cajoling me" and laid bare his allegiance to Morris. "He [Cosby] never forgave me."

In retelling the event, Colden, Morris, and Alexander all denounced Cosby for ruthlessly violating crown protocol by failing to consult with the council and obtain its consent to replace the chief justice. But all three may have overstated the charge. Neither Morris nor Alexander cited their authority or sources for claiming Cosby was derelict in failing to obtain council backing for his action, and Colden never stated he knew for certain the governor had not consulted members of the council beside himself about his decision beforehand. Technically, Cosby needed only three councilmen (out of a quorum of five, whom he might have assembled informally or secretly) to approve his decision, and there is reason to suppose he met the crown's minimum requirement for changing judges. Cosby was unlikely to have mulled the matter for as long as he did without broaching it to his two closest advisers on the council— Colonial Secretary George Clarke, a reflective man, and the governor's henchman Francis Harison, who both bore grudges against Morris and his coterie. And we know from Colden's final words on the subject that Cosby must have discussed it beforehand with DeLancey, whose judicial advancement was purchased by his own complicity. Colden wrote: "Mr. DeLancey excused his accepting of the commission [the chief justiceship] at the expense of his predecessor by saying that the governor could not be diverted from removing Mr. Morris and that if he did not accept of it, the governor resolved to put Mr. Harison in the office, a man nowise acceptable to anybody."

Because DeLancey was, Colden noted, "of a good family" with many powerful friends and there was never a suggestion that he had solicited Cosby to award him the prestigious post of chief justice, he escaped the resentment that now descended on the governor for his transparently vengeful dismissal of Morris. In humbling the old lion, Cosby and those who egged him on miscalculated how deeply (if not fondly) the chief justice was respected. Alexander, his closest ally, may have been less than objective but nonetheless likely reflected popular sentiment when he wrote a friend two months afterward about Morris's firing: "The late [former] chief justice had been in that office near twenty years. As to his integrity and skill in the law, [he] had established his character as much [as] or more than any judge in America ever did." If Cosby had been more politic and less a petty tyrant, he might have handled the matter in a more justifiable way, ordering his attorney general to draw up a bill of particulars that cited a pattern of alleged judicial misbehavior unbefitting the highest jurist in the colony. That he did not suggests the governor was either lax and irresponsible in discharging his duty or, more likely, that there were in fact insufficient grounds for replacing Morris.

His removal as chief justice left Morris after forty years of public service with only one inconsequential official post, senior member of the New Jersey Council, which Cosby rarely summoned and, if he did, likely overruled any initiative Morris might have tried to take, assuming he was ever advised by the governor when the council was due to convene. But if Cosby supposed he had bearded his bête noire and that Morris would now slink off into the night, no longer to hector him, he had failed to take the measure of a man who had labored indefatigably to bring down two previous governors. Within a week of his unceremonious dismissal, Morris wrote a long letter of protest to the Board of Trade that took liberties in describing how Cosby had abused his power by allegedly failing to obtain the council's required consent to replace the chief justice. Evidently relying solely on Colden's report to him, Morris wrote the ministry in London that after being told of Cosby's action, Colden asked the governor if he was merely advising the council of his decision or seeking its advice and consent, because if the latter purpose,

> he [Colden] would advise against it as being prejudicial to His Majesty's service. To which the governor replied that he did not, or ever intended to, consult them about it; he thought fit to do it and was not accountable to them *or words to that effect* [italics added].

The closing "or words to that effect" raises the suspicion that Morris may have been embellishing what Colden had related. Colden did not state in his version of the event that, in replying to his inquiry, Cosby had been openly disdainful of his accountability to the entire council—only that he had not sought Colden's advice. All that can be safely said, to judge by his own report of the council meeting, is that Colden was offended that he had not been consulted in advance; he did not explicitly say, nor should Morris have inferred—unless he polled all the councilmen—that Cosby had in fact failed to consult the requisite number before arriving at his decision.

Yet Morris had a far more legitimate basis for condemning Cosby: his failure to provide documentary evidence of misbehavior on the chief justice's part sufficient to merit his dismissal. Nor had the governor bothered to confront Morris with such charges and allow him an opportunity to explain and defend himself. "I make no doubt I should have been able to have answered them [allegations of judicial impropriety] to the satisfaction of my superiors," Morris asserted to the Board of Trade, "but since he has not done either [consult with the council or Morris himself on his fitness to continue on the bench], I have but too much reason to believe that I am displaced for the gratification of his ceaseless resentment. For any just cause I am sure he has not." In short, the dismissed chief justice was saying that Cosby had tried to rig New York's court system in order to deny Van Dam's right to a jury trial when the governor sued him for back salary, and Morris deserved not to be fired but commended for checking such an abuse of gubernatorial power.

His ire rampant, Morris would not limit his letter to London to self-defensive jabs at Cosby for unjustly discarding him. He counterattacked with sweeping charges of misconduct by the governor, yet in doing so, again mingled what was verifiable with what was not. In the first category was Cosby's acceptance of the £1,000 gratuity from the Assembly for his alleged efforts to protect New York colonists from the impact of the Molasses Act—in direct violation of the long-established rule against governors taking such potentially compromising gifts. There was a public record of this transgression, but none for Morris's further charge that Cosby had indulged in the habit of other governors by making land grants for "private profit . . . and the gratification of their friends . . . the little instruments of their tyranny and oppression and the tools to promote their purposes." Governors profited in two ways, Morris added in case the overseers of the realm were unaware—"by large presents made to [them] by the grantees . . . but [also by the grantees'] admitting the governors to become sharers in the grants." Then this boldly defamatory charge: "I am told the present governor (but how truly I don't know but believe there is something in it) will not grant any lands unless he comes in for one-third of them."

James Alexander would repeat this last charge a few months later in a letter to a London friend, mentioning "the governor's refusing to grant any lands without a third being secured to himself," as if the allegation were testified to by documents or witnesses to the extortionate demand. Again, we find Cosby's foes forfeiting their claim to higher moral ground by maligning him with charges no more specific and documented than the sweeping accusations the governor was fond of hurling at his adversaries. But within a few weeks of cashiering Morris, Cosby provided New Yorkers with further cause to fear him as a rash if not venal ruler.

III

In September 1733, his fourteenth month in office, Governor Cosby traveled to Albany, the second-largest settlement in New York colony, and during that tour of the north country, was asked to examine, apparently at the request of the unhappy Mohawk tribe, a deed that the natives had given to—and perhaps been paid for by—Albany's city magistrates. The deed was for a tract of land of indeterminate size that was the site of the Mohawks' ancestral meeting ground, not far from Fort Hunter, thirty miles northwest of Albany on the river named for the tribe. The natives, by all accounts, now felt (or were told) that the terms of the deed were unfair to them and at any rate were not being honored. After inspecting the deed, Cosby had it destroyed—in effect, returning the land to the Mohawks and infuriating Albany's leading citizens. Whether the governor performed an act of kindness to mollify the tribe or harbored an ulterior purpose—namely, to obtain the land for himself, as his detractors charged—is impossible to determine with any certainty. An examination of the few surviving accounts of the episode illustrates, if nothing else, how Cosby's own carelessness rather than rank dishonesty blackened his reputation.

Of the three eighteenth-century writers who recounted the fate of the Albany deed to the Mohawks' gathering place, the most reliable ought to have been Cadwallader Colden. Six years earlier he had published his pathbreaking study of the five-nation Iroquois Confederacy, of which the Mohawks were the easternmost people. Colden shared his fellow colonists' common perception that the natives were savages, remarking that they were "a poor, barbarous people under the darkest ignorance," but adding, "and yet a bright and noble genius shines through these black clouds. None of the great Roman heroes have discovered a greater love [of] their country or a greater contempt of death when life and liberty came in competition." He conceded that the natives were often ruled by "that cruel passion, revenge, which they think not only lawful but honorable to exert without mercy on their country's enemies"—and then asked, "But what have we Christians done to make them better?" Given his sympathies, it is not surprising to find that the 600-word sketch of the destruction of the Albany deed that Colden included in his rough-hewn, undated memoir of Cosby's administration suggests the Mohawks were ill used by both the governor and the Albany colonists.

According to Colden, who was not on hand to witness the event and so had to have relied on word-of-mouth to reconstruct it (but just whose word he did not tell us), Governor Thomas Dongan had issued a charter of incorporation to the city of Albany shortly after he took office in 1683 and included in it a provisional grant of 1,000 noncontiguous acres a long day's travel to the west, "where the Mohawks had their principal castle." Included in the grant, said Colden, was the right to buy those 1,000 acres from the Indians, "but the city had never been able to purchase it of them." In order to strengthen their security against attack and facilitate trade with the tribe, the city magistrates eventually talked the Mohawks into deeding them the tract. Just how Colden knew it consisted of 1,000 acres, he did not say, though he could have been shown the document in the course of researching his study of the tribes composing the Iroquois nation. The key to gaining the tribe's consent to grant the deed was apparently the city's agreement to hold the land in trust "for the use of the said Indians so long as any of them should remain to inhabit it." In other words, the city was to make the tract an Indian reservation that was off-limits to white settlers until the tribe was extinct. But unspecified problems arose—perhaps Albany had not been diligent in policing the outlying tract against white settlers' encroachments—and what Colden termed "defects" were found in the deed that the tribe asked Cosby to remedy on his visit.

The deeded Mohawk land, according to Colden, who as surveyor general of the colony was presumably an expert on the subject, was worth a pricey "£5,000 New York money," and Cosby, "being told of it and the defects of the Albany title, resolved to have it to himself." In thus vilifying the governor, Colden accused him of enlisting the commander of the royal garrison at Fort Hunter "to give the Indians some jealousy of the deed . . . and they were advised by him to complain that the city had procured the deed fraudulently and had inserted certain things into it which had not been interpreted or explained to them." In response, Cosby reportedly summoned the mayor of Albany to bring the deed to him, promising that it would be safely restored. As soon as the governor glanced it over in the presence of a delegation of Mohawks, on hand so Cosby could address their alleged grievances, he gave it to one of the Indians who, according to Colden's narrative,

> as was before concerted [instructed], tore it to pieces and threw it into the fire, and I have been told that after the Indian had the deed put into his hands, he stood some time in suspense till Colonel Cosby, with the motion of his hands, made him understand that he was to tear it and throw it in the fire. This destroying of deeds made a great noise and gave a good handle to Col. Cosby's enemies against him. The grand jury of Albany intended to indict him for it and certainly would had not the [Cosby-appointed] sheriff taken care to put some upon the jury and did all they could to intimidate the others. . . .

The mayor, anxious not to be perceived by his fellow citizens as having been in cahoots with Cosby, tried to get the matter investigated by the Assembly, but "Cosby's interest [influence] was so great as to prevent any public inquisition into this affair. . . . [But] his friends could not avoid the impression it made on people's minds that he would stop at no injustice to fill his pockets. It occasioned, however, so much clamor that his design was entirely defeated." Colden's palpable animus toward the governor, though, fed by Cosby's crude firing of Chief Justice Morris without a fig leaf to cover its impropriety, renders this account suspect. Why would Cosby have so coveted this particular tract and tried to wrest title to it from the incorporated municipality of Albany, thereby greatly alienating the powerful commercial interests of that important city, when as governor he could have had his choice of virtually any ungranted spread in either colony that he presided over—and far larger and better located land at that—simply by asking the crown to gift it to him? At the least, though, Cosby was guilty of dereliction of duty for allowing (if not ordering, as Colden charged) the deed to be destroyed rather than trying to have it revised to the satisfaction of the city and the tribe or directing the parties to have the dispute adjudicated.

The second account of this puzzling affair was by Lewis Morris, in an October 4 letter to the Board of Trade intended to further paint Cosby as a rogue unworthy of his office. After stating, without citing his source, that Governor Dongan had certified purchase of the Mohawk tract by residents of Albany for £500 or £600, Morris wrote that some forty-five years later, Governor Montgomerie came to suspect that the deed had been purchased fraudulently, but the Albany interests behind the deal were so powerful that no investigation was conducted until Cosby was asked to verify the legitimacy of the title. The governor declined to certify it, though, Morris charged, "unless he had one-third of the land. This made it necessary to enlarge [the] quantity asked for, which is now (as some of the persons connected told me) 30,000 acres, of which the governor is to have one-third, and his brother and his son-in-law are to be sharers with the other partners, who from the beginning were resolved (as I have been told) to try the validity of the Albany claim in a legal way, but the governor . . . had fallen on a much shorter method than the common forms of law would allow of," and then Morris repeats Colden's story that Cosby plotted to stir the Indians' unhappiness with the deed and coaxed them to destroy it.

Morris, to his discredit, offered no evidence or sources in support of his recitation. Who told him what Albany had originally paid for the land? How did he know Cosby demanded one-third of the Mohawk tract as his precondition for certifying Albany's title to it? Why did his alleged demand require the size of the deeded Mohawk territory to balloon from 1,000 to 30,000 acres? Who were the "connected" persons who Morris said told him what had transpired—if not phantoms, what were some of their names? Morris was unrestrained in his indictment, claiming that the manner in which Cosby had extralegally disposed of the Albany deed left the colonists under his sway dreading that any of their land titles could be similarly destroyed in an arbitrary and unjustifiable manner or retained only at an extortionate price. Then he assailed Cosby's administration for being corruptly staffed and run: "They [Morris's fellow colonists] find the offices of the government venal, some of them put into the hands of strangers necessitous and desperate in their fortunes; that money, and not merit, is the inducement of what is called his favor and the measure of his justice, and that he is incapable to distinguish between right and power."

The third surviving contemporary account of the event was by historian William Smith, Jr., whose lawyer father was a close associate of Alexander and a leading Morrisite supporter. Smith stated that the Mohawks, fearing a flood of white settlers, "had sagaciously . . . conveyed a very valuable part of their territory to the corporation [the city of Albany], to take effect on the total dissolution of their tribe," in order in the interim to enjoy the uninterrupted use of their traditional gathering place—until Cosby had "perfidiously" asked to examine the deed and, as Colden had reported, arranged for its destruction. If Smith's report was accurate, Cosby would have succeeded in angering both the Mohawks, for depriving them of the city's pledge to stanch the flow of white despoilers of their tribal homeland, and the city, for its loss of the deed ensuring its eventual title to the tract. Smith said the destruction of the Albany deed was of a piece with Cosby's entertaining the Oblong suit orchestrated by his henchman Harison and his "design against the people of Long Island . . . for a resurvey of old patents . . . [which] originated from the same motive: he hoped to enrich himself by the acquisition of lands already improved, as well as fees by the new grants." But again we look in vain for documented particulars.

Two more recent accounts shed little new light on the Albany deed brouhaha. Livingston Rutherford, a descendant and keen admirer of James Alexander—and unlikely to do Cosby any favors in the eyes of posterity—wrote in a 1904 study that the Mohawk land had been deeded to Albany "for protection against the rapid settling of the country" and "was destroyed because Cosby expected to receive certain fees when a new grant was executed." But no source is given for this alleged motive. Patricia Bonomi's *A Factious People*, issued by Columbia University Press in 1971, contends that the deed was for 1,200 acres and formally obtained from the tribe by the Albany corporation only in 1730, when Governor Montgomerie, according to Lewis Morris's version, balked at certifying it and left it for the next governor to resolve. But, in a rare concession to Cosby by modern commentators on his tenure, Bonomi suggested that from a legal standpoint, the governor "may well have had some reason to question the transaction's validity," given that while Albany's residents got on in a reasonably friendly manner with the nearby natives, "they were not above occasional sharp practices in matters of land."

To explain his conduct at Albany, Cosby used the columns of royal printer William Bradford's *New-York Gazette*, which served as a house organ for the governor's administration. The paper ran an unsigned letter to the editor in issue No. 428 (December 31, 1733) that read in part:

A corporation takes upon them to cheat the heathen out of their inheritance and fraudulently deprive them of their possessions. Here is a governor who is to be the father of this people, acquainted with this transaction and obtains the possession of the deed. Is he to give this deed back again and suffer the poor heathen to be abused? The answer is easy—no, he is to destroy it, and all the great clamor arose because a parcel of griping lawyers has not been employed to set it aside . . . to fill their ever craving pockets.

The letter concluded with one of the *Gazette*'s usual encomia to burnish the governor's scuffed image: "Cosby, the mild, the happy, good and great,/The strongest guard of our little state,/Let malcontents in crabbed language write,/ . . . Tho' they cannot bite,/He unconcerned will let the wretches roar/And govern just as others did before." With a touch less narcissism, Cosby later explained to the Board of Trade that the natives had been tricked into believing the deed they gave to Albany would block white settlers from occupying ancestral Mohawk land. Moreover, if he had not vacated the deed instead of ratifying or extending it to the city's advantage, the Indians would likely have gone over to the French side and favored their fur traders in the ongoing frontier rivalry.

Whatever his motives and whether he acted by impulse or design, Cosby may have been shrewder than his critics. His apologia for destroying the Albany deed as an act of statecraft that placated the Indians and kept them allied to Britain could have served the self-interested purpose that Colden, Morris, and Smith attributed to the governor but not in the fashion they ascribed. On January 2, 1734, according to official New York state records, a tract of 22,000 acres on both sides of the Mohawk River—but located well to the west of the tribe's gathering place at issue in the deed given to the city of Albany—was granted to "William Cosby and others" by the crown. Over the next four years Cosby and his heirs received five additional grants at dispersed locations in the Mohawk Valley that brought his family's total holdings in the north country to 71,400 acres. A feasible inference may thus be drawn that in the eyes of the masters of his kingdom, Cosby had acted astutely, not selfishly or despotically, in vacating the Albany deed, and was duly rewarded, much to the probable chagrin of his Morrisite antagonists.

IV

New York politics heated up that autumn. While Governor Cosby may not have thought of himself as competing in a popularity contest—he served, after all, at the king's will, not the people's—he had in fact lost standing among the colonists for, among other reasons, suing Van Dam, ousting Chief Justice Morris, and trashing the Albany deed. To be sure, he still enjoyed a solid power base, thanks to his continuing alliance with the Philipse and DeLancey families who controlled the Assembly and stoutly defended the royal prerogative. Cosby's antitax leanings, moreover, were helping the mercantile party gain converts among the land barons who had been a key element in the Morrisite coalition. Now Cosby acted to bind the Provincial Council to him more tightly as a puppet panel too spineless to question his more dubious political appointments, land grants, and policy decrees. He not only stopped inviting its three openly hostile members, Van Dam, Alexander, and Colden, to council meetings but formally asked the Board of Trade to approve his removal of the first two and his replacement appointees. (London, though, was in no hurry to oblige him.) Colden in particular became a thorn in his side because as surveyor general, he denied the governor a free hand to make profitable land grants to cronies and toadies; no titles could be officially transferred until Colden's office had surveyed and staked the property and certified its plat map—a process that could be interminably delayed. To rid himself of the righteous surveyor general, the governor complained to London that Colden was an obstructionist on the council (i.e., he voted against some of Cosby's bills), disclosed council secrets, and was a closet Jacobite (thus opposed to the legitimacy of the reigning Hanoverian dynasty)—all groundless charges. Colden's tenure was spared, at least in part, by the timely intervention of his friend Lewis Morris, who wrote an influential English acquaintance, the Marquis of Lothian, praising the New York surveyor general for keeping land grants honest and restraining the governor in his pursuit of personal gain. Cosby had better luck in purging the colonial government of Morrisite sympathizers at the county and local levels—a governor's traditional privilege but practiced with particular zeal by Francis Harison, his pet councilman and hitman. Harison also intensified his efforts as Cosby's chief propagandist, crafting regular insertions in Bradford's *Gazette*, with the publisher's compliance, to boost the governor's esteem with the reading public.

Morris, while shorn of power, was not content to send vitriolic letters to the Board of Trade in obvious reprisal for the governor's enmity toward him. The throaty old lion vowed to show the colony he was not yet toothless or clawless and meant to have Cosby's hide. Ironically, getting fired by the governor reinvigorated Morris's political energy, for now he could play the martyred victim of a corrupt and tyrannical governor against whom he intended to rally the colony to demand his recall to England. "Before that time," Colden wrote of Morris, "he was far from being a popular man." When the incumbent Assemblyman holding Morris's old seat for the borough of Westchester died in October, soon after the furor Cosby had stirred in Albany, the brooding lion saw his chance to leap back into the political arena.

Morris resuscitated his former coalition, now dubbed the People's Party, and built it around his son, Lewis Junior, who the previous year had won one of Westchester County's two Assembly seats, and his reliable brain trust of James Alexander, the best lawyer in New York; his younger legal associate, William Smith, father of the future historian, and upright Surveyor General Cadwallader Colden, the colony's leading intellectual. This formidable team, dedicated to Cosby's downfall, fashioned a campaign slogan—"King George, Liberty and Law"—aimed at attracting a mass following beyond the Westchester constituency of 500 freeholders eligible to vote in the Assembly contest Morris faced against Cosby's candidate, William Foster, clerk of Westchester's Court of Common Pleas. The slogan was shorthand for the party's holy trinity of principles: "King George" signaled its steadfast allegiance to the primacy of the crown over the allegedly mercenary and manipulative Walpole's ministry, which the Morrisites likened to Cosby's tendencies. "Liberty" signified the party's insistence that colonists be free from arbitrary treatment by royal officers, while "Law" conveyed their demand for property to be protected against illegal seizures. The populist party platform, spelled out in pamphlets and on the stump, called for impartial administration of justice; independence of the three branches of government (a coded putdown of Cosby's intrusiveness into his council's legislative deliberations); appointment of qualified and truly local officials (a slap at Cosby's patronage practice of hiring nonresidents who would pay whatever price Harison and his agents decreed for the job); and protection against crown usurpation of property rights. Furthermore, Morris and his campaigners assailed Cosby for the colony's stagnant economy—who else could be better to blame?

It was a broad-brush program meant to appeal to small freeholders throughout the colony, urban laborers and artisans, and prominent minorities like the Dutch and the Quakers. But behind their noble principles lurked the Morrisites' vitriol, stirred up because Cosby was in truth acting little differently from other governors, including Morris's patrons Robert Hunter and William Burnet, who rewarded their friends and disdained their enemies. Having formulated an aggressive line of attack, the People's Party leaders felt handicapped, given Cosby's overwhelming advantage in institutionalized power, for want of a mechanism to express their contempt, in a sustained and widely accessible manner, for this very model of a larcenous despot. A printing press was the only device then in existence capable of spreading their grievances across the landscape, but the governor controlled the leading print shop in the colony and co-opted its proprietor's drab newspaper into singing his praises on command. What Morris and his cohorts needed was their own paper, livelier than Bradford's *Gazette*, and a printer willing to risk turning out a publication that heaped scorn on Cosby for his arrant ways.

V

Abundant evidence exists that the *New-York Weekly Journal*, as its logotype announced its formal title to the world on Monday, November 5, 1733, was the brainchild and for the most part the work product of James Alexander, probably the foremost and perhaps wealthiest lawyer in New York. He would hardly have participated in the enterprise, of course, if he had not been the acolyte, professional beneficiary, and shrewd political adviser to Lewis Morris for the eighteen years since he had arrived in America. The germ for the idea of their starting up a paper in open opposition to the willful governor may have been planted a few months prior to Cosby's arrival in New York when Alexander, a serious bibliophile, attended an auction sale for the estate of the late Governor Montgomerie and purchased a copy of a book issued in Edinburgh and titled *The History of the Art of Printing* by Jean de La Caille and James Watson. Its subject was likely fresh in Alexander's mind when political events the next year roused the thought that a printing press was the only suitable weapon to bring Cosby down bloodlessly.

The depth of Alexander's aversion for the governor at the time may be gauged from a letter he wrote to former Governor Hunter in London a few days after the *Journal*'s debut, enclosing a copy of the first issue and remarking that Cosby "has long ago given more distaste to the people than I believe any governor that ever this province had." The reason for launching the paper, he added, was to let Cosby and his masters in London know that the colonists of New York "are not easily to be made slaves of nor to be governed by arbitrary power," and so the paper was designed "chiefly to expose [Cosby] and those ridiculous flatteries with which Mr. Harison loads our other newspaper which our governor claims and has the privilege of suffering nothing to be in but what he and Mr. Harison approved of."

Seven other newspapers were then being published regularly in four of the American colonies, but none of them—and none before them—had dared do what Alexander was proposing: to declare that the royal administration was accountable to the people for its abuses of power and that the press had a right to inform them on the matter. The prevailing view among colonial printers was that their shops were like public utilities, sanitized from partisanship but available for hire by whoever was prepared to pay to have their views published. Liberty of the press referred to the customers' right of access to the mechanism, not the printers' right to flaunt judgmental texts of their own or to favor the convictions of any particular political, religious, philosophical, or other kind of faction. Colonial newspapers were rather like community bulletin boards for posting diverse notices and readers' sentiments, but nothing that might inflame public discontent if their publishers wished to steer clear of government restraint. *Pennsylvania Gazette* publisher Benjamin Franklin's notion of press freedom likened newspapers to "a stagecoach in which anyone who would pay had a right to a place."

In proposing a paper that would rub against the grain of custom and the rigidity of British libel law, Alexander was being more wishful than defiant. A student of political trends, he was surely aware that advocates of free written expression had made headway as well as suffered setbacks at the hands of British law enforcement officers during the first third of the eighteenth century. Among the ranks of emerging press libertarians, none could have been more admirable in Alexander's estimate than John Tutchin, a Whig political satirist and pamphleteer whose journal *Observator* made a practice of offending unscrupulous government officials and financiers by revealing them for what they were. Oft-indicted and several times convicted and imprisoned by Parliament and the crown's law enforcers for seditious libel, Tutchin gained particular notoriety when tried in 1704 for charging that French agents were successfully bribing British ministers and that corruption was rife among the administrators of the Royal Navy. He refused to acknowledge that he had written the offending words despite his printer's testimony affirming it, then claimed he could not be convicted because he had not cited any of the miscreants by name. Chief Justice John Holt would have none of that, though, telling the jurors that the case was a classic instance of seditious libel. "To say that corrupt officers are appointed to administer affairs is certainly a reflection on the government," Holt asserted, adding that whoever made such accusations must be called to account "for possessing the people with an ill opinion of the government" or else "no government can subsist." Then he delivered the perfect rationale for tyrannical suppression of free speech and a free press: "For it is necessary for all governments that the people should have a good opinion of it [*sic*]. . . . Nothing can be worse to any government than to procure animosities as to the management of it . . . and no government can be safe without it be[ing] punished." In other words, the maintenance of even a corrupt and abusive regime took clear precedence over any claim of the people to be ably and justly governed.

The jury took fifteen minutes to find Tutchin guilty, but he was freed on a technicality—the writ originally served on him erred by one day in specifying when his accusations were published. He was not recharged, likely because of widespread if tacit acknowledgment that his reports were true, and was soon called to testify before a House of Lords committee inquiring into how a French fleet came to be furnished with naval stores and provisions from England. Still, Tutchin was hounded by infuriated officials for the rest of his days—he lived only three years more—and died in a Queen's Bench prison.

The relative infrequency of prosecutions and convictions for seditious libel was attributable to the chilling effect of the crown's ongoing scrutiny of writers and publishers, most of whom did not care to risk being dragged before the bench to answer charges and pay court costs, let alone being jailed for offending the impervious authorities. The government continued to issue warrants to search the homes and offices of whoever was suspected of propagating seditious or treasonous material. Soon, however, libertarian demands began to be voiced and published. In 1712, Joseph Addison, co-publisher with Richard Steele of *The Spectator*, urged critics of the government to express themselves so long as they took pains to do so truthfully, tastefully, and without malice. But then Addison, like most other contemporary advocates of press and speech freedom, hedged his provocative appeal by adding that Parliament's license of uncensored publications applied only to "whatever is not against the law." How, then, could press freedom have any meaning as long as the law said it was a serious crime to undermine public confidence in the government by criticizing it *even if* truthfully, tastefully, and earnestly?

This sanctioned muffling of dissent was perpetuated by the corpus of common law rulings of the courts of the realm, which were codified in a monumental two-volume compendium published in 1716 that served as unofficial holy writ in defining criminal law as it had evolved over the centuries. Written by William Hawkins, a respected barrister from the Inner Temple Bar and soon to become a serjeant-at-law, a member of the elite formal order of lawyers who dominated proceedings before the royal courts, *A Treatise of the Pleas of the Crown* was almost certainly priority reading in New York for James Alexander, especially in regard to its discussion of libel law.

Anyone who "in printing or writing" engaged in malicious defamation by blackening the memory of the dead "or the reputation of one who is alive and expose[s] him to public hatred, contempt, or ridicule" was subject to prosecution, Hawkins stated. Libel was viewed as particularly wicked for its tendency to invite "a breach of public peace by provoking the parties injured and their friends and families to acts of revenge." It did not matter if the offended party already had a bad reputation and, he added, more importantly, "that it is far from being a justification of a libel that the contents thereof are true . . . since the greater appearance there is of truth in any malicious invective, so much the more provoking it is." In other words, if the public was persuaded that the alleged government abuses of power had actually occurred, it was all the more likely to demand, perhaps violently, that the miscreants be punished or replaced—which, according to Hawkins's view of society, since he cites no other authority for his conclusion, would be a bad thing for the kingdom. So much for the common law of libel as a patron of social justice. In case his readers missed his point, Hawkins underscored it in a footnote: "The malicious publication of even truth itself"—an oxymoron of a high order—"cannot . . . be suffered to interrupt the tranquility of any well-ordered society." In the next section of his commentary, he propagated this authoritarian credo still a third time, writing that the seditious form of libel—that is, speaking ill in any fashion of those in control of the state—was to be treated as even more heinous than defaming private persons, for "reflecting on those who are entrusted with the administration of public affairs . . . has a direct tendency to breed in the people a dislike of their governors and incline them to faction and sedition." But breeding dislike of their corrupt or abusive governors was, of course, the whole point of speaking up lest the people grovel in dread of them forever.

This gospel of libel law according to Hawkins, now the high authority of the realm on the subject, also held that "not only he who composes or procures another to compose it [a libel] but also . . . he who publishes or procures another to publish it are in danger of being punished for it," notwithstanding that the publisher or printer might be ignorant or incapable of understanding the contents. These stipulations could not have escaped James Alexander in 1733 as he contemplated launching a paper explicitly intended to incite public enmity toward Governor Cosby. Whoever he enlisted to publish the Morrisites' sheet would be flirting with prosecution for libel no less than Alexander himself—and all the more so if the lawyer and anyone else he enlisted to compose the paper's published grievances cloaked their identities in anonymity.

With the arrival of the 1720s, political activity broadened as the aristocracy, landed gentry, and proprietors of commerce who ruled the realm began to recognize a need to admit—by modest increments, to be sure—the growing middle class and even aspiring elements among the masses to the national dialogue on social policies. Calls to extend voting rights were accompanied by insistence on the need to promote public awareness of contentious issues and invite constructive, peaceable criticism by those not previously heard from. Among the most ardent proponents of broadened free expression as both a civil right and a utilitarian virtue were a team of political journalists, lawyer and country squire John Trenchard and the reclusive Thomas Gordon, who wrote 138 essays under the joint pen name of "Cato" that appeared in British journals beginning in 1720. The "Cato" essays—the shared nom de plume was taken from the Roman statesman Cato the Younger, a fierce foe of political corruption and the tyrannical leaders Sulla and Julius Caesar—were collected in book form and published in six editions over thirty years, winning a substantial readership in America. Typical of their essay titles were "The Right and Capacity of the People to Judge of Government" and "Of the Restraints Which Ought to Be Laid upon Public Rulers." No colonist was a keener "Cato" enthusiast than James Alexander.

On the premise that free expression was every man's birthright provided only that it did not injure or limit the rights of others, "Cato" asserted that freedom of speech and security of property were inextricably linked, for "in those wretched countries where a man cannot call his tongue his own, he can scarcely call anything else his own." While governments ought to be praised so long as they deserved it, to allow them to do mischief "without hearing of it . . . is only the prerogative and felicity of tyranny." As trustees of the people's business, "Cato" wrote, all honest government officials ought to have their conduct "openly examined and publicly scanned. Only the wicked governors of men dread what is said of them" and deserved "to be publicly detested." To prevent their own downfall, such oppressors "have been loud in their complaints against freedom of speech and license of the press . . . [and] have browbeaten writers, punished them violently . . . and burnt their words."

Trenchard and Gordon's siren song beckoned a cadre of English libertarian writers into the open to challenge despotism in their own age, as Cato and Cicero had done in the last years of the Roman Republic. A dozen or more Whig journals began appearing in London in the 1720s and assailing public corruption in high places, especially Parliament and among the denizens of Robert Walpole's seemingly impregnable ministry, at times castigated as swindlers and stockjobbers who went unpunished for helping inflate the South Sea Company bubble and reaping fortunes before it burst. The most popular of these journals was *The Craftsman*, begun in 1726, whose principal backers and contributors (anonymous or pseudonymous to avoid Walpole's wrath) were a pair of peers, Henry St. John (Viscount Bolingbroke) and William Pulteney (the Earl of Bath). *The Craftsman*'s avowed mission was the exposure of political craft, in the sense of calculated or deceitful artifice, hence the journal's name. The Walpole regime was adept at parrying its critics' printed thrusts by clandestinely funding papers or journals loyal to the ministry or subsidizing them by free distribution through the postal system. A still more effective means of discouraging their fervid objectors was to prosecute them for seditious libel, and none was more relentlessly pursued than Richard Francklin, publisher of *The Craftsman*, who was tried by the government just a few months before William Cosby left London for New York. The outcome of Francklin's case just a year earlier must have given James Alexander pause in the autumn of 1733 as he contemplated establishing a newspaper with the identical antigovernment agenda.

Francklin's journal carried an anonymous 1731 report from The Hague revealing secret negotiations for a treaty among Britain, France, and Spain that the writer viewed as knuckling under by the Walpole ministry to the Catholic powers, betraying Britain's Protestant Dutch allies, and contrary to the nation's commercial interests. As such, the government indictment read, the article was subversive commentary serving to "vilify the administration of his current majesty's government" and "intended to break and violate the said treaty [and] thereby to raise and sow differences and discords [with] the French king and the king of Spain . . . and also to spread false news and rumors concerning the state of public affairs of the kingdom." In his defense, Francklin's counsel asked the jurors to determine whether the government's ministers had not in fact "deserved to have such things said of them"—a direct rebuke to the still-honored Star Chamber doctrine (per Hawkins's recent treatise) that truth could not justify defaming the government—and whether no distinction should be drawn between false news and true news, for if so, "we shall all live in darkness and ignorance." The prosecutor stuck to his guns, arguing that if *The Craftsman*'s objectionable words were hurled against the government, it was "immaterial . . . whether the matters or things published therein are either true or false." He claimed as well that the doctrine that truth cannot justify a libel antedated the discredited Star Chamber's reliance on it by three and a half centuries, citing a 1275 law but conveniently overlooking that the ancient act made it a crime "to tell or publish any *false* news or tales, whereby discord . . . may grow between the king and his people or the great men of the realm" (italics added).

All that was piffle to Chief Justice Thomas Raymond, who instructed the jurors that they were to return "a special verdict," a legalistic gambit that had found favor among judges over the previous century, limiting juries in some cases to decide only what the facts of a case were—in this instance, whether Francklin had indeed published the specified issue of *The Craftsman* and whether the words in question referred to the current monarch (George II) and his ministers—and then delegating to the judge the authority to decide whether, as Chief Justice Raymond stated it, "these defamatory expressions amounted to libel or not. This does not belong to the office of the jury but to the office of the court, because it is a matter of law, not of fact." But what if the applicable law was unjust on its face by being rooted in the circular rationale that to utter or publish *any* derogatory language about the government was a criminal act precisely because its purpose was to advise the citizenry it was being misgoverned? No matter—English courts like Francklin's that ordered so-called special verdicts were, on their own cognizance, abrogating a jury's right to determine whether a defendant was guilty of a criminal act even if the law misguidedly, arbitrarily, or irrationally defined it as such. If juries were left to determine only what the facts of a case were, regardless of mitigating circumstances, then a defendant's guilt or innocence became solely the province of judges, altogether eliminating the purpose of the jury system as the conduit—and living pulse—of communal opinion and values.

Francklin's jury did not choose, as a few others had in the past, to ignore the judge's directive and, since the facts in the indictment were indisputable, the verdict as to their criminality was left to the court, which ruled that the publisher was guilty as charged. He was sentenced to a year in prison, a £100 fine, and a seven-year surety of £2,000 to be held against any repetition of his provocative conduct.

Inspired by Francklin's journal but cautioned by his fate, Alexander faced a daunting challenge. How to create and sustain a periodical that delegitimized the loathsome William Cosby—to the point of getting him recalled to England—and yet not subject himself and any collaborators he enlisted to early arrest and prosecution for seditious libel, as much a crime in the colonies as in the British homeland? The governor had the colony's entire political machinery at his disposal to press charges and try to make Alexander pay as dearly for his temerity as he had done to Morris. And who in New York had more to lose in both a material sense and professional stature? Alexander's training as an engineer and land surveyor had given him hands-on familiarity with property law. Representing clients like Rip Van Dam and others in the maritime trade had required him to master admiralty law. His service on the Provincial Council and as attorney general of both New York and New Jersey had immersed him in civil law, and he was one of only eight New York attorneys licensed to practice before the Mayor's Court, which had original jurisdiction over much of the seaport's commercial and general litigation. If anyone in the colony had broader knowledge of the law than Alexander, it was Lewis Morris, who stood beside him in the contemplated journalistic venture. They were joined by Morris's assemblyman son, Lewis Junior; attorney William Smith, Alexander's younger law associate, educated at Yale and Gray's Inn in London; and, at least in spirit, Dr. Cadwallader Colden, New York's reigning savant, all of them accomplished writers who Alexander hoped would contribute to the new opposition paper. And then there was Alexander's wife, who in her own right was as formidable a figure in the colony as he was.

Mary Alexander was a native New Yorker whose father was a successful merchant from Glasgow and whose mother came from a Dutch family of goldsmiths. Her twice-widowed mother died three years into her third marriage—to a prominent Huguenot merchant—leaving Mary an orphan at eighteen and an heiress of considerable means. She soon married her step-uncle, a haberdasher, dry-goods importer, and real estate agent, invested some of her inheritance in his businesses, and opened a retail shop on Broad Street that sold merchandise her husband shipped in. In an age when ready-made clothing was rare, she stocked lace, crepe, silk, worsteds, and all the makings of women's finery as well as brightly colored plainer fabrics for everyday attire, turning her store into the colony's fashion hub. Widowed with three children after a nine-year marriage, Mary took a year to weed out the fortune-seekers among New York's eligible bachelors and in 1721, at age twenty-eight, married James Alexander, already one of the colony's leading lawyers, even as she had become one of its foremost merchandisers. The couple had seven children of their own, giving Mary a brood of ten whom she somehow managed to mother devotedly while directing her prosperous business. Shifting her religious affiliation from Dutch Reformed to Anglican, she rose in social rank beyond where mere entrepreneurial success had carried her and became a doyenne of New York society, yet found time to advance her husband's political career. In 1743, her personal fortune was said to be £100,000.

This like-minded cadre of close acquaintances, then, had the wealth, skills, and community standing to confront their royal governor but were not so brazen as to do it openly. They would not publicly attach their names to the *Gazette*'s new rival as its proprietors or authors of any of its contents—just as those high-minded men of means and position behind some of London's journals of social protest laid low to shield themselves from badgering by the government. But for centuries British law had required all publications to carry their printers' names, and there was just one man available in the colony for Alexander to engage as publisher of his paper—if he could be persuaded to compete publicly against his onetime master, William Bradford, the governor's royal printer.

In a memoir attributed to Peter Zenger and issued by his own shop in 1736, he somewhat disingenuously explained his involvement in the new weekly: "As there was but one printer in the province of New York that printed a public newspaper, I was in hopes, if I undertook to print another, I might make it worth my while." In fact, the memoir was written by James Alexander, who likely wished to conceal the true origin and purpose of the Morrisites' paper. It was not a venture that Zenger could have afforded to launch on his own even if he had been a more ambitious man. Though chronically struggling to keep his shop afloat, Zenger was likely not so strapped as to be easily seduced into playing sacrificial lamb for Alexander and his Morrisite circle. The printer knew, through long acquaintance with the Bradfords, father and son alike, of the past troubles each had undergone with government and sectarian watchdogs objecting to what they printed. Furthermore, if Alexander had been scrupulously honest with Zenger (and we have no basis for believing otherwise), he would have fully warned the printer of the prospective risks he faced for publishing the People's Party organ by pointing out that Richard Francklin had just completed a year in a London prison for issuing *The Craftsman*'s latest attack on the British government. At the least, Zenger must have sought assurances from Alexander that the lawyer and his colleagues would provide living wages for him and his assistants and cover any shortfall if the weekly's revenue from subscribers and advertisers did not pay for the required paper, ink, and equipment—and, as important, that they would serve as his defense counsel without a fee if he was prosecuted and support his family if he had to do jail time. There was almost certainly no written contract between them spelling out their understanding—its discovery would have imperiled the signatory parties' liberty and the paper's continued operation—but in agreeing to meet Zenger's terms, Alexander likely extracted the printer's pledge not to betray the identity of the venture's backers or to alter or object to any of the texts he was given to publish.

It may not have been a coincidence that the *New-York Weekly Journal* made its first appearance a week after the voters of Lewis Morris's home constituency decided whether to return him to the Assembly as their representative. The election contest was being closely watched throughout the colony because everyone knew it pitted Morris against a stand-in for the haughty governor who had rudely unhorsed him a few months earlier. The brand-new *Journal*'s account of the balloting made for livelier reportage than colonial readers had ever encountered.

6

A Superlative Monster Arises

CONSIDERING THE HIGH cost of paper and ink in colonial America, Peter Zenger's weekly was understandably miniature by modern standards. It consisted of a single 12-by-15-inch folio sheet folded in half and printed on both sides to produce a compact journal of four pages, each 12 inches high and 7.5 inches wide. Typographically it was somewhat more attractive and legible than the rival *Gazette*. Much of its text, running about 700 words per double-column page, was set in larger type with wider spacing between lines, giving it a less clogged look than Bradford's established paper.

Aesthetically, though, the newcomer was not much to look at. There was no display type to break up the grayness of the pages; there were no woodcuts or other illustrations, and no headings except two on the inside pages after the front-page leader, reading "Foreign Affairs" and "Domestic Affairs." The items beneath each, announced only by the place and date of origin, were filched and condensed from British or other American journals and had been written three or four months earlier. The type showed wear and tear, words set in italics took effort to decipher, grammar and punctuation were erratic, though proofreading was better than might have been expected from a shop with only a few hands to get out a weekly edition and tend to other jobs as well. Its prose, fussier than the *Gazette*'s, was intended to convey the elevated literary style common to English periodicals of the age. It cost 3 pence per copy or 3 shillings for thirteen issues, allowing subscribers a premium of one free issue quarterly. Advertisements, all-type only and resembling modern classifieds, cost 3 shillings (about $40 in early-twenty-first-century currency) for the first insertion and 1 shilling each time it ran thereafter (but the rates as listed in each issue did not indicate how many lines the advertiser was allowed for that price).

The top line of Zenger's proud new logotype contained only one word—"THE" set in small capital letters—and just below it, in far larger type, "New-York Weekly JOURNAL," and directly underneath, in elegant italics set off by top and bottom hairline rules, "Containing the freshest advices, Foreign, and Domestic." Then came the day and date of publication, which in its debut issue was sadly off by one month; it read "October 5, 1733" instead of November 5.

The page-one leader did not exactly make amends. The first line read "Mr Zenger," in keeping with the convention of the time, suggesting that what came next, like the rest of its original articles, had been submitted to the printer for inclusion at his discretion rather than written or solicited by him or an editor. The *Journal*'s initial offering was a turgid homiletic awash in moral and philosophical meandering, which urged readers to find in wisdom the consolation for all life's miseries and the surest way to cheat death. It ended with a painstakingly filigreed poem (much in vogue in that day) made still more unreadable by its tiny type. Page 2 offered items from Vienna about troop movements across Germany, a digest of sermons given in London and elsewhere in England, urging parishioners to help needy and persecuted souls resettle in the new American colony of Georgia, and an excerpt from a letter by the current Holy Roman Emperor to the Chief Bishop of Poland (likely of limited interest to mostly Protestants readers 5,000 or so miles away in the New World). But then at the bottom of the right-hand column of the second page, under the dateline "Westchester Oct 29, 1733" and consuming most of the rest of the issue, appeared something entirely unexpected—a truly fresh, lively news account of a major political event that modern journalists would recognize as creditable reportage. It also strongly suggested that Governor Cosby and his allies were gross abusers of democracy.

The succinct lead paragraph read: "On this day, the late Chief Justice of this Province, was by a great majority of voices, elected a Representative for the County of Westchester." It failed to include "to the General Assembly of New York" after "Representative," presumably because the writer did not wish to insult his readers' intelligence. The second graph, though, enticingly asserted that the vote had aroused "great expectation" since the contending parties had "exerted [themselves] (it is said) to the utmost." Then: "I shall give my readers a particular account of it, as I had it from a person that was present"—the "I" almost certainly being James Alexander, who, the article mentions, was on hand. Here was another innovation: an eye-witness narrative of an occurrence just a week earlier, enriched by graphic details but free of editorializing, letting the facts indict the Cosbyites—the purpose for which the *Journal* was created.

The account began by noting that Westchester's sheriff, Nicholas Cooper, the governor's appointee, like all sheriffs and county officials (though the paper didn't think it necessary to point that out), had posted notice at the local church and other public places of the day and site of the polling, Monday, October 29, on the Eastchester village green. But the posters failed to specify the time of balloting, "which made the electors on the side of the late judge [Lewis Morris] very suspicious that some fraud was intended," the paper reported. To alert Morris's backers in case the pro-Cosby voters suddenly appeared with the connivance of the sheriff, a vanguard of fifty Morrisites camped out on or stayed in homes near the green from midnight till sunrise while the main body of Morris supporters was assembling at nearby New Rochelle and feasting (also doubtless drinking heartily, though the article didn't say) to sustain them through the night.

At sunrise the Morrisite cavalcade streamed onto the green, led by two trumpeters, three violinists, and four "of the principal freeholders," bearing a gold-lettered banner that on one side read "KING GEORGE" in caps and on the other "LIBERTY & LAW," the People's Party motto. They were followed by candidate Morris himself at the head of two columns comprised of some 300 mounted freeholders, who were bona fide voters and said by the writer to be "a greater number than had ever appeared for one man since the settlement of the county." They made three circuits of the green, then retired to nearby homes for refreshment and to await the opposition.

At 11 A.M., Morris's foe, William Foster, appeared on the scene. The *Journal* identified him as a schoolmaster lately appointed by "his Excellency (the present Governor), clerk of the Peace and Common Pleas [court] in the county, which commission, it is said, he purchased for the valuable consideration of one hundred pistol[e]s" (roughly equivalent to $23,000 in 2014 currency, according to the leading authority on colonial currency). The public may have been aware that official positions were purchasable for the right price—very considerable, in this case—and thus been inured to what righteous moderns view as venal patronage peddling. Still, seeing the practice spelled out in so baldly revealing a manner must have startled many of the paper's readers. No source was cited for this intelligence, possibly because such transactions were common knowledge, and, in Foster's case, the report was probably both accurate and little cause for embarrassment, or else he might have sued the paper for libel. Even so, the *Journal*'s frank exposé of the going price for court clerkships qualified as its first public service.

Foster headed a group of 170 or so of his mounted supporters, trailed by Supreme Court Chief Justice James DeLancey and his colleague Frederick Phillipse, identified by the paper as "second judge of the province," who paraded twice around the green, calling out "No Land Tax," the motto of their well-heeled ranks. As he rode past, Justice Philipse "very civilly saluted the late chief justice by taking off his hat, which the late judge returned in the same manner"—and likely in good spirits because his side seemed to widely outnumber his opponent's. The congeniality soon ended as some Morrisites began to heckle Foster as a Jacobite supporter of the British crown pretender, which spurred Foster to yell back, "I will take notice of you."

The encounter grew more heated when Sheriff Cooper arrived around noon, resplendent in a ceremonial scarlet uniform with silver detailing, read out the royal authorization of the election, and directed the voters onto the green, where they were to assemble grouped by their choice of the two candidates. According to the write-up, "a great majority appeared for Mr Morris . . . upon which a poll was demanded, but by whom is not known to the relator [reporter], though it was said by many to be done by the sheriff himself." Morris promptly challenged the sheriff's order, asking several times "upon whose side the majority appeared, but could get no other reply but that a poll must be had." A two-hour delay ensued while benches, chairs, tablets, pen and paper were found for recording the votes to be cast aloud one by one.

Soon after the polling started, the anticipated Cosbyites' ploy was revealed. As the first of thirty-eight Quakers among the voters, all thought to be solidly behind Morris as a long-standing ally of their sect's rights, was called to state his choice, two of the sheriff's hand-picked inspectors intervened. Although the *Journal* described the Quaker as "a man of known worth and estate," the inspectors questioned whether he actually owned enough land to qualify as a voter. They directed the sheriff to make the man swear an oath "in due form of law" on the Bible, attesting to his status as a landowner, an act that would have forced him to violate the well known Quaker prohibition against sworn vows. This "he refused to do, but offered to take his solemn affirmation, which both by the laws of England and the laws of this province was indulged to the . . . Quakers and had always been practiced since the first election of representatives in this province to this time and never refused. But the sheriff was deaf to all that could be alleged." Despite being told by ex–Chief Justice Morris and his principal aides, Provincial Councilman Alexander and prominent attorney William Smith, that "such a procedure was contrary to law and a violent attempt [on] the liberty of the people," the sheriff denied the Quaker the vote as well as his thirty-seven coreligionists, "men of known and visible estates." Morris's legal team could have appealed to DeLancey and Philipse, the province's two highest-ranking judges, who were on hand and might have told the sheriff he was acting unlawfully. The pair of justices, however, were well known to be ill disposed toward Morris by long family enmity and beholden to Cosby for their recently elevated judicial rank, and so were unlikely to have intervened even if appealed to. The *Journal* dared not speculate in that fashion, but it did note, by way of implying the stratagem had been concocted in advance within the governor's coterie, that Sheriff Cooper was an outsider who owned no land in the county. Soon harsh words were flying in sympathy with the persecuted Quakers as well as repeated claims that Foster was disloyal to the king. None of the outcries mattered; by 11 P.M., when all the individual voice votes had finally been recorded, Morris prevailed by 231 to 151. If the thirty-eight Quakers had not been barred, Morris would have garnered nearly two-thirds of the vote.

Sheriff Cooper, his bludgeoning tactic having proven futile, wished the winner "much joy," while the loser said he hoped Morris "would not think the worse of him for setting up against him." Morris, rarely gracious to those he vanquished, replied that though he believed Foster was "put upon it against his inclinations," he was nonetheless culpable for the sheriff "making so violent an attempt upon the liberty of the people," and it would serve him right if the "people aggrieved" [i.e., the disenfranchised Quakers] sued him for £10,000, though he wouldn't urge them to. His supporters let out a triumphant "Huzzah," according to the *Journal*, as Morris reclaimed his status as local hero, but his victory went well beyond that. When he landed at the ferry dock in New York Harbor at 5 P.M. two afternoons later, "he was saluted by a general fire of the guns from the . . . vessels lying in the roads and was received by great numbers of the most considerable merchants and inhabitants of this city, and by them with loud acclamations of the people as he walked the streets, conducted to the Black Horse Tavern, where a handsome entertainment was prepared for him." Lewis Morris was back as a power player in the province's political maelstrom and now possessed a potent new means for attracting the public's support.

II

Probably because James Alexander was consumed with his legal practice and preparing most, if not all, of the *Journal*'s contents, so he could spare no time for further eyewitness reporting, the paper never again ran so vivid and engaging a narrative as its account of the

Westchester election. Its original articles, more literary and nuanced and thus less comprehensible, were filled with oblique references and sly innuendos that almost never named their targets.

Alexander devoted the first two pages of the second and third issues to a condensed rendering of several of Trenchard and Gordon's "Cato's Letters," which had begun appearing in London a dozen years earlier, dwelling especially on elegiac passages in praise of press freedom. Alexander was said to be so struck by these essays that he copied them down word for word in order to render them more persuasively, by selected quotation and faithful paraphrase, as lessons to the *Journal*'s readers. Here were the precepts the paper aimed to live by—and to use, though it was legally constricted from saying so, in order to bring down the despot in the governor's quarters. The first words of issue No. 2 were "The liberty of the press is a subject of the greatest importance, and in which every individual is as much concerned as he is in any other part of liberty." This was a novel idea to most readers, who had never been presented with critical allusions to their rulers. The essay went on: "No nation ancient or modern ever lost the liberty of free speaking, writing, and publishing their sentiments, but forthwith lost their liberty in general and became slaves." The free press was "a curb, a bridle . . . and a restraint on evil ministers" who ought to suffer "the lash of satire," and "the glaring truths" of their abuses ought to be shown to awaken their consciences, if any, "and render [their] actions odious to all honest minds."

But "Cato," as edited by Alexander, was not so wide-eyed in pressing his case that he failed to concede that some honest men were defamed by an unrestrained press. Even so, no worthy man would wind up hurt by printed calumnies, because his virtue would prevail and convince readers of the truth. Nor was Alexander an adherent of absolute press freedom, writing "abuses that dissolve society and sap the foundation of government are not to be sheltered under the umbrage of the liberty of the press" and that publications were not exempt from common-law holdings on the criminality, and thus punishability, of seditious libels. But Alexander, wearing "Cato's" mantle, insisted it was not up to governments or judges but juries of the people to decide when defamatory language was justifiable and whether its authors and publishers could be branded as enemies of society for performing an imperative public service.

The rest of issues Nos. 2 and 3 was given over to a list of ship arrivals and departures and a buffet of foreign news tidbits including results of parliamentary contests in Britain. Notably absent—and they would remain so—were fleshed-out reports of local occurrences and news from other colonies. There were two reasons for this omission, glaring in the eyes of a modern reader. First, the *Journal* had no role model; other American papers, like the *New-York Gazette*, Andrew Bradford's *American Mercury*, and Benjamin Franklin's *Pennsylvania Gazette*, were far from enterprising when it came to chronicling local events; objective reportage was in its fetal phase. Second, writing up hometown or provincial news could be risky; governments in colonies other than New York were no more tolerant of what might be taken for printed criticism and their legislatures no less avid in defense of "parliamentary privilege," forbidding press reports of their proceedings. *The Journal*, in readying its aim at the colonial authorities, had plunged into the cold stream of history and was swimming against the current.

Its fourth issue was tedious going, with an off-putting leader addressed to "Mr Zenger" from one "Philo-Patriae" (Lover of the Country), who wrote that since supreme rulers were charged with procuring "the good and safety of the community," its members should not countenance arbitrary acts of injustice by their administrators. But no malefactors' names or misdeeds were cited as examples. The rest of the issue consisted of items from Europe of remote concern to American colonists. But for the first time the *Journal* made use of a literary device—satire—increasingly favored by British wits to chide villainous and fatuous targets while hoping to avoid prosecution for libel. Artfully disguising their defamatory intent, English litterateurs often set their caustic parables, plays, or anecdotes in an earlier time or foreign or mythical place, used historical figures, fictive characters, or anthropomorphic animals to convey lacerating words in a way that could apply to the general human condition rather than real-life people or government officers who might charge the authors with a criminal activity. At times, writers employed initials to identify the butt of their ridicule, as the *Journal* did in leading off its advertisements in this issue with a bogus plea for the recovery of a lost dog, clearly meant to represent the governor's pet henchman and fawning publicist, Francis Harison:

> A large spaniel of about five foot five inches high has lately strayed from his kennel with his mouth full of fulsome panegyrics and in his ramble dropped them in the NEW YORK GAZETTE. When a puppy he was marked thus (FH) and a cross in the middle of his forehead; but the mark being worn out, he has taken upon him in a heathenish manner to abuse mankind by imposing a great many gross falsehoods on them. Whoever will strip the said panegyrics of their fulsomeness, and send the beast back to his kennel, shall have the thanks of all honest men, and all reasonable charges.

The taunt may have been too arch to turn Cosby's ardent retainer into the instant laughingstock that the *Journal* intended, but there could be little doubt in readers' minds what the paper was up to with the two-page anonymous leader in its next issue on December 5—a passionate defense of Englishmen's historic right to a jury trial, "the fortress and bulwark of their lives, liberties, and estates." Anyone who doubted as much had only to "look abroad in France, Spain, and Italy, and observe the miserable condition of the inhabitants" left to the mercy of often mercenary judges. "Deservedly," the *Journal* essay concluded, trial by juries has "ranked amongst the choicest of our fundamental laws, which whosoever shall go about openly to suppress, or craftily to undermine, does ipso facto ATTACK THE GOVERNMENT, AND BRING IN AN ARBITRARY POWER, AND IS AN ENEMY AND A TRAITOR TO HIS COUNTRY [capitals in the original text]." The right to a jury trial had long and often been "remembered by Parliament [as] the only security between the king and his subjects."

For a certainty, the article was meant to remind readers just how despotic and unpatriotic their governor had been the previous spring in trying to circumvent the jury system in his suit against Van Dam and by reported threats to use his power as chancellor to nullify disputed land titles (like the one to the Oblong, for example) or, as he had done summarily at Albany with the Mohawk deed to the city magistrates, to destroy them without recourse to a court of law. Cosby had, arguably, further imperiled the rights of the people by removing, without a stated cause, their staunchest defender of the jury system, Chief Justice Morris. If the *Journal*'s meaning had been too cryptic, the next issue's leader began:

> Some have said it is not the business of private men to meddle with government . . . but since it is the great design of this paper to maintain and explain the glorious principles of liberty and expose the arts of those who would darken and expose them, I shall here particularly show the wickedness and stupidity of the above saying, which is fit to come from no mouth but that of a tyrant or a slave, and can never be heard by any man of an honest and free soul without horror and indignation. . . . The difference between free and enslaved countries lies here, that in the former their magistrates must consult the voice and interest of the people, but in the latter, the private will, interest, and pleasure of the governors are the sole end and motives of their administration. . . .

But the *Journal* took care not to mention Cosby by name or cite any of his alleged abuses, just as in its first issue it had not explicitly charged him or his agents with trying to rig the Westchester election against Morris by denying the vote to his Quaker constituents. To report the undeniable facts of that episode was sufficiently bold and suggestive of Cosby's villainy. The men behind the paper were wily lawyers who were not about to hand their enemy a ready pretext for charging it—and them—with seditious libel; better to act as an irritant than wield a sledgehammer too easily turned against them by waiting prosecutors.

In its fifth issue, though, the paper ventured beyond the safety zone by including an article on its third page (of four) that began with a short report it had lifted, without attribution, from the *Gazette*. It stated that the French sloop *Le Caesar* had arrived in New York Harbor the previous week on a mission ordered by the governor of the Canadian fortress at Louisburg on Cape Breton Island at the eastern end of Nova

Scotia, purportedly to obtain provisions for the destitute inhabitants of the adjacent fortified town. The ship was permitted to fulfill its assignment by courtesy of Governor Cosby and his council. "They were while here entertained by His Excellency with great hospitality and kindness," the opening paragraph concluded, as if approving a humane intention on the British government's part. But then the *Journal* immediately turned skeptical without—yet—contending that any report in the *Gazette* on the governor's conduct was not to be taken at face value. "It's talk in town," Zenger's paper elaborated on the bare-bones item in Bradford's paper, "that one day in the fort [Fort George] as they were viewing the ramparts, one of [the *Caesar*'s crewmen] was overheard saying in French that he thought 'Three ships could take this place.' But as they were Frenchmen, it's to be presumed they meant 'Three ships could take such a French place.'" It was all the *Journal*'s writer needed to pounce on the governor's advertised kindheartedness and suggest it might instead have been an act of colossal folly: "As war is now proclaimed by France against Germany, wherein possibly Britain may by treaties and her interest be obliged to join against France, and we border on the French colonies, it were to be wished that all means were without loss of time to be taken to put Albany and this place [New York] in the best posture of defense that's possible; especially seeing there may be some reason to fear that the spying on our strength was more the Frenchmen's errand in coming here than to supply their pretended want of provisions; considering that their sailors have frankly owned there was no want of provisions at Cape Breton when they came from thence." The article wound up suggesting that perhaps the Assembly should be summoned to consult on the matter and speed defensive measures.

The upstart paper would not let the matter rest there. It undertook some authentic investigative reporting, and in its seventh issue on December 17, 1733—the first of several that would eventually be cited by Cosby's regime for propagating seditious libel—the lead article challenged as "far from true" the paragraph in the *Gazette* it had relied on earlier (and now admitted as much) in reporting, even if skeptically, *Le Caesar*'s visit to New York as a mission of mercy. In doing so, the *Journal* directly assailed its established rival for the first time, calling it "a paper known to be under the direction of the government" and claiming its printer was not allowed "to insert anything but what his superiors approve of." Then it presented three affidavits aimed at substantiating how the *Gazette*'s report had tried to mislead the public.

The first sworn statement was by a twenty-two-year-old Boston seaman whose vessel had been docked at Louisburg two months earlier. During his daily visits to the town, not only did he see no evidence that food and other provisions were in short supply but learned the fort itself was being expanded and strengthened to repel any foreign incursion. Still more condemnatory was the seaman's further report that, being in New York during *Le Caesar*'s recent visit, he had learned from crew members that French military officers and engineers were aboard the sloop and that as it navigated through New York Harbor they were busily mapping the shoreline and straits that converged on Manhattan, taking depth soundings of the waters, recording church steeples, flagpoles, and other landmarks of the city, and noting the layout and gunnery at Fort George. An affidavit from a second seaman concurred with the first, and a third deponent testified that on a visit to Montreal not long before, he had been harshly treated by the governor and other French officials solely because he was a British subject—an advisory clearly intended to contrast French hostility to foreign visitors with the clueless courtesy that Cosby's coterie had bestowed on the captain and crew of *Le Caesar.* Then to hammer the point home in the immediately following paragraphs, the *Journal* resorted to artifice, in the form of interrogative rather than declarative (and thus openly accusatory) wording:

It is agreed on all hands that a fool may ask more questions than a wise man can answer, or perhaps will answer if he could; but notwithstanding that, I would be glad to be advised in the following points of speculation that the above affidavits afford. . . .

Q. 1. *Is it prudent in the French governors not to suffer an Englishman to view their fortifications, sound their harbors, tarry in their country to discover their strength?*

Q. 2. Is it prudent in an English governor to suffer a Frenchman to view our fortifications, sound our harbors, etc.?

Q. 3. If the above affidavits be true, had the French a bad harvest in Canada? Or do they want provisions? . . .

Q. 5. Might not our governor as easily have discovered the falsehood of it as anybody else, if he would?

Q. 6. Ought he not to have endeavored to do it?

Q. 7. Did our governor endeavor to do it?

Q. 8. Was it not known to the greatest part of the town, before the sloop Le Caesar *left New York that . . . the French had sounded and taken the landmarks from without Sandy Hook up to New York? Had taken the view of the town? Had been in the fort? . . .*

Q. 12. Could we not, by seizing their papers and confining their persons, have prevented them in great measure from making use of the discoveries they made? . . .

Q. 14. Was it prudent to suffer them to pass through Hellgate, and also to discover that way of access to us? . . .

Having rhetorically skewered Cosby and his aides for consorting with the enemy while technically only asking questions, the paper followed with a further deft needling of the governor. In a short item, it informed the public—though not in so many words—that he had muted his Provincial Council's deliberative power of consent by usually summoning only six of its dozen members to meetings, most of them holders of one or more other offices at the governor's pleasure (their names and offices were listed). "Sundry others of the gentlemen of the council who have no offices nor expect any, live also in town [New York], but few of them have often the honor of being summoned to council," the *Journal* said. Of these intentionally excluded members, the article went on, "one . . . it is said, has not been once summoned since November 1732, tho' it is said he has been in town at the time of every one of the councils"—a reference, of course, to James Alexander, who almost surely wrote the piece himself to vent his frustration. The article concluded: ". . . As five [councilmen] do make a quorum, and when five do meet the *majority* of them do determine the point in question, it would seem it is thought there's no need of those (whom we beg leave to call) INOFFICIOUS MEN OF THE COUNCIL, seeing enough of more *fit* men are to be had." To readers who could parse the sarcastic elegance of the *Journal's* phrasing, it was saying, in effect, without resort to mentioning Cosby's name, "Your governor has insulated himself with a council of stooges in order to rule this colony despotically."

While Alexander was peppering the governor with carefully worded public obloquy—notice his use of "it is said" in the item just cited to cloak the charges as an allegation rather than an open accusation—Lewis Morris was mincing no words in a simultaneous private communication with the Board of Trade, describing the *Caesar* affair, which he wrote "gives much uneasiness to the inhabitants" of New York. But Morris, on a vengeful mission, seemed unfazed over the risk of defaming Cosby far more savagely than the *Journal* had dared. He wrote in a December 15 letter, "Whether as some suppose she [the sloop *Le Caesar*] was sent by the French government to sound our harbors and discover our [military] strength, or as others suppose, on a scheme projected by the governor and his brother, a major at Annapolis Royal (who is married to a French lady of that place [a British naval base in Nova Scotia]) to carry on a clandestine trade with the French, 'tis certain that the pretense of a bad harvest at Canada and want of provisions at Louisburg was but a mere sham." While he cited reports in the affidavits carried by the *Journal* that the French at Louisburg were not short of supplies and indeed were strengthening their military fortress there—and that far from welcoming British visitors as Cosby did the French crew, "they make prisoners of any Englishmen who come to Canada"—Morris offered no evidence to back the toxic rumor he passed on that the governor and his family were conspiring to trade clandestinely, illegally, and even treasonously with the crown's mortal foe. To top off his demolition job, Morris claimed to have an affidavit from an officer at Fort George stating that Cosby had been pocketing crown funds allocated for clothing and arming the several hundred soldiers of the New York garrison under his command as well as failing to buy and bestow gifts, as budgeted, for pacifying the native tribes on the frontier "in order to make a vast profit to himself."

We may reasonably suppose that if Morris, now returned to the colonial Assembly and determined to have Cosby removed from office, had hard evidence to support these grave charges, he would have presented it to both the New York legislature and the Walpole administration. But Morris did neither, likely because as a former jurist he feared his public allegations against Cosby would not withstand legal scrutiny, and so he had to hope his hectoring letters would soon trigger a thorough crown investigation of the governor's conduct.

While likely unaware of Morris's ongoing denunciations sent to the Duke of Newcastle as the Board of Trade's overseer, the governor knew full well who was behind the new paper in town and why it had been started. In a letter to the duke—his wife's cousin, remember—sent two days before Morris's latest diatribe to London, Cosby wrote that "I [have] found Alexander to be at the head of a scheme to give all imaginable uneasiness to the government . . . and making the worst impressions on the mind of the people. A press supported by him and his party [has begun] to swarm with the most virulent libels." He knew as well that Alexander's chief collaborator was Lewis Morris, "whose open and implacable malice against me has appeared weekly in false and scandalous libels printed in Zenger's Journal." Morris's aim, he added, was to prejudice the minds of "a deluded and unreasonable mob." Yet for all his fulminating, Cosby said he would not be lured, as he put it, into "a paper war" or defending his conduct and the authority of the crown in a courtroom.

But Alexander and Morris were just warming up, and their newspaper was catching on with New Yorkers, who had begun to appreciate the adroitness of the *Journal*'s jabs at the governor. The paper was selling out, and some weeks Zenger went back to press to print extra copies.

III

One reason for the immediate popularity of Zenger's sheet was that its essays, while often overly mannered and elusive in style, were both instructive and hortatory regarding political matters—qualities

Portion of southerly view of New York and its harbor from a 1717 engraving.

Map of New York Harbor published in 1735.

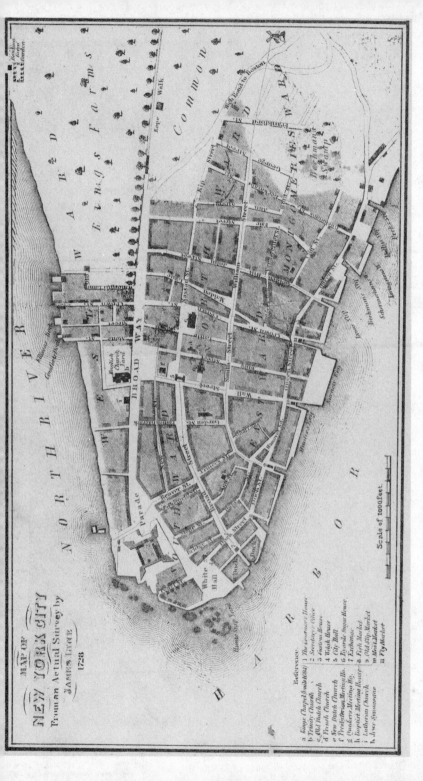

Map of New York City from a survey by James Lyne, 1728.

Harbor view of Fort George, where New York's colonial governors resided.

LEWIS MORRIS
Chief justice and political
power in colonial New York.

WILLIAM COSBY
Twenty-fourth royal governor
of New York (1732–36).

JAMES ALEXANDER
Zenger's lawyer and covert
editor of his paper.

CADWALLADER COLDEN
Civic reformer, historian,
longtime councilman.

Numb. XLIX.

THE
New - York Weekly JOURNAL

Containing the freſheſt Advices, Foreign, and Domeſtick.

MUNDAY October 7th, 1734.

Mr. *Zenger* ;

 Have received a Coppy of a Letter of Thanks from the People of *Goſhen* to their Repreſentative, who lives in that Neighbourhood, which I think eſerves te be made publick, with an Account of true Circumſtances that rarely at-nd Adreſſes of this Nature. I am told at only one Man refuſed, and that all the reeholders have ſigned who were not ab-nt at the Time of Signing. You will ſee y the Liſt of Names, that about 78 have gned, which proves that very few were ſent, I am told not above 3 or 4. This ddreſs came from thoſe Perſons who had ppoſed Coll. *Mathews's* Election, and who n be leaſt ſuſpected to have done it from rivate Views to ſerve him ; on the con-ary, every one (with the former ſingle xception) laid aſide their private Reſent-ents to ſhew their publick gratitude : *7hen* this is compared with what has hap-ened in other Parts of this Province, it ill be ſeen how juſtly the People are ſaid b be fickle and changeable, and whether he People have deſerted their Patriots, or heir Patriots have deſerted them ; for to ae the People ſeem ſteadily to purſue the ame Maxims of Liberty.

✱✱✱✱✱✱✱✱✱✱✱✱✱✱✱✱✱✱✱✱✱✱✱✱

Goſhen, Auguſt 21. 1734.
To Coll. *Vincent Mathews.*
SIR ;

WE the ſubſcribing Freeholders, Inha-bitants of the Precinct of *Goſhen* nd *Miniſink*, in the County of *Orange* take his Opportunity of returning you our hear-y Thanks for your Conduct in the laſt Seſ-ions of Aſſembly, while Matters of the reateſt Conſeqence for the Security of our Lives, Libertiy, and Property were under

your Conſideration : But we are ſurpriſed thoſe Things could have admitted ſo much Debate among the Repreſentatives of a free People, that they could not be brought to a Concluſion before you parted. For Sup-poſing the Arguments on both Sides of the Queſtion were otherwiſe of Equal Force, can the Lovers of Liberty heſitate in De-termining in Favour of Liberty, and in Oppoſition to what may be introductory of arbitrary Power ? The Laws themſelves being a dead Letter, which can do neither Good nor Hurt, but as they have Life and Force given them from thoſe who are in-truſted with the Execution of them ; it ſeems to us eſſential to our Freedom, that the Authority by which our Laws receive their Life, do not depend upon the Will and Pleaſure of any Man, or upon a mere Opinion of the Judges, who are only in-truſted to execute the Laws, or any other than the plain and poſitive Authority of thoſe who make them.

The Accounts we have of your Conduct, ſo conformable to the Sentiments of the People you repreſent, and of your Zeal to remove from all Truſt in the Execution of Juſtice, ſuch Perſons whoſe Characters and Actions have laid them under the juſt Su-ſpicion of the People of this Province, has indeared you to your Conſtituants. The Love and Eſteem of your Neighbours will give more real Satisfaction and Pleaſure than the Favour of any Man however great, and we hope you will find it a greater Secu-rity. Governours often ſmile one Day and frown the next ; nay, they may make a Sacrifice of thoſe that have loſt all other's Friendſhip by courting theirs ; and at beſt they are here to day and gone to morrow : But you we hope will remain long with us, and your Poſterity with ours. Your Inte-reſt is the ſame with that of the People a-mongſt whom you live, and therefore the
moſt

Last of four issues of the *Weekly Journal* burned by crown order.

Drawing in *Harper's Monthly* of officers burning copies of Zenger's paper on November 6, 1734, near New York's City Hall, site of public punishment (note stocks, whipping post, cage, and pillory).

Andrew Hamilton, portrayed at left, is shown (below) in *Harper's Monthly* illustration as he departs from New York's old City Hall, where Broad and Wall streets met, after defending Peter Zenger in his trial on August 4, 1735, on charge of libeling the British authorities.

in scarce supply in colonial reading matter. Its pages were also witty at times, as Bradford's *Gazette* never was. An early example was the leader in the eighth number of the *Journal*, published the day before Christmas 1733, and marking Lewis Morris's first known appearance in the paper, though it was unsigned, like most contributions (or carried pseudonyms like "Philo-Patriae," "Thomas Standby," and "Cato"). The unnamed narrator of Morris's jocular article claimed to have lately run into a gentleman greatly knowledgeable in occult teachings, who attributed cabalistic significance to certain initial letters of kings' and royal governors' names that predicted whether they would prove to be virtuous or villainous rulers. The narrator skeptically replied that he "had never imagined we had any secret friends or enemies among the letters of the alphabet"—letters were merely letters—until the soothsayer revealed that C was an especially noxious initial letter. This seemingly feckless claim prompted the interviewer to acknowledge the likely accuracy of the divination when applied to several governors of New York a generation earlier, naming Richard Coote (the Earl of Bellemont) and Lord Cornbury but leaving Cosby's name out and up to the reader to supply.

More pointed than this japery were two items near the back of the same issue, both aimed at further stigmatizing Cosby for his naïveté in allowing the French sloop to reconnoiter New York Harbor and its crew to inspect the town. The first item was a piece of enterprising reportage meant to cast the *Journal* as a patriotic organ, in contrast to the governor's hobnobbing with the enemy. It featured a woodcut, the first illustration to appear in the paper, of a map of Louisburg, revealing the captioned components of the French fortifications there as re-created from memory by a sailor who, according to his affidavit, had narrowly avoided being arrested for spying. This piece of quasi-espionage was immediately followed by two paragraphs still more suggestive of Cosby's gullibility. "It is publicly reported in town that Mr. Stephen DeLancey, a gentleman of well known honor, honesty, and veracity," read the first item, "has said that one of the gentlemen who came here in the sloop *Le Caesar* from Louisburg told him he hoped to see him again here, at the head of twenty thousand men," i.e., an army of occupation. The other item reported that "one of the French gentlemen extolling the civilities they had received from the governor and some of the gentlemen in town said: it was at present out of their power to [reciprocate] those civilities, but that when they were masters of the place, they would gratefully remember those gentlemen."

The next three issues of the *Journal* were scarcely confrontational, featuring didactic items like an essay by Sir Walter Raleigh on the glorious cause of liberty and more paraphrased "Cato" writing on why malicious rulers need not be revered. Faint as these references were to the government of contemporary New York, they added to the derogatory weight of the *Journal*'s challenge, and after just eleven issues, Cosby had read enough—notwithstanding his boast to Newcastle a few weeks earlier that he would not take legal steps against his detractors—to try to put a stop to it. His compliant chief justice, James DeLancey, charged the grand jury that met on January 15, 1734, to consider an indictment "necessitated by the recent publication of several papers . . . with a design and tendency to alienate the affections of His Majesty's subjects of this province from the persons His Majesty has thought it fitting to set over them. . . . [S]ome men of the utmost virulency have endeavored to asperse His Excellency and vilify his administration; they have spread about many seditious libels in order to lessen in the people's minds the regard that is due to a person in his high position."

These assaults had reached such a degree that "it is high time to put a stop to them," DeLancey asserted, because "all order and government is endeavored to be trampled upon." And if the grand jurors did not put an end to the abuses, the chief justice told them, "the ill consequences that may arise from any disturbances of the public peace may . . . in part lie at your door." His charge, the sort of proceeding initiated by a state's attorney rather than a judge in modern jurisprudence, was accompanied by a six-page memorandum on libel law as set out in Hawkins's 1716 treatise, said to be sufficient cause for the jurors to indict Zenger and his newspaper.

Cosby and his legal advisers might have been hoping that this sudden lightning bolt from Olympus would frighten the printer and his backers into submission rather than result in a criminal prosecution. And it might well have rattled Zenger, whose livelihood was precarious enough—his workforce appears to have been limited to a single journeyman assistant and his two oldest sons, both young teenagers, as apprentices. But his principal backers, Alexander and Morris, were well versed in the law and would likely have pointed out to the anxious printer that DeLancey's presentment was notably lacking in specificity—no individual issues, articles, or passages in the *Journal* were cited as defamatory, and nowhere could Cosby's name be pointed to among its pages as having been held up to ridicule. DeLancey had conceded, moreover, that "the authors [of the alleged libels] are not certainly known, yet it is easy to guess who they are." Indictments, though, were not generally validated by guesswork. Cosby's letters to the Board of Trade show he knew that Alexander and Morris were the principal perpetrators of the undertaking, but both men must have been careful to avoid being seen in contact with their printer, in case he and they were under government surveillance, and to hide any trace of their writings for the paper in case the governor ordered royal agents to search their homes or offices or Zenger's shop for manuscripts of the defamatory material. That Cosby's people had so far refrained from such oppressive policing and did not attempt to press charges against the Morrisites was likely due to their recognition that the *Journal* was the instrument of men whose resources, professional aptitude, and political accomplishments placed them at the apex of colonial New York's society and that to target them as enemies of the people might have incited the very insurrection the governor sought to avoid by trying to scare off the printer instead. For there was no mystery whatever about how the material so offensive to His Excellency was transmitted to the public; every issue of the *Journal* listed Zenger's name at the bottom of the last page as its printer and seller.

The grand jurors, perhaps enjoying the spectacle of their governor's discomfiture, declined to heed DeLancey's dire words and voted not to indict Peter Zenger. The jubilation in the *Journal*'s camp was evident from a letter of appreciation in the paper of January 28, listing the names of the nineteen grand jurors and commending them for their "tender concerns for the liberties of their fellow citizens. . . . [T]heir virtue and integrity merit them the title of patriots." It particularly admired "their noble and generous regard to the liberty of the press (which has been so openly attacked). . . ."

Cheered by the popular rebuff to the government's clumsy attempt to silence a suddenly emergent, passionately irreverent antagonist, Alexander and Morris now intensified their attack and drew Cosby's captive messenger, the *Gazette*, into a war of printed words unprecedented in colonial America. The leader in the next issue (January 21, 1734) of the *Journal*, bearing the mark of Morris's flamboyant style and white-hot enmity toward Cosby, sought to embolden readers to stand tall against their alleged oppressor. Governors were entrusted with great power, the essay began, and were worthy of it only so long as they bestowed "their favors upon the just and deserving. . . . That they can do, and have with impunity done, many injuries is but too evident to be denied. That our distance from the king makes applications to him [to punish abusive governors] difficult and in some cases impracticable I take to be the true reason that some of them, and the vile instruments of their avarice" have gone unchastened. "But because they do mischief with more safety than other men" was hardly reason "that we should therefore on any terms keep in with them . . . [which is] such a piece of logic . . . as any man but a wretch abandoned enough to become a tool to some governors would blush to assert. . . . Why don't we keep in with serpents and wolves on this foot—animals much more innocent and less mischievous to the public than some governors have proved." Then came this incendiary paragraph that, in keeping with the paper's disciplined self-censure, never mentioned Cosby but left little else to be imagined regarding its implied subject:

> A governor turns rogue, does a thousand things for which a small rogue would have deserved a halter. And because it is difficult . . . to obtain relief from him, therefore it is prudent to keep in with him and join in the roguery, and that on the principle of self-preservation. That is, a governor does all he can to chain you, and it being difficult to prevent him, [you] help him put them on and to rivet them fast.

There followed an awkward piece of verbal subterfuge to let readers know it was they who were culpable for licensing such tyranny. No people surpassed the Dutch in their devotion to liberty, the *Journal* harangued, "yet in their plantations [meaning New York as the successor to New Amsterdam] they seem to be lost to all sense of it. And a fellow that is but one degree removed from an idiot shall . . . govern as he pleases, dispose of them and their properties at his discretion, and their magistrates will keep in with him at any rate and think his favor no mean purchase for the loss of their liberty. . . . An ill governor not only enslaves the present generation but makes slavery hereditary . . . unless some SUPERLATIVE MONSTER arises and forces them, whether they will or no, to regain their liberty."

Such extravagantly accusatory language finally drove the *Gazette*, which had disdained recognizing the existence of the rowdy paper being issued by William Bradford's onetime apprentice, into the fray as Cosby's hired champion. In January it reminded readers that the governor was "the Father of his People," claimed his critics were "a parcel of griping lawyers," began referring to the *Journal*'s correspondents as "seditious rogues" and "disaffected instigators of arson and riot," and suggested that Zenger's name be understood as a synonym for "liar." It complained that its new rival, in lifting articles from British journals, had omitted material and juxtaposed passages in a way that distorted their original meaning. It scorned the *Journal*'s cheeky advertisements mocking its foes, like the one transforming Francis Harison into a runaway spaniel who often dropped off "fulsome panegyrics" at the *Gazette* office, and called them "secret arrows that fly in the dark." It took Morris's satiric bait by insisting Cosby was not to be compared with corrupt governors Coote and Cornbury just because all three of their names began with the letter C. It recalled that Morris, sitting as chief justice in 1727, had inveighed against the perils of treasonable words maligning the character of magistrates and, in his charge to a jury, warned New Yorkers not to speak or write disdainfully of their government. In its final issue that month, the *Gazette* declared in a letter to the editor "there is nothing so scandalous to a government and detestable in the eyes of all good men as defamatory papers and pamphlets."

This last rebuke prompted an unusually direct response in the next number of the *Journal*, marking the issue as the second of six that the government would later cite for seditious libel. Under the heading "Domestic

Affairs," Zenger's paper addressed an open letter to the *Gazette*, urging it not to waste words lecturing the *Journal* and the community about the fine points of libel law but instead "to come to what the people of this city and province think are the points in question, to wit: *They think as matters now stand, that their* LIBERTIES *and* PROPERTIES *are precarious, and that* SLAVERY *is about to be entailed on them and their posterity if some past things be not amended*" (italics and all-capital words in the original). The screed called for a dispassionate inquiry in both papers and the public arena into the contested issues lest their readers accede without protest to the establishment of "unbridled power," as evidenced by Chief Justice DeLancey's charge to the grand jury to indict Zenger. "The liberty of the press is now struck at which is the safeguard of all our other liberties."

The *Gazette* fired back the following week. In the guise, as usual, of a letter to the editor, likely written by Francis Harison, fingered by the *Journal* proprietors as the governor's obsequious advocate in Bradford's pages, the pro-Cosbyite paper declared, "I have reason to believe some of the people of the city and province think in relation to the paragraph in Zenger's paper, they think that it is an aggravated libel." The letter-writer added that the charge in the previous number of the *Journal* that "the liberty of the press is struck at" was baseless and asked of its author, "Who told him so? How is he warranted to publish this as a truth?"

It may be ventured that the *Gazette* and the Cosbyites were incapable of grasping, or conceding, the difference between "truth" and an opinion, just as they were dogmatic about labeling any protest, however justifiable, against government activity as criminal conduct because it might incite public unrest and complicate law enforcement. By the same token, one need not have been an authoritarian royalist or Cosby-lover to sense that the writers of the *Journal* were regularly indulging in hyperbole as they demonized the governor. Had his conduct in office really caused New Yorkers to feel that their liberties and properties were "precarious" and that slavery was about to be imposed on them by their "rogue" ruler?

William Cosby was hardly a majestic presence. He had sprung from the lowest tier of British aristocracy, posted an unexceptional military

record, been all but convicted of grand larceny while the royal administrator of a small island, and come by his exalted rank in the American
colonies almost entirely as the result of family connections. In the year
and a half since he was installed as governor of New York and New
Jersey, moreover, Cosby had shown himself to be a condescending, thin-
skinned, moody martinet given to rash, impolitic decisions. But posterity
has been left scant hard evidence that he was—as the *Journal* artfully and
relentlessly implied—an arrant defiler of his colonial citizenry's rights
and freedoms. In several highly visible instances, he and his minions had
tampered with legal procedures but to no avail; his suit against Van Dam
was thwarted and his surrogate candidate against Morris in the Westchester election had been defeated. His destruction of the Albany deed to
Mohawk land might have been excusable on humanitarian grounds. His
good-will gesture allowing the wily French to spy on New York Harbor
and its defenses might have been a diplomatic blunder, but it was hardly
evidence of treason. And his patronage practices and land grants were
no more partisan and self-serving, absent verifiable testimony to the contrary, than those of governors Hunter and Burnet, both greatly facilitated in their conduct of office by Morris, Alexander, and Colden. And if
Cosby was systematically barring contentious members from attending
his council meetings, why had they—all prominent citizens—not vehemently complained to the Board of Trade and the king?

IV

The significance of the antigovernment campaign by Zenger's
paper, if accepted as the earliest harbinger of defiantly free public
expression in America, does not depend on whether Cosby was a scoundrel and oppressor as charged or was the victim of a verbal mugging by
assailants aggrieved over being out of favor with the governor. There is
some room for debating that question. The real bone of contention, in
retrospect, was whether the *Journal*—or any publication or person—
could claim the legal right to object to the governor's conduct, whether
the charges were justifiable or not, and leave it to the public to decide the

answer. That issue became the focus of debate as New York's paper war spilled over into February.

The *Gazette* raised the argument that liberty of the press was not an unencumbered right—that government was entitled to halt and punish attacks, even veiled ones, that undermined its authority and thus its ability to function. The *Journal* shot back that while it agreed with its rival's contention that "envy, spleen, UNJUST clamors, and falsehood can never be introduced for the benefit of the community," it objected that "you rank CLAMOR in general, whether just or unjust, along with those low vices; for should just cause of clamor be given amongst a free people, [it] becomes a virtue and a duty." In an adjacent open letter to Bradford, the *Journal* added that "clamor" was indeed "the right of all freemen to make when cause is given for it," then invited the question "how shall we know whether it be just and right?" It replied:

> [I]f the actions clamored at be [deemed] just, then those who transacted them will never be afraid of submitting them to the judgment of the whole world by the press. . . . On the other hand, should the actors of things clamored at decline that test of their actions and by all ways and means endeavor to stop people's mouths, destroy the liberty of the press, and keep up the things clamored at unredressed, then there's reason to conclude the clamor is just.

That rationale was too permissive for the *Gazette*, which volleyed back by mocking Zenger's paper for claiming that the press was the safeguard of all English liberties. Printers, like ordinary men, were responsible—and liable—for the harmful effects of their spoken or written statements. It was "the abuse and not the use of the press that is criminal and ought to be punished." In reply, the *Journal* granted that abuses of the press ought perhaps to be punishable but pointed out that such a view begged the real question: "The difficulty lies [in determining] who shall be the judges of this abuse. Make our adversaries the judges, I don't well know what will not be a libel, and perhaps if we be the judges, it will be as difficult to tell what will. I would have the readers judges; but they can't judge if nothing is wrote."

Amid all this bandying of words about clamors by the press and how to distinguish its uses from its abuses, James Alexander, de facto editor of the *Journal*, made notes to himself after reading the *Gazette* of February 11 and growing incensed. One of its letter-writers had insisted there was no room for debating what constituted punishable printed defamation of the government because William Hawkins's *Treatise of the Pleas of the Crown* had definitively settled the matter eighteen years earlier in defining the elements of seditious libel, including the premise, fastened to a supposedly ironclad ruling by the notorious Star Chamber 127 years before, that a libel against the government and its officers was no less a libel for being true. Alexander would not accept the dictum that a writer or printer could justly be convicted of abusing the liberty of free expression for publishing the truth. In his view, Hawkins's tome was far from sacrosanct.

Alexander's notes, later to form the basis of Zenger's defense against a dogged government effort to silence his newspaper, asked "from whom he [the *Gazette* letter-writer] has heard that Hawkins has been looked on as good authority and for what reason a collector [Alexander's derogatory term for an editor] can give anything he collects more force than the thing from which he collected it. . . . [Hawkins says] a thing is law because he has collected it into that book." Alexander believed Hawkins was selectively compiling and interpreting the body of common law rulings in libel cases as he chose to, "yet I hope a private man's opinion will not determine what is or not law [or else] law would be very vague and uncertain if it depended on the pen or breath of a private man." Moreover, "is it not misleading [on Hawkins's part] to publish and declare those things for law for which no other authorities are offered but Star Chamber cases?" Those cases "can be of no more authority since the Star Chamber has been destroyed"—here Alexander was treading on less firm ground—and, he continued more on point, its rulings had been founded not on sound reasoning but on "the destruction of liberty and introductory of absolute slavery." Waxing more fervent as his notes lengthened, Alexander asked, "Are the facts he [Zenger] sets forth not true? . . . Are these things to be kept secret which so much concern all, [and] will the people be hoodwinked so as not to see things plain as the sun at noonday? . . . Should the people be reduced to those circumstances by wicked men [to] sit still and shut their ears from hearing, their eyes from seeing, and their mouths from crying out?"

In the February 18 issue of the *Journal*, Alexander translated his private fury into print by running the essence of a June 1721 essay by "Cato" that had directly challenged Hawkins's endorsement of the Star Chamber's *De Libellis Famosis* ruling that its defamatory effect, not its truth or falsehood regarding government behavior, was what made seditious libel a crime. On the contrary, the *Journal* asserted, terming exposure of "public wickedness . . . a duty which every man owes to truth and his country. . . . Whoever calls public and necessary truth libels does apprise us of his own character and arms us with caution against his own designs. . . . Knavish and pernicious [men] ought to be publicly exposed in order to be publicly detested." In short, defamation was the very purpose of protesting the abuses of government authority; otherwise, the compliant masses would remain forever victimized.

V

In the midst of all this heated jousting in print, Alexander found himself the prey of a bizarre plot very likely hatched by Francis Harison. As Cosby's scheming adjutant, pet "spaniel" (so caricatured by the *Journal*), and fawning defender in the pages of the *Gazette*, Harison had no doubt been infuriated by the grand jury's failure in mid-January to indict Zenger for libel and seems to have concocted a trap to ensnare not the poor printer of the paper tormenting him but its instigator and principal author.

On the frigid Friday evening of February 1, 1734, James and Mary Alexander had hosted a dinner party at their elegantly appointed home attended by prominent New Yorkers including Robert Lurting, in his eighth year as mayor of the city, who would still be holding the office when he died the next year. The party broke up around midnight when Alexander led his guests by candlelight to the front door, where one of them, social lioness Anne dePeyster, spotted a letter or a bill on the vestibule floor just inside the door. Since it was addressed to his wife, Alexander handed it to her, and she said to her friends, according to the testimony before the grand jury of another guest, "Let's see what's in it since I have no secrets from you." The midwinter night chilled the group standing there with the front door open, so Mary invited them all back into the parlor. James set his candle down on a small table beside the fireplace, and his wife read the letter to them aloud. Its contents made the night seem even colder.

The sender wrote that he "formerly was accounted a gentleman, but am now reduced to poverty, and have no victuals to eat, and knowing you to be of a generous temper, desire you would comply with my request, which is to let me have ten pistoles [roughly $2,500 in 2014 currency] to supply my necessaries and carry me to my native country." Failure to comply, the note added, would mean "you and your family shall feel the effects of my displeasure"—indeed, he threatened their destruction "by a stratagem which I have devised . . . I swear by God to poison all your tribe so surely that you shan't know the perpetrator." The letter instructed Mary to wrap the payoff in a rag and leave it by the cellar door the following night about 7 o'clock. and if the writer detected anyone on guard or hovering nearby, he would back away and strike later, but if his demand was met, he would never bother the Alexanders again.

The reading was interrupted by several exclamations on the villainy of the missive. Mrs. Alexander sat down, looking "much altered and concerned, [believing] she had not such an enemy in the world." Mrs. dePeyster offered to fetch her a drink to calm herself, but Mary declined. The male guests urged her not to be frightened, since intimidation was what the perpetrator was counting on to exact compliance.

Almost immediately, the handwriting of the note was recognized as closely resembling Francis Harison's—and the host and guests thought it was so intended. As official Recorder for New York City and a member of its Common Council, Harison signed a great many documents that passed beneath Mayor Lurting's eyes. Alexander had served with Harison for years on the Provincial Council (before the governor began disinviting him to its sessions) and was likewise familiar with his penmanship. Alexander's law associate William Smith, also present at the dinner party, had in the normal course of his commercial practice often come across Harison's writing rendered as part of his duties as an admiralty judge and customs official. Smith's historian son later recounted: "From the neglect to disguise the hand . . . it was conjectured that [the writer's] design was to provoke a criminal prosecution [based] on the proof of a similitude of hands." And if Alexander brought charges against Harison with no further evidence than the similarity of handwriting, which the defendant would of course contend had been counterfeited in order to frame him for attempted extortion, Harison would likely be exonerated (or, if not, surely pardoned by the governor) and then sue Alexander for slander and do grievous damage to his reputation and purse. Or even worse, if Harison had his way. Alexander, knowing Harison to be the author of all the political articles that ran in the *Gazette*, needed only to read two pieces running in consecutive issues of the rival paper at the end of January and beginning of February to confirm his suspicion that it was indeed Harison who had contrived the Machiavellian trap. In discussing libel and its heinous effects, the pair of *Gazette* articles prominently suggested that blackening someone's good name ought—unless the charges were proven—to be punishable not just by fine and imprisonment but by death.

Nobody's fool, Alexander evaded the transparent scheme by simply referring the matter to the colonial and municipal authorities and giving the letter to Lewis Morris, Jr., the son of his close friend, for safekeeping. In testimony before the grand jurors, Alexander urged them not to return an indictment against Harison based solely on the resemblance of his handwriting to that in the note. By mentioning Harison's name, though, he at least broached the suspicion that the governor's hatchet-man may have been intimately involved in the dirty business—but without accusing him of it. And by way of quashing any slander suit Harison had in mind, Alexander added that the jurors should jump to no such conclusion. The grand jury heeded his advice and took no action, instead referring the matter to the governor's council, where a special investigating committee was formed to review it. Still a councilman himself, even if *persona non grata* to the governor, Alexander refused to appear before the investigating panel because Harison was a member of it as well as a suspect in the crime, whatever its byzantine motive. Predictably, the council's report to Cosby fully cleared Harison of involvement in the incident, calling him a man incapable of such a foul deed, branding the letter a wicked forgery by malicious characters out to vilify an honorable member of His Majesty's Council, and asking the governor to offer a £50 reward for the discovery of the forger.

The desperation behind the extortionate letter, likely born of Harison's fury over the *Journal*'s growing popularity, was remarked on in a letter Alexander sent Morris as the plot against their party fizzled. "For how could they expect, as the handwriting of the letter was not much disguised . . . that I should have proclaimed to all the author of it[?]" Alexander asked. He supposed that if he had been foolish enough to name Harison as the perpetrator rather than leaving the writer's identity to others to investigate, Harison might, according to his articles in the *Gazette*, have claimed just cause if he killed Alexander for besmirching his name, and then "a petit jury could have been found to have brought in manslaughter from the heat of blood a man must be put into by hearing himself charged with such a villainy . . . and possibly they expected the murder of me would cause all the rest of us to fly to save our lives."

Foiled by Alexander's avoidance of entrapment, Harison had to content himself with the claim, in a letter to his fellow members of the New York Common Council, that he was the victim of a plot by political foes out to ruin him. As if to substantiate his claim, he said he had written several letters to Mary Alexander, ordering goods from her shop, so her husband—well known as Harison's archenemy—would have had access to samples of his handwriting. He prudently stopped short, however, of charging Alexander with actual responsibility for the allegedly counterfeit letter and arranging for its placement under his own front door. The Common Council never dignified Harison's letter with a response.

Alexander had yet another reason, perhaps the most compelling of all, for concluding that Harison was highly motivated just then to do him dirt. At the time the extortion note was delivered, Harison was facing trial on multiple charges of fraud brought by an accuser who had hired Alexander to argue his case. The suit was brought by Harison's former retainer, William Trusdell, a chronic debtor, whom he tried to use as a pawn to get his hands on all or some of the £200 Trusdell owed Boston businessman Joseph Weldon. Falsely claiming he had been engaged by Weldon to collect the money Trusdell owed him, Harison used his considerable political influence to prevail upon police officials to have Trusdell, his devoted former assistant, arrested in October of 1732 and kept in debtor's prison for nine weeks. Then, pretending it to be an act of compassion, he got Trusdell released, perhaps in hopes of a reward from both him and his Boston creditor. Nothing further would have transpired if Weldon, on a visit to Connecticut, had not happened to meet someone familiar with Trusdell's tribulations. Weldon headed for New York to straighten out the matter, and soon Harison found himself brought before the Mayor's Court of New York, where Alexander had filed charges in behalf of Trusdell, of whom he said, "The poor man had been his [Harison's] faithful servant, whom he rewarded with having a false action upon him for a large debt, in the name of a person who had given him no authority, and imprisoned him many weeks on that account."

The Mayor's Court found Harison guilty of fraud and fined him, as he may have anticipated after the grand jury indicted him not long before the extortion note was put under Alexander's door. Perhaps Harison had hoped to distract attention from his own treachery by implicating Alexander in the alleged forgery ruse and winning damages from him to cover any penalty he might have to pay Trusdell, Alexander's client. Whatever the truth, Harison's disreputability only grew. Yet he kept his political offices and place in the governor's good graces.

7

An End to Generous Pity

I N THE SPRING of 1734, as James Alexander labored behind the scenes to hasten the governor's downfall, Lewis Morris, both the spiritual leader and field commander of the anti-Cosby forces, spoke out publicly with fresh fervor toward that same end. His re-election to the Assembly the previous autumn and the grand jury's refusal in January to indict Peter Zenger for libels against the government no doubt strengthened Morris's confidence that his fellow colonists by and large sided with his party's accusations of despotic conduct by the administration. To display and denounce a prime example of this alleged tendency, the displaced chief justice wrote a lively pamphlet, running nearly 10,000 words, that Zenger's shop printed and announced for sale in the March 18 issue of the *Journal*.

Titled "Observations on James DeLancey's Charge," Morris deftly eviscerated his young successor as the colony's ranking jurist for behaving in effect as the governor's water-bearer by all but commanding the grand jury to return an indictment against Zenger instead of laying out the evidence of the printer's supposed crime for the jurors' consideration. "I have always thought it the proper business of the jury and not the judge to determine what papers were libels," Morris wrote, adding, "I was in some pain for Zenger, his judge having previous to any presentment declared his opinion." DeLancey's misplaced zeal to punish the printer, Morris argued, was aggravated by his total reliance, in stating the relevant common law, on cases adhering to the Court of the Star Chamber's infamous 1605 ruling in *De Libellis Famosis*. Under it, the courts "could construe any history of a bad prince or a bad great man . . . into a libel if they pleased," Morris wrote, and "it was not material whether the libel were true or the person against whom it was made . . . was of good or evil fame"—just to publish it by words, signs, songs or if they were found in private and not immediately burned or brought to a magistrate was a criminal act. Such a draconian edict "not only made it dangerous to write libels, but to write or speak or so much as whisper against any great or little man. . . . If it is, then the liberty of man will not long survive the liberty of writing and the liberty of the press"—freedoms that were "not only a proof of the liberty of the people but one great means of preserving [it] by exposing the persons and methods made use of to subvert it to that contempt they so justly deserve."

What DeLancey failed to grasp, Morris contended, was not only that the Star Chamber issuing that edict was "the great engine to enslave the nation" by making even "the most innocent expressions" into libels punishable "with the utmost cruelty and barbarity," but that a great deal of tumultuous history had transpired in the interim. The court "grew to be a general grievance, [and] was abolished by Parliament in the time of Charles I," whose head was likewise soon removed for his tyrannical disposition. True, after the Restoration and return of Stuart absolutism, "the same design of enslaving the nation [was] revived, writing disagreeable truths was [prosecuted], some of them made treason," and extreme fines and bloody punishments were inflicted, paving the way for the Glorious Revolution and the arrival of King William III, "the great redeemer of the English liberties." Since the Revolution, Morris asserted, there had been other decisions less slavishly reverential toward the Star Chamber's doctrine on seditious libel, even though Hawkins, the most prominent modern legal commentator, had been "tender and cautious"—in short, submissive—to that dead despotic court "as he is in other cases that admit of doubt." In Morris's eyes, Hawkins was plainly reluctant to concede that when old cases become obsolete, they ought to be discarded as guideposts to present-day standards of justice. And DeLancey, for his part, was forty years behind the times in insisting that judges may attribute to writings whatever meanings and innuendos they choose and brand them criminally libelous rather than leaving it to juries to determine when defamatory language may be justifiable and in the public interest.

Morris put his political as well as his polemical gifts to work that season whenever the Assembly was in session. His partisans were in the minority, but not by much, so he regularly introduced bills aimed at reducing Cosby's authority by, for example, limiting the salaries paid to crown officials, establishing an envoylike "agent" independent of the governor to represent New York at the British Court, and requiring sheriffs to be local men "of good and sufficient security"—not hacks imported from elsewhere to do Cosby's bidding. To embarrass Cosby personally, Morris offered a bill "to prevent clandestine marriages," a dig at the governor's daughter's secret wedding the previous spring to Lord Augustus FitzRoy lest his family and friends tried to intercede on learning the bride's family ranked several notches below the peerage. Morris's unflagging efforts to bedevil the governor, in reprisal for his rankling dismissal as chief justice, proved fruitless. The trade barons and their allies, still led by the Philipse and DeLancey families, retained control of the legislature—six years had passed since they won it, and so long as they remained loyal to Cosby, he had no motive to call for a new election that might have returned the Morrisites to power. The governor's authority to dissolve the Assembly when he chose posed a threat enabling him to press its members to spurn Morris's antiroyalist, pro-colonist agenda.

Fortunately for Morris, he enjoyed another means to get the governor's goat—namely, the *Journal*. Alexander was the driving force behind Zenger's paper, but Morris contributed to it frequently with pieces of barbed wit and extravagant style discernibly his own, though their authorship was never acknowledged. One such article, signed "No Courtier" (meaning the author was not an adherent of the Cosbyite

Court Party, as the Philipse-DeLancey alliance was then known), led off issue No. 23, appearing on April 8 and taking up more than half the paper. It succeeded so well in irritating the governor that it would become the third of six numbers of the *Journal* eventually charged with committing seditious libel. Like all the earlier antigovernment articles, it never mentioned Cosby's name but left readers in no doubt about who the target was.

Datelined "New Brunswick, March 27, 1734," the front-page piece took the form of an extended letter to "Mr. Zenger" from a writer who claimed to have lately visited a pub in that New Jersey town where he had come upon some people from New York, most of whom "complained of the deadness of trade" in the city that had especially affected "the industrious poor." One fellow pub-crawler, lamenting "the influence that some men (whom he called tools) had in the [Cosby] administration" and how many in the Assembly were susceptible to "the smiles and frowns of a governor, both which ought equally to be despised when the interest of their country is at stake," ranted on that

> I think the law itself is at an end. We see men's [property] deeds destroyed, judges arbitrarily displaced, new courts erected without consent of the legislature by which it seems to me trials by juries are taken away when a governor pleases. . . . Who is then in that province who call anything his own, or enjoy any liberty longer than those in the administration will condescend to let them do it?

There followed a wistful remark that "American assemblies that have only the power to make little paltry bylaws pretend to the power of a British Parliament" but cannot impeach an errant administration. The writer, nonetheless, posed a list of questions in the Socratic style favored by Morris, aimed at stirring the public to call the governor and his collaborators to task for their failings and asking first, "Is there any British subject [who] can commit a crime with impunity and is (if guilty of it) too big to be accused?" The answer was No. Next "Is the law and the administration of justice so weak and defective in the plantations [i.e., colonies] that any British subject cannot be tried for any crime and condemned or acquitted according to the merits of his cause?" Answer: "It is not." And then, "Cannot a grand jury indict (that is, accuse) any man a subject within their county (how great soever) of any crime?" Answer: "They may."

It is easy to see why Cosby and his regime detected insurrectionist incitement in such writing. But even dispassionate readers at the time might have noted the exaggerated nature of the charges against the governor in the April 8 *Journal*. Morris's fictive pubgoer in New Brunswick railed against "deeds [plural] destroyed, judges [plural] arbitrarily displaced, new courts [plural] erected without consent of the legislature," and trials by juries [plural] "taken away when a governor pleases," thereby blithely escalating isolated, if censurable, episodes during Cosby's tenure into multiple, repetitive transgressions. Where was Morris's and the *Journal*'s list of deeds destroyed other than the questionable Mohawk land grant? What judges were arbitrarily displaced other than Morris himself? What courts were erected without the Assembly's consent other than the failed effort by the governor and his council to extend the Supreme Court's power to hear equity disputes? What jury trials were taken away other than the also-failed attempt to deny one to Van Dam? Morris's surrogate accuser might have added to his list of grievances "elections [plural] in which freeholders were denied the ballot because of their religious beliefs," but this abuse, too, so far as historical records show, occurred but once, not habitually, as Morris's charge plainly states, and failed in its intention. Perhaps each (singular) of these incidents added up to enough misconduct for Morris and the *Journal* to claim literary license in conflating them into a pattern of rampant tyranny. But in so doing, Cosby's foes were themselves open to the charge of abusing freedom of the press. The question might then have become— had libel law permitted such latitude—whether overstatements of government misconduct in order to call it to the public's attention should be deemed criminal behavior. And who should have decided the answer? To Morris and Alexander, who conceded that press freedom was imperfect and open to abuse, government itself ought not to have been allowed to judge when it was being falsely or excessively pilloried; it should have been up to the people's juries.

Despite such arguable reservations about the purity or excesses of the Morrisites' literary vendetta against a governor plainly deficient in rectitude, popular and scholarly commentators have generally assigned an honorable and heroically daring character to Zenger's *Journal*. An example is Vincent Buranelli's 1957 volume *The Trial of John Peter Zenger*, which noted,

> Every Monday the lash fell across his [Cosby's] shoulders, the attacks varying through the gamut from airy satire to thundering condemnation.... [The paper was] always crammed with information about the officials and [drew] its material from dozens of plain citizens as well as from a "staff" of anti-Cosbyites. Because of the *Journal*'s popularity, a whole section of the people received a constant diet of critical journalism that showed them how influential their approval or disapproval was.... By creating political journalism in the true sense, it did as much perhaps as any single agent to create the American way of life.

Attributing such virtues and accomplishments to the *Journal* romanticizes its actual character and historical value to a faretheewell. The paper did not administer a weekly thrashing to the governor; it did intermittently apply some stinging satire and brazenly caricature Cosby as a despot. The paper transmitted next to no information about government officials, it ran few contributions from "plain citizens," had no known editorial staffers but Alexander, and it did not provide a "diet of critical journalism" nor create "political journalism" or any kind of journalism if by that word we mean the practice of assembling timely nonpartisan reportage or analyses of witnessed, recounted, or discovered events. Only the article in the first issue on the Westchester election and some of the disclosures about the visit of the French sloop *Le Caesar* to New York approximated the modern notion of journalism during the paper's early years. It offered little in the way of readily comprehensible news coverage; at its literary best, it delivered slyly attitudinizing commentary, veiled behind anonymous sources or none at all. The paper had, in fact, a *non*journalistic mission, which Buranelli accurately identified in writing that it "pointedly suggested that [Cosby's] London superiors should do something to alleviate the affliction they have imposed on their colony." Alexander's and Morris's close friend Cadwallader Colden, while sympathetic with their political program, saw their paper for what it was, a publication primarily intended to show the governor's actions "in the worst light they could place them" and included material "that could not be justified and of which perhaps the authors on more cool reflection are now ashamed, for in some of them they raked into men's private weaknesses and secrets of families which had no relation to the public." Modern commentator Alison Olson concurred, calling the *Journal* essentially "the mouthpiece of two of the governor's leading political opponents . . . bent on revenge for Cosby's dismissal of Morris . . . as Chief Justice of the colony."

While it is plainly a stretch to characterize the *New-York Weekly Journal* as an incubator of modern journalism and an illuminating conveyance of public information, functions the paper performed only in passing, it nonetheless served as a seminal contributor to freedom of expression as a benchmark of the American way of life. Zenger's paper was a journal of opinion, a vehicle for advocacy and persuasion rather than a news-deliverer aspiring to objectivity, and like lawyers arguing a case in court, it was not obliged to be evenhanded. Instead, it was exercising its putative license to select, present, and even exaggerate material supportive of its position and to castigate, downplay, or omit what was not, leaving it to the other side to raise counterarguments and to its readers to choose which set was more persuasive. The task the *Journal* set for itself was judgmental, and if that necessarily required defaming a governor it found oppressive—and, by definition, trafficking in seditious libel—it was a risk Zenger and his backers assumed, hoping their fellow citizens would decide that, so long as the *Journal* was in earnest and not the purveyor of intentional falsehoods, they should not be punished for having their say.

II

In March of 1734, the *Journal* began to widen its sphere of concern beyond condemnation of Governor Cosby to the economic travail besetting the colony. Over the spring months, the paper carried tirades against a perceived growth of selfishness among the wealthy, lampooning the Philipse mercantile clique in particular for its reactionary policies and practices.

The *Gazette* seemed to welcome this more sweeping approach, even remarking favorably on the broadened political debate and the Morrisites' partisan outcry as a healthy civic phenomenon: "Opposition is the life and soul of public zeal, without which it would flag and decay for want of an opportunity to exert itself." But hewing to the Cosbyite line, Bradford's paper played up the heated exchanges with its rival not as a symptom of discord and disaffection in the public arena but as evidence of the governor's beneficence: "The people of this province live under the influence of a free government; it is no wonder, therefore, if those in the administration meet with opposition, since it is the effect of free government."

Ignoring such flummery as smug propaganda in behalf of the royal administration, the *Journal* called for freewheeling public consideration of serious political reforms akin to those enacted during the Hunter and Burnet regimes. Some of the measures proposed went well beyond those earlier provisions. The tax code needed adjustment, the *Journal* asserted, so the rich would bear more of the cost of government. So ought election practices to be adjusted to allow voting by ballot instead of aloud as was commonly practiced. Economic reforms to help fund the needs of the working masses were required, like restoration of tonnage duties levied against foreign carriers of luxury imports and serving to boost the local fleet, which had lost much of its business to Bermudan vessels. Innovative programs, too, were endorsed, like allowing more local iron foundries and production of hemp for ropemaking. To reduce Cosby's sway through exercise of the royal prerogative, the *Journal* also pressed for proposals that Morris had thus far failed to push through the Assembly—and would have been subject, anyway, to the governor's veto. These included the popular election rather than the appointment of the mayors of New York and Albany; Assembly elections every three years to ensure a legislative body more responsive to public concerns; fixed salaries and fee schedules for government officials and services; jurisdiction of the courts to be prescribed by the Assembly, not the crown; judges to serve on good behavior and not otherwise replaced at the whim of the governor; and the appointment by the legislature of a provincial agent acting as New York's lobbyist-ambassador in London to give the colony a direct conduit to the ministry rather than allowing its needs and grievances to be filtered through the governor. The transcendent purposes of the *Journal*'s program, though never explicitly stated, were the spread of prosperity among all classes and the advancement of liberty over slavery as suffered under the rule of arbitrary and often oppressive colonial governors, of whom William Cosby was allegedly Exhibit A. Here were the seeds of the rising call for independence from Britain a generation hence.

Late that spring, Cosby confounded his Morrisite critics—and even some of his allies among the colonists—by acting as if he had been reading the *Journal* intently and had seen the light. This stunning conversion took the form of a raft of proposals in the governor's traditional message at the opening of the Assembly's term in April, all of them aimed at improving the colony's stagnant economy and porous military defenses. Cosby even had a broadside drawn up, likely written by Francis Harison, to let the public in on this remarkable awakening by their hitherto indifferent royal overseer.

The centerpiece of the economic program Cosby asked the legislators to enact sought to benefit both merchants and laborers by encouraging trade. It called for easing duties on imports so foreign shippers would buy more New York products for their return voyage, yet it also supported reimposing a modest tonnage tax on foreign carriers arriving in port and authorized subsidies and other forms of protection to stimulate local shipbuilding. Since flour was the colony's prime export, Cosby's prescription list would have commanded millers and bolters to better the purity and quality of the commodity and funded the hiring of additional inspectors to monitor the effort. The legislators were further asked to exclude the immigration of convict and Negro laborers in order to benefit the bargaining position of local laborers and artisans. To spread the tax burden and help defray the administrative costs of governance, Cosby recommended a stamp duty on all legal documents filed in court proceedings and on conveyances of all property titles. Responding to sharp criticism for having let the French sloop *Le Caesar* gather strategic information about New York Harbor and Fort George, the governor proposed strengthening the city's fortifications and erecting new ones at Albany and Schenectady. In a related and imaginative departure, he also called for creating a cadre of young smiths, mechanics, and other "artificers" to be sent among the Indians as instructors and thus woo them away from their French *amis*—the rough equivalent of the latter-day U.S. Peace Corps. Cosby even displayed openness to holding colonywide elections every two or three years, as the *Journal* had urged in the hope of dislodging the trade barons' grip on legislative power.

It was a very ambitious and conciliatory program, suggesting that Cosby possessed social awareness and political resilience not previously in evidence. Yet for his troubles, the governor was rewarded at first only with a lesson in the political orneriness among the American colonists, his friends and foes alike. Many of the measures on his Assembly wish list, recognizably originated by the Morrisites, were accurately perceived by them as co-opting their program, so they felt obliged to oppose them now lest Cosby gain primary credit for their enactment. The Morrisites also sniped at the particulars of the expanded military effort; Cosby, for example, wanted one large new fort to be positioned on an island in the middle of New York Harbor, while they wanted a ring of smaller installations to cover the channels converging at the foot of Manhattan. At the same time, Cosby's allies in the Assembly were leery of the populist nature of his proposals, yet eager to attract popular support by pressing the governor to yield more power to the colonists through enhanced Assembly oversight of his administration's conduct. About all he got from the lawmakers that spring was renewal of the tonnage tax on foreign shipping, but since vessels originating in New England and Philadelphia were exempted, even that concession didn't amount to much. Still, Cosby's initiatives were an encouraging sign that he was not wholly

oblivious to the criticism the Morrisites and their *Journal* had been lev-
eling at him.

The less damnable the governor's behavior appeared, of course,
the more foiled his enemies felt—which was likely Cosby's primary
intention—and so after the Assembly coolly received his program,
the governor displayed persistence rather than turning petulant as
usual when thwarted. As if to disprove reports of his haughtiness and
counter the *Journal*'s sneering portrayal of him as a greedy, bungling
despot, Cosby went on a charm offensive starting in June of 1734. He
invited citizens of modest means and station to dine or otherwise be
entertained at the governor's mansion in Fort George, mingled with
members of the pro-royalist Hum-Drum Club at Todd's Tavern to
talk politics, and met with merchants at a favored coffeehouse not
far from the fort to glean the concerns of the business community.
His outburst of sociability apparently served Cosby well, to judge
by a message he received that same month from the New York City
Corporation, congratulating him on the legislative program he had
presented to the balky Assembly, dominated by heedless mercantile
interests. Cosby might actually have derived solace from taking on
the aura, for the moment, anyway, of the people's governor.

While he retained working control of the Provincial Council, the
closely divided Assembly stood aloof from the venomous feud between
Cosby and Lewis Morris, who with his son Lewis Junior remained a
force to be reckoned with among their fellow legislators. Even though the
pro-Cosby Court Party outnumbered the Morrisites, the two sides were
allied as proud colonists against signs of oppressive rule by the mother
country. Thus, after an extensive June debate over the directive more
than a year earlier by the governor and council assigning the Supreme
Court equity powers to hear Cosby's suit against Van Dam without a
jury, the Assembly voted to deny the legality of the step because the lawmakers' approval had been neither asked nor given.

Having dealt the governor that bipartisan rebuke as an object lesson
to restrain his despotic tendency, the Court Party's thin majority passed
most of Cosby's economic reform package the following fall. Some of his
proposals were revised or watered down, and some new measures were

added. Among the latter were a large issue of paper currency to stimulate commercial activity—the very mechanism that Morris and Governor Hunter had employed twenty years earlier despite objections by the
creditor class—as well as tariffs on imported cider, barreled beef, salt
pork, and slaves to help pay for new military facilities, including one in
Suffolk, Long Island. The legislature, its makeup still unchanged since
1728 except for by-elections to replace retired or deceased members, even
felt compelled—with a push from the Morrisites and the *Journal*—to
support mandatory Assembly elections every several years and sent such
a bill to the council for its required approval. There it languished, as
Cosby and his clique had second thoughts, but the need had become a
growing grievance that the incumbents could no longer ignore.

In the end, the Morrisites, complaining that the governor had handed
out 110,000 acres to bribe reluctant legislators into backing his proposals, felt forced to vote against a program that included many reforms
they had long advocated simply because Cosby and the Court Party now
favored them. So much for civic virtue trumping rank partisanship.
Even so, the progressive awakening by the governor and his allies was in
no small measure a response to the onslaught by Zenger's paper, though
the Cosbyites would not have dreamed of admitting it.

III

While the lately reform-minded governor was bending the
Assembly to his will, partly on the strength of his denying
the public new elections that might have turned over the legislature to
his enemies, Cosby failed to win over the electorate in New York City,
nexus of the Morrisites' populist support. Its Common Council, which
occupied chambers in the west wing of City Hall across from where the
colony's General Assembly and its offices were quartered, held elections
at the end of September for its seven councilmen and their alternates,
the aldermen.

Cosby retained his grip on the council's executive officers, all royal
appointees, by renaming as mayor longtime incumbent Robert Lurting,

a popular nonpartisan figure (and friend of James and Mary Alexander), keeping on his conspiratorial *agent provocateur* Francis Harison as city recorder, and selecting a new and more pliable sheriff, John Symes. But the elected Common Council, with its joint legislative and judicial powers, was a different story. The Cosbyite slate was made up of merchants, backed by the wealthier element among the townies, while the Morrisites opted for candidates among the city's more numerous artisan community. Fewer of the latter met the voting qualifications, but enough of them did to give the Morrisites a landslide victory, losing only one of seven council seats to an incumbent who held the Dock Ward by a single vote out of seventy-five cast, and sweeping all seven contests for alderman. As the ballots were being counted, rumors flew that Morris's party had spread hundreds of pounds to buy working-class votes while Cosby's Court Party was said to have connived to get votes counted that were cast illicitly by soldiers stationed at the fort.

The night after the election, the city's streets swarmed with cheering celebrants, marching past the illuminated homes of the winning candidates and Morrisite leaders and singing ballads that jeered at the rebuked governor. The rowdy lyrics, to be sung to two popular tunes, had been circulated all over town in a broadside printed by Peter Zenger, likely less fearful of censure now since the grand jury had refused to indict him at the beginning of the year. The ballads caused a sensation; the words to one ran, in part:

> *Come on, brave boys, let us be brave/for liberty and law,*
> *Boldly despise the haughty knave/that would keep us in awe. . . .*
> *Our country's right we will defend,/like brave and honest men;*
> *We voted right and that's an end,/and so we'll do again. . . .*
> *Though pettifogging knaves deny/us rights of Englishmen,*
> *We'll make the scoundrel rascals fly/and never return again.*

Further irritating Cosby and his coterie were the two issues of the *Journal* immediately preceding the city election and the one just after, reporting its results. Issues No. 47 and No. 48 were devoted in the main to a highly technical, indeed almost impenetrable, discussion of the historical relationship between the governor and the New Jersey Assembly—in particular, which of them had the right to summon, suspend, and terminate sessions of the legislature. Buried in the stylized, wandering prose, likely the arcane handiwork of Lewis Morris, were charges that Cosby had been demanding to screen Assembly bills in New York before they were considered for approval by its Provincial Council; that he voted on ratification of the bills along with the councilmen, and that he summoned and adjourned the Assembly in his own name instead of the king's—all violations of the rules governors were instructed to follow. When the Board of Trade eventually learned of them, Cosby would receive a slap on the wrist from London. Issue No. 49 of the *Journal* (October 7, 1734) carried the final installment of the turgid essay, referred to at the time as "The Middletown [New Jersey] Paper," along with the results of New York's Common Council election, swept by a slate "put up by an interest opposite to the Governor's," the paper coolly noted and then commended "the virtue and vigor of the inhabitants" on their choice.

That same issue also carried a copy of a cryptic letter of gratitude from seventy-eight freeholders of Orange County in the Hudson Valley addressed to their assemblyman, Vincent Mathews, which, taken together with "The Middletown Papers" and the two acerbic election-eve ballads mocking the governor, would galvanize Cosby's inner circle to renew charges of seditious libel against Peter Zenger. The Orangemen's letter thanked Mathews for his efforts during the Assembly session ended the previous June "on matters of the greatest consequence for the security of our lives, liberty and property . . . in opposition to what may be introductory of arbitrary power." But the letter gave no clue what those vital matters were. Mathews had in fact asked his Assembly colleagues to recommend to the governor the removal of Francis Harison from the Provincial Council and "all offices of trust in the government" due to "the notorious and well known character of that gentleman." Harison had lately been convicted for perjury, and his penchant for fraudulent behavior had been revealed in the suit brought against him by his erstwhile lackey, William Trusdell. Mathews, though, who also served as judge and clerk of the Orange County Court of Common Pleas, had another score to settle with Harison. The judge had lately discovered forged writs and other legal documents in his own jurisdiction and adjacent Ulster and Dutchess counties indisputably linked to a pair of what he termed Harison's "tools," secret agents up to some unspecified dirty business—perhaps extorting payoffs from property-holders to retain their land deeds. The Assembly unanimously endorsed Mathews's recommendation to the governor, but Cosby ignored it. The vengeful Harison did not. In the months following the *Journal*'s publication of his constituents' appreciative letter to Mathews, he was fired by the governor as county court judge and clerk, other Orange County officceholders allied with him were replaced, and county residents who had signed the commendatory letter to Mathews were threatened with punishment. The county tax rolls were seized, moreover, with the intention, according to Mathews's disclosure to the Assembly the following year, of scouring the lists for those sympathetic to the sacked judge who had been delinquent in paying their modest quitrents to the colony and then suing them in Chancery Court—where Cosby alone served as judge and jury—for fines and court costs far in excess of their unpaid taxes.

Harison, still the governor's trusted lieutenant, vented his fury more immediately against Zenger and his Morrisite backers. The first clue of his renewed vehemence and its coming consequences was detectable in an anonymous letter to the editor in the October 7 issue of the *Gazette* that took the *Journal* to task for its three previous issues and condemned "the most insolent scurrilities and abuses" by the governor's enemies as rendered in the two anti-Cosby ballads, which were still being sung all over town. "The treatment our governor hath met with from the press of Zenger's correspondents is, I believe, hard to be paralleled in any history," the splenetic letter went on, "nor is the greatness of mind which he has shown in looking upon their railings with a generous pity and contempt, less extraordinary."

Cosby's "generous pity" ran out a week later. He and his camp concluded that the *Journal* was an incorrigible vehicle of mockery and invective and acted anew to silence it. On October 15, just as he had done at the beginning of the year, Chief Justice DeLancey—not the colony's chief prosecutor, Attorney General Bradley, as would become the practice in latter-day America—charged the grand jury to indict Zenger for defaming the governor and sullying the integrity of his administration. "All order and government [is being] trampled on," DeLancey told the jurors, and "reflections are cast upon persons of all degrees" that were certain to end in sedition if not prevented. "It is high time to put a stop to them." He likewise cashiered "two scandalous songs that are handed about. . . . Sometimes heavy, half-witted men get a knack of rhyming, but it is time to break them of it when they grow abusive, insolent, and mischievous." It was the jurors' duty, the chief justice told them, to determine the identity of the author and printer of the songs and order them prosecuted in accordance with the common-law definition of seditious libel as set down by the eminent legal commentator William Hawkins— namely, any words scandalizing the government and "reflecting on those entrusted with the administration of public affairs . . . with a direct tendency to breed in the people a dislike of their governors and incline them to faction and sedition."

The governor's camp seemed to be in denial of the results of the city election held just two weeks earlier. As Cadwallader Colden, among those councilmen at variance with Cosby, later wrote: "One might think after such aversion to [Zenger's] prosecution appeared from all sorts of people that it would have been thought prudent to have desisted from further proceeding, but the violent resentment of so many in the administration who had been exposed in Zenger's papers . . . blinded their eyes that they did not see what any man of common understanding would [have] seen and did see." Five of the nineteen grand jurors had served on the previous panel that had refused to indict Zenger, so it should hardly have surprised DeLancey and his royalist sponsors when the new grand jury likewise returned no indictment of the *Journal* and its publisher and added that it had not been able "upon a strict inquiry to discover either the author, printer or publisher" of the offending ballads—surely a disingenuous avowal since there were only two printers in the colony and one of them was in the governor's pay. Stymied once again by the jury, DeLancey's court ordered the "virulent, scandalous, and seditious" songs to be burned in front of

City Hall by the city (and county) hangman two days later, October 21, at noon in a symbolic act that punished nobody.

While the grand jury was still deliberating, Cosby's legal team took a more definitive step toward pressing its libel action by assembling a package of five publications Zenger had printed—the *Journal*'s issues No. 7 (featuring material about the French sloop *Le Caesar*'s suspect visit to New York Harbor), Nos. 47–49 (consisting largely of "The Middletown Papers" criticizing Cosby for ignoring crown rules on gubernatorial conduct), and the broadside containing the words to the two election-night ballads—and laid them before the Provincial Council as an incendiary menace to the colony. The councilmen, its pro-Morrisite brethren absent by Cosby's directive, found that Zenger's publications did indeed tend "to bring His Majesty's government into contempt . . . alienate the affections of the people of this province from [said] government, [and] raise seditions and tumults among the people." To put a stop to such "bold practices," the governor and his council directed a letter to the Assembly, recommending the creation of a joint committee between the two legislative entities to consider what action should be taken against Zenger and meanwhile to join in the Supreme Court's directive to have the hangman burn copies of the supposedly heinous publications.

Just why these particular issues of the *Journal* and the teasing songs were chosen by the guardians of the royal prerogative as intolerably rabble-rousing is hard to see through the mists of time. In the November 5 issue of the paper, Alexander dismissed the cited material as harmless stuff and challenged the government to "fix determinate meanings to sentences . . . which the authors have not fixed and to which better meanings can with equal justice be applied"—in other words, the songs named no names, so how could libeled victims be inferred from such vague ditties? As to issues 47–49 of the *Journal*, no modern reader would quarrel with Stephen Botein's comment in his 1985 pamphlet *Mr. Zenger's Malice and Falsehood* (issued by the American Antiquarian Society) that "it is somewhat difficult to understand why 'The Letter from Middletown' was considered exceptionally offensive, and quite a bit more difficult to believe that so complex and tedious a discussion could have inflamed the political imagination of any average reader." But Cosby himself left us a clear enough indicator of why Zenger's paper made him so irate. In a letter to New York's mayor and the city magistrates reprinted in the *Gazette* of October 14–21, the governor wrote:

> . . . You are well apprised what industry and pains are used to raise uneasiness in the people's minds at my administration by some men who under the specious and plausible pretense of liberty vent all the licentious bitterness and malice their private disappointments can suggest: surely the glorious name of liberty was never abused to worse purpose. These men have endeavored by the most false and scandalous misrepresentations of my conduct to less[en] the regard that is due to my character. . . . [T]hey have laid aside all manner of decency—they whose ai[m] seems to be to lead weak and unwary men into tumults and seditions to the disturbance of the public peace. . . . [Y]ou will exert yourselves as preservers of the peace which is entrusted into your hands and use the proper means to bring the offenders to consign punishment.

Cosby was likely hoping the City Council would at least join with his Provincial Council in ordering Sheriff Symes to have the hangman burn the specified issues of the *Journal* as an official rebuke—and warning—to its backers; perhaps, too, the city fathers would pressure the Assembly to accept his councilmen's request to meet with them and consider, without further resort to a grand jury, how to censure the indecent assailants of His Majesty's government. But within days of his appeal, the governor was spurned by both of the colonists' elected bodies.

On October 22, the Assembly, where Cosby retained nominal support of the majority, took up his council's request for a joint study/action committee on the Zenger problem, and after due deliberation voted to let the proposal "lie on the table"—that is, to do nothing about it. The Assembly's rebuff, just a week after the grand jury's continuing refusal to indict Zenger, was more than Councilman Harison could bear. The governor's scourge and apologist-in-chief came by the printer's house a few days later "and swore by the God that made him," Zenger would report in the December 23 *Journal*, "he would lay his cane over me the first time he met me on the street, with some other scurrilous expressions more fit to be uttered by a drayman than a gentleman." The printer thereafter took to wearing a sword when he went out in public.

By way of justifying a government crackdown on the *Journal*'s verbal harassment, the *Gazette*'s October 28 number asserted that "no restraint ought to be put on the press but what is sufficient to prevent the greatest abuses of it, abuses that dissolve society and sap the very foundation of government." Alexander answered in the November 4 *Journal* that he was "glad to see it owned in Mr. Bradford's paper" that only extreme abuses of the press ought to be prosecuted and dismissed application of such a charge to the four cited issues of the *Journal* and the election-night songs as "a ridiculous farce." Yet he sensed the imminent exhaustion of Cosby's patience, adding, "We are unpunished, it is true, but . . . how long shall we be so?"

IV

On November 2, the Provincial Council officially condemned Zenger for the allegedly seditious content of the specified issues and ordered them to be burned four days later in front of City Hall with the mayor and aldermen looking on. Accordingly, Sheriff Symes appeared on November 5 before the Court of Quarter Sessions of the City and County of New York, the upper house of the city's bicameral legislature (consisting of Mayor Lurting, City Recorder Harison, and the aldermen, who doubled as both magistrates and justices of the peace). As ordered by the Provincial Council, the sheriff directed the municipal authorities to command the hangman to burn the papers the following day between 11 A.M. and noon. But the mayor and aldermen, who only a few weeks earlier had contracted with Zenger to print the newly revised Charter of the City of New York, refused to allow the sheriff's order to be entered on its records. Over Francis Harison's strenuous protest, the Quarter Sessions Court ruled that neither it nor the city's Common Council had statutory power to issue such a directive, adding that obedience to an order unauthorized by any known law would be "opening a door for arbitrary commands" that might lead to "dangerous consequences." Bearing in mind that the Assembly "and several grand juries have refused to meddle with the papers when applied to by the [Provincial] Council," the municipal officials said they were instead "bound in duty . . . for the preservation of the rights of this corporation [i.e., the city] . . . and the liberty of the press" and the people of the province to have nothing further to do with the effort to punish Zenger and forbade the county hangman from burning the papers as the royal authorities had directed.

Thwarted by the city's governing body—whose almost unanimously anti-Cosbyite members had been elected only a month earlier—the sheriff had no option left but to order his own servant to carry out the council's orders to burn the papers on the appointed day. Also on November 6, Cosby made a similarly futile gesture by decreeing the four *Journal* issues and the Morrisites' mocking ballads to be seditious libels and offering rewards of £50 and £20 respectively for the identity of the authors of each.

Since repeated rhetorical denunciations of the *Journal*'s crusade against the governor had proven utterly ineffective, physical removal of the paper's principal mechanic seemed the only practicable solution—and aroused no qualms among the guardians of the royal prerogative. Zenger was taken prisoner ten days later on the Sabbath, even though he was known to be a regular congregant at the Dutch Reformed church. The governor's council issued the warrant for his arrest, signed by, among others, Chief Justice (and Councilman) DeLancey, on November 17 for printing seditious libels, and Francis Harison, accompanying the law officers who seized the printer, made sure the captive was not treated gently.

Zenger was committed to a jail cell in City Hall—some accounts say it was located on the third (top) floor, but sparse surviving documents indicate that prisoners were more likely held in the easier-to-access basement—where for several days, he later wrote, "I was put under such restraint that I had not the liberty of pen, ink, or paper, or to see or speak with people." The *Journal*, as the government intended, did not appear the next day—its first interruption since it began a year and ten days earlier. Zenger's backers grasped at once that their principal weapon to bring down Cosby from his royal pedestal might be lost if the printer was not quickly released from custody while they prepared, as he had no doubt been promised, to prevent his conviction.

Alexander put aside his editor's quill and donned his barrister's wig to represent Zenger, whose arrest was legally suspect. Before a large group of spectators in Chief Justice DeLancey's courtroom at City Hall on November 20, Alexander filed a habeas corpus writ challenging the government's complaint and arrest warrant. For them to be legal, Alexander insisted, the Assembly had to approve the arrest order by the governor and his council because, when sitting together, they were empowered to act as the province's final appeals court—so how could they ethically serve as prosecutor as well as judge and jury against the accused? The printer's rights were further abused, his attorney declared, by jailing him without any proof in support of the charges, which he said were no more than the opinions of the governor and his servile councilmen. At most, argued Alexander, his client was guilty of, if anything, a misdemeanor, so his bail ought to be set suitably low "according to the quality of the prisoner and the nature of the offense," in keeping with Magna Carta and subsequent declarations of the laws of the realm. The court ought therefore to consider, in determining reasonable bail, that the printer's net worth was but £40 exclusive of the tools of his trade and his family's clothing.

DeLancey heard detailed arguments over bail on Saturday, November 23, when Alexander stated that because the Provincial Council lacked authority to order Zenger's arrest and he was being held without firm evidence or explicit disclosure of what he was accused of, he should have no bail whatever and be discharged to await findings by the grand jury when it next convened. But if the court insisted on some bail, he asked that it be guided by the sworn statement he submitted of the defendant's paltry total worth.

DeLancey was unmoved. Also unrestrained in revealing his animus toward the prisoner. As Alexander would testify before an Assembly subcommittee in 1736, the chief justice, having signed the warrant for Zenger's arrest, now "imprudently announced to the spectators that 'a jury would near to perjure themselves if they found Zenger not guilty'—or words to that effect." DeLancey then set Zenger's bail at a harsh £400 (roughly $115,000 in 2014 currency) plus £200 to be put up in his behalf by "each of two sureties."

Whatever faint hope the Morrisites and their hired printer may have harbored that the governor's grateful choice for chief justice would preside impartially, let alone mercifully, over Zenger's prosecution all but vanished on the spot. In an account of the proceedings against him published in 1736 and attributed to his authorship, the printer wrote, "As this was ten times than was in my power to countersecure any person in giving bail for me, I conceived I could not ask any to become my bail on these terms; and therefore I returned to gaol . . . where I lay until Tuesday the 28th of January, 1735," the final day of the Supreme Court's term, as the government punitively protracted his jail stay to await yet a third grand jury hearing on the charge of seditious libel.

His captors, too, though, were in for a disappointment. If they had supposed that an unjustly high bail keeping the *Journal*'s printer locked up would cause it to cease publication forthwith and for good, they had not long to wait to learn otherwise. The paper reappeared on Monday, November 25, having missed only one issue in Zenger's absence, and its first words on the front page were a message from the imprisoned publisher. It began, "As you were last week disappointed of my Journal, I think it incumbent upon me to publish my apology, which is this"— and recited how he had been arrested and isolated until finally allowed contact with his lawyer and given "the liberty of speaking through the hole of the [cell] door to my wife and servants by which I doubt not you'll think me sufficiently excused for not sending my last week's *Journal*, and I hope for the future . . . through the hole of the door of the prison to entertain you with my weekly *Journal* as formerly. And am your obliged humble servant, J. Peter Zenger."

And the paper did carry on without him, much as before though more cautious in its content until Zenger's fate could be determined. Here was irrefutable proof that editor James Alexander, not the publisher, was the indispensable figure in the *Journal*'s operation. The shop hands apparently consisted of only a single journeymen printer, Zenger's two eldest teenage sons, and his wife, Anna, likely now in charge of proofreading (as she may have been all along) and finances when not visiting Peter at the jail to receive instructions and keep up his spirits.

Whether the *Journal*, with its publisher absent indefinitely, could stay the course was not immediately evident, but his seizure, at any rate, was a cause for celebration by the *Gazette*. In its December 9 issue Cosby's house organ gloated over Zenger's tribulations and needled him with mock sympathy by claiming that his backers were unwilling to raise the money to bail him, even while the paper's correspondents were "every hour undermining the credit and authority of the government by all the wicked methods and low artifices that can be devised." The rival sheet hazed Zenger by adding that his friends were at pains to ensure their own safety "but neglect that of their poor printer."

It was a telling point—why didn't the eminently successful Alexander, his wealthy wife, his frequent co-counsel William Smith, and their rich associates, Lewis Morris and Rip Van Dam, all of them core supporters of the *Journal*, bail Zenger instead of letting him languish behind bars as their sacrificial lamb? Unless one is prepared to characterize Alexander in particular as a manipulative coward—when his life's work testifies to the opposite—there is every reason to heed the few trenchant sentences in Kent Cooper's otherwise artless and unconvincing 1946 bionovel, *Anna Zenger: Mother of Freedom*: "It is inconceivable that a man of Alexander's character, who had sufficient wealth to bail himself out of jail on most any charge and defend himself successfully in any proceeding, would sit idly by and see Zenger, the poor printer, persecuted if Alexander himself had any guilt at all." Cooper's risible explanation is the device on which he based his novel, that Peter's wife Anna Zenger, not Alexander, was the genius behind the *Journal* and its chief writer—a premise altogether lacking documentary evidence. The most compelling explanation for why the *Journal*'s brain trust left Zenger in jail is that Alexander was indeed not sitting idly by while guiltily allowing the printer to be his fall guy; rather, Zenger was more useful to their mission of doing in Cosby by remaining in jail than by regaining his liberty. Even though Alexander and his confreres certainly could have afforded to put up the returnable bail money, they were also, as Stanley

Katz put it, "shrewd enough to value the sympathy aroused by the news of Zenger's hardships." No doubt they were also cautious enough to fear continued prosecutions—perhaps against them as well as Zenger—and forfeiture of their bonds if they had posted the money in his behalf.

Perhaps a more interesting question is why didn't Zenger, with a family to feed and his livelihood cut off, purchase his freedom by turning state's witness and apprising law enforcement officials that Alexander & Company were the real forces behind the *Journal* while he was a mere job printer trying to earn a living. Novelist Cooper's fanciful thesis was that Peter, depicted as an earnest clod, was just trying to protect his wife, supposedly the inspiration behind the paper as well as its principal writer, from the government's bloodhounds. Dismissing this absurdity out of hand, we turn to the simplest and most plausible reason Zenger did not betray the principals behind his paper—that he had a firm understanding with them to serve as their front man and in return would be rewarded with financial security for himself and his family, expert legal defense if need be, and celebrity status. And Zenger was an honorable man who stood by their arrangement. It is likely, too, that Cosby's prosecutorial team had no need to press Zenger to identify the authors of the *Journal*'s defamatory content because they already knew the answer and how problematic a task it would have proven to charge these powerful and resourceful colonists with seditious intent against the crown. Why risk a violent uprising by the Morrisite partisans when jailing their printer would serve as well to disarm the firebrands? Alexander, moreover, out of both self-concern and the need to keep Zenger's morale up and his lips sealed, must have assured him that his arrest and the privations of imprisonment were stirring ever-deeper public resentment against the governor and his minions. Indeed, each passing day of his confinement was making martyrs of the printer and his large, suffering family while hastening the hour of Cosby's recall to England. At any rate, Zenger's prospect was for a jail stay of no longer than six or so weeks until the grand jury reconvened and, the odds were, again refused to indict him.

But the governor controlled New York's judicial system, and to hear the *Journal* tell it, he had nasty, tyrannical habits.

V

Two days after Peter Zenger's arrest, New York Assemblyman Lewis Morris was granted permission by his fellow legislators "to go home, being indisposed," so he might recuperate from an ailing leg. "Home" was understood to mean his Westchester estate, but instead he hurried to his large manor near the New Jersey coast and within the week, joined by one of his younger sons, Robert Hunter Morris, he slipped away from America on a ship bound for England.

The timing of this seemingly hurried and decidedly clandestine departure suggested to his biographer, Eugene Sheridan, that Morris might have been fleeing William Cosby's jurisdiction in case the combustible governor had decided to rid himself of his regime's most incessant critic, not just Zenger, their foes' spear-carrying mercenary. Perhaps so, but it is likely that Morris's voyage to Britain—his first since his successful mission in behalf of his fellow New Jerseyans thirty-three years earlier—was no spur-of-the-moment impulse. His ongoing series of letters to the Board of Trade in London, claiming that Cosby was an oppressive and imprudent ruler of the two colonies under his command, had availed the dismissed chief justice nothing. The governor remained free of reprimand, and the Morrisites had failed to stem his control of the provincial government (if not of the Common Council of New York City)—witness the Assembly's recent passage of most of Cosby's legislative proposals.

Morris had made no evident headway in undermining the governor's hold on his post in large part because Cosby retained powerful protectors in England, while the American-born colonist lacked comparable advocates and connections there. But as a longtime jurist, Morris should also have recognized that his complaints were steeped in his own bile and deficient in the kind of hard supporting evidence needed to sway the overseers of the empire, who were disinclined to heed querulous colonists. This was especially the case because Morris's grievance against the governor was by then well known at Whitehall, so the Board of Trade—and especially Secretary of State Newcastle, Grace Cosby's cousin—"wanted incontrovertible proof of Cosby's maladministration in the form of properly authenticated testimony from relatively disinterested parties in New York," in Sheridan's view. By late November of 1734, Morris finally realized the only strategy likely to achieve his two main purposes—getting Cosby removed from office and his own job back presiding over New York's high court—was to cross the ocean and argue his case in person to every crown officer, even the king, if need be, who would give him a hearing.

Although his party of New York malcontents could not afford to send a delegation to Westminster in support of their feisty captain, neither did it allow him to travel as a lone-wolf predator, foraging as he went. While hardly a pauper, Morris left America bearing a list of 297 subscribers to his mission, including names from some of the most prominent families in the colony—Schuyler, Beekman, and Livingston among them—who contributed funds to cover the living, legal, and secretarial costs of the expedition and not leave him roaming London's streets as a mendicant in case his efforts took longer than a season to succeed. The most generous of his supporters, not surprisingly, were Alexander and Van Dam, who provided £200 each, but many of the signatories, who included Zenger, donated shillings rather than pounds to the cause. To gather what amounted to a sizable petition of protest against Cosby's conduct must have taken some time, suggesting that Morris's leave-taking was premeditated, although it might have been accelerated by Zenger's arrest. He also carried with him further evidence of careful planning—a memorandum listing the objectives and priorities of the venture, drawn up by Alexander with help from William Smith and Lewis Junior.

Their design called for Morris to first gather a circle of British friends and allies who could best help him storm the citadels of power, starting with the Board of Trade, to obtain a hearing in the great capital; meanwhile, back in New York, Alexander and his colleagues would assemble "further proofs and materials" in the form of affidavits attesting to Cosby's abuses and forward them to England as soon as possible. Alexander also hoped to transmit additional endorsements of Morris's undertaking from members of the Assembly and New York city councilmen and aldermen to lend weight to his plea for relief. Ideally, Morris should have already had in hand all the incriminating evidence he needed before departing, so there is some reason to suspect that Zenger's arrest may have hastened Morris's seemingly abrupt embarkation. At any rate, once he received the additional materials from New York, Morris was to complete his analysis of the compiled record and, with the aid of London legal counsel, draw up a thorough petition of complaint against the governor, to be presented to Cosby's friends and supporters for serious scrutiny in the hope they would come to the only seemly conclusion: lamentably, New York and New Jersey required a new and right honorable royal governor. If, as seemed likely, this overture was rejected, Morris was to take this compendium of grievances to the king's Privy Council, members of Parliament, and the press to force the issue.

Beyond forcing Cosby's expulsion, Morris's priority list included, of course, restoration of his chief justiceship as well as the award of a number of commercial benefits to his fellow colonists, such as official encouragement of native industries that wouldn't compete with British manufacturers. The Morrisites were realistic enough, moreover, to anticipate that if they failed to gain all they sought, the crown might be amenable to a compromise allowing Cosby to retain his post provided he agreed to a series of reform measures. Among those suggested were the immediate election of a new Assembly (the incumbents had been sitting for seven years); acceptance of Assembly laws clarifying the colonial court system and specifying the qualifications of sheriffs and other royal officers; barring the governor's presence from the Provincial Council while it sat in a legislative capacity—and, not incidentally, requiring him to remove the execrable Francis Harison from the council.

Cosby, who was certainly aware of Morris's voyage since the *Gazette* repeatedly chided the governor's archenemy for his furtive departure, sent several letters to Newcastle in December, as Morris was crossing the Atlantic, berating the former chief justice and his friends Alexander, Van Dam, and Colden as "infamous fellows" and "profligate wretches" for their "newspaper vendetta" against him. But he failed to mention that he had locked up their printer or to warn his London superiors of Morris's impending visit lest he seem concerned that they might swallow any of the sour grapes the American traveler would try to sell them.

For his part, Alexander saw to it that the *Journal* continued to appear, even if he pulled in its horns a bit until Zenger's case was resolved. In its December 4 issue, he reprinted one of "Cato's Letters" dealing with libels by way of implicitly protesting Zenger's imprisonment. Parts of the "Cato" essay, readily applicable to Cosby for his alleged abuses of power, asserted that some rulers and administrators were "unwilling to be interrupted in the progress of their ambition and of making their private fortunes by such ways as they could best and soonest make them, and consequently have called every opposition to their wild and ravenous schemes, and every attempt to preserve the people's right, by the odious names of Sedition and Faction and charged them with principles and practices inconsistent with the safety of all government."

In its last issue of the year, while Peter Zenger remained holed up in a chilly cell in City Hall, his *Journal* officially acknowledged Morris's ambitious expedition and offered him its belated blessing, more doggerel than poetry:

> *Ye gods, be kind unto the worthy Chief;*
> *Conduct him safely soon to get Relief*
> *Where Great Augustus Reigns; there may he find*
> *An easie Access, and the Sov'reign kind.*

8

Whiffs of Torquemada

To apply continual pressure on the *Journal* operating without its printer—and cause him maximum discomfort—the government's law enforcement officers kept Peter Zenger in jail till the end of January, when the Supreme Court term expired, to bring its libel charges against him before a grand jury for the third time. In the interim, James Alexander, as the paper's de facto publisher as well as its owner's defense counsel, had used the *Journal* to whip up public resentment against Zenger's imprisonment. In a letter addressed to the captive in the paper's January 26, 1735, issue, for example, a "correspondent" asked with reference to his tormentors, "Is it possible the people can forget the attempts to silence you and destroy the liberty of the press . . . purely to hinder their vile actions from being made public? Can they forget the arbitrary removal of judges and the bold attempts made to establish arbitrary courts?"

Since no record has survived showing how Chief Justice DeLancey's charge to the third grand jury differed significantly from the prior two failed efforts, we can only guess at why he and the Cosby coterie hoped for a different outcome. In all likelihood, they did not expect it—they might have been simply going through the motions to dispel further accusations by their enemies that they were disdainful of lawful procedure. But the grand jury's reluctance to indict Zenger no longer mattered, for the government had decided to make him stand trial by resort to another expedient. On January 28, as Zenger later recounted, "the grand jury having found nothing against me, I expected to have been discharged from my imprisonment. But my hopes proved vain, for the attorney general then charged me by *information* for printing . . . parts of my *Journals* No. 13 and No. 23 as being *false, scandalous, malicious, and seditious.*"

An "information" was a complaint that the government's law officers could file with the courts to put an alleged offender on trial before a petit jury rather than first having to obtain an indictment from a grand jury. The stratagem, even if sanctioned by law, irritated the public, which perceived the device as high-handed and oppressive. "In an admittedly political trial," colonial historian Stanley Katz surmised, "this procedure doubtless alienated many otherwise neutral New Yorkers, and made the prosecution even more unpopular." To substantiate his charges against Zenger, Attorney General Richard Bradley took a precaution that the government had neglected in its presentments to the grand jury. Disregarding the four issues of the *Journal* previously cited as seditiously libelous and symbolically burned on orders of the governor and his council—without the consent of the colony's General Assembly or New York City's Common Council—Bradley cited explicit passages in two other issues that were particularly offensive to Cosby and his staff. Among them were the words, in issue No. 13, that "the people of the city and province of New York . . . think, as matters now stand, that their liberties and properties are precarious and that slavery is like to be entailed on them and their posterity, if some past things be not amended." Issue No. 23 was objected to for its reported exchange at a New Brunswick tavern between a complaining New York visitor and a listening New Jerseyan who suggested the other man move across the Hudson, only to be told there would be no point to the transfer since both provinces "are under the same governor. . . . We see men's deeds destroyed, judges arbitrarily displaced, new courts erected without consent of the legislature by which trials by jury are taken away when a governor pleases; men of known estates denied their votes. . . . Who is there in that province [New York] that can call anything his own or enjoy any liberty longer than those in the administration will condescend to let them?"

Bradley must have been confident that such accusations were so absurdly overblown that Zenger's counsel could hardly disprove their falsity. But even if Alexander attempted to provide testimony in support of the claimed government abuses, the attorney general could have had few fears about the trial's outcome. Almost certainly, Chief Justice DeLancey, presiding over the proceedings, had confided to him that, at the close of the arguments, he intended to resort to a directive that would remove the jury's power to decide whether the defendant was a criminal as defined under the common law on libel. DeLancey would instruct the jurors to return "a special verdict," as English courts sometimes did in cases of seditious libel and other complex transgressions, limiting them to determine only "the facts" in the case—specifically, in Zenger's trial, whether the accused had actually printed the defamatory matter and which government officials it referred to—and then leaving it to the court to decide if the texts constituted a criminal act as defined by the common law. The King's Bench had done just that only three years earlier in the famous case of the Crown against Richard Francklin, publisher of the anti-Walpole journal *The Craftsman*; the jury obeyed the court's instruction, and the printer was harshly punished for casting aspersions on the claimed benefits of the ministry's pending treaty with France and Spain.

Filing the government's "information" against Zenger meant he had to remain in jail to await trial until the Supreme Court reconvened in April—unless Alexander petitioned the court to reduce the printer's bail substantially or release him on his pledge not to flee the colony. Neither step would have suited the government's priority of closing down the *Journal*; the longer Zenger was locked up, the more likely his paper was to cease publication. Ironically, Alexander was content to let his client linger where he was—but for precisely the opposite reason: the longer Zenger was kept in durance vile, the greater the public's grievance toward a seemingly heartless government. In its issue of February 23, the *Journal* carried letters addressed to Zenger surely meant to fuel its readers' animus toward Cosby. One of them urged the printer, "Go on prosper and whilst you continue to breathe liberty and curb oppression, may you ever reign triumphant over your adversaries." Another letter asked baldly, "Have the enemies of the liberty of the press gained anything by the imprisonment and prosecution of John Peter Zenger?"

At the same time in London, Lewis Morris, corresponding regularly with Alexander, did something rare in their exchanges—he mentioned Zenger by name. The two astute lawyers were ordinarily careful to make no written references to their deep involvement with the *Journal* or its printer, no doubt fearing that discovery of such evidence might well subject them to prosecution by Cosby's officers as complicit in the paper's alleged libels. In his February 24 letter to Alexander, Morris provided the only extant proof that Zenger's chief backers did not feel obliged to rescue him from jail by putting up his bail—or harbor guilt for not doing so. Morris's comment, due to the two-to-three-month transoceanic time lapse, referred to Zenger's bail hearing in November, but his comment would have applied with equal or more force to the printer's freshly extended stay in jail following the government's decision at the end of January to prosecute him by means of the so-called information. "You were right in not entering into any security for Zenger," Morris advised Alexander, explaining,

> for those who can construe names into any meaning would not have failed to have made you sensible of the mistake. The case of [Richard] Francklin, the printer of the Craftsman here, is parallel with Zenger's; his printing house is in our neighborhood at Covent Garden, but the man himself is a prisoner in . . . Southwick, and his writers won't become security for his good behavior in any large sum because they well know in whose power it is to construe words. But he like Zenger prints on and leaves those concerned to make the best on it.

Morris's conscience had been further assuaged by the time he wrote Alexander a month later that he had reliably learned the chief writer and backer of *The Craftsman* was a figure of renown in London comparable to Morris's own in the far smaller pond of New York—Henry St. John, Viscount Bolingbroke, a leading Tory politician and gifted polemicist, who had not been willing to expose himself to Prime Minister Walpole's prosecutors by putting up security to ensure that Francklin could publish further assaults on the government. Rather, Bolingbroke was said to rationalize that his reluctance to pay the price for lifting the government constraints imposed on the printer was proving a boon to *The Craftsman*'s circulation.

Morris and Alexander's own rationalized self-interest would consign Zenger to six more months in prison from the day the information was filed against him by the government. Yet his newspaper soldiered on, growing more, not less, strident in its populist protest as the trial date loomed. In its February 17 issue, for example, it accused Cosby's trade-baron allies in the Assembly of selling their votes to the governor:

> Almost everyone of them enjoys places of profit, honor, and power
> under him, by which they keep their neighbors in awe and advance
> their private fortunes and those of their friends and relations . . . and
> the governor . . . [is] ready to oblige them at all times with the grant
> of land and other private favors.

Few well-to-do colonists were to be found among those most lamenting Peter Zenger's plight.

II

As he arrived in London in midwinter of 1735, his mission there would have weighed heavily even on a far younger man than Lewis Morris, who at age sixty-four was unaccustomed to the swirl and din of British politics and society. Without a legitimizing commission from the New York Assembly, of which he was a member, or allies among the English aristocracy or in the commercial houses ever more influential in how the realm was run, Morris had to rely more than he liked on prominent London lawyer Ferdinand Paris to plead his case against Cosby and for his own reinstatement as chief justice of New York.

Both causes had to be pursued outside the courtroom, for Morris had neither legal standing nor witnesses nor affidavits to bring a formal action against Cosby's conduct in office, "the sole intent of which," as Morris put it to Alexander, "was the making of a purse." The governor, moreover, had possessed the legal authority, if not sufficient justification, to send him packing from the bench. To convince London's keepers of the empire that Cosby had dismissed him solely because he had ruled against the governor in his salary dispute with Van Dam, Morris had his exhaustive legal opinion in the case printed up—and while he was at it, also reproduced and distributed the Privy Council's ruling more than a decade earlier against Cosby's larcenous conduct while governor of Minorca. Morris's chief obstacle, he shortly discovered, was not that he lacked well-placed sympathizers in the inner offices, antechambers, or corridors of the government or that his charge against Cosby for firing him without cause lacked merit—or even that Cosby had powerful patrons in crown circles; in fact, Morris learned, the governor was far from a popular figure in fashionable London or its temples of power. The most obstinate problem the American visitor encountered was the government's institutional ennui, at times shading toward palpable hostility, when confronted with colonists' complaints of ill treatment by crown officers.

Morris's disenchantment over the coolness of his reception was painfully evident in his February 24 letter to Alexander, remarking, "Governors are called the king's representatives [who] must be treated with softness and decency—the thing complained of is nothing near so criminal [to] them as the manner of complaint in the injured." A month later, he drove home the point again to Alexander. "Your instructions are good, but you have very imperfect notions of the world on this side of the water," the traveler wrote home. "They are unconcerned at the sufferings of the people in America." Faced with the chilly atmospherics of Parliament and the ministry, where influence was routinely bought and sold and sordid dealmaking was standard procedure, the affronted colonist—himself not above ethically dubious politicking when it suited his priorities—confessed his frustration in trying to raise a clamor against his archenemy. "Everybody here agrees in a contemptible opinion of Cosby," Morris reported, "and nobody knows him better, or has a worse opinion of him, than the friends he relies on, [but] maybe you will be surprised to hear that the most nefarious crime a governor can commit is not by some counted so bad as the crime of complaining of it [because] the last is an arraigning of the ministry that advised the sending of him, exposing them to censure."

Rather than wallowing in self-sorrow after his initial discouragement, Morris and his son Robert applied themselves tirelessly to widening the normally blinkered eyes of British officialdom to their grievances. Little was beneath their dignity while trying to connect with those who wielded power, starting with the need to find low-level secretaries amenable, when their palms were crossed with guineas, to placing Morris's petition for relief on the right desks at succeeding levels up the administrative ladder. Even while persisting, Morris feared that the lassitude and indifference plaguing Britain's imperial establishment were systemic and that his efforts would forever fall on deaf ears. "And who is there that is equal to the task of procuring redress?" he asked Alexander despondently. "Changing the man [an abusive governor] is far from an adequate remedy, if the thing remains the same. . . . [W]e had as well keep an ill, artless governor we know as change him for one equally ill with more art that we do not know."

In such perceptions, reflecting the strained forbearance of a small but growing number of formidable colonists, lurked the germ of revolution beginning to take hold in America.

III

As he arranged his thoughts for Zenger's defense before the Supreme Court at its spring session, James Alexander had good reason to hope the trial jury would be no more inclined to find his client guilty of criminal behavior than had the three grand jury panels that rejected the government's call for his indictment. On the face of it, Zenger had become a more pitiable figure while he had been imprisoned and so the more likely to be acquitted by the trial jury.

To judge by his pretrial notes, probably written in March of 1735, Alexander was not greatly worried by the possibility—the likelihood, even—that Chief Justice DeLancey would instruct Zenger's jurors to return a "special verdict," ordering them to determine only two salient "facts" in the case—who actually printed the cited texts and which officials they were intended to sully—and leaving it to the court to decide if the defamatory language was sufficiently flagrant to warrant punishment. Alexander's notes show he saw no point in trying to force the prosecution to prove Zenger had in fact printed the material in question. The evidence he had done so was so overwhelming, he believed, that it might "give an ill turn to the minds of the jury to lay any stress on want of proof of his printing and publishing."

But Alexander was surely mindful of the Walpole ministry's recent successful prosecution of *The Craftsman*'s Richard Francklin, thanks to a "special verdict," so he had to be ready, if DeLancey issued the same directive, to challenge it. To do so, it would be essential to establish that Zenger stood accused not merely of printing passages explicitly or inferentially alluding to the governor and his administration but also of printing particular words, the meaning and context of which tainted them as *criminally* defamatory. Both these charges were inseparably included in the complaint against Zenger, so a juror voting to convict had to find him guilty of both acts, not just the first while leaving the second for the court to decide. The jury, he would argue, was not required to surrender its power of acquittal to the bench; in determining the relevant "facts" in the case, jurors were entitled to consider, after Alexander called witnesses to Cosby's transgressions, whether the defamatory words were factually based. If the accusations in Zenger's paper were provable or credibly testified to, they were justifiable expressions of a free press and qualified as public service, not criminal defamation. Justice, in short, demanded that inconvenient truth should prevail over an abusive regime's vested interest in obscuring it.

Alexander's notes show he had in mind another, more direct stratagem that would have altogether prevented DeLancey from imposing a "special verdict" directive—or having anything whatever to do with the trial; he was planning to ask the chief justice to step down from the bench because of a manifest bias against Zenger. On three occasions DeLancey had ardently urged grand jury panels to indict the printer, and as a member of the Provincial Council, he was among those supporting the arguments against Zenger's *Journals* in the conference between the council and the Assembly to arrange for four issues of the paper to be burned as libelous. As a councilman, too, DeLancey had signed the order for the attorney general to arrest and press charges against Zenger, and at his habeas corpus hearing, the chief justice had been overheard to remark that a jury that failed to find the printer guilty would surely be charged with perjury.

Did Alexander really suppose DeLancey would recuse himself from presiding at the Zenger trial? Such a display of judicial rectitude might have seemed farfetched, but DeLancey had in fact declined to participate in hearing Cosby's suit against Van Dam after then–Chief Justice Morris stomped out of the courtroom, vowing never to sit as a member of the Supreme Court exercising equity powers without authorization by the Assembly. Justice DeLancey's explanation was that as a councilman, he had supported Cosby's demand for half the salary Van Dam was paid while acting governor, and thus, unless he absented himself from hearing the suit, the appearance of his impartiality would have been fatally compromised. But Alexander's brainstorm seems misbegotten in historical retrospect. For even if DeLancey, with renewed scruple, would have bowed to Alexander's request and similarly declined to participate in the Zenger trial, his departure would have left only a single Supreme Court justice, inexperienced Frederick Philipse, to hear the case and instruct the jury. In that event, Cosby would almost certainly have named another justice to fill the still-vacant third seat on the court and join Philipse— someone as likely disposed as DeLancey to side with the government against Zenger. Perhaps Alexander's ulterior motive for his contemplated effort to shame the chief justice from presiding at the trial was to publicize how avidly Cosby's choice to succeed Lewis Morris as New York's ranking jurist was doing the governor's bidding to put the

Journal out of business and leave its printer in jail for an extended stay as a deterrent to other malcontented colonists.

Even if Alexander somehow convinced DeLancey to step aside, Zenger's counsel still had to convince the trial jury that the common law was far from settled in positing the criminality of seditious libel. The weight of legal authority, summarized by Hawkins's encyclopedic treatise, was plainly against him; so was the latest precedent, the conviction of Richard Francklin, just a few years earlier. The Star Chamber's *De Libellis Famosis* finding of 1605 stood as a seemingly immovable object in Alexander's path.

As a student of legal history and theory, he had detected the glaring disconnect between the Star Chamber's assignment of criminality to all defamatory expression directed at the government (i.e., seditious libel) and the only justification for doing so as stated within the ruling itself—namely, the premise that nothing could prove more unsettling to the king's subjects than the claim that wicked and corrupt men had been appointed to rule over them. How did it logically follow, though, that the law should deem it a criminal act to protest that dishonorable men were *in fact* ill-serving both the king who had placed them in office and his subjects whom they were treating unjustly or abusively? Wasn't it the corrupt crown officers who should have been charged with criminal acts—and not the complainants who accurately excoriated them? The Star Chamber ruling did not say. Its silence on this critical missing link in logic, as well as on why creditable complaints of misconduct by royal administrators ought not to be tolerated (if not eagerly welcomed) by the crown, spoke volumes.

Alexander's plea in convincing the jury to disregard *De Libellis Famosis* might plausibly have begun by pointedly suggesting why the Stuarts had displayed zero tolerance for any public criticism of the royal regime. At the core of the dreaded Star Chamber's modus operandi was unswerving devotion to the king's divine right to reign, which the Stuart dynasty proclaimed when it took the throne three years before the *De Libellis Famosis* decision. Given providential authorization, the crown could do no wrong, and therefore neither could the monarch's appointed officers be corrupt or wicked men; even to accuse them of wrongdoing was to muddy the crown and undermine the peace of the realm by inciting insurrection. But what if, in fact, Alexander might have asked the Zenger jury with Cosby in mind, some or many of the king's officers were demonstrably rotten apples—why should a just sovereign tolerate their continuance in office? Why should His Majesty not wish to be apprised of their waywardness and have them punished rather than punish those who revealed the culprits for what they were? Was the king's majesty not undermined more by sheltering an unjust and abusive government than by conceding its soiled character? Ought not oppressive magistrates, ministers, and their scoundrel aides to be purged from government and those who correctly identified them be commended for attempting to enhance, not diminish, the king's grace in the eyes of his subjects? Yet this seemingly unexceptionable logic had long been shunted aside by common-law rulings fanatically faithful to the Star Chamber's implicit doctrine that king and government were without sin.

Thus, the time had come, Alexander's notes suggested, for courts to recognize that the authority of *De Libellis Famosis* and subsequent rulings adhering to it had been invalidated by the destruction of the Star Chamber and the Revolution of 1688 following the Stuart Restoration under Charles II and James II. Their reigns, Alexander noted, were rife with "manifest partiality and exorbitancy . . . as the judges then being at the discretion of the ministry [were] pushed and willed for its purposes." Therefore, any reliance by Cosby's attorney general on these old, discredited legal authorities in trying Zenger would be misplaced and ought to give way to more lucid and compassionate arguments.

However enlightened, Alexander's view was nonetheless a radical proposition. While his notes referred to some open-minded opinions by judges and courts hearing seditious libel cases since *De Libellis Famosis*, none had pierced the doctrinal heart of that pernicious ruling. Alexander had to stay focused on how to overcome common-law insistence that any defamation of the government was, ipso facto, a seditious libel. He would argue instead that "defamation must be charging another with something false or scandalous or more . . . [because] giving one's true fame cannot be a defamation." The historical record showed that all indictments and informations for libel that ever were do plainly point out what's requisite to make a paper a libel[er], viz., to be false, malicious, seditious, scandalous, but if a paper not be proved to be these, but on the contrary to be true, twelve upon their oaths could never justly find a defendant guilty of such [charges as raised by the] information.

Rather than directly challenging the dictum first enunciated in *De Libellis Famosis* that the truthfulness of defamatory language did not make it any less a libel, Alexander might have considered turning the coin around during the trial. Attorney General Bradley's complaint against Zenger repeatedly listed the characteristics of the *Journal* excerpts that he said made them libels, and in each case the list began with the words "false" or "falsely," followed by "scandalous," "seditious," and sometimes "malicious." It was the alleged falsity of the paper's contents that appeared to serve as the linchpin of Bradley's case against the printer, even as falsity had been the essence of libel under English law for centuries before the Star Chamber ruled that the truthfulness of antigovernment criticism served only to compound its criminality by all the more inviting disobedience to state authority. But why, then, Alexander might ask the jury, had the attorney general bothered to begin his formal complaint by characterizing the cited words in Zenger's paper as "false"—untrue—if their truthfulness, according to the Star Chamber doctrine, would have made them no less a crime? And since the prosecutor stressed that the words were false, making that allegation an inextricable element of the charge, was he not obligated to prove as much? Or, at the least, why shouldn't defense counsel be permitted to produce evidence intended to establish the truthfulness of the questionable passages in order to discredit the charge of falsity on which the prosecution depended? The jury was entitled to know, Alexander might argue, whether the attorney general's allegation was valid before reaching its verdict. If not, if any and all criticism of government—whatever its merits, whether verifiable or not—was punishable as seditious libel, then only laudatory words about administrative officials, in the manner practiced by the *New-York Gazette*, could be published with impunity.

Such restricted freedom of the press was no freedom at all but a travesty of liberty and no better than the prepublication censorship that Parliament had allowed to expire in 1694.

As for the other three defamatory characteristics asserted in the complaint against Zenger, each might have been similarly challenged by his lawyer as legalistic window-dressing. To argue that the cited *Journal* language was "scandalous" meant, by the generally accepted definition of the word, that the paper damaged the government's reputation by accusing it of violating morality or propriety. But this was merely another way of saying that the language in question was indeed defamatory, and intended to be, in view of the government's alleged misconduct—and if the accusation was *not* false, then the jury could be told that the scandal was not the newspaper's doing but the government's and so Cosby and his regime deserved to have their reputations blackened. To brand the paper's words as "seditious" meant that they advocated resistance to or the replacement of lawful authority. But suppose, Alexander might ask the jury to consider, the government was exercising its authority in an *unlawful* manner; shouldn't it then be resisted until the misconduct ceased or a new and better regime assumed power? For the attorney general to label the *Journal*'s words as "malicious," moreover, was to assign them the intention to cause pain, injury, or distress among the traducers of upright governance. Inflicting discomfort on such abusers of power, though, could scarcely be treated as a crime since it was merely incidental to the paper's primary purpose: to rid the government of misbehavior. And which was by far the graver sin, wounding the government's feelings with just accusations of iniquity or the pain, injury, and distress Cosby's regime stood accused of inflicting on the people?

The real problem for both sides with invoking the truth or falsity of the words at issue in order to determine if they should be punishable was the ambiguity of human experience. Neither truth nor falsity, when weighed by real-life vagaries, is an absolute. Accounts of actions or events, attributions of character traits, descriptions of circumstances and contexts—all are often partial truths at best, open to debate, and susceptible to conflicting personal opinions, interpretations, and predispositions rather than qualifying as objective, incontrovertible fact. To assess how near the preponderance of the trial evidence came to complying with any given community's consensual paradigm of The Truth was supposedly, in Alexander's day as well as ours, the function of juries. Thus, it was to the jurors Alexander hoped to appeal by convincing them that English common law as applied to alleged libels against the government stood as an outdated impediment, not an intelligible guide, to the delivery of justice for the accused and ought not to weigh like a lodestone on the jury's collective conscience.

IV

Among the goings-on in New York that James Alexander kept Lewis Morris, his mentor of twenty years, apprised of during the latter's London stay was the sudden resurfacing early in 1735 of Francis Harison's vengeful scheming—in particular, his effort to wrest away the 50,000-acre Oblong grant along the New York-Connecticut boundary from a group of Morrisite investors.

The big speculative real estate transaction had been engineered by New York Surveyor General Cadwallader Colden, who played a key role in settling the border dispute and later invited Morris, Alexander, and other friends to participate in the venture. Governor Montgomerie had granted them provisional title to the land in September of 1730 for a fee of £750, with final transfer to await the land company's completion, at its own considerable expense, of staking and running the formal boundary line between the two colonies. That task was finished in June of 1731, but in the interim, Harison, sulky because he was only belatedly admitted to the Morrisite investment group despite having helped facilitate the whole arrangement, had hurriedly assembled a rival group of wealthy investors in England, headed by Lord Chandos, who petitioned the crown in March 1731, to grant them title to the same highly desirable Oblong tract. Aristocratic pull by the Chandos consortium succeeded in gaining the royal seal just two months later—and a few weeks before title was transferred to the New York group by Montgomerie, who was kept in the dark about the competing English claim.

Harison's dark plot required a challenge to the Morrisite investors' grant in the New York courts, but the conniver knew that no colonial jury would likely side with the Chandos group's maneuver, even if it bore the royal imprimatur. Harison marked time until he had won favor with the incoming governor before suggesting to Cosby that, in his capacity as chancellor presiding over the New York Chancery Court without a jury, he could hear the dispute (because it involved the transfer of royal property), rule in favor of the Chandos group, and vacate the Morrisites' title to the Oblong. The grief Cosby had endured from the Morrisites over his suit against Van Dam likely made the governor receptive to Harison's ploy, as did the prospect of a large fee from the Chandos group when title to the property was transferred to the English investors. Beset, though, by legal and political squabbles with the Morrisites, Cosby was in no rush to add fuel to the fire. After two years of waiting, Harison proposed a variation on his earlier legal strategy—instead of his filing a motion in behalf of the Chandos group to have the New Yorkers' title to the Oblong vacated, the governor would instruct his attorney general to sue in the king's name since, after all, the crown had approved the Chandos grant. By then, too, the Morrisites had heard—though no hard evidence was ever produced—that the English group had offered to contribute a share of the disputed tract to Cosby if, as chancellor, he ruled in their favor.

In a postscript to his February 4, 1735, letter to Morris, Alexander reported he had been credibly informed that Attorney General Bradley would shortly petition the Chancery Court in behalf of the king to set aside the Morrisite investors' Oblong title. If the report was true, Alexander worried, "it will alarm the province more than anything that has been done in this administration, for I am pretty well assured that there's scarcely a patent [property title] in the province can stand the test if [our group's] patent will not. . . . [E]very freeholder in [New York] is liable to have his patent called in question the same way and to have his lands given away to great men in England. What the consequence of this will be time only can show, but I dread it."

Bradley filed suit three weeks later, apparently undeterred by the brazenness of Harison's effort to steal the Oblong from the Morrisite leaders and Cosby's obtuseness when the subject at hand was legal procedure. Ever since Britain had established a colonial presence in America, the crown had assigned the power to grant land titles to either the royal governors it appointed or to the proprietors it gifted provinces to outright, like William Penn, Berkeley and Carteret in New Jersey, and the Calverts of Maryland. The perquisite was one of the principal lures for enlisting governors, allowing them to garner wealth and influence in their provinces. Awarding virgin tracts to owners residing in the colonies, moreover, had the further virtue of quickening their use as farmland—and thus adding to the riches of the realm—rather than the crown's bestowing them on absentee owners back in Britain who might let them lay idle overseas indefinitely.

The blatant irregularity of the crown's grant to the Chandos group was bitterly denounced by Colden, who knew more about the history of the Oblong than anyone else. In his memoir on the Cosby administration, he wrote there was no justification "to grant in England lands in New York after the king had given full powers to grant the land there" to the royal governors who "solely and without once any interposition of the king or other authority had exercised that power for above seventy years." The Chandos grant had been nothing but an indulgence to a group of cosseted aristocrats, so, as Colden added, "it seemed no less odd for a suit to be brought in Chancery in the king's name who had no interest in it to vacate the New York grant in favor of that in England." Colden was forced to conclude that "such a course of proceeding [Bradley's suit in the king's name] would not have been attempted before any Chancellor but such a one as Col. Cosby, who had no notion of either natural justice or of equity or of the law of the land."

Alexander, as counsel to the Morrisite investors in the Oblong, filed written "exceptions" to Bradley's suit, pointing out the irregularities of the grant to the Chandos group, arguing the king had no vested interest in authorizing Cosby's attorney general to sue to vacate Montgomerie's fully authorized title transfer to the New York grantees, and challenging Cosby's right to sit in sole judgment of the suit because he had a vested interest in the outcome—namely, that if, as chancellor, he voided the grant to the Morrisites, he stood to collect, as governor then awarding the Oblong to Chandos's or some other group, a fee as large as, if not greater than, the £750 paid to Montgomerie four years earlier by the New York group.

When the Oblong suit was heard in Chancery on April 12, 1735, Chancellor Cosby seemed plainly out of his depth. After Bradley rose to answer Alexander's written objections to the case being heard by that court, Cosby sat him down and said he had already made up his mind that the suit could go forward. Once again, the governor appeared to open himself to the charge of exercising power in a precipitous, arbitrary fashion. Fortunately, he had on hand his principal adviser and confidant, Provincial Secretary and Councilman George Clarke, who played an impromptu role in the brief courtroom drama. When Alexander then stood to speak, Bradley assumed it was to protest Chancellor Cosby's summary ruling and objected that the matter was now closed. Alexander answered that he wished to bring another matter to the court's attention, and as Colden later recounted,

> The governor seemed not to know what to do—whether to hear him [Alexander] or not—but looked to Mr. Clarke [and] took his directions by Mr. Clarke's behavior; when Mr. Clarke stopped from going out (for he got up in order to go away as soon as the governor had overruled the exceptions), the governor stopped and seemed as if he would hear what Mr. Alexander had to propose, but Mr. Clarke beginning again to move away, the governor moved from the bench and would hear nothing [further], and the defendants were obliged to put in their answer [in writing] not being allowed to plead or demur to the bill, which being done this affair rested there.

Clarke, who for nearly a decade had been alienated from the Morrisites but remained the closest approximation of a political non-partisan among the royal officeholders in the colony, may well have intended to write to crown legal authorities back in London before counseling Cosby how to rule on the disputed Oblong grants. He doubtless saw through his fellow Councilman Harison's whole conspiracy, but the two men shared—along with Cosby himself—a deep antipathy toward

Morris and his friends. When the one-judge Chancery Court reconvened seven weeks later, the governor ruled that he was fully empowered by his royal instructions to hear the Oblong dispute and, noting that Governor Hunter among other of his predecessors had acted as chancellor to rule on equity suits, dismissed the exceptions raised by the Morrisite holders of the 50,000-acre grant.

Alexander could not have been sanguine about his chances of prevailing in the Oblong dispute any more than in Zenger's defense.

V

A few days after Governor Cosby had refused to step aside from hearing the suit to strip away the Morrisites' Oblong grant, James Alexander returned to courtroom combat, this time for the April 15 opening of the spring term of the New York Supreme Court and the first moves in the trial of John Peter Zenger. Freeing him was certainly the attorney's primary goal, but Alexander and his co-counsel, William Smith, also hoped to show that the government's relentless efforts to criminalize the printer were part of a pattern of persecution against Cosby's foes and further reason to have the governor recalled to England.

After mulling his tactical options for several months, Alexander decided to drop his initial inclination to challenge Chief Justice DeLancey's role as the presiding official at the trial on the ground of his manifest enmity toward Zenger—not to mention, as indeed the defense counsel could not, the DeLancey family's well-known animus toward the Morrisite leaders who backed the printer's newspaper. The evidence supporting a motion to exclude the chief justice for prejudice was abundant. Indebted to Cosby for anointing him the colony's highest-ranking jurist, DeLancey had compliantly and repeatedly led the legal effort to have the *Journal*'s printer prosecuted, had imposed an onerous bail requirement, and had made biased comments in open court at the bail hearing about Zenger's likely guilt. Still, even if DeLancey was almost certain to deny Alexander's motion that he step aside from the trial, the request would likely call the public's attention to the chief justice's collusive relationship with the government's oppressive tendencies. It might also have served to cow DeLancey into behaving more judiciously in his rulings during the trial. But trying to embarrass the chief justice into being on his mettle was also to risk further antagonizing him, to the likely detriment of his client's case. And if, against all expectation, DeLancey should agree to recuse himself, how would that have helped Zenger? Cosby would surely replace him with someone certain to do his bidding alongside second justice Frederick Philipse, whose family's hostility to the Morrisites was no less than the DeLanceys'.

Instead, Alexander adopted a subtle variation of his earlier plan. Rather than an *ad hominem* attack on DeLancey's alleged bias against Zenger, he entered a pair of "exceptions" that challenged the right of both justices to hear the case—or any case, for that matter—on the ground that the commissions issued by the governor advancing them each one rank after Morris had been dismissed from the court were fatally flawed. Cosby's appointment decree stated that the two jurists were to serve only "during the pleasure" of the governor, meaning he could dismiss them whenever he chose if their rulings did not sufficiently accord with his wishes, whereas under long custom in England, judges were permitted to sit only "during good behavior," leaving them susceptible to impeachment by Parliament or summary removal by the crown or its ministry upon due consideration of misconduct charges. Cosby, furthermore, according to Alexander and Smith, had failed to win formal approval from his council before making the two judicial appointments, a violation of his—and every governor's—instructions from the Privy Council.

Alexander's objections may have been shrewder than they appeared. DeLancey seemed likely to brush aside the defense counsel's complaint about the legitimacy of his and Philipse's appointments as a mere diversionary tactic. But what if, in a suddenly conciliatory shift, the chief justice were to acknowledge the objections Alexander raised were valid? The alleged flaws in the appointment commissions were technical in nature and could have been easily remedied if Cosby elicited his council's tardy blessing of the two appointments and then issued revised commissions stating that the justices were to serve "during good behavior" in conformity with the English practice. Such a concession would have splendidly suited Alexander's real purpose, which was to insinuate that the existing wording of the justices' commissions, tying their tenure to the governor's pleasure, made them creatures of Cosby's arbitrary and at times despotic will and thus likely to rule in accord with his dictates. And had the wording of their commissions been altered, DeLancey and Philipse might even have proven thankful to Zenger's counsel for freeing them from the governor's yoke—or so Alexander might have hoped.

If so, the hope proved short-lived. As soon as defense counsel tried to file its motion challenging the justices' commissions, DeLancey seemed surprised and then riled by the innuendo behind it. A more seasoned jurist might have calculated that satisfying the defense's objections—which might be readily accomplished with Cosby's cooperation—could have strengthened their independence from the governor and likely prolonged their tenures. But DeLancey must have sensed that Cosby would not agree to any changed wording that served to diminish his control of the colony's judiciary. The chief justice urged Zenger's lawyers to consider carefully the meaning and consequences of their "exception"—meaning that it was, in effect, an expression of contempt for the legal standing of the court's two members and, by extension, the legitimacy of its very operation. Smith assured the bench that they had fully thought through the matter, indeed to the point where he would stake his life on the illegality of the judges' appointments. Faced with resolute adversaries, DeLancey said he would ponder the question overnight.

He may have devoted some of that evening to discussing the defense counsel's challenge with Cosby and his legal advisers, for when DeLancey appeared in court the next day, he took a drastic step far beyond what Alexander's pro forma motion justified. According to the *Brief Narrative* of the trial published by Zenger the following year, the chief justice rebuked defense counsel Smith with sharp, stunning language: "You thought to have gained a great deal of applause and popularity by opposing this court as you did the Court of Exchequer [created by Cosby within the Supreme Court to hear his suit against Van Dam]. But you have brought it to that point that either we must go from the bench, or you from the bar. Therefore we exclude you and Mr. Alexander from the bar." Then he handed the court clerk an order not only removing the two attorneys as Zenger's counsel but barring them from further law practice within the colony.

Since there were no more highly accomplished and widely esteemed practitioners in New York than Alexander and Smith, the chief justice's order seemed designed to crush Peter Zenger's chances of escaping conviction, longer imprisonment, and a fine probably ruinous to his occupation—and, of course, to his *Journal*. As Livingston Rutherford remarked in his account of the Zenger case, "This remarkable order of disbarment well illustrate[d] the intense and bitter partisanship which characterized the actions of the government."

There was, to be sure, one other New York lawyer supremely qualified to replace Alexander and Smith as Zenger's defense counsel—and it would have been poetic justice for him to have taken on the task, given that he had ignited the whole firestorm over Cosby's conduct in office and helped create the *Journal*. But Lewis Morris was in London just then, battling to unhorse the governor. So on April 18, Zenger asked DeLancey to appoint competent counsel to represent him at his trial, and the justice, mindful of the heavy blow he had inflicted on the defendant in peremptorily disbarring his skilled lawyers, obliged. Though still in his mid-twenties, John Chambers was one of only eight New York City lawyers licensed to practice before the Mayor's Court; his credentials may be further inferred from his later service on the Provincial Council and as a Supreme Court justice. But Chambers was known to be a satellite orbiting Cosby's coterie. Having earlier signed a public declaration supporting the governor's administration, he had been chosen to run on the Cosbyite slate for New York City's Common Council the previous September, only to be trounced 35 to 5 in the balloting. As consolation, he was appointed recorder of the council, roughly equivalent to the modern position of New York City corporation counsel, succeeding the reprobate Francis Harison. Chambers's abilities as an advocate, according to the history of colonial New York by William Smith's son, were dismissed by Zenger's lawyers as "more distinguished for a knack of haranguing than his erudition in the law." Alexander had no choice but to rely on Chambers's professional integrity and hope he would provide the printer more than a perfunctory defense.

Zenger's substitute counsel immediately pleaded his client not guilty, then showed that he would not be manipulated by Alexander and Smith's directives as he spurned their suggestion to ask the court to include in the record the bench's dismissal of the exceptions filed to the judges' commission as a possible basis for appealing the outcome of the trial. But Chambers had the presence to ask the court to delay the start of the trial so he might have enough time to prepare Zenger's defense and to request a "struck jury" to be impaneled for the trial, now rescheduled for early August when the court's next session opened. A "struck jury" meant that the clerk of the court would choose—presumably at random—forty-eight bona fide New York freeholders from the official registry, with the prosecution and defense each allowed to challenge twelve names; twelve others were then picked from the remaining twenty-four. Chambers's motion was intended to head off the often-used (and sometimes abused) expedient of letting the sheriff, a political appointee, choose whatever jurors he saw fit to have serve. The court reserved judgment on the struck jury request until the new term.

In the intervening spell of more than three months, with Zenger still imprisoned in City Hall, Alexander and Smith could do little more than fret and try to steer Chambers toward preparing a bold defense, arguing that the common law on seditious libel was by no means as rigid as Hawkins's treatise asserted and calling witnesses to substantiate the truth of the *Journal*'s attacks. Chambers's surviving notes from that pretrial period, however, reveal his intention of making a far narrower argument to the jury. The accusations and sarcasm printed in the *Journal*, he planned to claim, were too vague and indefinite in their subjects and objects to validate the prosecution's surmises about whom and what they really referred to and thus could hardly have incited civil unrest and disrespect for government authority as charged in Bradley's complaint. Even if it was common knowledge who the target was of the paper's assaults, Chambers's approach was "a technically adequate peg upon which a jury could safely find factual basis for an acquittal," in the view of Columbia law professor Eben Moglen. The success of such a strategy would depend on the selection of a receptive trial jury, but the defense could not count on that even though three grand juries had proven sympathetic to Zenger. At trial, the jurors were more likely to be intimidated by the chief justice, who might well direct them to deliver a "special verdict" and force them to pretend, if they were to ignore the bench's instruction and acquit Zenger, that they were ignorant of who the *Journal*'s target was—a fiction tantamount to perjury, as DeLancey had injudiciously forecast at Zenger's bail hearing.

Evidently convinced that Chambers lacked the skill and conviction to prevail at the trial, Alexander began casting about for a more experienced and confident lawyer to argue the case. Finding no takers among New York attorneys willing to risk the intemperate governor's wrath and contend with the grinding legal machinery at his disposal, he searched for practitioners beyond Cosby's jurisdiction who might be imported to handle the case. The largest and nearest pool of outside legal talent was in Philadelphia, then a larger city than New York, and Alexander thought he had his man in forty-two-year-old John Kinsey, son of a Friends minister and a prominent member of the Pennsylvania Assembly—he would later become speaker of that body and then chief justice of the commonwealth. Such was Alexander's own reputation that Kinsey replied to his inquiry by saying he was inclined to serve at the New Yorker's invitation "in any just cause in which I am at liberty." But he was unable to take on Zenger's case, he apologized, because "Diverse letters have lately passed between the governor [Cosby] and myself, which tho' they do not relate to this [Zenger] affair, are of such import that I cannot undertake against him without subjecting myself to be reflected upon as doing what is dishonorable."

There was another, equally prominent Philadelphia attorney, currently serving as speaker of the Pennsylvania legislature, but he was fifty-nine, suffering from gout, and an unpromising candidate to endure the travails of travel and the midsummer heat in a New York courtroom. Likely out of growing desperation that no replacement for Chambers could be found, Alexander drafted a pair of brief statements he hoped Zenger would be allowed to address to the court and thereby win sympathy from the jury that Chambers's performance would likely fail to stir. The first statement dealt with the very issue that Alexander had elected to set aside for fear it would exacerbate DeLancey's hostility if delivered by Zenger's defense lawyer, yet might give the chief justice pause if the printer himself spoke the words. The remarks Alexander prepared for Zenger to deliver before the trial got underway were an appeal to DeLancey that he "ought not to sit as judge on my trial" because he was one of "the honorable Council that ordered a warrant to consign me to jail and then was one of the managers at a conference with the General Assembly in which . . . Your Honor was pleased to insist that all my *Journals* were scandalous libels," and, furthermore, he was one of the Council members who ordered his papers "burned by the Common Hangman." In sum, Zenger was to say he believed the chief justice "has prejudged the case . . . and can't hear what I have to offer in my own defense with that impartiality that is necessary." The printer was to add that at his bail hearing, "Your Honor . . . was pleased to declare that if any jury acquitted me, they would go near being perjured."

The second statement Alexander drew up for Zenger, which he hoped DeLancey would allow him to deliver at the end of the trial, was more emotionally compelling. "You gentlemen of the jury know me, that I have lived very peaceably in this province," it would begin, "[and] that . . . I have followed my trade for the support of my family." Then he was to contend, regardless of what Chambers might have said or omitted saying in his behalf, that the government had not proven "the papers I am prosecuted for are either false, scandalous, fictitious or seditious, but have produced strong proof of the contrary." He would remind the jurors he had been in jail the better part of a year, during which his family might have starved but for the "charity of good honest people." He would tell them that as a youngster accompanied by his parents he had "fled from a country where tyranny, oppression, and arbitrary power had ruined almost all the people"—and "if for declaring the truth I am to suffer still greater punishment, let it be such . . . as will make an end of my life, for I can't bear the thought of having my family starving. . . . To punish a man, gentlemen, for telling the truth, no human law can exact because it opposes divine laws of God set forth in his Holy Scripture."

No corroborative evidence survives but even a dim imagination can picture Peter Zenger in his stifling cell that July, trying to memorize the words his faithful friend James Alexander wished him to recite before an audience that held his fate in their hands—and praying to his Maker for the strength to do so and for his ordeal to end, for the printer was a pious man.

VI

The *Journal* issued in the last week of July, on the eve of the trial, disclosed Alexander's grave worry that the chief justice, whose actions on and off the bench had seemed rife with the zealotry of a Torquemada in his quest to destroy Zenger and his press, would take the case out of the jury's hands. The paper that week ran an essay its editor hoped would attract attention among would-be jurors in New York County, instructing them that even if a judge directed a special verdict in a libel case, the jury was at liberty to disregard the instruction and decide for itself, rather than leaving it to the court's discretion, whether the defamatory words themselves—not just who printed them and whom they assailed—were criminal in nature and intended to incite a civil uprising. Unless a jury was impaneled with the fortitude to defy judicial orders in reaching its verdict, Zenger's chances would be slim at best.

Thus, how the two justices ruled on defense counsel John Chambers's motion for a struck jury, taken under advisement three months earlier, would be all-important as the Supreme Court convened for a pretrial hearing on July 29, six days before the case was to be argued. Happily for the printer, James DeLancey—for the moment, at any rate—overrode prior evidence of his prejudicial mindset as he ruled twice on the jury question, first on the method of selecting the panel and, soon after, on the honesty with which it had been carried out. The young chief justice, for all his evident entanglement with Cosby's regime, was too faithful to the ethical strictures of his calling to ignore the age-old right of British subjects to a legitimate jury trial by their peers. That meant Zenger was entitled to a jury chosen at random from the list of officially registered freeholders and not cherry-picked with ulterior design by lackeys of the government regime. Despite DeLancey's order to that effect, Sheriff John Symes and the clerk of the court, who served at the governor's behest, had other ideas.

The selection process began that same day about 5 P.M. with a number of Zenger's counselors and friends on hand to observe the manner in which the clerk of the court created the list of forty-eight would-be jurors. But instead of producing the Freeholders' Book—it contained fewer than a thousand eligible names, so it was common knowledge who everyone listed in it was—and publicly drawing out four dozen of them to "strike" the jury pool in the prescribed fashion, the clerk presented a prechosen list that Sheriff Symes claimed had been taken out of the Freeholders' registry. On examination, the list was quickly found to be a transparent fraud. Zenger's advocates recognized that many on the list were not certified freeholders. Others held offices and commissions bestowed on them by Cosby and retained "at the governor's pleasure." Still others were former city magistrates who had been voted out of office the previous September when the Morrisites took control and, as Zenger wrote a year later in his ghosted account of the event, "must be supposed to have [had] resentment against me for what I had printed concerning them." Finally, and most egregiously, the clerk's prearranged list included tradesmen in the governor's service (among them his baker, his tailor, his joiner, his shoemaker, and his candlemaker). Zenger further recounted that Attorney General Bradley, on hand to advance the prosecution's interest in the makeup of the jury, took careful note of the "few independent men who were on the list" with the intention of having them struck as objectionable to the crown.

The clerk of the court refused to accept Chambers's objection to the unsubtly skewed list, so Zenger's counsel appeared in court the next morning to protest the attempt by the governor's subservient law officers to rig the jury. The crudity of their action must have jarred even DeLancey, whose comparably overwrought action in disbarring Alexander and Smith may have inspired the sheriff and clerk to suppose Zenger was fair game for dismemberment under the color of law. The chief justice promptly ordered the sheriff's list of jurors to be scrapped for a new one drawn solely from the Freeholders' Book in the presence of both parties. The result was a dramatic improvement in the defendant's chances for a fair trial.

Only one potential juror, known to be a Morrisite, in the newly drawn pool of forty-eight names was challenged by the attorney general, although six of them were secretly among the 297 subscribers to the fund gathered to support Lewis Morris's trip to London. Of the final twelve chosen, half were believed to lean toward the Morrisite political faction, including foreman Thomas Hunt. As many as seven jurors may have been of Dutch ancestry and nursed a grudge against Cosby for his zealous effort to bring Van Dam, their leading Knickerbocker kinsman, to heel. And one of the selected jurors, Hermanus Rutgers, had served on the January 1734 grand jury that first heard the libel charges against Zenger and declined to indict him.

The composition of the trial jury pointed up the risk Cosby and his legal corps had faced in bringing the action to silence the *Journal* and the clamorous Morrisite faction behind it. New York County's citizenry was preponderantly and perennially cool toward the crown's chosen administrator of their colony, and Zenger's paper had provided a welcome outlet for their disdain, which, in fairness, would likely have been, as in the past, directed at any preening aristocrat sent from the mother country to reign over them. On the other hand, Cosby was the certified embodiment of the royal prerogative and held imperial sway over the colony's law enforcement and judicial personnel. His calculatedly chosen chief justice was about to wield the gavel at the Zenger trial and would seek to orchestrate its outcome by rulings on every motion and objection and his final instructions to the jury. The common law of the realm, moreover, was solidly on the government's side. In the 130 years since the Star Chamber ruling in *De Libellis Famosis*, only two notable trials on the charge of seditious libel had ended with the defendants escaping conviction. One was due to a technicality; the prosecution had misstated by a single day when the libel was published. The other case ended when most of the nation rose up in support of seven bishops who dared assert that James II had illegally set aside Parliament's statute barring Catholics and other non-Anglicans from public service—and then unceremoniously booted the monarch out of the kingdom.

Valiant Peter Zenger could count on no comparable happenstance. Even if a far more gifted lawyer were on hand to defend him, the anguished printer faced a brutal day in court when it finally convened on Monday, August 4, 1735, to consider the charges against him.

9

Philadelphia Lawyer

T HE TRIAL DATE fell on a Monday, normally press day for the *New-York Weekly Journal*, but out of necessity the paper had been printed the day before, even though it was the Sabbath. Zenger's shop was to be stripped of its labor force that Monday because, as he explained to his readers, "not only my journeymen but my two little sons are subpoenaed as evidences [witnesses] against me." The prosecutor planned to call them to the stand to verify that Zenger had supervised the printing of the two allegedly libelous numbers of his paper, and that, along with the identity of the person against whom the paper's defamatory words were directed would be all the evidence required to convict him, according to the prosecutor. But there was another, equally compelling reason to produce and distribute the *Journal* a day early: by circulating it on the eve of the trial, the Morrisites hoped to alert New York's citizenry to the signal event and attract a sizable audience to the courtroom sympathetic to the defendant's cause.

The plan succeeded. Long before the assigned hour, milling crowds pushed through the three graceful archways that formed the entrance to City Hall and flowed upstairs to camp outside the doors to the second-floor courtroom. It was not a large chamber—one prominent account of the trial, by Livingston Rutherford in 1904, describes it as "a little room" and says it was filled "to its utmost capacity" when the bailiff called the court to order. At a guess, the audience numbered between 250 and 300, and, to rely on Rutherford's words again, "Every class in the community was represented." The author, though related to Alexander and plainly out to memorialize his efforts in behalf of press freedom, was likely not far off the mark in writing:

> The majority of the people felt that they had assembled not merely to witness the trial . . . but that here the last fight was to be made against the administration which was so arbitrarily oppressive. If Zenger should be found guilty, surely their last hope of relief would be gone, they would be powerless to resist any hardship the governor might see fit to impose. On the other hand, Zenger's acquittal would mean a decided check to the evils from which they suffered, a vindication of their demands and of the principles for which they contended, and would give them courage to continue their efforts to rid themselves of their despicable governor.

The trial opened with the prosecutor, Attorney General Richard Bradley, reading the charges against the prisoner and the text of the passages that he asserted were false and seditious libels by which the governor had been "greatly and unjustly scandalized as a person who has no regard to law or justice." Cambridge-educated, Bradley was nearing the midpoint of his twenty-nine-year tenure as the colony's chief law enforcement officer. Detractors credited his longevity less to his skills than to his avid compliance with the wishes of whatever governor was in office at the moment. His foes in the Assembly and among the Morrisite populists whispered that the attorney general was prone to abuse his power by issuing "informations" with insufficient cause and then extracting payoffs to drop the prosecutions. Like much of the criticism against Cosby and his lieutenants, documented evidence of such venality was lacking or ambiguous.

After Bradley read out the charges for acts that he said had caused "great disturbance of the peace" throughout the province and required

Zenger's conviction, he recited the allegedly libelous passages. In doing so, he was mindful of the requirement under common law as set forth in Hawkins's treatise that a libel had to defame a specific individual or group, and so he took the liberty of telling the jurors parenthetically that each time the word "governor" was mentioned, it referred explicitly to the incumbent officeholder. Cosby's name, though, never appeared in the cited texts.

Defense counsel John Chambers then pleaded his client not guilty. It was at this point that Alexander had intended—until a few weeks prior—to have Zenger stand and ask permission to direct remarks to the bench, written for him by his then-disbarred lead counsel and asking the chief justice to step down as the presiding jurist because of his arrantly prejudicial conduct toward the printer over the previous year and a half. Alexander had decided, however, that it would be too risky a move, certain to be rejected by DeLancey and only further antagonize him. More to the point, Alexander had lately succeeded in obtaining another and far more promising weapon, shortly to be unsheathed, to compensate for Chambers's limitations as an advocate. And so the young lawyer proceeded to make his opening remarks, only partially guided by the line of argument that Alexander and Smith had urged on him.

Absent court reporters with mechanical means or as yet uninvented shorthand techniques to create a complete, literal transcript of the proceedings, we cannot be certain of the precise words uttered at the Zenger trial. But posterity has been given a likely close approximation, thanks to notes prepared both before and after the trial by the defense counsel and Alexander, who used them to create the *Brief Narrative* of the event that he wrote and Zenger published the following June. Thus, we know for a near certainty that in his opening statement for the defense, Chambers stressed two principal points. The first was that the attorney general had to prove not merely that Zenger printed the quoted words but that they were libelous because they were untruthfully defamatory. To do so, the government had to convince the jurors that the offending language was, as Hawkins and other authorities had posited in their distillation of common-law rulings, "false, malicious, seditious, and scandalous" as charged and thus a criminal act. Heeding Alexander's planned brief and noting that a libel had been repeatedly defined as "a malicious defamation," Chambers argued that "to defame is falsely and maliciously to take from a man his good name and character, or to endeavor to do so." Therefore, according to the accepted definition, every libel had to be false and malicious, and the prosecutor had to call witnesses to establish that the *Journal*'s words met that test—and not just that Zenger had printed them.

Chambers then turned to his other main argument—a hobbyhorse he wished to ride but Alexander thought was lame to begin with: the government's legal obligation in a "special verdict" proceeding to establish the identity not only of the printer but also of the defamed individual. "I conceive it is incumbent on Mr. Attorney [General]," Chambers's notes show he intended to declare, "fully to prove and make appear, not by innuendoes, probabilities and farfetched insinuations, but by plain, positive and convincing evidence [who the intended target of the libel was]. Otherwise, you will acquit the defendant."

At this point, just before the defense was about to yield the floor to the prosecution to present its case, a venerable figure unfamiliar to onlookers arose from the cluster of Zenger's advisers seated behind Chambers's table and traded places with the printer's young counselor. The pulse and drama of the trial were at once transformed. The newcomer identified himself to the bench as Andrew Hamilton, a certified member of the Pennsylvania bar, and thereby stirred a murmur of surprise and anticipation in the thronged hall, especially among those in the profession who knew his reputation as the most accomplished barrister in the American colonies.

For nearly two decades, he had been a dominant force in the politics of his colony, serving at that moment as speaker of the Pennsylvania Assembly, second in power only to the governor, against whom he was embroiled in conflict in his role as longtime attorney to the family and heirs of the province's proprietary founder, William Penn. Hamilton's array of gifts—masterful command of language, a feel for the theatricality of the courtroom, deft touches of wit and irony, and, as one contemporary admirer put it, "confidence which no terror could awe"—at once set him apart as an advocate whose like had never been seen before in the courts of New York.

In his search to replace the callow and unadventurous Chambers as Zenger's trial lawyer, James Alexander had little hoped to entice Hamilton to accept the engagement, given his many official commitments, busy court calendar, advanced age of fifty-nine, and reduced mobility due to gout. But Alexander had persisted in his quest. Though fifteen years his junior and lacking Hamilton's eloquence, he was a friend of the Philadelphian and had much in common with him beside their profession. Both were native Scots, brought great energy and ambition with them to America as immigrants in their early twenties, built flourishing legal practices linked to their political acumen, gathered extensive law libraries (often lending their books to each other)—and kept their origins and youthful run-ins with royal authority wreathed in mystery.

No reliable record of his ancestry or upbringing survives, but young Hamilton's family were likely people of at least modest means, for in 1690 at age fourteen, he entered St. Andrew's, Scotland's oldest university, earned his degree in three years, undertook postgraduate studies in Glasgow, and then attended the University of Edinburgh, apparently to begin learning law. While there, he was rumored to have been caught up, just as Alexander would be the following decade, in conspiratorial Jacobite activities devoted to expelling the imported Dutch-born monarch William III and restoring the Stuart dynasty, even if Catholic-leaning, as the legitimate rulers of the realm. Besides fearing his disclosure and capture as a subversive by government officers, Hamilton may also have been implicated in a murder or possibly a fatal duel, and upon reaching his majority, reportedly changed his name to Trent for a time, the better to help him flee to America with an untainted identity.

Andrew took shelter as an unobtrusive private tutor in Northampton County on Virginia's Eastern Shore, where he was soon befriended by a wealthy, childless couple named Foxcroft, who gave him lodgings in exchange for managing their large estate and introduced the well-spoken and learned young man into prominent social and political circles. Hamilton connected with a highly regarded attorney in whose office he resumed his legal studies and before long was admitted to practice. His patron Isaac Foxcroft died in 1702 and his widow Bridgett two years later. By her will, the bulk of the Foxcroft fortune passed to Hamilton, whom she called "my beloved friend," causing some local tongues to wag that the young heir was an unscrupulous fortune-seeker who had exercised undue influence over the couple and might have pursued an immoral relationship with Bridgett while both wife and widow. No evidence emerged that Mrs. Foxcroft's affection for Andrew was anything other than maternal and platonic; much of the talk was no doubt stirred by envy of his evident brains, charm, and luck. At any rate, by age twenty-eight he had achieved financial security that allowed him freedom from pandering to acquire dubious clients and suffering fools in the course of his law practice—an independence of character that cost him in popularity despite his abundant legal aptitude.

Moving north to Maryland, Hamilton quickly gained professional prominence, married a daughter of an influential Quaker family, who helped him gather a profitable new clientele, and bought a 600-acre estate near Chestertown, across Chesapeake Bay from Maryland's capital at Annapolis and its urban center, Baltimore. To burnish his legal credentials, he returned to England, joined a firm at Gray's Inn, one of the four leading societies for London barristers, and was called before (i.e., admitted to) the English bar, gaining invaluable connections before returning to America. His Quaker in-laws now opened doors for him in Philadelphia, where in 1713 he was contacted by the Penn family's agent to handle ongoing disputes over proprietary rights originally granted to them by the Duke of York before he took the throne as James II. Hamilton's relationship with the Penns greatly added to his standing in Philadelphia, where he bought a residence and set up an office even while gaining entrée to Lord Baltimore's family and entering elective politics as a member of Maryland's House of Delegates. There he soon made his mark by leading the effort to codify the colony's laws. In 1717, he transferred his activities entirely to Pennsylvania, where he argued frequently before the province's Supreme Court, was appointed attorney general of the colony, then elevated to membership on the Provincial Council, and became both recorder for the city of Philadelphia and master of the rolls (i.e., chief clerk) of the Supreme Court, to which he would no doubt have been appointed had he been willing to abandon his private practice. Elected to the Pennsylvania Assembly in 1726, he was two years later awarded the speakership, the ranking elective office in the province, which he still held when his friend James Alexander solicited him to defend Peter Zenger at his trial.

Hamilton's credentials for the job did not include a reputation as passionate defender of press freedom—quite the opposite. As a member of the governor's council, he had twice joined in that body's censure, prosecution, and punishment of Andrew Bradford, Philadelphia publisher of the *American Weekly Mercury*, for committing seditious libel. In 1722, Bradford was charged for printing an anonymous pamphlet and publishing in his paper an article taken from it that complained of "the dying credit of the province," interpreted as an impermissible slur on the government. Bradford got off with a stern warning never again to publish any commentary on the public affairs of Pennsylvania without the approval of the governor or his surrogate. Seven years later, the *Mercury* carried a letter signed "Brutus" urging readers "to throw off all subjection" to the king and his government, presumably including Pennsylvania's, which got Bradford jailed by order of the council, again with Hamilton's approval; the publisher was released only after his abject apology.

Still, advocates with Hamilton's virtuosity were quite up to arguing either side of a legal dispute, so landing him to try to win Zenger's acquittal was a considerable coup for Alexander. Hamilton's celebrated talents aside, he had the added advantage for the defense of being an out-of-towner, little known to the New York public at large, and thus was free of taint as a partisan in the province's increasingly heated political climate. He could command the stage—and the jurors' ears—at City Hall as no local practitioner might. From Hamilton's standpoint, it was worthwhile to make the effort in behalf of the poor printer, even if he was asked—and agreed—to do so without charging a fee. Hardly averse to celebrity, he often came to the aid of impecunious clients, and besides, he had been under assault for several years by the *Mercury*'s Bradford for siding with Penn descendants against the governors of Pennsylvania. The Zenger trial provided a ready-made arena for Hamilton to strike a blow at Bradford's father, William, whose *Gazette* was Cosby's slavish supporter.

Alexander's enlistment of such a luminary was kept secret until the moment of his court appearance in order both to unnerve the attorney general and deny other government officials, especially the chief justice, the opportunity to fashion a pretext for barring Hamilton from appearing in court as Zenger's cocounsel. Hamilton very well may not have been licensed to practice in New York, for example, and DeLancey would have been under no obligation to waive such a requirement as a professional courtesy. But because of Hamilton's reputation, Zenger later wrote in his account of the trial, "they did not dare to proceed to such an arbitrary length"—especially, he might have added, after having summarily denied the defendant James Alexander's valuable services.

In the brief period between Hamilton's clandestine arrival in New York and the opening of the trial, Zenger's dismissed counselors worked intensively with their stellar visitor to give him the benefit of all their research and suggested a tactical approach to the courtroom argument that Chambers was hesitant to adopt. Certainly, though, Chambers had to be told he was to yield the lead defense counsel role that had been imposed on him; otherwise, had the news been sprung on him in court that morning, he might have publicly objected and fed DeLancey a reason to deny the substitution. Probably to ensure Chambers's cooperation after receiving notice of his demotion, spare him his dignity, and keep him from revealing the identity of his high-caliber replacement to the Cosbyite camp, where his usual loyalties—but not his present ethical duty—lay, he was allowed to deliver the defense's opening statement. Most of it, anyway. Having done so without much helping or hindering his client, the novice yielded the floor to the virtuoso.

II

His eloquence at times sounds long-winded to modern ears, but from his first remarks that day Andrew Hamilton exhibited the vivacity, wit, and incandescent presence of a great Shakespearean actor. He thoroughly enthralled his City Hall audience.

He did not much care for the segment of Chambers's opening argument on the government's need to prove that Zenger had printed the alleged libels and that they were explicitly directed at Cosby; these were distractions and beside the essential point, which for the Philadelphian was the truth or falsity of the offending words. So, hewing to the strategy Alexander had laid out in his notes before his disbarment, Hamilton told the court at the outset that he could not properly deny "without doing violence to my own principles . . . the publication of a complaint which I think is the right of every free-born subject to make when the matters so published can be supported with truth. And therefore I'll save Mr. Attorney the trouble of examining witnesses to that point, and I do, for my client, confess that he both printed and published the two newspapers set forth in the information—and I hope in so doing he has committed no crime."

He did not bother to admit further that the defamatory passages were directed at the governor—that intention was as self-evident as the identity of their printer. But in conceding the two charges, which together were the only elements required for a jury to convict a libeler under a special verdict directive from the bench, Hamilton was taking a grave risk. The chief justice could have halted the proceedings then and there on the basis of the defense's admissions and in effect directed the jury to return a guilty verdict, leaving it to the court to say if the published words were libels. Why DeLancey failed to do so is puzzling. Perhaps the august advocate's unexpected first words momentarily stunned the chief justice's mind. Or perhaps, as Stanley Katz has written, "The answer may possibly lie in the fact that DeLancey was so inexperienced, and that the Governor was particularly vulnerable to the charge that his administration condoned abuses of the legal privileges of Englishmen." Behind this latter hypothesis lies the reasonable surmise that DeLancey preferred to let the proceeding run its course rather than summarily impose a special verdict directive at the very start and thus invite harsh criticism that he had trampled on the defendant's right to a fair jury trial.

Still more puzzling, though, is why the attorney general did not ask the court on the spot to stop the trial and instruct the jury to return a guilty verdict. Instead, Bradley told the bench that since he had no further need of the witnesses he had planned to call to attest to the charges Hamilton had just confessed to, he asked for and received permission to discharge them, including Zenger's journeyman printer and two sons. A curiously protracted silence followed, during which Bradley might well have been mulling whether to ask the court to stop the trial abruptly and order a special verdict. Or perhaps he was giving DeLancey a brief interlude to reflect on taking such a step without the prosecutor's calling for it. If so, the chief justice was disinclined, for as the lull persisted, he finally asked Bradley, "Well, Mr. Attorney, will you proceed?"

The prosecutor chose not to take the question as a spur for him to seize the initiative by requesting a special verdict then and there, but he left the jurors no room to doubt what their eventual finding had to be. "As Mr. Hamilton has confessed the printing and publishing of these libels, I think the jury must find a verdict for the king," said Bradley, "for supposing they were true, the law says that they are not the less libelous for that; nay indeed, the law says their being true is an aggravation of the crime." His cited source for this latter claim was the sixth section dealing with libels in Hawkins's 1716 treatise, stating that "since the greater the appearance there is of truth in any malicious invective, so much the more provoking it is." In other words, the more factual or accurate the disclosure of governmental foul play, the more likely it was to incite a disturbance of the peace by informed victims of official misconduct and cause them to demand a remedy for their grievances—a far worse transgression, according to the common law.

Hamilton pounced at once on Bradley's smug assumption. "Not so neither, Mr. Attorney," he broke in. "There are two [parts] to that bargain [Zenger's confession]. I hope it is not our bare printing and publishing a paper that will make it a libel. You will have something more to do before you make my client a libeler; for the words themselves must be libelous— that is false, malicious, and scandalous, or else we are not guilty."

Alerted that he had a fight on his hands, Bradley ignored the objection and presented the heart of his case—the rationale behind the criminality of seditious libel. Since government played a paramount role in protecting the lives, religion, and property of subjects of the realm, the attorney general averred, assiduous care had always been taken to prevent everything that might tend to scandalize magistrates and others concerned with the administration of the government, "especially the supreme magistrate [i.e., the king]." And since "it is a very great offense to speak evil or to revile those in authority over us," there had been "many instances of severe judgments and punishments inflicted on such as had attempted to bring the government into contempt" by publishing "false and scurrilous libels against it . . . to the great disturbance of the public peace." To support this narrative, Bradley invoked Hawkins's authoritative treatise with its multiple references to case law, going back to *Coke's Reports* on *De Libellis Famosis* in the Star Chamber era but citing more modern rulings as well. He read excerpts defining the nature of libel as a criminal act excoriated "by the law of God and man," citing a passage from Acts of the Apostles, XXIII:5, which read, "Then, said Paul, I wist not, brethren, that he was the high priest. For it is written, thou shalt not speak evil of the ruler of thy people." Gathering a head of steam, Bradley went on, "Mr. Zenger has offended in a most notorious and gross manner His Excellency our governor," and the Provincial Council and Assembly had likewise been scandalized by the *Journal*'s claim that the people's liberties and properties were now "precarious and that slavery is likely to be entailed on them and their posterity," that the Assembly "ought to despise the smiles and frowns of the governor," and that "the law is at an end" in the province since trials by jury were taken away whenever it pleased the governor. "If these assertions are not libels," Bradley said, "then I don't know what is. . . . [Accordingly] the governor has directed that this prosecution take place in order to put a stop to this scandalous and wicked practice."

With the attorney general's stern denunciation of Zenger's papers still ringing across the thronged gallery, Chambers opened the defense's argument by pointing out that Bradley's condemnation of the words cited in the *Journal* as libelous did not make them so, and the government, to win a conviction, had to prove its charge that the words were in fact false, malicious, and seditious. After that, no more was heard from the young attorney as Hamilton took the floor and held forth for the remainder of the trial.

"I agree with Mr. Attorney [General] that government is a sacred thing," he began, "but I differ very widely from him when he would insinuate that the just complaints of a number of men who suffer under a bad administration is libeling that administration." The case at hand was just such an instance, Hamilton said, contending that the complaints in Zenger's papers prompting the government to accuse him of criminal activity were evidently of wide concern in the province, to judge by "the extraordinary appearance of people of all conditions which I observe in court upon this occasion." As an aside to win favor with the audience, he added, "I have reason to think that those in the administration have by this prosecution something more in view, and that the people believe they have a good deal more at stake than I apprehended."

Hamilton then got down to business by launching an assault on the Star Chamber precedents that he said the prosecutor was relying on "to support his cause." Calling them "those dreadful judgments" that he hoped "had long ago [been] laid aside" because they had been issued by "the most dangerous court to the liberties of the people of England that ever was known in that kingdom," he expressed his ironic wish that Bradley, "knowing this, would not have attempted to set up a Star Chamber here nor to make their judgments a precedent for us." But just as the attorney general's fulminating that Zenger's paper had committed criminal acts did not prove it had in fact done so, neither could Hamilton's reviling the Star Chamber for handing down evilly arbitrary rulings alter the reality that its pronouncement on libel, especially when directed against the government, remained on the common-law books as the governing precedent. As an artful advocate, Hamilton was forced to steer around this immovable object, and the balance of his argument came down to urging the court and the jury to abandon past dogma for a more just and justifiable standard in determining the criminality of defamatory words directed at an abusive government. For it was well known, he said, that what was considered to be treason for a man to speak in those Star Chamber days "has since . . . been practiced as lawful." And there were numberless other instances of laws that applied once in one place being set aside as inapplicable to later times and other places.

For another thing, the attorney general erred, said Hamilton, in his understanding of seditious libel by citing cases that assumed all the obedience and regard properly due the king as supreme magistrate of the realm was likewise due to all his subordinates. But could anyone, he asked, with another ironic thrust, "give an instance that the mayor or the head of a [municipal] corporation put in a claim to the sacred rights of majesty?" Nor, he implied, could a governor, for another example, do likewise to render himself blameless. "Let us not . . . make bold to transfer that allegiance to a subject which we owe to the king only."

The trial then began turning into a debate as Bradley rebutted that even though the otherwise nefarious Star Chamber had been dissolved nearly a century earlier, its doctrine on seditious libel stood as valid and pertinent as ever. And since Hamilton had admitted Zenger published the papers in question, he kept on harping, without altering his tune by even a sharp or a flat, "nothing is plainer than that the words [cited in the information] are scandalous . . . tend to sedition, and to disquiet the minds of the people of this province. And if such papers are not libels, I think it may be said that there can be no such thing as libels." And as his adversary had done in seeking to circumvent the ongoing, if pernicious, authority of the Star Chamber's *De Libellis Famosis* ruling, so Bradley ignored the central question that Hamilton had posed—whether defamation of bad magistrates and abusive public officers should be reckoned a criminal act.

Hamilton countered by acknowledging that there were indeed such things as libels, but what his client was charged with did not constitute one. What Zenger was confessing to that morning was only that he had published the words that were discomforting to the government, not that the words were libelous, meaning criminally defamatory. The two men sparred briefly about whether Bradley had included the word "false" in describing to the court the texts Zenger had published, and the prosecutor, after saying he thought he had not omitted the word, replied that it was of no relevance because, either way, "it has been said already that it may be a libel notwithstanding it may be true."

To Hamilton, the distinction went to the heart of the argument he was about to unleash, and he turned on Bradley's dismissive air.

"In this I must differ with Mr. Attorney," he said, and again stressed that he had in actuality pleaded Zenger not guilty to the charge in the information, which explicitly asserted the printer had published "a certain false, malicious, seditious and scandalous libel. This word 'false' must have some meaning, or else how came it there? I hope Mr. Attorney will not say he put it there by chance. And I am of the opinion that his information would not be good [i.e., valid] without it." The falsity of the texts was the central issue, for the *Journal's* language could not be both false and demonstrably (or at least arguably) true. Hamilton wondered, rhetorically, whether "if the information had been [brought] for printing and publishing a certain *true* libel, would that be the same thing? Or could Mr. Attorney support such an information by any precedent in the English law?" The question was a flagrant feint, of course, since Hamilton could not, by the same token, claim any precedent for his implied defense that truthful defamation had never been—and could or should not be—legally held to be a crime. Before his opponent could answer, Hamilton rushed on, "No, the falsehood makes the scandal, and both make the libel." Indeed, to save the court time and the attorney general the trouble, he agreed that if Bradley could "prove the facts charged upon us to be false, I'll own them to be scandalous, seditious and a libel" and that his client was guilty as charged.

By arguing, in effect and without common-law precedent or statutory authority, that truth was a decisive defense in a libel action, especially one of seditious libel when the societal consequences could be broad indeed, even politically seismic, Hamilton was breaking new ground. He was proposing what a just law of libel should be, not what the contemporary legal consensus said it was. Alexander had faced the same encumbrance, his notes show, and the two men must have been aware, when they conferred in the days leading up to the trial, that they were flirting with alchemy in seizing on truth as the magic elixir to ward off criminal charges for defamatory criticism of the government. For the absence of legal precedent or statutory authority for their position was, on analysis, less problematic than their insistence that freedom of expression ought to be conditioned on speaking and writing only what is true. Such an argument, while tempting, apotheosized the concept of truth to a pristine and universally recognizable state of grace, as if it were objectively definable and possessed with mathematical certainty or irrefutable logic like Descartes' famous postulate *cogito, ergo sum,* on self-knowledge of human existence. "Hamilton did not appreciate," observed legal historian Leonard W. Levy, "that the truth is a mischievous, often an illusory, standard that often defies knowledge or understanding and cannot always be established by the rules of evidence . . . [and] that one man's truth is another man's falsehood or that political opinions, which notoriously differ, may not even be susceptible of proof."

Such fault-finding with Hamilton's grasp of semantics and the often squirmy, elusive nature of truth likely devalues his considerable intellect and worldliness. Hamilton might well have been hoping that Bradley had neither the quickness nor depth of mind to raise the point Levy makes about the unruliness of truth. But if Bradley had done so, Hamilton could have raised with equal force the very same objection to the words "false," "falsity," or "falsehood" that the attorney general's case arguably relied on. In doing so, however, Hamilton would have left himself vulnerable to an even more perilous counterthrust by the prosecution. For if falsity was as blurry and volatile a concept as truth— and therefore the government would have great difficulty in proving its charge that Zenger's defamatory passages were, first and foremost, false—then Hamilton could hardly seize on truth-telling as the immunizing panacea against prosecution for seditious libel. Worse still, a shrewder thinker than Bradley could have pointedly added that since both truth and falsity are far from absolute and finite notions but, rather, imprecise and susceptible to tortuous interpretation, the Star Chamber court had been fully justified in ruling out both as a determinant of whether a libel was sufficiently defamatory to be punishable; thus, true or false, it was a heinous crime to defame the government and thereby incite civil disorder.

But Bradley was a pedestrian advocate and missed the opportunity, resorting to cant instead. "We have nothing to prove," he said, because Zenger had confessed to printing the libels, "but if it was necessary—

and I think it is not—how can we prove a negative?" For him the point was that even "supposing all the words to be true, that will not help them [the defense]," and he cited the opinion of Chief Justice John Holt of the King's Bench in *Tutchin's Case*, rendered in 1704, almost a full century after the Star Chamber's severe codification of libel law. Claimants of abuses by royal officials, Holt wrote, had to be held to account for "it is very necessary for all governments that the people should have a good opinion of it [*sic*]."

Dodging Holt's pronouncement, Hamilton opted to dispute the prosecutor's claim that a charge could not be proven false, for it could indeed be, he said, if it were shown, for example, that the victim of an alleged murder was in fact still alive or that a supposedly stolen horse had never left its stable—or, he might have added, by an alibi that the accused was verifiably far from the scene when the crime occurred. Nevertheless, Hamilton offered, with mock magnanimity, to relieve Bradley of the chore of proving Zenger's defamations false by instead allowing the defense to summon witnesses "to prove those very papers that are called libels to be true."

The gambit at once drew DeLancey's intervention. "You cannot be admitted . . . to give the truth of a libel in evidence," the chief justice asserted. "A libel is not to be justified, for it is nevertheless a libel even if it is true."

But DeLancey had put his finger on the heart of Hamilton's case: that truth both justified and decriminalized the publication of defamatory language. "I am sorry the Court has so soon resolved upon that piece of law," the defense counsel retorted. "I expected first to have been heard to that point. I have not in all my reading met with an authority that says we cannot be admitted to give the truth in evidence for an information upon a libel"—meaning, without saying it in so many words, that truthful accusations were justly meant to be defamatory and alert the people to their government's abuses, but that did not transform the libel into a criminal act.

DeLancey would not acknowledge the distinction. "The law is clear," he said, "that you cannot justify a libel."

III

A ndrew Hamilton had not come to New York to be humbled by a judge barely half his own age. Persisting at that critical juncture, he granted the bench that a libel was always undeniably a libel to the extent that it was defamatory, even as a murder or assault and battery were undeniable acts that could not be pleaded as not guilty if the defendant in fact performed them. "Yet it will not be denied he may, and always is [allowed to] give the truth of the fact or any other matter in evidence, which goes to his acquittal—as in murder, he may prove it was in defense of his life, his house, etc., and in assault and battery, he may give in evidence that the other party struck first, and in both cases he will be acquitted."

The apposite rationale gave DeLancey pause. "I pray show that you can give the truth of a libel in evidence."

The opening set Hamilton's silver tongue in rapid motion. It was a stretch, though, for him to cite cases with outcomes that could clearly satisfy the chief justice's test. He began with the late-fourteenth-century prosecution of firebrand John of Northampton, charged with libel for writing a letter to a member of the king's Privy Council remarking that he supposed the royal judges of the realm "would do no great thing"— taken to mean an illegal act or ruling—on orders from the crown. The remark was deemed libelous for inclining the king to think worse of his judges for even suspecting he might order them to act illegally. The case was allowed to lapse without a conviction largely because there was neither truth nor falsity in the words, which were merely a hypothesis or opinion about an act that hadn't occurred and might never. By citing the case, Hamilton hoped to leave the inference that truth had won out because the words at issue were not shown to be false.

He came a bit closer to the mark by invoking the renowned 1688 *Case of the Seven Bishops*, who were charged with falsely derogating King James II in their published petition to him asking that they be relieved from his order, as head of the Church of England, to all clerics to read aloud to their congregants his royal decree dispensing with acts of Parliament that denied non-Anglicans the right to serve in the government or military. The prelates pleaded they had not libeled the monarch but only given their studied opinion, based on ample statutory citations, that the crown was exceeding its authority by setting aside duly enacted laws of the realm. The four judges hearing the case were evenly split on the question of whether the bishops' contention was true or false; the jury declined to convict the churchmen and heeded the defense counsel's argument that the issue was really a legal judgment over the extent of the royal prerogative, not a malicious assault on the king. Hamilton said he offered the case to show that "the falsity, malice, and sedition of the writing were all facts to be proven . . . [and] we are not the first to insist that to make a writing a libel, it must be false," for as Justice Powell had told the *Seven Bishops* jury, he found no falsehood in the clergymen's petition, so there was no libel. But neither had the truth of the petition been established as the exonerating factor, which was what DeLancey had asked Hamilton to show; all the case really illustrated was that the truth or falsehood of offending words might be indeterminable and thus not dispositive of whether the libel was a criminal act.

Hamilton thought he found more compelling support, finally, in an early-eighteenth-century proceeding—*Fuller's Case* of 1702, in which the defendant was charged with falsely and wickedly publishing a claim sworn by a certain Mr. Jones that (1) he was paid £5,000 by representatives of the king to ruin Fuller's reputation and (2) the king of France paid £180,000 in bribes to English officials, the latter being an allegation of treason on the recipients' part. The extreme provocation for the government's libel charge—reported gross acts of corruption by representatives of the crown—prompted Chief Justice Holt to ask Fuller, "Can you make it appear they [Jones's claims] are true?" Subpoenas would be issued by the court to bring in witnesses to the claim, Holt assured the defendant, because for him to have published "such things as you are charged with, it lies upon you to prove them true, at your peril. If you have any witnesses, I will hear them. How came you to write those books which are not true?" Notwithstanding that Fuller failed to produce evidence corroborating what he had published, Chief Justice Holt—whom

Hamilton lionized in passing as a great jurist—must have believed that defendants in seditious libel cases were entitled to prove their defamatory words true and thus void of criminality, or else why had Holt put the question to Fuller?

Alas, Hamilton was still stuck with Holt's contradictory opinion in *Tutchin's Case* two years after the Fuller matter was heard, in which the chief justice asserted that it was imperative for the peace and stability of the realm that the public hold a good opinion of the government, so even truthful defamations of its officials should not be left unpunished. With sinuous reasoning, Hamilton tried to turn *Tutchin's Case*, which he said "seems to be Mr. Attorney's chief authority," against the attorney general. For during his trial, defendant Tutchin was asked by the king's counsel to state whether the reports in his papers of misconduct by crown officers were true (and thus presumably mitigated the charges), but "as he never pretended that they were true," Hamilton said, trying to put a positive spin on Tutchin's publication of unsubstantiated accusations, "the chief justice was not to say so"—that is, had no cause to opine on the issue of whether truth might justify publishing defamatory material.

Hamilton's sleight of hand did not altogether hide that he was grasping at a straw as he asked the court's permission, under what he characterized as Holt's rule, to bring forth witnesses attesting to the truth of Zenger's cited papers. DeLancey was sufficiently respectful of the defense counsel's assurance, if not his dubious citations, to ask to see the law books Hamilton had with him and examine their references to the precedent cases he had raised. According to Zenger's account of the trial, the chief justice studied the texts for "a considerable time."

This interlude invites a moment's reflection on what might have transpired if Hamilton had at this point won over DeLancey and been allowed to parade witnesses who presumably could establish the truthfulness of William Cosby's maladministration of New York as charged by the *Journal*. Whom did the Philadelphian have at his disposal willing and able to risk the governor's fury by testifying against his allegedly despotic and illicit conduct? Were any of Cosby's denounced actions, with the exception of his high-handed dealings with the Provincial Council—such as failing to summon hostile members like Alexander and Van

Dam to its meetings and sitting in on and sometimes voting during its legislative deliberations—technically and provably illegal? Or was Cosby just another royal magistrate exercising his rightful power in ways that struck those he did not favor as wanton and arbitrary? Was Hamilton physically up to the ordeal, if allowed, of examining witnesses over a protracted proceeding, one that would also have allowed the attorney general the chance to discredit them all on close cross-examination? Would Cosby permit such a spectacle to unfold and in the process find himself subjected to further endless aspersions on his character? And suppose the Philadelphian dared to subpoena the governor and subject him to the indignity of testifying on the accuracy of the *Journal*'s charges, in effect making his own conduct, not Zenger's, the subject of the trial? The dauntless Hamilton might well have tried to do so, given his running disputes with the governors of Pennsylvania. And if Cosby had refused the subpoena in the unlikely event the court issued it, he would have been in contempt of the judicial system that he himself ruled over.

None of these diverting possibilities, however, would come to pass. After weighing Hamilton's cited cases, the chief justice asked the prosecutor what he had to say about the defense counsel's contentions. Bradley declined to address any of the particulars his opponent had introduced and mulishly insisted, "The law in my opinion is very clear—they [the defense] cannot be admitted to justify a libel, for by the authorities I have already read to the court, it is not the less a libel because it is true. . . . The thing seems to be very plain."

DeLancey, mindful that his courtroom might at once erupt into a circus of discord and recrimination, nevertheless agreed with the attorney general. "The Court is of opinion you ought not to be permitted to prove the facts in the papers," he said and quoted Hawkins anew: "It is far from being a justification of a libel that the contents thereof are true . . . since the greater appearance there is of truth in any malicious invective, so much the more provoking it is." This colloquy followed:

> *Hamilton:* These are Star Chamber cases, and I was in hope that practice had been dead with the court.
>
> *DeLancey:* Mr. Hamilton, the court has delivered their opin-

ion. And we expect you will use us with good manners.
You are not to be permitted to argue against the opinion
of the court.

Hamilton: With submission, I have seen the practice in very
great courts and never heard it deemed unmannerly to—

DeLancey: After the court have declared their opinion, it is
not good manners to insist upon a point in which you are
overruled.

Hamilton: I will say no more at this time. The court, I see,
is against us on this point . . . I hope I may be allowed
to say—

DeLancey: Use the court with good manners, and you will
be allowed all the liberty you can reasonably desire.

"I thank your honor," Hamilton replied, and the next instant he all
but invited a contempt-of-court charge as he turned away from the bench
toward the jurors' gallery, where he directed virtually all his remarks for
the remainder of the proceeding. It was to be a trial in which not a single
witness would be called and at the end of which, Hamilton could now
be certain, the chief justice would direct the jurors to return a special verdict, leaving it to the bench to decide Zenger's fate, and expect them to
obey him. Hamilton hoped not; his next words were: "Then, gentlemen
of the jury, it is to you we must now appeal for witnesses to the truth of
the facts we have offered and are denied the liberty to prove."

DeLancey's gavel might have come crashing down then and there,
dismissing Hamilton and leaving neophyte John Chambers to flounder
amid the detritus of Zenger's defense.

IV

For the second time, the chief justice drew back from wielding the
maximum judicial power at his disposal and allowed the imposing
defense counsel to display defiance of the bench. DeLancey, after all,
would have the last word before the jury retired to deliberate.

To embolden the jurors not to quake before the court's final directives, Hamilton began by saying to them, "Let it not seem strange that I apply myself to you in this manner [that] I am warranted to do both by law and reason." The law, he said, supposed the jurors "to have been drawn out of the neighborhood where the [crime] is alleged to be committed . . . because you are supposed to have the best knowledge of the fact that is to be tried." And if they found against his client, they had to take it upon themselves to say that "the papers referred to in the information . . . are false, scandalous and seditious, but of this I can have no apprehension." The jurors were citizens of New York and knew "the facts that we offered to prove were not committed in a corner—they are notoriously known to be true, and therefore in your justice lies our safety."

As common-law precedent for the jury's ultimate power to decide a defendant's guilt or innocence as it and not the bench determined, Hamilton relied on *Bushel's Case.* In that proceeding, a 1670 English jury disregarded the court's instruction to find William Penn guilty for holding a Quaker prayer meeting in London of 300 worshipers who the government claimed were "unlawfully and tumultuously assembled, to the disturbance of the peace." The jurymen were fined for their defiance, but juror Bushel refused to pay the fine, was jailed, appealed his conviction, and was acquitted by Chief Justice John Vaughan of the Court of Common Pleas. His words, Hamilton told the Zenger jury sixty-five years later, remained the people's safeguard against courts dictating verdicts to juries. If a judge, from the evidence as he interpreted it, shall first resolve what law is to apply to the facts—rather than letting the jury determine the facts as variously testified to and whether the law applied to them—and order the jurymen to find accordingly or be punished themselves, Vaughan wrote, "what either necessary or convenient use can be fancied of juries, or to continue trials by them at all?"

Hamilton's message to the jury was clear; like the heroic Bushel, they should decide on Zenger's guilt or innocence of their own accord and not leave the verdict to the court. He conveniently omitted reference to the ruling thirteen years later by Chief Justice George Jeffreys, the notoriously pro-Stuart "Hanging Judge," who held in the seditious libel case against Algernon Sidney, a brave foe of Charles II's despotic suppressions, that it was the bench's sworn duty to define what the law was in such cases and, in view of the sufficiently proven facts, to order the jury to find accordingly. (And it did; R.I.P., Algernon Sidney.)

To buttress his case, Hamilton now baited the prosecutor into spelling out for the jury just what the common law and its commentators said the crime of seditious libel consisted of. When Bradley obliged by quoting the words in Hawkins's reputedly definitive treatise, Hamilton chided them for vagueness and asked, "By what certain standard rule have the books laid down" to determine whether offending passages were "malicious" or "defamatory," whether they really tended to incite a breach of the peace and were "a sufficient ground to provoke a man, his family, or friends to acts of revenge," especially when the cited words were ironic or scoffing?

In the debate that followed between the bench and the two advocates as to whether scornful or satirical words could be considered scandalous and really cause a breach of the peace, DeLancey remarked that it was up to "those who are to judge the words" to determine if they were scandalous. At once Hamilton shot back, "I am glad to find the court of this opinion. Then it follows that [these] twelve men [the jury] must understand the words in the information to be scandalous—that is to say false." But DeLancey cut him off: "No, Mr. Hamilton—the jury may find that Zenger printed and published those papers and leave it to the court to judge whether they are libelous. You know this is very common—it is in the nature of a special verdict, where the jury leave the matter of law to the court." Finally, the chief justice had explicitly divulged his intention to resort to a special verdict directive, widely detested among colonists as an authoritarian practice aimed at shrinking the role and power of juries.

Hamilton promptly challenged this assertion of judicial power. The jury, he argued, might indeed defer to the bench in the matter of stating the law, "but I do likewise know they may do otherwise. I know they have the right beyond all dispute to determine both the law and the fact, and where they do not doubt the law, they ought to [be free to] do so." In an allusion to *Bushel's Case* and Chief Justice Vaughan's words on appeal freeing the defendant, Hamilton insisted that to leave it to the bench to determine if the words cited in the charge against Zenger were libelous or not "in effect renders juries useless."

Far from bending under the weight of his task and his years, the indefatigable defense counsel moved on to "examine the inconsistencies that must inevitably arise from the doctrines Mr. Attorney has laid down." This required him first and foremost to eviscerate *De Libellis Famosis*, acknowledged as the leading case on libel and the one to which almost all others deferred. It was true, Hamilton said, that "in times past it was a crime to speak truth, and in that terrible Star Chamber, many worthy and brave men suffered for so doing." Happily, though, he added, that 1605 ruling as understood by the attorney general and chief justice "is not law at this day." He agreed it was "base and unworthy to scandalize any man. . . . But when a ruler of a people brings his personal failings, but much worse his vices, into his administration, and the people find themselves affected by them, either in their liberties or properties, that will alter the case mightily." For "all the high things that are said in favor of rulers and of dignities and upon the side of power will not be able to stop people's mouths when they feel themselves oppressed—I mean in a free government."

Hamilton grew still more daring now, yet was careful to avoid exposing himself to charges of preaching treason. "All men agree we are governed by the best of kings," he said, but despite the duty and reverence the attorney general said were due to men in authority, "they are not exempt from observing the rules of common justice . . . and the laws of our Mother Country know no exception." Then, without citing Cosby by name, he took unmistakable aim at him to focus the jury on what he insisted the trial was all about. "Men in power are harder to come at for wrongs they do . . . especially a governor in the plantations, where they insist upon an exception from answering complaints of any kind." The only recourse open to the public in such cases was some form of civil disobedience, justifiable because the people were "not obliged by any law to support a governor who goes about to destroy a province or colony or their privileges, which by His Majesty he was appointed and by law is bound, to protect and encourage." Indeed, he hammered home the point:

It is natural, it is a privilege, I will go further, it is a right which all freemen claim and are entitled to . . . when they are hurt—they have a right publicly to remonstrate the abuses of power in the strongest terms . . . to put their neighbors upon their guard against the craft or even violence of men in authority, and to assert with courage the sense they have of the blessings of liberty.

And since that was precisely what Peter Zenger was doing with his *Journal*, the jury's duty was clear, Hamilton indicated, for "of what use is this mighty privilege if every man that suffers [at the hands of an abusive governor] must remain silent [and] if a man must be taken up as a libeler for telling his sufferings to his neighbor?"

As if, near the end of his soaring recitation, he wished to throw the prosecutor a bone while really doubling down on his radical argument against Bradley's dogmatic stand, Hamilton conceded that lawful restraints upon the natural right of subjects to complain or remonstrate against their rulers "can only extend to what is false. For as it is truth alone that can excuse or justify any man for complaining of a bad administration, I as frankly agree that nothing ought to excuse a man who raises a false charge or accusation. . . . Truth ought to govern the whole affair of libels." This, of course, was his way of saying that the demonic common-law precept at the core of seditious libel—that truthful content did not serve to decriminalize it—should be overturned, starting with the case at hand. His words had a sonorous, seductive tenor, to be sure, but the malleable and evanescent nature of "truth" as a beatific attainment made it a threadbare fabric for the glittering garment with which Hamilton's bravura rhetoric sought to adorn his central premise. Luckily, his opponent failed to point out this shortcoming to the jury by way of justifying the Star Chamber doctrine that whatever the degree of truth or falsity in defamatory expression could and should not factor into its criminality. Hamilton did not explain, moreover, and apparently felt he had no need to, how the public came by its "natural right" to complain about abusive rulers, for by now he was making a political, not a legal, argument against the remnants of injustice still clinging to the common-law definition of seditious libel.

In passing, he again tweaked the attorney general by alluding—more than a touch fancifully—to what he called a growing diversity of views among judges and juries about what a libel was. Hamilton suggested that this alleged trend had been paralleled by evolving perceptions in the area of religion and faith. Views could now be expressed with impunity, he noted, that two centuries before might have caused the speaker to be burned at the stake. Attorney General Bradley, he said, was fortunately not pressing prosecutions for unorthodox religious beliefs, for "it is pretty clear that in New York a man may make very free with his God—but he must take special care with what he says about his governor."

While he was at it, Hamilton rebutted the prosecutor's earlier invocation of the Bible to show that it was against God's law for the people to defame their rulers. To the contrary, the defense counsel cited Isaiah IX:16, which says, "The leaders of the people cause them to err, and they that are led by them are destroyed." If a New Yorker dared to recite this passage, Hamilton mocked, Bradley would likely twist the words to suit his purpose, namely, to silence a just critic of the government when its officials turned abusive. The courtroom audience's receptivity to such displays of Hamilton's oratorical élan may be inferred from a comment by Cadwallader Colden (who likely was present) on this biblical allusion: "Mr. Hamilton here took great liberty, but the applause with which it was received by the numerous auditors and the approbation they gave it by their countenances made the Court think proper to pass it over without notice."

Despite the draining summer heat and having been on his feet for many hours—we have no record of just how long the day's proceedings lasted or whether court recessed at any point—the veteran barrister ascended to the peak of jurisprudential eloquence in his peroration. Praising the defendant's fortitude in *Bushel's Case* and his fellow jurors' defiance of the judge's instructions, Hamilton urged Zenger's jurors to likewise vote their consciences: "As the verdict, whatever it be, will be yours, you ought to refer no part of your duty to the discretion of other persons"—he of course meant DeLancey and the second justice, Frederick Philipse, who had silently deferred to the chief justice throughout the trial and was certain not to dissent from his directive to the jury. "If you should be of opinion that there is no falsehood in Mr. Zenger's papers," Hamilton declared, "you will, nay—pardon me for the expression—ought to say no . . . it is your right to do so, and there is much depending on your resolution as well as upon your integrity." Then came this grand metaphor:

> Power may justly be compared to a great river. While kept within its due bounds, [it] is both beautiful and useful; but when it overflows its banks, it is then too impetuous to be stemmed; it beats down all before it and brings destruction and devastation wherever it comes. If then this is the nature of power, let us at least do our duty and, like wise men who value freedom, use our utmost care to support liberty, the only bulwark against lawless power, which in all ages has sacrificed to its wild lust and boundless ambition the blood of the best men that ever lived.

After thanking God that he lived under a government "where liberty is well understood and freely enjoyed," he added wistfully that experience had shown how government authority can go wrong. And so "I cannot but think it mine and every honest man's duty that—while we pay all due obedience to men in power—we ought at the same time to be on our guard against power wherever we apprehend that it may affect ourselves and our fellow subjects." He paused at this point to add an affecting personal note. "You see I labor under the weight of many years, and am broke down with many infirmities of body. Yet old and weak as I am, I should think it my duty, if required, to go to the utmost part of the land where my service could be of any use in quenching the flame of prosecutions . . . to deprive a people of the right of remonstrating—and complaining, too—of the arbitrary attempts of men in power." Finally came this exhortation:

> The question before the court and you gentlemen of the jury is not of small or private concern. It is not the cause of a poor printer nor of New York alone, which you are now trying. No! It may in its conse-quence affect every freeman that lives under a British government on

the main of America. It is the best cause. It is the cause of liberty, and I make no doubt but your upright conduct this day will not only entitle you to the love and esteem of your fellow citizens, but every man who prefers freedom to a life of slavery will bless and honor you as men who have baffled the attempt of tyranny and who, by an impartial and uncorrupt verdict, have laid a noble foundation for securing to ourselves, our posterity, and our neighbors that to which nature and the laws of our country have given us a right—the liberty—of exposing and opposing arbitrary power in these parts of the world by speaking and writing truth.

While some historians and legal commentators have taken issue with parts of his courtroom performance—in particular, for straining to make the shoe fit in a number of his cited case references—Andrew Hamilton's words that day, extolling the freedom to protest by voice or pen the misconduct of government, are regarded by nearly universal consensus of those familiar with them as among the most exhilarating in the annals of American politics and jurisprudence.

Overwhelmed by this torrent of rousing verbiage, the stolid prosecutor chose to close briefly by damning his opponent with faint praise and an ill-concealed hint of envy. Hamilton had gone out of his way, Richard Bradley told the jurors, to make his listeners "very merry." But he insisted nothing the defense counsel had said and none of the cases he had cited had much to do with the case before them. Declining to rebut any of Hamilton's arguments, the attorney general stuck to his guns; there could be "no doubt" that the papers Zenger had confessed to printing were scandalous and reflected highly unfavorably on His Excellency, the governor. According to the brief paraphrase in Zenger's memoir of the trial, Bradley likely omitted the word "false" from his final remarks on the defamatory nature of the *Journal*'s words. If so, it was in acknowledgment of how tellingly Hamilton had riddled the government's unwillingness and inability to substantiate that allegation. He had "no doubt," Bradley wound up, that the jury would find the defendant guilty "and would refer to the court for their direction"—a final slap at Hamilton for citing *Bushel's Case* and the arrant disregard by its jurors for the sanctity of the bench.

DeLancey was acutely aware of the defense counsel's blatant appeal to the jury throughout his remarks to make up its mind independently of the court's strictures. Yet he had not cut Hamilton short, indeed had given him wide latitude and endless time to say his piece, even tolerating his repeated insistence that the truthfulness of defamatory language ought to insulate it from criminal charges despite the youthful chief justice's equally vehement rulings that the law said otherwise. In the end, though, DeLancey could not restrain his pique. "The great pains Mr. Hamilton has taken to show how little regard juries are to pay to the opinion of the judges," he told the jurors, "is done no doubt with a design that you should take but very little notice of what I may say on this occasion." And then he gave them a short, highly ambiguous instruction that seemed both to dismiss and concede Hamilton's point.

DeLancey began by claiming that "the facts or words in the information are confessed," allowing the inference that Zenger had admitted that "the facts or words" cited in the prosecutor's complaint were, as charged, "false, scandalous, malicious, and seditious." But Hamilton had emphatically stated that his client was *not* confessing he had libeled— only that he had printed the cited issues of the *Journal*. DeLancey, perhaps more wily than Hamilton gave him credit for, glossed over the distinction. Given Zenger's confession, the chief justice continued, "the only thing that can come in question before you is whether the words as set forth in the information make a libel." That was semiclarifying yet semiconfusing, since it left open whether Zenger had or had not confessed to publishing texts containing classifiable libels. "And that is a matter of law, no doubt," DeLancey said, "which you may leave to the court." Why "*may* leave" to the court instead of "must" or "are required to" or "I am instructing you to"? Was it a slip of the tongue or a subtle bow to Hamilton's harangue that juries would be without purpose if judges could bully them into surrendering their precious right to determine a defendant's guilt or innocence? As if fearing the jurymen were inclined to heed the ardent defense advocate's plea to flex their collective backbone, DeLancey wound up by reminding them of "the words of a learned, upright judge," Chief Justice Holt, in *Tutchin's Case*: If malcontents "should not be called to account for possessing the people with an ill opinion of the government, no government can subsist, for it is very necessary for all governments that the people should have a good opinion of it."

No judge, no ruler, no philosopher or savant had ever offered a more brutally candid instruction on how tyranny sustains its taloned grip on power. Did Peter Zenger's jurors see this insidious rationale for what it was? If so, would they dare embrace the freedom of the printer and his backers to rouse—justly or unjustly, truly or falsely—an ill opinion of their government without suffering for it at the hands of the king's men? The royal authorities, invoking the common law of the realm, denied the existence of any such liberty, which Andrew Hamilton claimed was the people's "natural right." Would twelve good men of New York City agree with him and declare that bad laws ought to be abandoned and abusive governments upbraided? Or would Peter Zenger, on the afternoon of August 4, 1735, rue the day twenty-five years earlier when he had come to America for a better, freer life?

10

Indelible Ink

THE EVENING THAT followed the long day's trial was the last in the nearly nine months Peter Zenger spent behind bars. The stayover prevented his attendance at the celebratory dinner for forty guests at the Black Horse Tavern, a Morrisite hangout, in honor of Andrew Hamilton. The jury had tarried a short time—one report said its deliberation lasted just ten minutes—before returning. Foreman Thomas Hunt told the clerk of the court that the jurors had found the defendant not guilty of publishing libels as charged, "upon which there were three huzzahs in the hall, which was crowded with people," Zenger later recounted, "and the next day I was discharged from my imprisonment."

He did not say whether he was among the well-wishers who saw Hamilton off on his return shipboard trip to Philadelphia. His great triumph had been to transform the trial from an assessment of the printer's guilt into, in effect, a condemnation of the governor for alleged abuses of royal power—a verdict the adroit attorney had won without calling a single witness to corroborate the defamatory words Zenger's paper had printed. But a jury of New Yorkers believed those words, and the city, paying tribute with salvos of cannon fire from vessels in the harbor—none of them, presumably, flying the royal ensign—bid a grateful farewell to the brilliant barrister for inspiring its blatant rebuke to His Excellency William Cosby.

Neither the *New-York Gazette*, the governor's house organ, nor other colonial papers—not those in Boston or Ben Franklin's and Andrew Bradford's in Philadelphia—carried news of the event, and Zenger's own sheet ran no account of it the following week. There was only a modest note from the unshackled proprietor that read, "The printer, having got his liberty again, designs God willing to finish and publish the charter of the City of New York next week," but no fortissimo exulting about justice prevailing or his ongoing intention to hold aloft the free press as the torch of liberty. The *Journal* confined itself to a brief account of the trial in the following week's edition.

From the nearly complete absence of reportage elsewhere, Zenger's victory might have been taken for a strictly local phenomenon, reflecting the bumptious nature of New Yorkers and their chronic insubordination toward their rulers. Even their joyful outburst over the trial verdict grew quickly muted, perhaps out of fear the impulsive Cosby might react with draconian measures like declaring martial law, arresting random Morrisites as insurrectionists, or bringing fresh charges against Zenger if his paper resumed hectoring the governor. But Cosby, however poor a model of rectitude, was no fool and likely mindful that the resident hostility toward him might erupt in violent resistance if he provoked it further.

After a six-week lull of caution on both sides, the people's lingering, if low-key exultation over the outcome of the Zenger imbroglio was manifested at a September 16 session of the New York City Common Council presided over by Mayor Paul Richards, who had been a member of the first grand jury of the three that declined to indict the *Journal*'s publisher. That day the city fathers voted to present Andrew Hamilton "the freedom of this Corporation," certifying him as an honorary citizen of New York, and two weeks later issued a decree of gratitude to the Philadelphian for "the remarkable service done to the inhabitants of this city . . . [by] his learned and generous defense of the rights of mankind and the liberty of the press, in the case of John Peter Zenger, which he cheerfully undertook under great indisposition of body and generously performed, refusing any fee or reward." As a tangible token of appreciation, some of the councilmen and other gentlemen of the community joined to purchase an oval, five-and-a-half-ounce gold box, three inches long by two inches wide and three-quarters of an inch deep, engraved with the city's arms. When Alderman Stephen Bayard traveled to Philadelphia to present the gift, its lid was inscribed with a Latin motto, translated as "Though the laws are sunk and liberty trembles at the deed, yet shall they rise again." The underside of the lid bore a second incised tribute: "Gained not by money but virtue."

Hamilton's performance has been celebrated ever since by the American bar not for its deft untangling of the thorny legal thicket that confronted him and his client but as a paradigm of the noblest aspirations of his calling; he had demonstrated that, as legal scholar Eben Moglen has written, "lawyering was not merely a trade—the virtue of lawyers was the pursuit of justice."

II

In the immediate wake of the Zenger verdict, there was no apparent shift in New York's political power structure. While the Morrisites and their anti-Cosbyite allies dominated the city government, the governor still held sway over the Provincial Council and the colony's law enforcement machinery, even if his control of the judiciary had been defied by the Zenger jury, and had kept the Assembly in check by denying the people a new election of its membership. For all Lewis Morris's feverish efforts in London to have the governor's conduct censured, there was no sign he was succeeding or that Cosby's standing in official circles was shaky. Quite the opposite, in fact. In August, soon after the Zenger verdict—not learned of in London, of course, for several months—the Board of Trade approved Cosby's request to remove James Alexander and Rip Van Dam from his council and sent it on to the crown's Privy Council for confirmation. The military high command, moreover, advanced the governor's army rank from colonel to brigadier general and made him a vice admiral for good measure, emblemizing his authority over all the armed forces garrisoned in the two colonies over which he exercised civil rule.

By mid-autumn, though, the governor's fortunes had turned. On November 6, the New York Assembly took note of Cosby's reported intention to rule on the Oblong suit, initiated by scheming Councilman Francis Harison to strip the consortium of Morrisite leaders of their 50,000-acre grant along the New York-Connecticut boundary and hand it to a group of upper-crust British speculators. The dispute had been stalled since early in the year in the juryless Court of Chancery, where the governor, presiding as the sole judge in his ex-officio role as chancellor, had hesitated to deal a heavy-handed blow to his political enemies and likely awaited further guidance from British authorities on the legality of the crown's conflicting—and irregular—Oblong grant to the investors Harison had inveigled into his vengeful plot. But by the fall of 1735, Harison had fled from the colony, reportedly back to Britain to escape creditors, court fines, and a sordid reputation as Cosby's bagman. Cosby was likely eager now to rid himself of the irksome problem and pay back the Morrisites for humiliating him at the Zenger trial—and how better than by vacating their title to the Oblong tract and handing it to titled Englishmen for a hefty fee. Before he got around to it, the New York Assembly caught wind of Cosby's pending Oblong decision. With their historic antipathy to royal tribunals that sat without juries in equity matters and could strip colonists of their land titles as the governor dictated, the colonial lawmakers resolved that "a Court of Chancery ... in the hands or under the exercise of a Governor without consent of [the] General Assembly, is contrary to law, unwarrantable, and of dangerous consequence to the liberties and properties of the People." Likely sensing that he would be stirring up a hornet's nest similar to his own never-resolved suit against Van Dam, Cosby took no further action on the Oblong matter.

Twenty days later in London, the Privy Council dealt the governor another embarrassing rebuke. For most of his year-long campaign in London to gain the attention of government authorities with his laundry list of complaints against Cosby, Lewis Morris had been snubbed. But it was not in his proud nature to go away quietly. In raising his charges of misconduct against Cosby, Morris failed for the most part to provide hard supporting evidence or official endorsement of his efforts from the Assembly. But he mounted a more substantive case arguing that the governor had stripped him of the chief justiceship solely because he had ruled against Cosby in the Van Dam suit. Morris's petition to have his firing reversed finally prompted the Privy Council to instruct Cosby to reply to the accusation. Furious over the indignity of having to answer the insolent Morris, the governor overplayed his hand. According to a November 8 letter James Alexander received from a London correspondent with access to high crown circles, "the governor's spleen, pique, and prejudice were so notoriously seen through the whole charge [his rebuttal to Morris] there was no supporting it."

Morris was permitted to attend and address the Privy Council, whose members included a number of outright Cosby backers, among them Lord Halifax, his father-in-law, and the Duke of Newcastle, his wife's first cousin. Nothing daunted, Morris soon got into a row with Newcastle by charging that the Board of Trade, over which the duke presided, had acted without precedence in instructing the financially needy Cosby to help himself to half of Van Dam's salary for his service as acting governor. After a number of sessions at which the matter was aired, Newcastle absented himself from the decisive meeting, an admission he had given up trying to excuse cousin Cosby's sacking of Morris. On November 26, King George signed the Privy Council ruling that Morris had been removed as New York's highest judge without sufficient cause.

It was a hard-won victory for Morris but a decidedly limited one. The king's council declined to recommend that he be reinstated as chief justice. One reason bandied about in court and ministry circles and relayed to Morris was that he had violated the rules of British establishment etiquette by going public with his grievance—"appealing to the country," it was said, by daring to publish at his own expense the extensive opinion he had delivered in the Van Dam case and the accompanying letter he had addressed to Cosby saying that there was nothing personal about his decision. More to the point, since the keepers of the imperial realm were nothing if not pragmatists, the Privy Council knew that if it had ordered Morris's dismissal reversed, Cosby's authority would have been fatally undermined, leaving two royal colonies in a political vacuum. The successor chief justice, James DeLancey, furthermore, was well connected to the Walpole administration and in no danger of being demoted to second justice even though the government now acknowledged that Morris had been unfairly replaced. And DeLancey, enjoying his new eminence, lacked the grace to step back, especially to accommodate Morris, toward whom his family held a long-standing grievance. DeLancey would remain in office for the next twenty-four years until his death and twice served as acting governor for a total of nearly four years.

On November 24, two days before the king confirmed the Privy Council's de facto apology to Morris for his unmerited sacking, Cosby had suffered a far graver setback. He was stricken with tuberculosis, according to most contemporary accounts of his medical condition, and remained a fevered, mostly bedridden invalid for the next sixteen weeks.

By the time Cosby fell ill, word had arrived from the Board of Trade confirming his suspension of Van Dam and Alexander from the Provincial Council. The governor summoned the council to his bedside, formalized the two Morrisite members' suspension pending the Privy Council's approval, and named his confidant George Clarke, with the most seniority after Van Dam's, as the new council president—and thus the prospective acting governor if Cosby's health failed. Civil strife, quiescent since the Zenger trial, flared anew. Van Dam challenged the legitimacy of his removal on the ground that the Privy Council had not yet ratified the Board of Trade's pliancy toward Cosby and insisted Clarke's elevation to council president was premature. The *Journal* found its caustic voice anew, chastising the Cosbyite retinue for its naked power grab, while Van Dam petitioned the Privy Council to block what he characterized as a renewed outbreak of despotism. Clarke, with his firm ties to the British aristocracy and long tenure as New York's colonial secretary and auditor, simultaneously urged the Board of Trade to confirm his status with dispatch and head off civil discord.

In this potentially incendiary atmosphere, James Alexander conceived the idea, probably in the closing weeks of 1735 or January of the new year, of exploiting the popularity of the Zenger trial verdict the previous summer and reaping fresh political advantage from it. The vehicle was to be a published narrative of the legal proceedings that had show-cased the justice of the Morrisite cause and Hamilton's dazzling advo-cacy that had made it appear that it was the governor, not the printer, who deserved censure. Alexander himself was to write the account, of course, posing under Zenger's byline, even as he had remained the undercover creator of the *Journal*'s editorial content. To shed his ano-nymity now would likely have given the whole game away and made him seem to have dishonorably exploited Zenger, who had bravely taken the rap for his paper's defamatory content. Alexander's openly authoring the narrative would have been practically confessing his role all along as Cosby's principal tormentor in print and would probably have dimmed the lawyer's hope of early readmission to the New York bar. So he set about the task as Zenger's ghost writer by asking the three participating lawyers for their trial notes. Attorney General Bradley flatly declined, likely suspecting that any account emerging from the Zenger camp would portray his courtroom performance disdainfully. John Chambers apparently balked at first, perhaps out of bitterness that his part in the case had been so thoroughly upstaged by Hamilton's last-minute heroics. Hamilton himself agreed to send his friend Alexander a set of his trial notes as soon as he could find the time to edit them. But as the winter lengthened and Cosby's health declined, Alexander grew more eager to publish his account of the trial to provide heady Morrisite propaganda, yet Hamilton's notes, crucial to the project, failed to arrive.

Meanwhile, Morris in London, unaware of Cosby's condition and feeling scarcely vindicated by the Privy Council's slap on Cosby's wrist for humiliating him, renewed and broadened his assault on the governor. He formally petitioned the ministry to remove Cosby for gross misman-agement of his office that had sapped the confidence of New York and New Jersey colonists in his—and the crown's—authority. Morris put his writing talent to use drafting a 12,000-word indictment of Cosby, a grab bag of every negative report at his disposal, however loosely substanti-ated. Morris added petitions that his backers had gathered from similarly disaffected New Yorkers and set about trying to deliver the whole pack-age of grievances to King George himself.

The process was grueling and expensive. Morris wrote to Alexander early in January 1736 that every charge against Cosby had to be filed in the form of an affidavit. "If you complain of 20 things, there must be 20 references—20 orders, 20 duplicates," which cost him about £10 sterling for each petition. However gently or forcefully the government might admonish Cosby, Morris predicted that in the end the governor would continue to do what he liked, then added forlornly, "This must mend sometime, but when, God knows. . . . In a word, we cannot help ourselves on our own side of the water; we must learn to bear our miseries as well as we can till chance or providence relieves us." Except for a Privy Council order to Cosby to desist from sitting and voting with his Provincial Council when it met to consider legislative business, none of the other abuses Morris had attributed to the governor was addressed in the early part of 1736.

Morris's relentless crusade turned moot on March 10 when Cosby died at the age of forty-six, having been little loved by his subjects and too extravagantly reviled by his foes for disfavoring them. The Morrisite vehemence against him was captured in parting disparagement soon after Cosby's passing by an anonymous letter-writer to the *Journal*: "As a true lover of this province, I can't help wishing that the measures of his administration may rather serve as beacons of danger . . . to be avoided than as an example to future tyrants; in this very much depends the quieting of the minds of a people long distressed with arbitrary power."

Cosby's holdover council quickly anointed Clarke acting governor, to the chagrin of the Morrisite faction supporting Van Dam's candidacy, absent the Privy Council's confirmation of his dismissal at the late governor's behest. The Assembly was not in session and could only be summoned by the governor, so the legislature could hardly put a brake on Clarke's installation, even if it were so disposed. But that prospect was far from certain, for Clarke, a prominent member of Long Island's landed gentry, was a good deal more politic and less grasping than Cosby, understood the rule of law, and knew all the nooks and crannies of colonial administration. As a temperate, even cunning, crown officer, he pledged to restore peace and reconcile the warring camps. But Alexander and the other Morrisite leaders were out to regain power, not share it with Cosby devotees, and kept sounding the tocsin of strife. Clarke urged them to calm down while they all awaited instructions from London; meanwhile, he put the Fort George garrison on alert against any civil outburst like the Leisler revolt half a century earlier.

On the day Cosby died, Hamilton coincidentally sent off a packet to Alexander enclosing his Zenger trial notes and an attached letter that began "Dear Jim" and ended "Your affectionate and humble servant." In between, the Philadelphian apologized for his delay in meeting Alexander's request, blaming it on the press of his duties as speaker of the Pennsylvania Assembly and his courtroom caseload. "I have sent it [his edited notes] ill done as it is," he added sheepishly. "I have had no time to read it over but once since it was finished. . . . The meaning of all this is to beg you to alter and correct it agreeable to your own mind."

Offered carte blanche by the central figure in the courtroom drama, Alexander set to work melding Hamilton's, Chambers's, and his own notes—and, to be sure, his keen memory—to fashion a simulated transcript of the trial, prefaced and interspersed with some narrative under Zenger's byline. As a disclaimer against charges of partisanship, Alexander noted that "Mr. Attorney [General Bradley] has not been pleased to favor us with [a copy of] his argument," and scrupulously kept disparagement of the prosecutor from slipping into the text. Nor were there glowing encomia or sly asides glorifying Hamilton's words—but of course Alexander had the privilege to choose which words to include or omit. Behind a façade of impartiality was an obvious imbalance in presentation between the defense attorney's long and impassioned speeches and the prosecutor's bland, paraphrased, and far briefer remarks. The June 21, 1736, issue of the *Journal* announced the publication and sale of *A Brief Narrative of the Case and Trial of John Peter Zenger, Printer of the* New-York Weekly Journal, a forty-page, tightly packed pamphlet that quickly found a wide readership. It ran through several printings in New York, was soon issued in Boston and circulated throughout the American colonies, had five editions in London the following year, and was reprinted periodically over the remainder of the eighteenth century. Thanks to the *Brief Narrative*, Zenger's case became, along with the Salem Witch Trials, the best known of American colonial-era courtroom dramas, and the printer and his defense counsel have passed into legend as intrepid champions of press freedom.

III

The availability in print of a detailed account of the Zenger trial invited, besides admiration for the defense counsel's forensic derring-do, the gimlet-eyed scrutiny of fellow attorneys unabashedly devoted to the crown and its venerable prerogative to smother objections to abusive government practices. One such naysayer wielding a particularly acidic pen took the pseudonym "Anglo-Americanus" and produced a pair of articles appearing in the summer of 1737 in *Keimer's Gazette*, published out of Barbados, where the reputed author, Jonathan Blenman, served as king's counsel for the colony. His stinging dismissal of Hamilton's virtuosity, while voiced from a small British outpost in the Caribbean, was soon amplified throughout the empire by reprints in pamphlet form, prominently circulated in London and by the Bradfords, William and Andrew, who issued copies from their print shops in New York and Philadelphia respectively, in an effort to demythologize Zenger's eloquent defender as a slayer of royal dragons.

Asserting at the outset that it was his duty to unmask "the bad law, false reasoning . . . [and] gross absurdities" of Hamilton's courtroom presentation, Anglo-Americanus (hereafter referred to as A.-A.) assailed Hamilton's citation of cases in which he claimed truth served as a defensive shield against libel charges. They were "gross misrepresentations," A.-A. asserted, inapplicable to the Zenger case and turned on issues other than the truth as a decisive consideration. Invoking them was such a distortion that A.-A. wondered if they were offered "from ignorance or disingenu[ousness]." Hamilton had nonetheless insisted the defamatory texts published by Zenger couldn't be libels because they were true and "puts it upon the king's counsel to prove the facts to be false"—hardly an unreasonable request, A.-A. might in fairness have noted (but did not), since the government's complaint had charged that the defamatory words were false. Instead, A.-A. lamented that, after the prosecutor replied that falsehoods couldn't be proven and Hamilton offered to prove instead the truth of the complaints against Cosby, the court held that truth could not justify a libel and halted the defense counsel's gambit. For it was doubtful, A.-A. argued with relish, that based on the true facts, Hamilton could have proven "habitual misuse of power" by the governor as the *Journal* charged. It was the hallmark of libelers "to multiply and exaggerate facts" as Zenger's paper did, A.-A. contended, in claiming that under Cosby's regime judges (plural) were arbitrarily displaced (two were, and not entirely without justification) and that courts (plural) were illegally erected (one attempt, on at least debatable grounds, was made and foiled). Could Hamilton have proven, A.-A. asked, that "the law itself was at an end," as a *Journal* article contended, or that "trials by jury were taken away when a governor pleased" when "if I mistake not, [Hamilton] was at that time speaking to a jury in a regular court of law."

Homing in on his target, A.-A. then challenged Hamilton for failure "to show a single instance [case] where witnesses have been produced by counsel *and admitted by the courts* to prove the truth of a libel [italics added]. When he does this, it will deserve consideration." But here A.-A. was the one being disingenuous, because he knew that the courts, hewing to the Star Chamber dictum, had for the most part disallowed defense counsel to introduce testimony in order to show that cited defamatory language was true and ought to mitigate the charge. Indeed, Hamilton had met A.-A.'s supercilious challenge by making the opposite argument at the trial—that no case had yet been cleanly adjudicated in which a defendant was convicted of seditious libel by the jury for writing or publishing words denunciatory of the government that were demonstrably true. What A.-A., like Attorney General Bradley, failed to argue in rebutting Hamilton's reliance on the truth defense was that the flexible nature of truth and falsehood—both often objectively unprovable and residing in the realm of personal judgment—made them inadequate criteria for determining whether defamatory words in specific contexts were criminal weapons. Hamilton might better have been criticized by a commentator without A.-A.'s bias for failing to argue that the Star Chamber ruling of 1605 was an abrupt departure from three centuries of English statutory law holding falsehood to be the essence of criminal libel. Even if this long line of statutes had been held inapplicable because they had either expired and not been renewed as required by Parliament or when a new sovereign took the throne, falsity as the central determinant of a libel could have been cited at the Zenger trial as a historic fact that the Star Chamber should not have arbitrarily—and dictatorially—brushed aside, leaving *De Libellis Famosis* as eminently ripe for reversal.

The longer Anglo-Americanus went on, the more he disclosed not Hamilton's shortcomings as an advocate but the writer's own predilections as an antidemocrat. Because Hamilton "seems to be above having his points of law decided by the authorities of the law," A.-A. decried, the defense counsel had relied on political arguments instead, ignoring that the rule of law depended on maintaining the social fabric rather than the moral worth of individual acts "and their tendency to hurt the community, whose peace and safety are their [the law's] principal objects." Citizens had no statutory or "natural right," as Hamilton had argued, to go public with their criticisms of government unless they did so "in a lawful way," which A.-A. defined as bringing their "just complaints" to magistrates, the courts of justice, Parliament, even the king himself, but excluded the right to share their complaints with their neighbors because the state as well as the individual had a right to protect itself "from injurious criticism." Discontented citizens ought to take their grievances first to the very parties they claimed were victimizing them—regardless of how costly, time-consuming, and unavailing that process might prove (as A.-A. did not trouble to concede)—instead of trying to arouse community-wide support by spoken or published words composed to help pressure their abusers to reform their allegedly wicked ways. Serenely confident in the just administration of the realm, A.-A. claimed that if half the abuses that Zenger's paper had alleged were proven true to the royal administration's satisfaction, Cosby would surely have been replaced.

Lest he be accused of opposing freedom of the press, A.-A. pointedly vowed, "I think it the bulwark of all other liberty and the surest defense against tyranny and oppression." Then he revealed his unsettling authoritarian inclination by adding, "But still, it is a two-edged sword, capable of cutting both ways, and is not therefore to be trusted in the hands of every discontented fool or designing knave." Who, though, was to draw that distinction in a free society where one man's "discontented fool or designing knave" might be the next man's inspired champion of liberty? Anglo-Americanus, like so many others of his era, was a stranger to the precept that genuine freedom of the press meant those you despise as fools or knaves are blessed with the very same liberty as you to express themselves however they wish.

But other voices arose and views emerged in the mother country that were relayed back to the American colonies in support of Hamilton and freer public expression of political protest. According to a report from its London correspondent in the May 18, 1738, issue of Franklin's *Pennsylvania Gazette*, the Zenger trial had become "the common topic of conversation in all the coffee houses, both at the court end of town and in the city [financial district]." The writer added:

> Our political writers of different factions, who never agreed in anything else, have mentioned the trial in their public writings with an air of rapture and triumph. A Goliath in learning and politics gave his opinion of Mr. Hamilton's arguments in these terms: "If it is not law, it is better than law, it ought to be law, and will always be law wherever justice prevails." The [*Brief Narrative*] of the trial has been reprinted four times in three months, and there has been a demand for it by all ranks and degrees of people. . . . We look upon Zenger's advocate as a glorious asserter of public liberty and of the rights and privileges of Britons.

In his final years, Hamilton retained his place among the foremost civic figures of his colony, continuing to serve as speaker of both the Pennsylvania and Delaware legislatures, chief admiralty judge, and active member of the small committee chosen to oversee the design and construction of the Pennsylvania State House, where the legislators would meet. Hamilton was incorrectly credited by some with the design of the building, which a generation later became known as Independence Hall, but Hamilton did some of the early design drawings. The long-term project, the most imposing public structure in the colonies, was not completed until a dozen years after his death in 1741, six years to the day that he argued for Peter Zenger's—and all humanity's—right to publicly criticize those who govern them without having to fear for their lives or liberty. In its obituary on August 6, 1741, the *Pennsylvania Gazette* wrote of Hamilton:

> He lived not without enemies, for, as he was himself open and honest, he took pains to unmask the hypocrite and boldly censured the knave without regard to station and profession. . . . He steadily maintained the cause of liberty. . . . He was no friend to power as he had observed an ill use had been frequently made of it in the colonies, and therefore was seldom on good terms with governors. . . . He was long at the top of his profession . . . and tho' stern and severe in his manner, he was compassionate in his nature and very slow to punish. . . . [He] was indefatigable in endeavoring to remove the prejudices of others[,] . . . was the poor man's friend, and was never known to withhold his purse or service from the indigent or oppressed. . . .

A generation after Hamilton's death, perhaps the harshest words ever written about his Zenger defense—the touchstone of his fame—were published by attorney-historian William Smith, Jr., who was seven years old when his father and namesake sat at the printer's trial alongside his close professional associate, James Alexander (with whom he had been disbarred at the same time that spring by Chief Justice DeLancey). One might suppose that the younger Smith, in his history of New York colony, would have had kind words for Hamilton, whose oratory had won the day for his father and his Morrisite allies, Zenger's chief backers. Instead, Smith excoriated Hamilton. By belaboring his "ignorant audience" in the jury box and the courtroom with rhetorical flimflam, the Philadelphia counselor had managed to "artfully convert the guilty nakedness of the cause of his client into a defense," Smith charged. Having "captivated [the jurors'] minds into a belief that if the scandals were true, Zenger was not [a] criminal," Hamilton attributed to past events and libel cases meanings that were "tortuously extracted from them beyond any precise endorsement of his contention" that truth legitimized defamatory publications. Indeed, "such was the fraudful dexterity of the orator, and the severity of his invectives upon the governor and his adherents that the jury . . . pronounced the criminal innocent because they believed them [their rulers] to be guilty."

For Smith to label Zenger "the criminal" was of course to evade the central issues of his case and trial: Could—and should—a citizen be convicted for daring to question or criticize in any way, whether truthfully or falsely, factually or by distortion, the government's conduct if the complainant's objections could be said to diminish public trust in or satisfaction with the state's authority—which was, certainly, the author's very intention in putting pen to paper.

What Smith failed to grasp—or at least to grant—was that Hamilton in his defense of Zenger was doing what great advocates do when a harsh and inhumane law stands in the way of justice for their clients; he urged that it be superseded by good sense and fair judgment. Such boldness was, arguably, not "fraudful" but purposeful advocacy. A modern, monumental instance of such advocacy was the 1953 argument before the U.S. Supreme Court by Thurgood Marshall and his NAACP Legal Defense Fund colleagues that racial segregation of schoolchildren, though six times upheld by the high court under the "separate but equal" doctrine since it was pronounced in 1896, ought to be set aside as inhumane and unjust *even if* such discrimination had long been practiced under the color of law—and *even if* its destruction could be accomplished only at the likely cost of widespread social upheaval and violent resistance.

A more charitable—and fitting—judgment of Hamilton's Zenger defense than William Smith's diatribe was delivered a few decades later by another descendant of the families that were most closely associated with the printer's cause. Gouverneur Morris, who was a brilliant lawyer like his grandfather Lewis Morris, and a member of the Continental Congress as well as among the principal drafters of the U.S. Constitution, called his fellow Philadelphia attorney Andrew Hamilton "the Day-Star of the American Revolution"—the beacon who had lighted his countrymen's path toward liberty and away from captive colonialism.

IV

In the spring of 1736 before word of William Cosby's death had reached London, his patron the Duke of Newcastle tried to quell Lewis Morris's incessant badgering of crown personnel to punish the governor for his alleged abuses of power. In a none too subtle ploy that would have served to remove the tireless agitator from the New York scene so Cosby could continue to function unharassed, the duke as overseer of the American colonies offered Morris the governorship of New Jersey, shortly to be separated from joint rule by the governor of New York.

For Morris, still supposing himself the absentee senior member of the New Jersey Council, the offer must have been sorely tempting. More than thirty years before, he had lusted for that royal post as a reward for having masterminded New Jersey's surrender as a renegade proprietary province to crown sovereignty. But in a notable display of principle, he now declined the alluring bribe on the ground that he had come to London not to rehabilitate his personal standing, though that would have gladdened him, but primarily to press for Cosby's downfall and reforms that would allow the colonists a greater say in their government.

His selfless gesture availed Morris little. The king's councils and ministers kept the American provocateur from presenting his case against Cosby to the monarch in person. By midyear, when news of the governor's death reached Britain, the point of Morris's mission had been blunted, along with his hopes for systemic reforms in imperial governance. He soon set sail for home and arrived on October 8, 1736, to find New York on the precipice of political anarchy as the colony awaited for London to choose between George Clarke and Rip Van Dam as claimants to the Provincial Council presidency and the role of acting governor. Greeted by cheering crowds who remembered his muscular, if at times abrasive, brand of leadership, Morris presented himself as the colony's political savior, offered to resume his purloined post as chief justice under Van Dam's authority as acting governor, and assured all who would listen that when he left London, he was aware of no imminent orders granting Clarke's petition to succeed Cosby, at least temporarily. Suspecting a neo-Cosby crackdown by Clarke and the mercantile faction that backed him if the crown ignored Van Dam's counterclaim to rule the colony, Morris was heard to cry out to his frenzied supporters, "If you don't hang them, they'll hang you." A few days later he led a pack of followers to the barred doors of the Assembly, then nine years in power, to demand that it dissolve itself—since Clarke would not—and hold elections that would reflect the colony's true political sentiment. By then Clarke, hanging on to power by his fingertips and his partisan council's backing, had taken refuge in Fort George in case the Morrisite forces moved to seize power by force.

The insurrectionist threat ended abruptly on October 13 when the brigantine *Endeavour* arrived in New York with Privy Council orders confirming Clarke as council president; a further directive followed, naming him lieutenant governor and commander-in-chief of the colony's military. Morris quickly lost his charisma with the public after having spread what Cadwallader Colden retrospectively called the "false intelligence" that Clarke was not slated to gain the crown's nod to govern New York. Morris retreated in haste to New Jersey, where, seemingly clueless that his political star had dimmed to near-invisibility, he further tarred his reputation. Claiming still to be the senior member of the Provincial Council on which he had first sat forty-five years earlier, he said he was entitled to serve as acting governor while the Privy Council went about finalizing the intended separation of New Jersey from Clarke's jurisdiction. The second-longest-serving New Jersey councilman, who had taken the post as acting governor after Cosby's death, at once denied Morris's claim by pointing out that under crown rules, any councilman absent from the province for more than one year—Morris had been away far longer—without the governor's permission forfeited his seat. Unfazed, Morris insisted he was in the right and began issuing proclamations until a warrant was issued for his arrest. The limping old lion barely escaped back to Morrisania, his family refuge in Westchester, where he waited for Clarke and his retinue to falter, allowing what was left of the Morrisite coalition to reclaim power.

Morris would wait in vain. Clarke, though an anti-Morrisite for a dozen years after being deprived of a portion of his power during Burnet's governorship, remained a conscientious bureaucrat rather than a partisan politician. Once invested with the crown's imprimatur as acting governor, he made shrewd moves to conciliate the colony's warring factions. With the council under his control, he dissolved the Assembly in May of 1737 and called for new elections, a significant concession to Morris's party, which had been demanding without success that Cosby do likewise from the day he arrived. Morris himself had fallen precipitously from Olympian heights but even as a minor deity was able to lead his party to a big Assembly victory, perhaps in populist protest over the crown's reticence to clean the slate after the unpopular Cosby's demise. James Alexander, who had been sorely victimized by the Cosby regime, was elected as one of New York County's representatives in the Assembly; both Lewis Morrises, father and son, were returned to the legislature from Westchester, with Lewis Junior chosen Assembly Speaker, and in what must have seen to him a providential act of redemptive justice, John Peter Zenger was named to replace William Bradford as the colony's royal printer.

It was an exhilarating time for Alexander especially. With young Morris's backing, he introduced reform measures to prevent Assembly members from accepting gifts (especially land grants) or patronage jobs to buy their influence—a proposal that their less idealistic fellow legislators ultimately rejected. But in a key concession by Clarke to secure the Morrisites' cooperation, the acting governor pushed the Assembly to legislate Alexander's and William Smith's reinstatement to the New York bar from which Chief Justice DeLancey had impetuously suspended them two and a half years earlier. Alexander celebrated his rehabilitation by building a splendid mansion on Broad Street, decorated with his wife's knowledge of elegant home furnishings and adjoined by a large garden renowned for its roses. As an enlightened civic leader, he pushed vigorously to sanitize the city's streets, docks, and waterways.

Legislative cooperation and political calm returned as Clarke's star rose, soon costing the Morrisites their grip on New York City's government in the General Council elections and then support throughout the colony. The damage was partly self-inflicted. When Clarke successfully co-opted the formerly high-principled Morrisites by offering patronage to their titular leader and his son, they accepted, empowering them to fire Cosbyite judges and other hostile officeholders in Westchester, their bailiwick, and install their own slate. This crass indulgence in the political spoils system was precisely what Lewis Morris and his allies had railed against when Cosby practiced it—arbitrarily firing officeholders disloyal to his will and replacing them with cronies or cringing flunkies. Their glaring hypocrisy drained the Morrisites' leadership credibility, and their whole party structure collapsed in October of 1738 when Lewis Morris suddenly resigned from the Assembly and transferred his waning but not-yet-depleted political energy to the arena where he had first flexed it nearly half a century earlier—New Jersey.

In order to facilitate Clarke's efforts to stabilize and solidify his hold on New York's government, the crown unexpectedly appointed Morris the first independent governor of New Jersey since it had become a royal colony—belated recognition, in part, for Morris's role in that transition at the turn of the eighteenth century. For all the feathers he had ruffled, especially the Duke of Newcastle's, during his London mission to do in Cosby, Morris had shown himself to be a formidable advocate with a legitimate personal grievance and a man of character for having turned down the earlier offer of the New Jersey governorship if he would only quit hounding Cosby and haunting the power-wielders of the realm. Discredited in his native province of New York, Morris was pleased to cross the Hudson and accept the executive political authority he had long coveted, even if it now amounted to a consolation prize.

In the March 1739 elections that Clarke called after dissolving the New York Assembly in the hope of putting the Morrisites to rout, the trade barons' forces still led by the Philipse and DeLancey clans charged their foes with extravagant spending in the previous session and recaptured the legislature. Lewis Morris, Jr., while retaining his seat, was replaced by former Speaker Adolph Philipse; the four assemblymen newly representing New York City were all anti-Morrisite as even James Alexander was defeated. The incoming Assembly, begrudging Peter Zenger his role in sullying the character of William Cosby, fired him as the colony's official printer after holding the sinecure barely a year, and returned it to William Bradford. George Clarke skillfully retained the governorship for seven relatively serene years.

Only after Clarke was succeeded by George Clinton, admiral of His Majesty's fleet, in 1743, would Alexander and his colleague William Smith return from private practice to public life as close advisers to the new governor. Clinton reappointed Alexander to the Provincial Council, from which Cosby had so savagely banished him a decade earlier, and retained his close friend and fellow native Scotsman, Cadwallader Colden, who by then had become the longest-serving councilman, while remaining the colony's surveyor general. Colden's reputation as New York's leading scientist had been burnished the same year Clinton took office by a series of essays he produced, correlating the city's filthy living conditions with the serious yellow fever epidemic of 1741–42—a notable pioneer study in the annals of American public health.

V

Lewis Morris's lifelong career was a power trip. He battled ardently and effectively against those in authority who used it in ways that denied him his purposes, turning them by his lights into tyrants he had to bring down. Yet when he himself attained power, he grew intoxicated with it, forgot his better instincts, and degenerated into the sort of ogre he had fulsomely denounced. And so it was when he at last assumed the royal mantle as governor of New Jersey.

Morris no sooner took office than his chameleon habit of shedding inconvenient principles drove him to abandon his outspoken aversion to what he regarded as Britain's indifference toward and maladministration of its American colonies. With fatal mistiming, he now embraced the crown's ironclad dominion over its outlying territories—and thus his own derived omnipotence over his subjects—in an age when the provinces were evolving into a loose federation of self-governing commonwealths. Instead of the obedience Morris demanded from it, the New Jersey Assembly refused to allow him and his council to amend money bills, prompting him out of spite to veto many of the democratic reform measures the lawmakers had passed, including mandatory elections every three years (or more often), one of the key demands Morris had brought with him to London to check Cosby's alleged despotism. The governor turned into such a fierce proponent of the royal prerogative, with its reflexive impulse to beat back any perceived encroachments by the people and their elected representatives, that at one point he urged the Board of Trade to propose a bill to Parliament requiring all revenues collected abroad by the crown in the colonies to be transmitted to the king for disbursal through his colonial administrators as they saw fit. Such a proposition signaled a 180-degree reversal of Morris's career-long advocacy of colonists' rights to participate in their government's activities like true Englishmen in the mother country. He even reversed his long-held support of the Quakers' right to serve in public office by asking Newcastle to cancel it.

The supreme irony of Morris's gubernatorial tenure was that he adopted the self-aggrandizing hauteur of his dead archenemy, William Cosby—and then some. He appointed his twenty-six-year-old son, Robert Hunter Morris, to the New Jersey Council, where he could serve as his father's eyes, ears, and tongue, as well as chief justice of the colony, as if to compensate for his own loss of that same high office in New York. In petty greed, too, he seemed to ape Cosby by bristling when he was voted a meager (to him) salary of £1,000, even though it was a good deal more than what New York governors had formerly received for serving jointly as overseer of New Jersey's affairs. More telling, his preference for imperial authority over local needs cost him the initial majority he had commanded in the Assembly. He would dissolve it five times in the hope of adding to his slender clique in the legislature but never succeeded.

His power to bully his foes gone, Morris's seven-year term as governor was marked by ceaseless rancor and mutual distrust between him and the citizenry he lorded over. When he died in office on May 21, 1746, at age seventy-four, he had made himself a reviled figure, his colony was nearly bankrupt, and riots over disputed land titles were once again plaguing the province.

The tragic final chapter in a career of brilliant promise repeatedly wasted by fatal flaws of character helps explain history's reluctance to credit Lewis Morris's sizable—if always self-serving—contribution to the cause of liberty and social justice advanced by American colonial statesmen. His studied outrage led to the downfall of three deeply flawed royal governors and the establishment of the first newspaper in the New World created for the purpose of protesting, at dire risk, alleged abuses of British crown power. That the *Journal*'s protests may have been overstated to gain public attention should not distract posterity from recognizing the valor of its pioneering effort to elevate freedom of the press to a core value of the American people.

Just two months after Morris's death, John Peter Zenger, the printer who had steadfastly served his ends, also died. At age forty-nine, he left a wife and six children and a reputation as a loving husband and tender father. His widow, Anna, continued as proprietor of the *New York Weekly Journal* for two-and-a-half years before handing the responsibility to John Zenger, Peter's son from his first, short-lived marriage, for three more years. The paper's final issue, No. 1017, appeared on March 18, 1751.

It is worth noting that during the five years he outlived the *Journal*, James Alexander, its creator, editor, and principal contributor, never acknowledged his central role in the paper's operation, just as he had refrained from doing so while it existed. We can only guess at the motive behind his reticence. To have functioned in the open as the outspoken paper's driving force would have compromised his standing as a leader of his colony's legal profession and tagged him a subversive in the eyes of the royal authorities. Once the Morrisite leadership decided that no useful purpose would be served if Alexander stepped forward to admit writing or editing the articles that prompted the libel charges against the *Journal*—indeed, his detention and prosecution would have even more certainly imperiled the paper's survival than Zenger's incarceration— Alexander was obliged to cede the printer historical credit for fronting the whole printed assault on the fallible governor and, as a result, stoically enduring extended jailtime for doing so. No doubt his lawyer would have appeared cowardly if, only after the trial's favorable outcome, he had come forward to claim accolades as the *Journal*'s guiding spirit, and would have seemed even more dishonorable if he had done so after the

Zengers were no longer on the scene and could not have contested or objected to his disclosure. And so James Alexander, who masterminded the whole clamorous Zenger mission and inked most of its diatribes against authoritarian government, has been snubbed by history as just another colonial lawyer.

The last survivor of the Morrisite cabal, Cadwallader Colden, had been an idealistic Whig in his early years as a uniquely useful civil servant thanks to his scientific, political, and literary skills and intellectual range. Government derived its authority from the people, he believed, and when its officers failed to protect the public's well-being, Colden favored their replacement, even as he resented and sought to check the power of wealthy merchants and land barons. In eclipse during the decade-long Cosby-Clarke gubernatorial tenure, he emerged as a political force advising Governor Clinton during his ten-year term but phased, imperceptibly at first, into a strong supporter of the royal prerogative. By 1760, when as senior member of the Provincial Council he began the first of his four terms as acting governor, Colden sided with the crown against the Assembly and its elitist majority, later complied with the hugely unpopular Stamp Act of 1765, and was burned in effigy by mobs for his order to turn around the guns at Fort George and aim them at the city to discourage armed uprisings against further tax levies.

Even when seeking political compromise, Colden kept losing popular support. In 1769, he supported an Assembly measure allocating £2,000 to supply British troops, opposed by New Yorkers as an occupation force rather than, as the crown claimed, a safeguard against foreign or Native American incursions; in exchange, the Assembly won royal approval to float a £120,000 bond issue to meet public debts and bolster the economy. When merchant and political activist Alexander McDougall, a leader of the sub rosa Sons of Liberty movement, published a tirade titled "To the Betrayed Inhabitants of the City and Colony of New York" denouncing the deal as a betrayal of colonists' rights and a step toward enslavement by the royal government, the Assembly—with Acting Governor Colden's hearty approval—brought charges against the writer for seditious libel. After McDougall refused to plead, demanding his right to a jury trial, Colden ordered a grand jury hearing by a panel stacked with well-heeled citizens opposed to the antiroyalist movement. The writer was indicted but refused to put up bail, though he could well afford to, and remained in jail to gain support from the mass public, as Peter Zenger had done thirty-five years before. Indeed, Zenger's case was pointedly invoked, and a new edition of the *Brief Narrative* of his trial sold well in the city, yet Colden, once a Morrisite stalwart and practitioner of press freedom, now took the side of repressive government. McDougall was spared only when the key witness against him, the printer of his incendiary pamphlet, died just before his jury trial was to begin.

By the time of Colden's final term as acting governor (1773–74), he was as reviled as Lewis Morris had been at the end of his political career, and not only for his Tory sympathies but for corrupt administrative practices of the very sort he had faulted Cosby for, such as lavish land grants to friends and allies whose fees for such favors much increased Colden's wealth. He died in Queens County, at age eighty-seven, in September of 1776, four days before British troops seized New York City from George Washington's hastily retreating little army.

VI

On what basis, if any, was the storm brewed by John Peter Zenger and his newspaper's creators noteworthy beyond the parochial circumstances of its time and place?

Should the episode be regarded simply as a compelling morality play in which the righteous victims of oppression grittily triumphed over their thoroughly contemptible ruler? The foregoing account suggests this would be a naïve reading of what likely transpired. Governor William Cosby was almost surely an ignoble character during his three-and-a-half-year tenure in New York, but if he was in fact half the villain his colonial critics claimed, they failed to marshal firm evidence of it. Nor were his Morrisite enemies immaculately aligned on the side of the angels. Zenger's backers, according to Stanley Katz, a leading authority on the social dynamics of colonial New York at the time, "were, in fact, a somewhat narrow-minded political faction seeking immediate political gain rather than long-term governmental or legal reform." Nor did Zenger's paper itself, while a cut or two above its colonial peers, provide its readers with much in the way of hard information nor often ascend to the realm of literature. It had a different purpose, one that justifies history's attention even now when Zenger's fame has largely receded.

Nineteenth-century historians like James Grahame and George Bancroft valued the Zenger case as a still resonating *cause célèbre* and the beginning of the struggle for American liberty wrenched from an arbitrary and dictatorial empire. Bancroft wrote in 1868 that the *Journal* had been founded "to defend the popular cause"—which in reality hardly existed if he meant an antiroyalist movement—and that the outcome of Zenger's trial caused American colonists to exult in "the victory of freedom." Scholars a century later, however, took a far more subdued view of the subject. In his 1960 essay "Did the Zenger Case Really Matter?" Leonard Levy, Pulitzer Prize–winning constitutional historian and author of *Emergence of a Free Press*, asserted,

> The persistent image of colonial America as a society which cherished freedom of expression is a sentimental hallucination that ignores history. . . . It is traditional, of course, to state that colonial times were troubled by a continuing struggle between "the royal judges" and American writers and printers who demanded freedom to criticize the government. . . . No such struggle really existed. Moreover, the Zenger case had no appreciable effect on the freedom, or the lack of freedom, of the press in colonial New York.

Stanley Katz went even farther down this debunking road in the lucid introduction to his 1963 edited version of the *Brief Narrative*, remarking that the Zenger case was not "a landmark in the history of law or of the freedom of the press. . . . The reformation of the law of libel and the associated unshackling of the press came about, when they did, as if Peter Zenger had never existed." At the close of his introduction thirty-three pages later, Katz nevertheless goes on to state that, despite excessive claims of the case's importance, its fame is "by no means undeserved, for the arguments brought forward in Zenger's defense represent an early appreciation of the emerging popular basis of American politics, full recognition of which would ultimately lead to reforms of both politics and law."

Let us accept Katz's second thesis that the Zenger case was symptomatic rather than directly causative of the remarkable divergence in the mindset of American colonists from that of their British countrymen in the home isles. The mechanism behind the social turmoil of 1732 to 1735 in New York was the Morrisite newspaper and the example it set by daring to protest—in the open and for the first time in America, leave aside its proprietors' ulterior motives—alleged abuses of the crown's power and thereby risking their liberty in the face of the prevailing law of the realm. Here is how the Zenger affair foreshadowed the coming of the free press in America: by heralding it as the indispensable catalyst for the creation and sustenance of a democratic society empowered to criticize its rulers when they strayed from rectitude. Zenger's writers may have been no more honorable or selfless than the targets of their heated invective, but as Patricia Bonomi's *A Factious People* noted, in commending the Morrisites' skill at popularizing issues to attract broad public acceptance of their own values and policies, they "contributed directly to the growth of the press and . . . effectively used printed propaganda as an opposition weapon."

Zenger's *Journal*, it may then be ventured, helped implant in the public mind that open protest against an imposed and arguably unjust government was both a social necessity and a civil right. By encouraging juries not to vote to suppress free expression as a criminal activity, the outcome of Zenger's trial advanced journalism as a meritorious profession and directly challenged the mindless Star Chamber dictum that "the greater the truth, the greater the libel."

The events in and around New York City in those years when the names Cosby, Morris, and Zenger were at stage center thus hastened the dawning conviction that British colonialism, even when practiced with benign neglect, was intolerable because the crown was committed to exploitative, cost-free operation of its overseas holdings. The American colonies were, fundamentally, outright possessions, utilities, distant satellites of the home islands, their orbits firmly tethered and their inhabitants less British countrymen than feudal tenants. If the Cosby-Morris clash, intensified by Zenger's weekly, did not result in an urgent call for radical reform of America's constitutional status, the drama nonetheless presaged events in the decades immediately following, when the press, its fiery pamphleteers, and stinging satirists had a profound influence.

Scholars may fairly minimize the impact of the Zenger trial on the subsequent legal status of seditious libel, since only judges' rulings, not jury verdicts, got factored into the critical mass known as the common law. And no post-Zenger court cases or bench opinions in Britain or its colonial tribunals seriously questioned the criminality of defamatory assaults on the government and its officers. For the remainder of the colonial period, moreover, neither Parliament nor the American legislatures contemplated statutes that would immunize protesters from punishment for venting their political grievances. When British jurist and Oxford law professor William Blackstone's four-volume *Commentaries on the Laws of England* began to appear thirty years after the Zenger trial, it reconfirmed the Star Chamber and Hawkins definition of seditious libel as "the malicious defamation of any person, especially a magistrate . . . in order to provoke him to wrath or to expose him to public hatred, contempt, and ridicule. The direct tendency of these libels is the breach of the peace," and thus they were criminal acts. Blackstone did not define what constituted "malicious" defamation or allow for complaints intended not to breach the peace but to press the government to rule more justly and equitably. In perpetuating the doctrine that "it is immaterial with respect to the essence of the libel whether the matter of it be true or false, since the provocation, not the falsity, is the thing to be punished criminally," Blackstone at least sensibly added, "though, doubtless, the falsehood of it may aggravate its guilt and enhance its punishment."

But to trivialize Zenger's mission for what it did not achieve in transforming the common law on libel is shortsighted. As University of Maryland historian Alison Olson has written, skeptics who have dwelled on the absence of verdicts and court rulings that explicitly claimed Zenger's triumph as a binding legal precedent have "made us miss what the Zenger trial really did accomplish"—namely, in her view, the "dynamic growth of political expression in the colonies by making it relatively safe for American writers to publish political humor—particularly satire—of men in office. . . . After the trial, any politician was a fool to take a satirist to court."

In fact, after the Zenger trial was publicized through relatively wide distribution of its *Brief Narrative*, almost no colonial juries convicted writers or editors charged with seditious libel. By the 1740s, publishers from Massachusetts to North Carolina were being acquitted upon presenting evidence of the truth of the statements that had prompted defamatory charges against them. Crown officers, moreover, were supplanted as the principal antagonists of a free press by colonial legislators. Insisting on the same privilege of immunity from public scrutiny of their activities as was enjoyed by both houses of Parliament, American lawmakers continued to regard press reports on their proceedings and votes as a breach of their sacrosanct status. Free of any requirement to summon a grand jury to indict or a petit jury to convict, legislatures acted as self-appointed tribunals-of-the-whole, prosecuting at will anyone who questioned or publicized their activities without first being licensed to do so. Here was a different but no less lamentable abuse of power by men elected to represent their neighbors, to whom they nonetheless wished to remain unanswerable for how they conducted the people's business. Happily, those who offended the privileged characters in the New York Assembly were rarely dealt with harshly, usually escaping punishment with a humiliating apology. But encouragement of an informed public through reportage by a free press remained a mischievous fancy among colonial lawmakers.

Yet the press grew more assertive once Britain introduced the Stamp Act in 1765, the first revenue measure with a serious impact on colonial America and at once perceived as a dire threat to printers' livelihoods. They began openly denouncing the royal administration as despotic; by March 1768, the *Boston Gazette* was proclaiming that "There is nothing so fretting and vexatious, nothing so justly terrible to tyrants and their tools and abettors as a free press. . . . [I]t is ever watched by those who are forming plans for the destruction of the people's liberties, with an envious and malignant eye." Enforcement of seditious libel became practically impossible among an aroused citizenry. But, as Leonard Levy has comprehensively chronicled, popular approval of a free press did not also embrace the concept of an impartial press, incompatible with political reality in an ever more polarized society. To stay in business throughout the revolutionary period, most newspaper owners had to cater to the rabidly antiroyalist popular will.

Washington's 1781 victory at Yorktown marked the end of crown rule over the American colonies but hardly liberated the press of all legal restraints. To be sure, some of the thirteen new states, mindful of the press's contribution to the success of their rebellion, began to incorporate pledges of free expression into their statutory language. Virginia's 1783 constitution, for example, adopted while Jefferson was still governor, outlawed all prior restraint of printed matter, yet still hewed to Blackstone's strictures by allowing prosecution for libel as false defamation. When the U.S. Constitution was drawn up four years later, it was silent about the sanctity of a free press. This shortcoming was emphatically corrected two years later with the adoption of the Bill of Rights, declaring in its very first amendment that "Congress shall make no law . . . abridging the freedom of speech, or of the press, or the right of the people peaceably to assemble," and distinguishing the infant nation as the first on earth to include by written compact with its people the assurance of free expression among its fundamental precepts of governance. But how free was the press's freedom? The First Amendment did not, for example, explicitly protect the press from prosecution for seditious libel under the English common law, still the backbone of the new American legal system. Equally important, the amendment was conceived as a bar to incursions on press freedom only by Congress; it did not extend to anti-press activity by either state governments or the other two branches of the federal apparatus, the executive and the judicial.

Determining precisely what a constitutionally ensured "free press" means has been slow in coming, though its first severe test occurred just seven years after the Bill of Rights was enacted. Faced with their fading political prospects and adopting a narrow view of the First Amendment's protections, President John Adams and his Federalist Party tried to cling to power by passing the Alien and Sedition Acts of 1798, which held it a crime to publish "false, scandalous, and malicious writing" against the government and its chief executive. The Adams camp then invoked the new act to prosecute and silence its critics who favored Vice President Jefferson's rising Republican Party. Jefferson's friend and chief ally, James Madison, who played a central role in drawing up both the Constitution and the Bill of Rights, arose in wrath to denounce the Sedition Act as nothing but an American version of British seditious libel law and, as such, anathema to the First Amendment. His passionate 1799 Virginia Report asserted that "to the press alone, checkered as it is with abuses, the world is indebted for all the triumphs which have been gained by reason and humanity." Thus the "security of the freedom of the press requires . . . an exemption not only from the previous inspection of licensers but from the subsequent penalty of laws." Had antisedition acts, like the 1798 statute forbidding every publication that might bring government authorities into contempt or disrepute, "been uniformly enforced against the press," Madison asked, "might not the United States be languishing at this day . . . [as] miserable colonies groaning under a foreign yoke?" To Adams apologists who argued that the new law would punish only false and malicious statements and allow authors and publishers to prove the truth of their defamatory statements, Madison rebutted that even "where simple and naked facts alone are in question, there is sufficient difficulty in some cases, and . . . trouble and vexation in all, of meeting a prosecution from the government with the full and formal proof necessary in a court of law." And when the offending words took the form of opinions, inferences, and conjectural observations, proving "truth" in court was still more problematic. As to refuting the "malicious" element of an alleged libel, "it is manifestly impossible to punish the intent to bring those who administer the government into disrepute or contempt without striking at the right of freely discussing public characters and measures, because those who engage in such discussions must expect and *intend* to excite those unfavorable sentiments, so far as they may thought to be deserved."

Madison's righteous fury over the press-throttling statute helped elect Jefferson to the presidency the following year, and his party let the Sedition Act expire in 1801 before the Supreme Court could weigh its constitutionality. A long road had then to be traversed until the latitude and immunities of "a free press" as pledged by the First Amendment would be explicated. The power to abridge press freedom was not denied to the states as well as the federal government until 1866 with the passage of the Fourteenth Amendment. Another sixty-five years passed before the Supreme Court, in *Near v. Minnesota*, struck down a statutory ban against the publication of scurrilous invective as unconstitutional "prior restraint" of press liberty, even when the publication in question grossly affronted common decency.

Still another generation was required before the nation's highest court finally and firmly—if not quite absolutely—put seditious libel to rest as a lurking toxic menace to press freedom. In its 1964 decision of *New York Times v. Sullivan*, the justices reversed a ruling by the Alabama Supreme Court upholding large damage awards to Montgomery city officials who claimed they were criminally defamed as a result of minor factual errors in a full-page advertisement protesting brutal police repression of desegregation advocates. True defamatory statements had long been acknowledged by American courts and juries as sufficient grounds for rejecting libel claims, but the burden had generally rested on the defendant to prove the truth of the offending passages. Protecting truthful defamations was not enough, though, to satisfy the First Amendment's mandate, the Supreme Court held in *Sullivan*. A free press also required constitutional protection—call it breathing room—for publishing some false or erroneous material; otherwise, reporters and editors might well hold back in self-censorship from presenting evidence of misconduct out of fear some minor errors might result in ruinous monetary judgments in favor of an otherwise justly criticized plaintiff. A free press was entitled to immunity from libel suits for "erroneous statements honestly made," Justice William Brennan wrote for the unanimous court, as the burden was now shifted to the plaintiff, unlike in Britain, to show that the falsity was other than an honest mistake. The Constitution required "a federal rule that prohibits a public official from recovering damages for a defamatory falsehood relating to his official conduct unless he proves that the statement was made with 'actual malice'—that is, with knowledge that it was false or with reckless disregard of whether it was false or not."

Seditious libel was thus virtually eliminated as a criminal offense under American law. Eradicating the pox had taken 231 years of hard labor, initiated by Peter Zenger, James Alexander, Lewis Morris, and their little journal that lives on, indelibly.

EPILOGUE

From Zenger to Snowden

O N THE FACE of it, press freedom in America has attained a degree of vigor that would have been as unimaginable to Peter Zenger and his contemporaries as today's man-made vehicles traveling to the edge of our solar system. In the half-century following the landmark ruling in *New York Times v. Sullivan* (1964), proliferating news media have seen their expanded liberty consolidated even while venturing into the hazardous terrain of cyberspace, where technology has revolutionized the field of communications no less than in the Gutenberg age.

On closer examination, though, these gains have not come without fresh challenges—and by one measure, at least, free expression remains nearly as imperiled as when Britain's Star Chamber ruled that to maintain the peace of the realm its government was fully entitled to silence all voices of protest and dissent. Nowadays in the United States, we speak of "national security" as the primary—and usually the only—rationale for policing the press, and to safeguard our people, First Amendment rights have at times been deemed less than absolute. In twenty-first-century America, there is little or no interference with transmitting information and opinion that might have formerly been considered subversive (i.e., endangering law and order or inviting insurrection by undermining public faith in the government). But in the age of global terrorism and nuclear armament, there is notably lower tolerance for protecting the sources that provide the media with some of their most important and disturbing revelations.

Packaging information for readers, viewers, and listeners from sources that eagerly provide it has long been a basic service of the news media to abet the public's health, safety, and convenience. Many sources, of course, provide the press with information of a primarily self-serving nature to gain profit, power, and celebrity, and so the media have long been licensed by law and custom to determine which items they will select from this outpouring and how they will refine the raw material to edify, gratify, or influence their consumers. But investigative journalism—ferreting out and reporting illegal, immoral, or otherwise antisocial activity that its perpetrators do not wish to be publicly known—has often proven a far more hazardous enterprise. Sometimes the indicting evidence is just sitting there, awaiting discovery by the persevering reporter. More frequently the critical element in reportage of this sort is leaked from disaffected inside sources—whistleblowers—who require reporters to keep their identities confidential for fear of reprisal. While no legal impediments stand in the way of publishing such revelations other than the *Sullivan* exception for malicious defamation, law enforcement officials have often requested—and sometimes gone to court to obtain—disclosure of reporters' confidential sources when the subject is criminal behavior that appears to justify prosecution. But if it became generally known that reporters were unable to assure skittish informers that their identities would be protected, investigative journalism would be hobbled and the latitude of press freedom seriously compressed. The issue needed to be adjudicated.

In its 1972 decision of *Branzburg v. Hayes,* the Supreme Court denied reporters the same privileged communication with their sources that lawyers are accorded with their clients, doctors with their patients, and clergymen with their parishioners, so they cannot be compelled to testify in court proceedings about their confidential exchanges. *Branzburg* held that journalists had no more right than any other citizens to withhold information sought by prosecutors and that any resulting impingement on the press's ability to gather confidential information on a pledge not to reveal its sources had to yield to society's need to maintain the fair administration of justice—an interest with roots said to run deeper and date back farther than freedom of the press. A dissenting opinion, however, by Justice Potter Stewart, since widely invoked by lower courts, proposed a balancing test to require prosecutors to show that they were not engaged in fishing expeditions for incriminating information by forcing reporters to break their vows of secrecy; that the public had a compelling interest in the information sought; that it had a direct bearing on the misconduct charged, and that it could not be obtained in any other way. At first, the *Branzburg* ruling seemed a heavy blow to investigative journalism. And some reporters have been jailed or threatened with jail for defying court orders to testify, but prosecutorial power has been sparingly applied, perhaps because public opinion has favored reporters' principled resistance to government coercion, and sentences have been short. In the highest-profile case yet, *New York Times* reporter Judith Miller served eighty-five days for refusing to name the leaker in a national security matter.

The *Branzburg* decision, moreover, allowed that the states and Congress could, if they chose, pass "shield" laws granting reporters the professional privilege of not having to disclose confidential sources, and every state except Wyoming has since awarded journalists at least a qualified privilege under the First Amendment or its own state constitution not to testify, with Justice Stewart's balancing test to be applied in some places. A few states like California and Alabama have allowed the press blanket immunity from testifying while others have tests to ensure that the reporters are certifiably professional journalists. Determining just who qualifies as a "real" journalist has prompted an ongoing judicial debate; the New Hampshire Supreme Court, to cite one tribunal, has adopted a broad standard by granting eligibility to Internet practitioners like bloggers and website curators on the ground that "freedom of the press is a fundamental personal right, which is not confined to newspapers and periodicals." As print media have receded and the public has turned increasingly to electronic images on screens for information and opinion, online providers have made headway in winning legal protection under the First Amendment. Their gains have come notwithstanding that the new breed of information purveyors often lacks the responsible supervisory support systems of traditional news organizations and may be described in some instances as vanity media. Still, if free expression really means what it says, how can a democracy constitutionally impose admissions standards limiting who is entitled to the protected use of the megaphone to address the World Wide Web?

A yawning gap remains in shield-law protection for journalists guaranteeing their freedom from disclosure of news sources: there is no federal statute granting that privilege. Congress has taken up the matter but repeatedly shied from enacting such a measure, largely for fear that it would encourage leaks from within the national security community. It may be safely said that no issue holds greater importance to the vitality of the free press since the *Sullivan* ruling than the growing tension between the federal government's duty to safeguard the nation's security by whatever means it deems necessary and the public's competing right to be informed of these protective measures and decide whether they are warranted or an imposition of authoritarian power alien to a just and open society. It is in essence the very issue on which Peter Zenger's prosecution was brought.

The parameters of national security policy have been the subject of public controversy for the past century of America's ongoing hot and cold wars. One need not be dismissed as a pacifist or traitor to inquire, especially during the second half of this protracted period of far-flung strife, whether the perceived national security threat at any given time was substantive or overblown—and whether the government response was proportionate or an indulgence in chauvinist hubris and global adventurism. It was, after all, President (and retired five-star General) Dwight Eisenhower who warned in his farewell remarks to the nation that it had best beware of the threat to its freedom posed by "the military-industrial complex." That partnership has strengthened since Eisenhower delivered his cautionary words and evolved into a triumvirate with the addition of a much-enlarged, deeply entrenched, and avidly covert intelligence establishment difficult for transient presidential administrations to rein in.

Starting in 1971 with the publication of the so-called Pentagon Papers by the *New York Times* and the *Washington Post*, the press has delivered three major, deeply troubling revelations about the government's national security activities arising from America's post-Korea Asian wars. These reports were based on information conveyed by government whistleblowers subject to prosecution under the U.S. Espionage Act of 1917 for aiding the enemy in wartime, but in none of these three instances was the press itself found guilty of criminal activity. Quite the opposite in the case of the Pentagon Papers, drawn from the Defense Department's forty-three-volume history, classified "Top Secret," of the U.S. involvement in the Vietnam War, revealing the dubious rationale of the undertaking, the brutal nature of its conduct, and how officials deceived Congress and the public about the illegal scope of the conflict and its exorbitant cost in blood and money. The government asked the judiciary to halt publication of the self-indicting documents on the claim that it would endanger U.S. soldiers still in combat, hinder diplomatic efforts to end hostilities, and slow the recovery of American POWs. But the Supreme Court ruled 6 to 3 that the government had failed to prove the disclosures would "surely result in direct, immediate, and irreparable damage to our nation or its people." Branding the term "national security" as a "broad, vague generality," Justice Hugo Black wrote in his opinion, "Only a free and unrestrained press can effectively expose deception in government. . . . The guarding of military and diplomatic secrets at the expense of informed representative government provides no real security for our republic." Due to illegal evidence-gathering and other procedural errors, espionage charges were dropped against the Pentagon Papers whistleblower, Daniel Ellsberg, a U.S. military analyst employed by the RAND Corporation.

The efforts of the government intelligence community did not abate no matter who occupied the White House, stirring the *New York Times*'s Anthony Lewis, among the most knowing journalists ever to report on American civil rights and liberties, to observe in his 1991 book *Make No Law*: "Presidents have used the needs of national security in [our] age to justify cloaking more and more of the vital business of government in secrecy. The intelligence agencies spend billions of dollars every year, but the public is not allowed to know the amount or the justification for it."

Ten years later, when the 9/11 disaster visited the worst national security calamity on American soil since the Japanese attack on Pearl Harbor and plunged the country into what has become known as the Global War on Terrorism, the U.S. military-intelligence apparatus ramped up frantically, with the blessing of a manipulable president and a jittery Congress, to find and vanquish a shadowy, fanatical enemy. Inevitably, the Patriot Act and the creation of the National Security Agency have worked at cross-purposes with the free press, which at times and under government pressure has been overly credulous in scrutinizing U.S. counterterrorist methodology. In two recent landmark disclosures, though, the news media have roused public concern that government interventionist initiatives, however well intended, may be doing more harm than good while unwittingly turning America into a perpetual garrison state.

Starting early in 2010, eight years into major American military incursions in Iraq and Afghanistan, twenty-three-year-old U.S. Army intelligence officer Bradley Manning extracted some 750,000 secret or sensitive documents from State and Defense Department databases and transmitted them to WikiLeaks, a nonprofit, self-styled "disclosure portal." Based in Sweden, where the law is hospitable to whistleblowers, and run by Australian Julian Assange, a so-called Internet activist, WikiLeaks alerts global media about war atrocities and other forms of oppressive governmental behavior.

The material published by the American press via Manning and WikiLeaks graphically dealt with, among other subjects, deadly collateral damage to civilians in war zones under assault by U.S. forces, strategic and tactical details of their ground operations, a quarter-million secret cables sent from 271 American embassies and consulates in 180 countries going back to the Vietnam War, and the holding of Afghans and Pakistanis, ranging in age from fourteen to eighty-nine, for years of interrogation at the Guantánamo detention center even though there was minimal or no evidence that they posed a danger to the United States. This torrent of testimony to the ugly character of the war on terrorism fed apprehension across the country that the use of massive firepower—

and even torture, repugnant to most Americans—to pacify fratricidal Muslim sects halfway around the world was not strengthening America's national security but inflaming and multiplying its enemies. The U.S. government seemed nonplussed, commenting, for example, in an April 2011 statement, "It is unfortunate that *The New York Times* and other news organizations have made the decision to publish numerous documents obtained illegally by WikiLeaks concerning the Guantanamo detention facility . . . [which] may or may not represent the current views of a given detainee." "Unfortunate" in the government's view, perhaps, but it made no attempt to suppress the disturbing media reports. Manning, though, was demoted to private, convicted of espionage, and sent to prison for thirty-five years.

Still closer to Americans' hearths—and all the more alarming to their sensibilities—than the Manning/WikiLeaks disclosures were the revelations that the *Washington Post* and *The Guardian* of Great Britain began publishing in June 2013. Drawn from a reported 1.7 million documents copied from the National Security Agency's secret cyberfiles, the articles described the immense scope of global surveillance operations by the sixteen agencies comprising the U.S. intelligence community. The whistleblower was Edward Snowden, a thirty-year-old computer wizard, who had been employed by the Central Intelligence Agency, other NSA components, and two private companies contracted to perform supervisory security work for the spy agencies.

Snowden's stolen trove disclosed, among other stunning news, that the NSA had obtained a secret court order, permitted by the Patriot Act, directing telecom giant Verizon to provide the agency with the daily phone records of millions of Americans, showing what numbers they called and how long the conversations lasted. The NSA, moreover, was using court-approved access to monitor ordinary citizens' log-ons to Google and Yahoo search engines and, in addition, had tapped undersea cables to collect data from hundreds of millions of those companies' account holders worldwide. The NSA had also been harvesting millions of email and instant-messaging contact lists and searching their contents. And it had spied on countless residents of Germany, France, and Brazil, eavesdropped on the private phone conversations of thirty-five world leaders including German Chancellor Angela Merkel, was track-ing the location of cellphones globally and utilizing the same tools as Internet advertisers to pinpoint targets for government hackers. Snowden further divulged that the U.S. government had budgeted $62 billion to fund intelligence activities in 2013 and that NSA boasted in a mission statement it expected by 2016 to be able "to gather intelligence on anyone, anytime, anywhere." In making these sensational disclosures of what he said were gross violations of the Fourth and Fifth amendments (against illegal searches and denials of due process) as well as the Universal Dec-laration of Human Rights, Snowden said he had done nothing wrong because every individual had a duty transcending national obligations of obedience to prevent crimes against peace and humanity. He added that he had repeatedly complained by email to colleagues and supervisors that the government surveillance operations he eventually revealed were unlawful, but his objections were ignored. The problem with internal whistleblowing, he said, was that "you have to report the wrongdoing to those most responsible for it." The NSA rebutted that it could find no record of Snowden's alleged expressions of concern beyond a solitary inquiry. At this writing, he remains a fugitive charged with espionage.

The magnitude of the NSA's invasion of the privacy of millions of Americans, 90 percent of whom Snowden claimed were in no way sus-pected threats to the nation's security, sufficiently shocked the public, as the Patriot Act was about to expire in the spring of 2015, to force Con-gress into imposing a measure of constraint on the security agency's indis-criminate gathering of megadata. Henceforth, phone companies would hold on to their customers' records and allow NSA access to individual accounts only after the agency had obtained a court-approved search war-rant. But none of the other secret surveillance practices Snowden docu-mented was curbed. When last-minute objections to the ongoing scope of the Patriot Act were raised in the Senate before its renewal deadline, President Obama warned the lawmakers that letting the domestic spying programs expire could lead to terrorist attacks on America. "I don't want us to be in a situation in which for a certain period of time those author-ities go away and suddenly we're [in the] dark," he said. "Heaven forbid we've got a problem where we could have prevented a terrorist attack or apprehended someone who was engaged in dangerous activity, but we didn't do so simply because of inaction in the Senate." In its article on these remarks by Obama, the *New York Times* added, "But civil libertarians say the administration's warnings amount to fear-mongering and efforts to thwart a much-needed overhaul of the government's surveillance powers."

The Snowden disclosures have presented Americans with a profound dilemma. They can uncritically accept their government's syllogistic argument that runs: (1) terrorists pose an unprecedented and ceaseless threat to world peace and stability; (2) to protect our national security the United States has no choice but to lead the global war on terrorism; (3) to do so effectively and interdict terrorist activities, the government must use all the technological tools at its disposal; (4) this massive surveillance program must be conducted in secret, so we cannot reveal the methods, scope, or cost of our global intelligence campaign—but (5) trust us; we, the government, are not violating the liberties of you, the people—unless you are doing something you shouldn't be.

Or Americans can ask with reason why they must uncritically and indefinitely trust their government in matters of national security after its officials—leave aside that various people have been in charge over the years—distorted and lied about its conduct of the disastrous war in Vietnam, led the nation into interminable combat in Iraq (on a false premise) and ungovernable Afghanistan, and has been shamelessly spying on their private lives on a massive scale.

Compliant or resistant, Americans may wish to pause and consider that the world they live in is divided between democratic nations ruled with the consent of the governed and nations that are not, which is to say police states ruled to a greater or lesser extent by tyranny. For a nation to be and remain a genuine democracy, the approval of the governed must be *informed* consent, not extracted by coercion or deceit. How, though, if whistleblowers are to be crucified, can the press faithfully inform an easily distracted public that its democracy may be facing a threat, no less inimical to its cherished values than global terrorism, from a government that endows its national security officers with a higher priority than the people's right to a free and open society?

ACKNOWLEDGMENTS

Three people, each at a different stage in the process, were of invaluable help in this undertaking. At the outset, I was encouraged by Stanley N. Katz of Princeton University's Woodrow Wilson School of Public and International Affairs and director of its Center for Arts and Cultural Policy Studies, who began his academic career by producing two books that proved essential to my research and generously pointed me to other sources. I was equally fortunate to enlist as my principal research assistant Sarah Cramsey, then completing her dissertation in European history at the University of California–Berkeley and now on the faculty at Tulane University; she was resourceful and persistent in accumulating vital source material and offered me a number of useful insights. And my wife, Phyllis, as always and with a keen eye, performed the unenviable task of reviewing multiple versions of a spouse's handiwork and suggesting improvements.

I am also grateful for the assistance kindly provided by Michael Ryan, head librarian at the New-York Historical Society, and Tammy Kiter, manuscript reference librarian, and several of her colleagues at that institution; Thomas G. Lannon, assistant curator in the Manuscripts and Archives Division of the New York Public Library; Steven Tettamanti, acting executive director of the New Jersey Historical Society; and Jack McPeters, a staff member at New York State Archives, an affiliate of the New York State Library. Reference librarians at the University of

313

California's Doe Library and the law school library at Boalt Hall in Berkeley were endlessly patient with my repeated pleas for aid. I was the beneficiary, too, of the expertise of John J. McCusker, emeritus professor of American history and economics at Trinity University, San Antonio, Texas, for providing me with computations on the modern monetary equivalents of colonial currency. And a special note of thanks to Judith Crawford and John K. Doyle for leading me to and helping me explore their set of the amazing *Iconography of Manhattan Island*.

Finally, without the enthusiasm of my literary representative, Georges Borchardt, and the confidence in the project of John Glusman, editor-in-chief at W. W. Norton & Company, and his colleagues, this book would never have emerged from America's blessedly free press.

—R.K.

A NOTE ON SOURCES

Although the John Peter Zenger affair has been written about, often peripherally, in a number of books and articles, both scholarly and popular, there has been no previous book-length narrative dealing with the events and circumstances of his career and trial. This void is in large part explainable by the fact that the celebrated but modest printer left virtually no trace of his personal life, political views, or business dealings—or if he did, they were destroyed by time and heedless caretaking. As a result, there has been dogged misunderstanding of the actual role Zenger played in the creation and operation of his newspaper, the *New-York Weekly Journal*. To cite one example, Wikipedia, the useful, universally consulted, but too often inaccurate online research tool, says that Zenger's occupation was "Newspaper Writer." There is no extant documentary evidence that Zenger wrote a single word that appeared in the paper he published; his merit resided in his willingness to front for a group of antiauthoritarian colonists who wished to bring down a British governor by decrying in print his alleged abuses of power but were unwilling to risk the wrath of the crown and the prevailing law on libel for daring to do so under their own names.

The author's effort to open the lens of history and place Zenger's—and, more to the point, his editorial and financial backers'—pathbreaking journalistic mission within the wider context of American politics and the struggle for the liberties at its core has been made possible by the survival of two indispensable primary sources: copies of most of the issues of Zenger's newspaper, published between 1733 and 1751, and several annotated versions of *A Brief Account of the Case and Trial of John Peter Zenger*, a pamphlet issued by Zenger's own press a year after his trial and purportedly written by the defendant himself but actually the creation of James Alexander, Zenger's principal attorney and the editorial hand that crafted his newspaper. Many university, some public, and several private libraries hold microfilm or digitalized files of the *Journal*—the author utilized the resources of the University of California's Doe Library in Berkeley, the New-York Historical Society, and the New York Public Library for this purpose. Nearly two-thirds of the 1,017 issues of the paper published by Zenger, his widow, and his son John are accessible through the Readex division of NewsBank's Archive of Americana (see its collection "America's Historical Newspapers" under "Colonial Societies, 1730–1753"). Of the three leading editions of the Zenger/Alexander account of the August 4, 1735, trial, all of which include prefatory remarks by their editors in addition to the full, recreated "transcript" of the courtroom proceedings in New York's City Hall, by far the most valuable is the Harvard University Press edition edited by Stanley N. Katz. Its trenchant introduction, meticulous annotation, and illuminating appendices, along with Katz's subsequent book, *Newcastle's New York: Anglo-American Politics, 1732–1753*, establish his work as the starting point for any attempt to compass Zenger's world. Also useful but of decidedly secondary value are Livingston Rutherford's *John Peter Zenger, His Press, His Trial* and *The Trial of Peter Zenger* by Vincent Buranelli, who also wrote several lively articles for scholarly journals dealing with aspects of the Zenger affair (see the author's Selected Bibliography for full citation of all publications mentioned in this note).

To sense the broader social and political landscape that Zenger and the leading colonial figures of his day occupied, three books proved of special utility, starting with *A Factious People: Politics and Society in Colonial New York* by Patricia U. Bonomi. An equally rich source was Eugene R. Sheridan's lucid biography *Lewis Morris, 1671–1746: A Study in Early American Politics*, which, along with Sheridan's four-volume edition of Morris's letters and related documents, makes it clear that the brilliant if volatile Morris was the dominant player in the Zenger drama, without whose burning passion to avenge himself against Governor William Cosby for firing him as chief justice of the New York Supreme Court there would have been no *New-York Weekly Journal* and Zenger's name would be unknown to posterity. A treasure house of the vagaries of colonial politicking in Zenger's day, with often startling reverberations in its modern and sadly sordid practice, is the unpublished Ph.D. dissertation completed in 1936 at Stanford University by Beverly McAnear—"Politics in Provincial New York, 1689–1761." Of recent scholarly writings on the Zenger case and its larger context, none surpasses Eben Moglen's 1994 article in the *Columbia Law Review,* "Considering Zenger: Partisan Politics and the Legal Profession in Colonial New York," which with justification treats the subject primarily as a collision between legal and political factions whose yearning for power was of greater concern than their expressed passion to advance freedom of the press in pre-Revolutionary New York.

For an overview of Britain's governance of its American provinces, the two leading authorities are *The American Colonies in the Eighteenth Century* by Herbert L. Osgood and *Royal Government in America* by Leonard W. Labaree. For a closer study of Zenger's specific orbit, the reader is directed—after Katz's absorbing *Newcastle's New York*—to William Smith, Jr.'s two-volume *History of the Province of New York,* an idiosyncratic and often subjective study but of particular interest because it is our only serious contemporary chronicle of the period, and Michael Kammen's kaleidoscopic *Colonial New York: A History.* The early phases of freedom of the press as both a theoretical construct and a highly problematic political concern are comprehensively treated by Fredrick S. Siebert in *Freedom of the Press in England, 1476–1776,* and in its evolution in America by Leonard W. Levy in his engaging study *The Emergence of a Free Press* and his edited collection of documents, *Freedom of the Press from Zenger to Jefferson.* Interestingly, but unconvincingly in this author's estimate, Levy, a highly creditable constitutional scholar, has downplayed the role of Zenger's paper in the nurturing of press freedom in America despite its unique mission as the first colonial periodical created for the explicit purpose of criticizing how the British government administered its power.

The most important archival material pertinent to the Morrisite political coalition and its relationship to Zenger's paper is to be found in James Alexander's papers in the Rutherford Collection at the New-York Historical Society, the Manuscripts and Archives Division of the New York Public Library, and the holdings of the New Jersey Historical Society in Newark. Some of the documents in this last group were edited by William A. Whitehead and printed in *Documents Relating to the Colonial History of the State of New Jersey* (see *Archives of the State of New Jersey*, first series, vol. V, 1720–37).

NOTES

1: A Perilous Trade

4   **Zenger's birthplace:** While all sources give Zenger's birthplace as the Palatinate, the likely most authoritative source I have found specifies Rambach, a picturesque community of about 500 people. See Ann T. Keene, entry for John Peter Zenger in *Immigrant Entrepreneurship: German-American Business Biographies, 1720 to the Present*, vol. 1, ed. Marianne S. Woceck (German Historical Institute, last update 2013). See also Henry Z. Jones, Jr., *The Palatine Families of New York, 1710* (Universal City, CA, 1985), 1202.

8   **The Palatines' transatlantic crossing:** Irving G. Cheslaw, *John Peter Zenger and "The New-York Weekly Journal,"* 4.

17   **in twenty-first-century dollars:** John J. McCusker, Ewing Halsell Distinguished Professor of American History and professor of economics, Trinity University, email to the author, June 15, 2014 (see Bibliography).

22   **punishable as subversive or even treasonable:** Leonard Levy, *The Emergence of a Free Press*, 3–15.

24   **"it is a greater offense":** *De Libellis Famosis*, in Edward Coke et al., *The Reports of Sir Edward Coke*, vol. 3 (Part V): 254–56, new edition (1826).

25   **Siebert on falsity as key to libel:** Fredrick Siebert, *Freedom of the Press in England, 1476–1776*, 118–19.

29   **Literacy was higher there:** See, for example, Daniel J. Boorstin, *The Americans: The Colonial Experience*, 294.

30   **"I thank God":** Levy, *op. cit.*, 18.

30   **James II's instructions to Andros:** William. S. Reese, *The First Hundred Years of Printing in British America*.

33   **so if the defiant Bradford:** Levy, *op. cit.*, 22.

2: Stormy Petrel

37 **"an assertive and combative landed aristocrat":** Eugene R. Sheridan, *Lewis Morris, 1671–1746*, x.

38 **"a little whimsical in temper":** William Smith, Jr., *The History of the Province of New York*, 1:179.

39 **keeping parties in lawsuits:** Beverly McAnear, *Politics in Provincial New York, 1680–1761*, 252.

39 **not by temper "fitted to gain popularity":** Cadwallader Colden, *Letters and Papers of Cadwallader Colden*, IX: 305–12.

39 **Turner's estimate of Morris:** *Proceedings of the New Jersey Historical Society* 67, no. 4: 261.

43 **Morris's uncle's will:** Anonymous, *History of the County of Westchester*, 292.

44 **maidservant Becky confessed:** "Correspondence Relating to the Morris Family," *Proceedings of the New Jersey Historical Society* 17 (1922): 41–48.

45 **demanding but affectionate male head:** Sheridan, *op. cit.*, 7; Morris, *The Papers of Lewis Morris, Governor of New Jersey from 1738 to 1746*, 4.

45 **Benjamin Franklin's recollection:** Sheridan, *op. cit.*, 8.

45 **Lewis regarded his black bondsmen:** *Ibid.*, 11.

47 **"those who had the greatest material stake":** *Ibid.*, 16.

50 **4,000-acre spread in Monmouth:** *Ibid.*, 3–4.

54 **"very dregs and rascality of the people":** *Ibid.*, 34, and see 214n33.

56 **The Assembly passed Morris's program:** Deposition of John Johnston before the New Jersey Assembly, May 1, 1707, 207–209. This underhanded exercise is discussed by Sheridan, *op. cit.*, 57, and at 217n4.

57 **"does give his tongue too great a liberty":** Sheridan, *op. cit.*, 61.

58 **without regard for or loyalty:** *Ibid.*, 65.

3: Power Plays

64 **the Van Cortlandt fortune:** Patricia U. Bonomi, *A Factious People*, 60–68.

67 **trade-related imposts:** *Ibid.*, 80.

72 **lavishly dispensing royal land:** *Ibid.*, 72.

73 **Morris justifying his tax plan:** Sheridan, *op. cit.*, 108.

75 **to strengthen the maritime trade:** McAnear, *op. cit.*, 267.

77 **"Not many in the colony":** Eben Moglen, "Considering *Zenger*," moglen.law.columbia.edu/publications/zenger.html (1998).

77 **Livingstons on Morris's self-interest:** Stanley N. Katz, *Newcastle's New York*, 72.

77 **On *Androboros*:** Sheridan, *op. cit.*, 117–18. While attributing joint authorship to the work, Morris's biographer acknowledges that Hunter was the play's principal creator, though both men were skilled satirists.

78 **"probably the best of the [colonial]":** R. M. Naylor, "The Royal Prerogative in New York, 1601–1775," *Quarterly Journal of the New York State Historical Association* V, no. 3 (July 1924): 223.

79 **Zenger went to Philadelphia:** Vincent Buranelli, ed., *The Trial of John Peter Zenger*, 4.

79 **marriage to Mary White:** Ann T. Keene, *Immigrant Entrepreneurship: German-American Business Biographies, 1720 to the Present.*

79 **500 pounds of Maryland tobacco:** Keene, *op. cit.*

81 **mingling freely with colonial society:** Smith, *op. cit.*, 164–66.

82 **used his judicial office to intimidate:** Sheridan, *op. cit.*, 124–26.

84 **"men of estate and ability":** Katz, *Newcastle's New York*, 41.

84 **"men of learning and good morals":** Smith, *op. cit.*, 166.

87 **Burnet's land grants to Morrisites:** McAnear, *op. cit.*, 319.

87 **Clarke's multiple appointments:** Naylor, *op. cit.*, 238.

88 **Clarke's broad oversight:** On Clarke's character, career, and political acumen, see Smith, *op. cit.*, II:44ff.; chap. 6 of Katz, *Newcastle's New York*; and Bonomi, *op. cit.*, 130–35.

91 **"little acquainted with any kind of literature":** Smith, *op. cit.*, 187.

92 **2,000 gallons of Madeira:** Jill Lepore, *New York Burning*, 28.

92 **Colden on Montgomerie:** McAnear, *op. cit.*, 370.

92 **"scandalous, unjust and false reflections":** Sheridan, *op. cit.*, 144.

93 **Morris urged the Board of Trade:** William A. Whitehead, ed., *Documents Relating to the Colonial History of the State of New Jersey*, V (1720–1737): 319.

94 **Bradford's reprimand:** Leonard W. Levy, *The Emergence of a Free Press*, 49.

94 **Franklin first ran into a storm:** *Ibid.*, 30.

95 **Zenger's "grasp of the English language":** Buranelli, *op. cit.*, 4.

4: Bending the Rule of Law

99 **"Let sleeping dogs be":** Katz, *Newcastle's New York*, 10.

99 **Churchill on Walpole's reign:** Winston S. Churchill, *A History of the English-Speaking People*, III, "The Age of Revolution," 105.

100 **"indefatigable industry for the minutiae":** Katz, *op. cit.*, 12.

101 **Cosby's ancestry:** *Ibid.*, 32; Livingston Rutherford, *John Peter Zenger, His Press, His Trial*, 6.

103 **"that what [Cosby] had suffered":** Colden, *The Letters and Papers of Cadwallader Colden*, IX:286.

103 **word from London about Cosby:** James Alexander letter to Colden, *New-York Historical Society Collections of Documents* (1918), 49–50.

103 **for fair-weather hunting:** Rutherford, *op. cit.*, 6.

105 **"virtually unrestrained":** Katz, *A Brief Narrative of the Case and Trial of John Peter Zenger*, 37; Katz, *Newcastle's New York*, 31, 37; Rutherford, *op. cit.*, 3–4; Naylor, "The Royal Prerogative in New York," *Quarterly Journal of the New York Historical Association*, no. 4 (1921): 221; Labaree, *Royal Government in America*, 60.

106 **New York's heterogeneous population:** "Estimated Population of American Colonies, 1630–1780," Bureau of the Census, U.S. Department of Commerce, see *1988 World Almanac and Book of Facts*, 378.

108 **the virtues of his fellow New Yorkers:** William Smith, Jr., *The History of the Province of New York*, II: 227.

108 **"quacks abound":** *Ibid.*

108 **Morris as acting governor of New Jersey:** In a letter to Cosby that Morris appended to a document dated April 20, 1733, he remarked that on the half dozen or so times the two men had met by then, they had exchanged only a few words except for the first occasion, which he indicates was when he presented the governor with the royal seal of New Jersey, as discussed in the text immediately below, about a week after Cosby's arrival in New York. Why Morris did not attend the welcoming ceremony for Cosby at City Hall is unclear—perhaps he felt, as the temporary governor of the adjacent colony, he would have been humbling himself to appear among a crowd of lesser dignitaries; better for this Mohammed to come to Mount Morris to present his credentials. See Sheridan, *The Papers of Lewis Morris*, II (1731–37): 49–50.

108 **"willing to show his disposition":** Colden, *op. cit.*, 286.

110 **Morris's dishonorable methods:** Whitehead, *Documents Relating to the Colonial History of the State of New Jersey*, V:520ff.

110 **vote to amply fund:** Colden, *op. cit.*, 287.

111 **$280,000 in 2014 currency:** Author's correspondence (May 22–June 8, 2014) with John J. McCusker, professor of history emeritus, Trinity University, and author of *Money and Exchange in Europe and America, 1600–1775*.

111 **"Damn them":** W. Smith, *op. cit.*, 4.

111 **"Our party differences seemed over":** Whitehead, *op. cit.*, V:360.

111 **"a man of rather strong personality":** Herbert L. Osgood, *The American Colonies in the Eighteenth Century*, II:444.

111 **early letter to Newcastle, lamenting:** Whitehead, *op. cit.*, 322.

112 **services rendered by the acting governor:** Colden, *op. cit.*, 289–90.

117 **Morris's rebuke to Cosby:** Sheridan, *The Papers of Lewis Morris*, II: 49–50.

118 **"[H]is known very bad character":** For Cosby's December 18, 1732, letter to Newcastle, see the New-York Historical Society's Collections of Documents, V:955, cited in Buranelli, *The Trial of Peter Zenger*, 25–26.

120 **a lengthy written opinion:** Buranelli, *op. cit.*, 13.

121 **"made up for his lack":** Bonomi, *op. cit.*, 107.

121 **Alexander expects Morris to be suspended:** Alexander letter to Ferdinand John Paris, March 19, 1733, *New Jersey Archives*, V:329–31, cited in Katz, *Newcastle's New York*, 97.

122 **"if judges are to be intimidated":** Sheridan, *The Papers of Lewis Morris*, II: 49.

124 **intended to replace the chief justice:** Buranelli, *op. cit.*, 13–14.

5: Battle Lines

127 **Assembly refusing to pay for boundary survey:** NYGenWeb, *History of Putnam County*, New York, chap. 8, www.rootsweb.ancestry.com/~nyputnam/history /chapVIII.

128 **surveying and running the line:** McAnear, *op. cit.*, 406–8.

129 **Harison parlayed his pull with Cosby:** Colden, *op. cit.*, 309.

130 **Colden's dim view of Cosby:** *Ibid.*, 311.

131 **"in the hands of such an ignorant":** *Ibid.*, 305.

131 **governors were required to seek:** Labaree, *op. cit.*, 101.

132 **Colden's account of the event:** Colden, *op. cit.*, 298–99.

133 **failing to consult with the council:** Colden, *op. cit.*, 298; Whitehead, *op. cit.*, 349, 362; Buranelli, *The Trial of Peter Zenger*, 15, citing *New-York Historical Society Collections of Documents*, V:955.

133 **vengeful dismissal of Morris:** Colden, *op. cit.*, 299.

134 **"more than any judge in America":** Whitehead, *op. cit.*, 362.

134 **Colden "would advise against it":** Buranelli, *op. cit.*, 15.

135 **"but since he has not done":** Sheridan, ed., *The Papers of Lewis Morris*, 2 (1731–37): 52–57.

136 **"I am told":** Whitehead, *op. cit.*, 354.

136 **as if the allegation were testified to:** Alexander's letter of December 4, 1733, to "Secy Popple," see Whitehead, *op. cit.*, 363.

137 **"But what have we Christians done":** Seymour J. Schwartz, *Cadwallader Colden: A Biography*, 40.

138 **"being told of it":** Colden, *op. cit.*, 304.

138 **"Cosby's interest":** *Ibid.*, 305.

139 **Morris repeats Colden's story:** Sheridan, *The Papers of Lewis Morris*, 2: 61–63.

140 **"design against the people":** Smith, *The History of the Province of New York*, II: 22.

141 **"was destroyed because Cosby":** Rutherford, *John Peter Zenger, His Press, His Trial*, 21.

141 **"they were not above occasional sharp practices":** Bonomi, *op. cit.*, 121.

142 **the Indians would likely have gone over:** Cosby letter to the Board, June 19, 1734, *New-York Historical Society Collections of Documents*, VI:6.

142 **Mohawk Valley grants to Cosbys:** See "Grantee Index to Colonial Patents," New York State Library and Archives, A4684-99, Land Management Bureau, Office of General Services.

144 **"Before that time":** Colden, *op. cit.*, 299.

144 **meaning of the Morrisites' slogan:** Gordon B. Turner, "Governor Lewis Morris and the Colonial Government Conflict," 272.

146 **"chiefly to expose":** Buranelli, *op. cit.*, 26. Alexander's letter to Hunter was dated November 9, 1733.

146 **Franklin's notion of press freedom:** Stephen Botein, ed., *Mr. Zenger's Malice and Falsehood*, 8.

147 **"For it is necessary":** Leonard W. Levy, *The Emergence of a Free Press*, 9.

148 **"in printing or writing":** William Hawkins, *A Treatise of the Pleas of the Crown*, 1:352–55.

149 **he contemplated launching a paper:** *Ibid.*

150 **the joint pen name of "Cato":** Levy, *op. cit.*, 109.

150 **"in those wretched countries":** *Ibid.*, 110.

152 **"these defamatory expressions":** *Ibid.*, 12.

154 **her personal fortune was:** John N. Ingham, ed., *Biographical Dictionary of American Business Leaders* (Greenwood Press, 1983).

154 **Zenger's hopes for the paper:** Katz, *A Brief Narrative of the Case and Trial of John Peter Zenger*, 41.

6: A Superlative Monster Arises

159 **price of Foster's clerkship:** Correspondence between the author and John J. McCusker (see Bibliography).

163 **disguising their defamatory intent:** Alison Olson, "The Zenger Case Revisited," 223–45.

169 **"Whether as some suppose":** Sheridan, *The Papers of Lewis Morris*, II (1731–37): 72–73.

170 **"paper war":** Katz, ed., *A Brief Narrative of the Case and Trial of John Peter Zenger*, 10; Sheridan, *The Papers of Lewis Morris*, 2:73.

170 **The paper was selling out:** No records of the *Journal's* circulation figures have survived. A reasonable guess would be that its press run during the first several years of its existence was about 500 copies per week, but for some more outspoken issues it may have been closer to 750 copies sold throughout the colony.

171 **Morris's first known appearance:** Sheridan, *op. cit.*, 80.

175 **Zenger's name be understood:** Vincent Buranelli, "Governor Cosby's Hatchet Man," *New York History* 47, no. 1 (January 1856): 26–39.

175 **"there is nothing so scandalous":** *New-York Gazette*, January 21–28, 1734.

176 **"The liberty of the press":** *New-York Weekly Journal*, January 28, 1734.

178 **"[I]f the actions clamored at":** *New-York Weekly Journal*, issue 14, February 4, 1734.

178 **"the abuse and not the use":** *New-York Gazette*, February 11, 1734.

178 **"The difficulty lies":** *New-York Weekly Journal*, February 11, 1734.

179 **Alexander's notes:** James Alexander Papers, Manuscripts & Archives Division, New York Public Library.

180 **a letter or a bill:** *Ibid.*

181 **text of the letter to the Alexanders:** Rutherford, *John Peter Zenger, His Press, His Trial*, 34–35; Moglen, "Considering Zenger," emoglen.law.columbia.edu/publications/zenger.html (1998); W. Smith, *A History of the Province of New York*, 2:8–9.

182 **"From the neglect":** Smith, *op. cit.*, 9.

183 **if he killed Alexander for besmirching:** Rutherford, *op. cit.*, 36.

183 **Council never dignified Harison's letter:** Colden, *The Letters and Papers of Cadwallader Colden*, 315.

7: An End to Generous Pity

186 **"I was in some pain for Zenger":** Sheridan, *The Papers of Lewis Morris*, II (1731–37): 95.

190 **"Every Monday the lash fell":** Buranelli, "Governor Cosby's Hatchet Man," 160–61.

191 **"in the worst light":** Colden, *The Letters and Papers of Cadwallader Colden*, 318–19. These remarks suggest that Colden, while in accord with the paper's immediate political mission, may not have actively contributed to the *Journal's* pages.

191 **"the mouthpiece of two"**: Olson, "The Zenger Case Revisited," 223–45.

192 **"tirades against a perceived growth"**: McAnear, *Politics in Provincial New York*, 420–21.

192 **The *Gazette* seemed to welcome**: *New-York Gazette*, March 11, 1734.

192 **evidence of the governor's beneficence**: McAnear, *op. cit.*, 422.

194 **"Cosby even displayed openness"**: W. Smith, *A History of the Province of New York*, vol 2:11; McAnear, *op. cit.*, 434–45.

194 **the expanded military effort**: McAnear, *op. cit.*, 422.

198 **a slap on the wrist from London**: Buranelli, *op. cit.*, 28.

198 **"the notorious and well known character"**: *Journal of the General Assembly of the Colony of New York*, entries for October 21–25, 1735.

199 **the anti-Cosby ballads**: McAnear, *op. cit.*, 425; Katz, *A Brief Narrative of the Case and Trial of John Peter Zenger*, 110–11.

200 **"All order and government"**: Rutherford, *op. cit.*, 39.

200 **"One might think"**: Colden, *op. cit.*, 535.

201 **"to bring His Majesty's government"**: Katz, *op. cit.*, 42–43.

201 **Alexander dismissed the cited material**: *Ibid.*, 14.

204 **city officials refuse to punish Zenger**: Rutherford, *op. cit.*, 43.

204 **Zenger committed to jail**: Phelps Stokes, *The Iconography of Manhattan Island*, V:272. It is stated here that the third floor was added to City Hall during renovations made in 1763. The only surviving drawing of the building before that date was made in 1818 by David Grim, then eighty-two years old, who depicted it from memory the way it looked during his youth. Grim's rendering shows the building with just two full stories and only a low-ceilinged attic above with small windows, more suited to storing furniture and supplies than housing prisoners, who would likely have found confinement there unbearable during New York's hot summers.

204 **"I was put under such restraint"**: *New-York Weekly Journal*, November 25, 1734.

205 **"imprudently announced to the spectators"**: Katz, *A Brief Narrative*, at 139 deals with DeLancey's grievous slip of the tongue as raised in Alexander's notes for his trial brief; see also n. 50 on page 219.

207 **Cooper on Alexander's character**: Kent Cooper, *Anna Zenger*, 331.

208 **"shrewd enough to value"**: Katz, *op. cit.*, 19.

209 **fleeing William Cosby's jurisdiction**: Sheridan, *Lewis Morris, 1671–1746*, 193.

210 **"wanted incontrovertible proof"**: *Ibid.*, 161.

211 **this compendium of grievances**: Katz, *Newcastle's New York*, 91–95; Sheridan, *The Papers of Lewis Morris*, II: 118ff.; and Sheridan, *Lewis Morris, 1671–1746*, 163–66.

212 **acknowledged Morris's ambitious expedition**: *New-York Weekly Journal*, December 30, 1734.

8: Whiffs of Torquemada

214 **"the grand jury having found"**: Rutherford, *op. cit.*, 47–48.

214 **"In an admittedly political trial"**: Katz, *A Brief Narrative*, 20.

216 **"You were right in not"**: Sheridan, *The Papers of Lewis Morris*, II: 143.

217 "Almost everyone of them": McAnear, *op. cit.*, 422.

219 "Everybody here agrees": Bonomi, *A Factious People*, 127, quoting Morris letter of March 31, 1735.

219 "And who is there": Sheridan, *op. cit.*, 24–25.

220 The evidence he had done so: Katz, *op. cit.*, 139.

223 Alexander on the Restoration judges: *Ibid.*, 140–41.

224 "all indictments and informations": *Ibid.*, 141.

227 if, as chancellor, he ruled in their favor: Sheridan, *op. cit.*, 2:132n9.

227 "it will alarm the province": *Ibid.*, 131.

228 "to grant in England": *Colden, The Letters and Papers of Cadwallader Colden*, 311.

229 Cosby deferring to Clarke: *Ibid.*, 312.

232 Faced with resolute adversaries: Rutherford, *op. cit.*, 49; Katz, *op. cit.*, 52–53.

233 "This remarkable order of disbarment": Rutherford, *op. cit.*, 51.

233 Chambers's legal abilities: W. Smith, *A History of the Province of New York*, II:19.

234 Moglen on Chambers's approach: Moglen, "Considering Zenger," 38.

235 Kinsey unable to defend Zenger: Rutherford, *op. cit.*, 57.

236 the chief justice "has prejudged the case": Katz, *op. cit.*, 147.

238 instead of producing the Freeholders' Book: Rutherford, *op. cit.*, 60.

238 having them struck as objectionable: Katz, *op. cit.*, 56.

239 secretly among the 297 subscribers: Rutherford Collection, II:75, New-York Historical Society; Rutherford, *op. cit.*, 62.

239 juror Hermanus Rutgers: Rutherford, *op. cit.*, 62; *New-York Weekly Journal*, January 28, 1734.

9: Philadelphia Lawyer

242 "a little room": Rutherford, *op. cit.*, 61.

244 "I conceive it is incumbent": Katz, *A Brief Narrative*, 146–150.

244 Andrew Hamilton, a certified member: This was not the same Andrew Hamilton discussed in chap. 2, nor was he related to that colonial governor of New Jersey, who admired young Lewis Morris.

244 "confidence which no terror could awe": W. Smith, *The History of the Province of New York*, II:21–22.

245 Hamilton's wide connections: Foster C. Nix, "Andrew Hamilton's Early Years in the American Colonies," *William & Mary Quarterly*, (3rd series, vol. 21, no. 3 (1964): 390–407.

248 But because of Hamilton's reputation: Rutherford, *op. cit.*, 63.

249 "without doing violence": *Ibid.*, 69.

249 "The answer may possibly lie": Katz, *op. cit.*, 226n22.

250 "since the greater the appearance": Hawkins, *op. cit.*, 353.

250 "There are two [parts]": Katz, *op. cit.*, 62.

250 Bradley on the sanctity of government: *Ibid.*, 63.

251 "If these assertions are not libels": *Ibid.*, 64.

252 "I agree with Mr. Attorney": *Ibid.*, 65.

252 **Bradley, "knowing this":** *Ibid.*, 66.

253 **"Let us not":** *Ibid.*, 66–67.

253 **"nothing is plainer":** *Ibid.*, 68.

255 **"Hamilton did not appreciate":** Levy, *Freedom of the Press from Zenger to Jefferson*, xxxii.

255 **"We have nothing to prove":** Rutherford, *op. cit.*, 80.

256 **"it is very necessary":** *Howell's State Trials*, XIV, 1128.

256 **"A libel is not to be justified":** Katz, *op. cit.*, 69.

256 **"I expected first to have been heard":** *Ibid.*, 70.

257 **"Yet it will not be denied":** *Ibid.*

258 **"such things as you are charged with":** *Ibid.*, 74.

260 **"It is far from being":** *Ibid.*

263 **shrinking the role and power of juries:** Katz, *op. cit.*, 76–77; Rutherford, *op. cit.*, 93.

263 **"but I do likewise know":** Rutherford, *op. cit.*, 93.

264 **"base and unworthy":** Katz, *op. cit.*, 79.

265 **"of what use is this mighty privilege":** *Ibid.*, 79–83.

265 **"Truth ought to govern":** Katz, *op. cit.*, 84; Levy, *op. cit.*, 54–55; Rutherford, *op. cit.*, 101.

266 **"Mr. Hamilton here took":** Colden, *op. cit.*, 337.

267 **"If you should be of opinion":** Katz, *op. cit.*, 96.

267 **"You see I labor":** *Ibid.*, 99. Hamilton was not exactly ancient, though made himself seem so to win sympathy from the jury, as Katz no doubt correctly surmises; the attorney was fifty-nine years old at the time.

267 **"The question before the court":** *Ibid.*

269 **a short, highly ambiguous instruction:** *Ibid.*, 100.

10: Indelible Ink

272 **Hamilton praised by New York Council:** At the same New York Common Council meeting on September 16, 1735, Zenger, who had apparently recuperated from his extended imprisonment, delivered six copies bound in parchment of the new charter of the City of New York that the magistrates had commissioned him to print before his arrest the year before. The charter is considered an example of Zenger's craftsmanship at its best.

273 **"Gained not by money but virtue":** Katz, *A Brief Narrative*, 230, nn. 59 and 60.

273 **"lawyering was not merely":** "Considering Zenger," 47.

275 **removed as New York's highest judge:** Katz, *Newcastle's New York*, 117.

278 **"This must mend sometime":** Bonomi, *op. cit.*, 126–50.

278 **Cosby's death unlamented:** *New-York Weekly Journal*, March 15, 1736.

279 **Hamilton sends notes to Alexander:** Burton Alva Konkle, *The Life of Andrew Hamilton*, 108.

280 **Hamilton criticized by "Anglo-Americanus":** Katz, *A Brief Narrative*, 239n1.

281 **Could Hamilton have proven:** *Ibid.*, 152–81.

284 **Smith on Zenger's "guilty nakedness":** Smith, *op. cit.*, 2:20.

286 **Van Dam's authority as acting governor:** Bonomi, *op. cit.*, 131–33.

287 **"If you don't hang them":** Sheridan, *Lewis Morris*, 178.

289 **Zenger fired as official printer:** Katz, *Newcastle's New York*, 154.

291 **reversal of Morris's career-long advocacy:** Turner, "Governor Lewis Morris and the Colonial Government Conflict," 271.

291 **Morris's seven-year term:** *Ibid.*, 262.

294 **"were, in fact, a somewhat narrow-minded political faction":** Katz, *A Brief Narrative*, 1.

295 **"The persistent image":** Leonard Levy, "Does the Zenger Case Really Matter?" 35–60.

295 **Katz's evaluation of Zenger case:** Katz, *op. cit.*, 34.

296 **"contributed directly to the growth of the press":** Bonomi, *op. cit.*, 136.

297 **"dynamic growth of political expression":** Olson, *op. cit.*, 224.

298 **"There is nothing so fretting":** Levy, *Emergence of a Free Press*, 67.

299 **still hewed to Blackstone's strictures:** Levy, *Freedom of the Press from Zenger to Jefferson*, liii.

301 **Brennan's opinion in *Sullivan*:** *The New York Times v. Sullivan* (376 U.S. 254).

Epilogue: From Zenger to Snowden

307 **"Presidents have used the needs":** Anthony Lewis, *Make No Law*, 242.

308 **intelligence officer Bradley Manning:** After undergoing transsexual procedures, Manning's first name is now Chelsea.

311 **"But civil libertarians":** *New York Times*, May 30, 2015.

SELECTED BIBLIOGRAPHY

Andrews, Charles M. *The Colonial Period of American History*, vol. 2 (Yale University Press, 1934–38).

Anonymous, *History of the County of Westchester*, vol. 2 (New York, 1848), collection of the New-York Historical Society.

Bonomi, Patricia U. *A Factious People: Politics and Society in Colonial New York* (Columbia University Press, 1971).

Boorstin, Daniel J. *The Americans: The Colonial Experience* (Random House, 1958).

Botein, Stephen, ed. *Mr. Zenger's Malice and Falsehood: Six Issues of the New-York Weekly Journal, 1733–34* (American Antiquarian Society, 1985).

Buranelli, Vincent. "Governor Cosby's Hatchet Man," *New York History*, vol. 37, no. 1 (January 1956): 26–39.

———. "The Myth of Anna Zenger," *William & Mary Quarterly*, vol. 13, no. 2 (April 1956): 57–68.

———, ed., with introduction and notes. *The Trial of Peter Zenger* (NYU Press, 1957).

Cantor, Norman F. *The English: A History of Politics and Society to 1760* (Simon & Schuster, 1967).

Cheslaw, Irving G. *John Peter Zenger and "The New-York Weekly Journal": A Historical Study* (privately printed ca. 1952; title page cites author as "Lecturer in History, Columbia Univ.").

Churchill, Winston S. *A History of the English-Speaking People*, vol. 3, "The Age of Revolution" (Dodd, Mead, 1957).

Colden, Cadwallader. *The Letters and Papers of Cadwallader Colden*, vol. 9 (New-York Historical Society, 1937).

Cooper, Kent. *Anna Zenger: Mother of Freedom* (novel; Farrar, Straus, 1946).

DeArmond, Anna Jenney. *Andrew Bradford: Colonial Journalist* (Kessinger Publishing, 1949), originally a University of Pennsylvania doctoral dissertation, 1947.

Epps, Garrett, ed. *The First Amendment—Freedom of the Press: Its Constitutional History and the Contemporary Debate* (Prometheus Books, 2008).

330 | *Selected Bibliography*

Hawkins, William. *A Treatise on the Pleas of the Crown*, vol. 1, 6th ed. (Gale ECCO Print Editions).

Kammen, Michael. *Colonial New York: A History* (Oxford University Press, 1975).

Katz, Stanley N., ed. *A Brief Narrative of the Case and Trial of John Peter Zenger, Printer of the New York Weekly Journal* by James Alexander (Harvard University Press, 1972).

———. *Newcastle's New York: Anglo-American Politics, 1732–1753* (Harvard University Press, 1968).

Keene, Ann T. Entry for John Peter Zenger in *Immigrant Entrepreneurship: German-American Business Biographies, 1720 to the Present*, vol. 1. Edited by Marianne S. Woceck (German Historical Institute, 2013).

Konkle, Burton Alva. *The Life of Andrew Hamilton* (National Publishing Co., 1941).

Kornstein, Daniel J. *Thinking Under Fire: Great Courtroom Lawyers and Their Impact on American History* (Dodd, Mead, 1987).

Labaree, Leonard W. *Royal Government in America* (Yale University Press, 1930).

Lepore, Jill. *New York Burning: Liberty, Slavery, and Conspiracy in Eighteenth-Century Manhattan* (Knopf, 2005).

Levy, Leonard W. "Does the Zenger Case Really Matter? Freedom of the Press in Colonial New York," *William & Mary Quarterly*, vol. 17, no. 1 (January 1960), 35–50.

———. *The Emergence of a Free Press* (Ivan R. Dee, 1985).

———, ed. *Freedom of the Press from Zenger to Jefferson* (Bobbs-Merrill, 1966).

Lewis, Anthony. *Make No Law: The Sullivan Case and the First Amendment* (Random House, 1991).

McAnear, Beverly. "Politics in Provincial New York, 1689–1761," Stanford University doctoral dissertation, 1935.

McCusker, John J. *How Much Is That in Real Money? A Historical Price Index for Use as a Deflator of Money Values in the Economy of the United States* (American Antiquarian Society, 2001).

———. *Money and Exchange in Europe and America, 1600–1775* (University of North Carolina Press, rev., 2001).

Moglen, Eben. "Considering Zenger: Partisan Politics and the Legal Profession in Colonial New York," 94 *Columbia Law Review* 1495 (1994), with a postscript; also available online at moglen.law.columbia.edu/publications/zenger.html (1998).

Morris, Lewis. "The Opinion & Argument of Lewis Morris to Governor William Cosby, 1733," *Proceedings of the New Jersey Historical Society*, vol. 55, no. 3 (1937).

———. *The Papers of Lewis Morris, Governor of New Jersey from 1738 to 1746* (New Jersey Historical Society/G.P. Putnam, 1853), no editor cited, with anonymous "Introductory Memoir."

Naylor, Rex Maurice. "The Royal Prerogative in New York, 1691–1775," *New York Historical Association Quarterly Journal*, no. 4(1921): 221–255.

Olson, Alison. "The Zenger Case Revisited: Satire, Sedition, and Political Debate in Eighteenth Century America," *Early American Literature*, vol. 35, no. 3 (2000).

Osgood, Herbert L. *The American Colonies in the Eighteenth Century*, vol. 2 (Oxford University Press, 1924).

Phelps Stokes, I. N., ed. *The Iconography of Manhattan Island, 1498 to 1909*, 6 vols. (New York: Robert H. Dodd, 1915–1928).

Reese, William S. *The First Hundred Years of Printing in British America: Printers and Collectors* (American Antiquarian Society, 1990).

Rutherford, Livingston. *John Peter Zenger, His Press, His Trial . . .* (Dodd, Mead, 1904).

Schwartz, Seymour J. *Cadwallader Colden: A Biography* (Humanity Books, 2013).

Sheridan, Eugene R. *Lewis Morris, 1671–1746: A Study in Early American Politics* (Syracuse University Press, 1981).

———, ed. *The Papers of Lewis Morris*, vol. 1, 1698–1730; vol. 2, 1731–37 (New Jersey Historical Society, 1991 and 1993).

Shorto, Russell. *The Island at the Center of the World* (Doubleday, 2004).

Siebert, Fredrick Seaton. *Freedom of the Press in England, 1476–1776* (University of Illinois, 1952).

Smith, Joseph H., and Leo Herskowitz. "Courts of Equity in the Province of New York: The Cosby Controversy, 1732–36," *American Journal of Legal History* 14 (1972).

Smith, William, Jr. *The History of the Province of New York*, 2 vols. Edited by Michael Kammen (Harvard University Press/Belknap Press, 1972).

Turner, Gordon B. "Governor Lewis Morris and the Colonial Government Conflict," *Proceedings of the New Jersey Historical Society*, vol. 67, no. 4: 260–303.

Whitehead, William A., ed. *Documents Relating to the Colonial History of the State of New Jersey*, vol. V, 1720–1737 (Daily Advertiser Printing House [Newark N.J.], 1882).

IMAGE CREDITS

1. Detail from "A South Prospect of Ye Flourishing City of New York in the Province of New York in America," 1717 entire view, by John Harris after William Burgis, engraving from four plates on four sheets, for sections, see 43057, 20340; neg #32098. Photography © New-York Historical Society.

2. "A New Map of the Harbor of New York," printed by William Bradford and first advertised for sale in his *New-York Gazette* of March 24–31, 1735, cartographer and present owner unknown. First reproduced in *The Iconography of Manhattan Island, 1498–1909*, six volumes (New York: Robert H. Dodd, 1915–1928), from which this image was scanned.

3. Detail from "Map of New York City from an Actual Survey by James Lyne, 1728." From the collections of the Museum of the City of New York (X2011.5.140).

4. "A View of Fort George with the City of New York from the Southwest," ca. 1740, painting by Carington Bowles and J. Carwitham. From the collections of the Museum of the City of New York (52.100.30).

5. "Governor Lewis Morris," ca. 1726, oil on linen, 30 ¹⁄₁₆ x 25 inches, by John Watson (American, 1685–1768), detail. Brooklyn Museum, purchased with funds given by John Hill Morgan, Dick S. Ramsay Fund, and Museum Collection Fund, 43.196. [Actual date of work may be later than 1726 since Morris did not become governor of New Jersey until 1739, although that title may have been added to the earlier work after he assumed the office.]

6. William Cosby, colonial governor of New York (1732–36), woodcut dated 1736. North Wind Pictures Archive (PUSA3A-00087).

7. James Alexander, from painting in Livingston Rutherford's book on John Peter Zenger; Portrait File, PR 052, box 3, Folder: James and Mary Alexander; neg #3181 (detail). Photography © New-York Historical Society.

8. Portrait of Cadwallader Colden, ca. 1749–52, by John Wollaston (ca. 1710–1767), oil on canvas, 30 x 25 inches, detail. Bequest of Grace Wilkes,

1922 (22.45.6). The Metropolitan Museum of Art. Image copyright © The Metropolitan Museum of Art. Image source: Art Resource, New York.

9. Front page of *The New-York Weekly Journal*, October 7, 1734, copy obtained online at Doe Library, University of California at Berkeley, from Readex division of NewsBank's Archive of Americana collection, "America's Historical Newspapers—Colonial Societies, 1730–1753."

10. Drawing by Harry Fenn titled "Burning of Zenger's *Weekly Journal* in Wall Street, November 6, 1734," appearing in *Harper's Monthly*, May 1908, page 839.

11. Painting of Andrew Hamilton (1676–1741) by Adolph Wertmuller, 1808, detail. Courtesy of the Philadelphia History Museum at the Atwater Kent, the Historical Society of Pennsylvania Collection (HSP.1852.7).

12. Drawing titled "Andrew Hamilton Departing from the City Hall, August 4, 1735," appearing in *Harper's Monthly*, May 1908, page 843.

INDEX